MICROSOFT

Windows 98

Introductory Concepts and Techniques

Gary B. Shelly
Thomas J. Cashman
Steven G. Forsythe

COURSE TECHNOLOGY
ONE MAIN STREET
CAMBRIDGE MA 02142

an International Thomson Publishing company 

SHELLY CASHMAN SERIES®

CAMBRIDGE • ALBANY • BONN • CINCINNATI • LONDON • MADRID • MELBOURNE
MEXICO CITY • NEW YORK • PARIS • SAN FRANCISCO • TOKYO • TORONTO • WASHINGTON

Printed in the United States of America

For more information, contact:

Course Technology
One Main Street
Cambridge, Massachusetts 02142, USA

ITP Europe
Berkshire House
168-173 High Holborn
London, WC1V 7AA, United Kingdom

ITP Australia
102 Dodds Street
South Melbourne
Victoria 3205 Australia

ITP Nelson Canada
1120 Birchmount Road
Scarborough, Ontario
Canada M1K 5G4

International Thomson Editores
Saneca, 53
Colonia Polanco
11560 Mexico D.F. Mexico

ITP GmbH
Konigswinterer Strasse 418
53227 Bonn, Germany

ITP Asia
60 Albert Street, #15-01
Albert Complex
Singapore 189969

ITP Japan
Hirakawa-cho Kyowa Building, 3F
2-2-1 Hirakawa-cho, Chiyoda-ku
Tokyo 102, Japan

ISBN 0-7895-4299-4

PHOTO CREDITS: *Project 1, pages WIN 1.4-5* Young Bill Gates, Paul Allen and Bill Gates, Courtesy of Lake Side Middle School; Microsoft Company Photo, Bill Gates, Microsoft Campus, Courtesy of Microsoft Corporation; Intel Microprocessor Chip 4004, Courtesy of Intel Corporation; *Project 2, pages WIN 2.2-3* IBM Personal Computer, Courtesy of International Business Machines Corporation; Xerox Mouse, Courtesy of Xerox PARC; *Project 3, pages WIN 3.2-3* Telephone Booth, © The Stock Market/Anthony Redpath, 1998; Hard Drive, Courtesy of Seagate Technology; Italian Castle, Courtesy of Corel Professional Photos CD-ROM Image usage; Volkswagen, Courtesy of Volkswagen of America, Inc.; Pentium II Microprocessor, Gordon E. Moore, Chairman of the Board, Intel Corp., Courtesy of Intel Corporation.

5 6 7 8 9 10 BC 03 02 01

MICROSOFT

Windows 98

Introductory Concepts and Techniques

C O N T E N T S

PROJECT THREE

File, Document, and Folder Management and Windows 98 Explorer

Preface

The Shelly Cashman Series® offers the finest textbooks in computer education. The Microsoft Windows 98 books continue with the innovation, quality, and reliability consistent with this series. We are proud that both our Microsoft Windows 3.1 and Microsoft Windows 95 books were used by more schools and more students than any other series in textbook publishing.

The Windows 98 interface includes a new Quick Launch toolbar on the taskbar, additional toolbars you can add to the taskbar, and a choice of three desktop views (Web style, Classic style, and Custom style). The Web style turns on the Active Desktop™ that places the Internet Explorer Channel bar and constantly changing Web content on the desktop, lets you point to an icon to select it and single-click the icon to open its window, and displays folders that look and respond like Web pages.

In our Microsoft Windows 98 books, you will find an educationally sound and easy-to-follow pedagogy that combines a step-by-step approach with corresponding screens. The Other Ways and More About features offer in-depth knowledge of Windows 98. The all-new project openers provide a fascinating perspective on the subject covered in the project. The Shelly Cashman Series Microsoft Windows 98 textbooks will make your computer applications class exciting and dynamic and one that your students will remember as one of their better educational experiences.

Objectives of This Textbook

Microsoft Windows 98: Introductory Concepts and Techniques is intended for a one-unit course that covers Windows 98. No computer experience is assumed. The objectives of this book are:

- To teach the fundamentals and skills necessary to adequately use Windows 98
- To provide a knowledge base for Windows 98 upon which students can build
- To expose students to real-world examples and procedures that will prepare them to be skilled users of Windows 98
- To encourage independent study and help those who are working alone in a distance education environment

When students complete the course using this textbook, they will have a basic knowledge and understanding of Windows 98.

The Shelly Cashman Approach

Features of the Shelly Cashman Series Microsoft Windows 98 books include:

- Project Orientation: Related topics are presented using a project orientation that establishes a strong foundation on which students can confidently learn more advanced topics.
- Screen-by-Screen, Step-by-Step Instructions: Each task required to complete a project is identified throughout the development of the project. Then, steps to accomplish the task are specified and are accompanied by screens.
- Thoroughly Tested Projects: Every screen in the textbook is correct because it is produced by the author only after performing a step, which results in unprecedented quality.
- Two-Page Project Openers: Each project begins with a two-page opener that sets the tone for the project by describing an interesting aspect of Windows 98.

Microsoft Windows 98

MOORE and More Storage

Cramming Data in Small Places

Is it any doubt that you are an expert when it comes to cramming? You cram for final exams, cram books into heavy backpacks, and cram clothes into tiny closets. Only a few decades ago, college students held contests to see how many people could cram into telephone booths and Volkswagen Beetles. About the same time, Gordon Moore, a semiconductor engineer, realized cramming was a good thing when it came to computer chips.

In 1965, Moore observed a trend when he was drawing an illustration for a speech: every 18 to 24 months a new memory chip was being released with double the number of transistors as its predecessor. He predicted that this growth would continue exponentially, and he was correct. Today's Pentium II processor has 7.5 million transistors, which is nearly 3,200 times more than the 2,300 transistors found on a chip released in 1971.

1. Click expanded folder icon, press MINUS SIGN
2. Click expanded folder icon, press LEFT ARROW
3. Click expanded folder icon, double-click folder icon

- **Other Ways Boxes for Reference:** Microsoft Windows 98 provides a variety of ways to carry out a given task. The Other Ways boxes displayed at the end of most of the step-by-step sequences specify the other ways to do the task completed in the steps. Thus, the steps and the Other Ways box make a comprehensive reference unit.
- **More About Feature:** These marginal annotations provide background information about the topics covered, adding interest and depth to learning.

More About

Desktop Views

The Classic style was included in the Windows 98 operating system to allow Windows 95 users to upgrade easily to the newer Windows 98 operating system. Responses from people in the Beta Test program, which is a program designed to test software prior to the public sale of the software, indicated that most Windows 95 users had little difficulty switching to Windows 98, and experienced users liked the Web style and Active Desktop.

Organization of This Textbook

Microsoft Windows 98: Introductory Concepts and Techniques consists of three projects, as follows:

Project 1 - **Fundamentals of Using Microsoft Windows 98** In Project 1, students learn about user interfaces and Microsoft Windows 98. Topics include launching Microsoft Windows 98; mouse operations; maximizing, minimizing, moving, sizing, and scrolling windows; describing the Internet and World Wide Web; recognizing the Classic, Web, and Custom styles; launching an application program; using Help; and shutting down Windows 98.

Project 2 - **Working on the Windows 98 Desktop** In Project 2, students work on the Windows 98 desktop. Topics include creating a document on the desktop by starting an application; creating and naming a document on the desktop; opening, saving, printing, and closing a document on the desktop; storing documents in folders on the desktop; opening, modifying, and printing documents within a folder; copying a folder onto a disk; opening multiple documents; creating shortcuts; deleting documents, shortcuts, and folders; turning on the Active Desktop; adding active desktop items to the desktop; and using Microsoft Support Online.

Project 3 - **File, Document, and Folder Management and Windows 98 Explorer** In Project 3, students manage windows and files on the desktop and use Windows 98 Explorer. Topics include using My Computer; displaying drive and folder contents; opening a document from a window; launching an application program from a window; cascading and tiling open windows; copying, moving, and deleting files from windows; Windows 98 Explorer; displaying files and folders in Explorer; displaying drive and folder contents; expanding a drive or folder; launching an application from Explorer; copying, moving, renaming, and deleting files in Explorer; displaying object properties; finding files and folders; and the Run command.

End-of-Project Student Activities

A notable strength of the Shelly Cashman Series Microsoft Windows 98 textbooks is the extensive student activities at the end of each project. Well-structured student activities can make the difference between students merely participating in a class and students retaining the information they learn. These activities include:

- **What You Should Know** A listing of the tasks completed within a project together with the pages where the step-by-step, screen-by-screen explanations appear. This section provides a perfect study review for students.
- **Test Your Knowledge** Four activities designed to determine students' understanding of the material in the project. Included are true/false questions, multiple-choice questions, and two other unique activities.

- **Use Help** Users of Windows 98 must know how to use Help. This book contains extensive Help activities. These exercises alone distinguish the Shelly Cashman Series from any other set of Windows 98 instructional materials.

- **In the Lab** These assignments require students to make use of the knowledge gained in the project to solve problems on a computer.
- **Cases and Places** Unique case studies allow students to apply their knowledge to real-world situations. These case studies provide subjects for research papers based on information gained from a resource such as the Internet.

Instructor's Resource Kit

A comprehensive Instructor's Resource Kit (IRK) accompanies this book in the form of a CD-ROM. The CD-ROM includes the Instructor's Manual and other teaching and testing aids. The CD-ROM (ISBN 0-7895-5571-9) is available through your Course Technology representative. The contents of the CD-ROM follow.

- **Instructor's Manual** The Instructor's Manual is made up of Microsoft Word files that include lecture notes, solutions to laboratory assignments, and a large test bank. The files allow you to modify the lecture notes or generate quizzes and exams from the test bank using your own word processor. Where appropriate, solutions to laboratory assignments are embedded as icons in the files.
- **Figures in the Book** Illustrations for every screen in the textbook are available. Use this ancillary to create a slide show from the illustrations for lecture or to print transparencies for use in lecture with an overhead projector.
- **Course Test Manager** Course Test Manager is a powerful testing and assessment package that enables instructors to create and print tests from the large test bank. Instructors with access to a networked computer lab (LAN) can administer, grade, and track tests online.
- **Interactive Labs** Eighteen hands-on interactive labs solidify and reinforce computer concepts.

Acknowledgments

The Shelly Cashman Series would not be the leading computer education series without the contributions of outstanding publishing professionals. First and foremost among them is Becky Herrington, director of production and designer. She is the heart and soul of the Shelly Cashman Series, and it is only through her leadership, dedication, and tireless efforts that superior products are made possible.

Under Becky's direction, the following individuals made significant contributions to these books: Doug Cowley, production manager; Ginny Harvey, series specialist and developmental editor; Ken Russo, graphic designer and Web developer; Mike Bodnar, Stephanie Nance, Dave Bonnewitz, and Mark Norton, graphic artists; Jeanne Black, Quark expert; Marilyn Martin, proofreader; Marlo Mitchem, administrative/production assistant; Cristina Haley, indexer; Sarah Evertson of Image Quest, photo researcher; and Susan Sebok contributing writer.

Special thanks go to Jim Quasney, our dedicated series editor; Lisa Strite, senior editor; Lora Wade, associate product manager; Tonia Grafakos and Meagan Walsh, editorial assistants; and Kathryn Coyne, product marketing manager. Special mention must go to Becky Herrington for the outstanding book design, Mike Bodnar for the logo designs, and Ken Russo for the cover design and illustrations.

Gary B. Shelly
Thomas J. Cashman
Steven G. Forsythe

Instructions for Selecting the Default Desktop View Settings

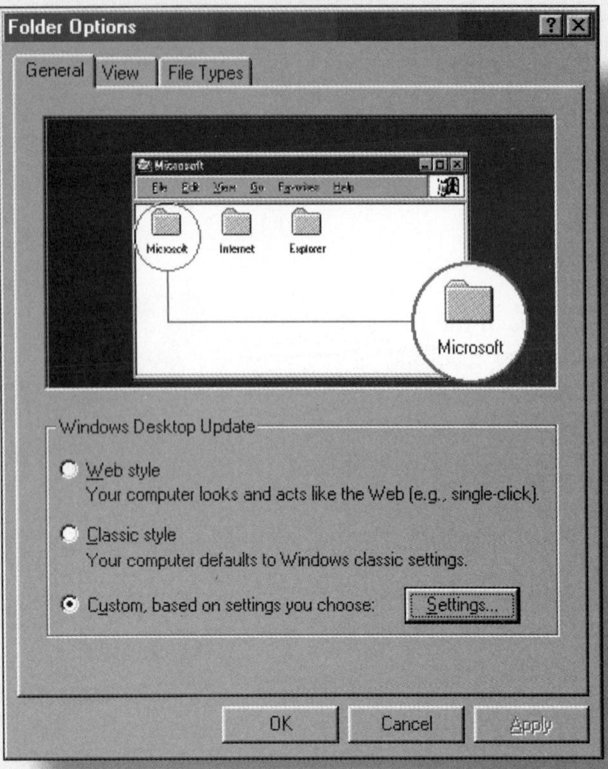

FIGURE 1a

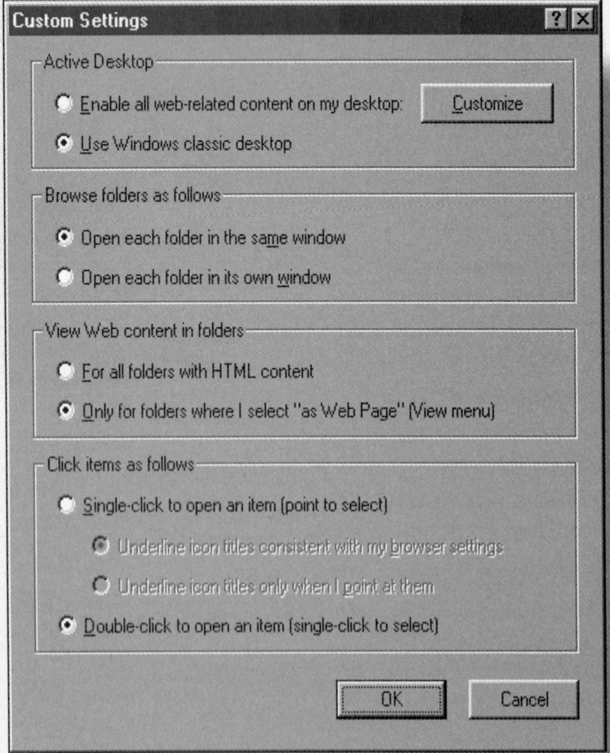

FIGURE 1b

The projects and assignments in this textbook are presented using the default desktop view settings (default Custom style), as chosen by Microsoft Corporation. With the exception of the Open each folder in the same window option, the default settings are those of the Classic style. To ensure your success in completing the projects and assignments, the Windows 98 operating system must be installed on your computer system and the default desktop view settings must be selected. The following steps illustrate how to use the Folder Options dialog box and Custom Settings dialog box to select the default settings.

1. Click the Start button on the taskbar.
2. Point to Settings on the Start menu.
3. Click Folder Options on the Settings submenu to display the Folder Options dialog box (Figure 1a).
4. If necessary, click the General tab in the Folder Options dialog box to display the General sheet.
5. If necessary, click Custom, based on settings you choose to select the option.
6. Click the Settings button in the Folder Options dialog box to open the Custom Settings dialog box (Figure 1b).
7. On a piece of paper, write down the name of each option button that is selected in the Custom Settings dialog box.
8. Click Use Windows classic desktop to select the option.
9. Click Open each folder in the same window to select the option.
10. Click Only for folders where I select "as Web Page" (View menu) to select the option.
11. Click Double-click to open an item (single-click to select) to select the option.
12. Click the OK button in the Custom Settings dialog box.
13. Click the Close button in the Folder Options dialog box.

As a result of selecting the default settings, you can perform the steps and assignments in each project of this book. If, after finishing the steps and assignments, you must reset the desktop view to its original settings, perform steps 1 through 6 above, click the option button of each setting you wrote down in step 7, and then perform steps 12 and 13.

Microsoft
Windows 98
My Computer
Select an item to view

Microsoft Windows 98

Fundamentals of Using Microsoft Windows 98

OBJECTIVES

You will have mastered the material in this project when you can:

- Describe Microsoft Windows 98
- Explain a user interface
- Identify the objects on the Microsoft Windows 98 desktop
- Perform the basic mouse operations: point, click, right-click, double-click, drag, and right-drag
- Open, minimize, maximize, and restore a Windows 98 window
- Close a Windows 98 window
- Move and resize a window on the Windows 98 desktop
- Scroll in a window
- Understand keyboard shortcut notation
- Describe the Internet and World Wide Web
- Differentiate between viewing the Windows desktop in Classic style, Web style, and Custom style
- Launch an application program
- Use Windows 98 Contents Help and Index Help
- Shut down Windows 98

The Best Job In The Whole World

Bill Gates Uses His Leave Wisely

"My job probably is the best job in the whole world." No wonder Bill Gates makes this claim: as founder and CEO of Microsoft, he is the richest person on the planet with a net worth estimated at $50 billion—not bad for a Harvard College student "on leave."

His computing efforts began in grade school when he and a classmate, Paul Allen, learned the BASIC programming language from a manual and programmed a mainframe computer using a Teletype terminal purchased with proceeds from a rummage sale. In 1968, they wrote a program to play tic-tac-toe. Then they developed more complex programs, including one resembling the board game Risk with the objective of world dominance.

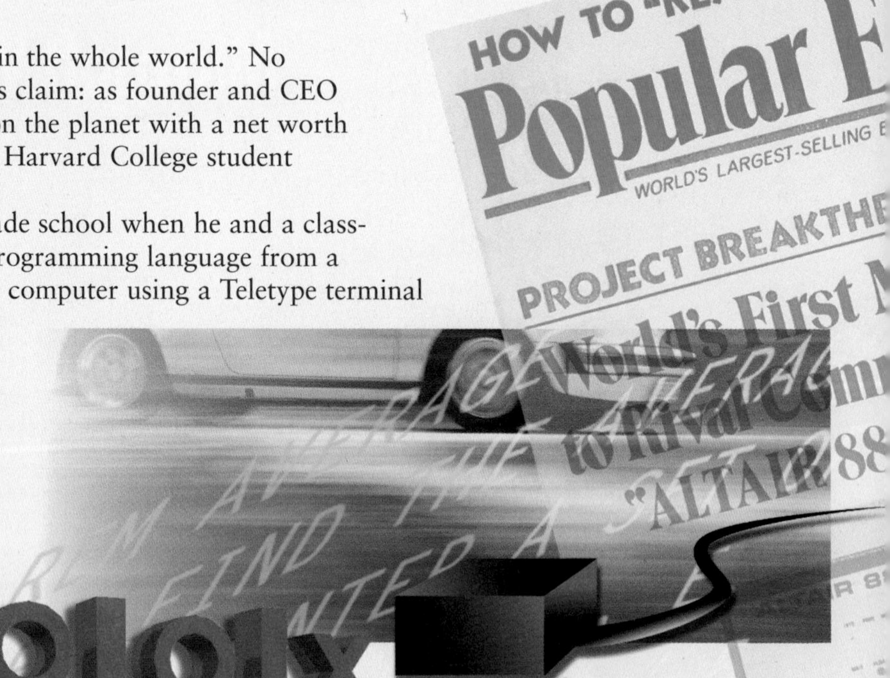

In high school, Gates and Allen had a thirst for more computing power than the Teletype terminal could offer. They wrote custom programs for local

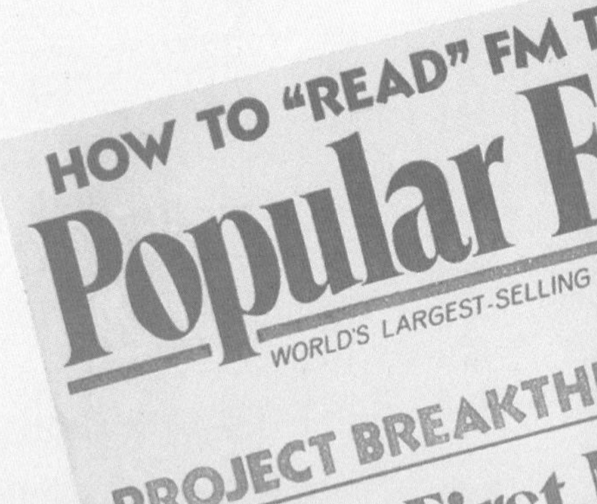

businesses during the summer and split their $5,000 salaries between cash and computer time, which cost them about $40 per hour. In addition, they debugged software problems at local businesses in return for computer use. In Gates's sophomore year, one of his teachers asked him to teach his computer skills to his classmates. Also, he boasts that he wrote a program to schedule students in classes and changed a few lines of code so he was the only male in a class full of females.

When Gates was 16 in 1972, he and Allen read a ten-paragraph article in *Electronics* magazine about Intel's first microprocessor chip. They requested a manual from Intel, experimented with pushing the chip to its limits, and formed the Traf-O-Data company. This pursuit involved developing a device about the size of a toaster oven with a rubber hose connected to a metal box containing a paper tape. When a car ran over the hose, the device punched a hole in the tape. They used the Intel chip to analyze the tape and subsequently to determine traffic flow in several cities.

Gates entered Harvard College in 1973, and Allen landed a job programming Honeywell minicomputers in Boston. They continued to scheme about the power of computers. In Gates's sophomore year, they saw a picture of the Altair 8800 computer on the cover of the January 1975 edition of *Popular Electronics*. That computer was about the size of the Traf-O-Data device and contained a new Intel computer chip. For five weeks, they spent sleepless nights writing BASIC for that computer, and Gates says that on some of those days, he did not see anyone or eat.

At that point they formed the world's first microcomputer software company: Microsoft Corporation. They realized they needed to make some sacrifices to achieve their goal of "a computer on every desk and in every home," so Allen quit his job and Gates left Harvard. Gates says he always planned to return to earn his degree, and he considers himself "on a really long leave." In the interim, he has added 25,000 employees to help him achieve yearly net revenues surpassing $11 billion.

Microsoft Windows 98

Fundamentals of Using Microsoft Windows 98

CASE PERSPECTIVE

Everyday from locations around the world, millions of Windows 98 users turn on their computers. When the computer starts, the first image on the monitor is the Windows 98 desktop. If these users did not know how to launch an application program, manipulate files and objects on the desktop, send and receive e-mail, and obtain information using the Internet and/or intranet, their computers would be useless.

You have just acquired a computer with the Windows 98 operating system. Your task is to learn the basics of Windows 98 so your computer will be useful to you, and you will be able to assist others who may come to you with questions and requests.

Introduction

An **operating system** is the set of computer instructions, called a computer program, that controls the allocation of computer hardware such as memory, disk devices, printers, and CD-ROM and DVD drives, and provides the capability for you to communicate with your computer. The most popular and widely used operating system for personal computers is **Microsoft Windows.** **Microsoft Windows 98** (called **Windows 98** for the rest of this book), the newest version of Microsoft Windows, allows you easily to communicate with and control your computer.

Windows 98 is easy to use and can be customized to fit individual needs. Windows 98 simplifies the process of working with documents and applications, transferring data between documents, organizing the manner in which you interact with your computer, and using your computer to access information on the Internet and/or intranet. In Project 1, you will learn about Windows 98 and how to use the Windows 98 user interface.

Microsoft Windows 98

Microsoft Windows 98 is an operating system that performs every function necessary for you to communicate with and use your computer. Windows 98 is called a **32-bit operating system** because it uses 32 bits for addressing and other purposes, which means the operating system can address more than four gigabytes of RAM (random-access memory) and perform tasks faster than older operating systems. Windows 98 includes **Microsoft Internet Explorer (IE)**, a software program developed by Microsoft Corporation, that integrates the Windows 98 desktop and the Internet. Internet Explorer allows you to work with programs and files in a similar fashion, whether they are located on your computer, a local network, or the Internet.

Windows 98 is designed to be compatible with all existing **application programs**, which are programs that perform an application-related function such as word processing. To use the application programs that can be executed under Windows 98, you must know about the Windows 98 user interface.

What Is a User Interface?

A **user interface** is the combination of hardware and software that you use to communicate with and control your computer. Through the user interface, you are able to make selections on your computer, request information from your computer, and respond to messages displayed by your computer. Thus, a user interface provides the means for dialogue between you and your computer.

Hardware and software together form the user interface. Among the hardware devices associated with a user interface are the monitor, keyboard, and mouse (Figure 1-1). The **monitor** displays messages and provides information. You respond by entering data in the form of a command or other response using the **keyboard** or **mouse**. Among the responses available to you are responses that specify what application program to run, what document to open, when to print, and where to store data for future use.

The computer software associated with the user interface consists of the programs that engage you in dialogue (Figure 1-1). The computer software determines the messages you receive, the manner in which you should respond, and the actions that occur based on your responses.

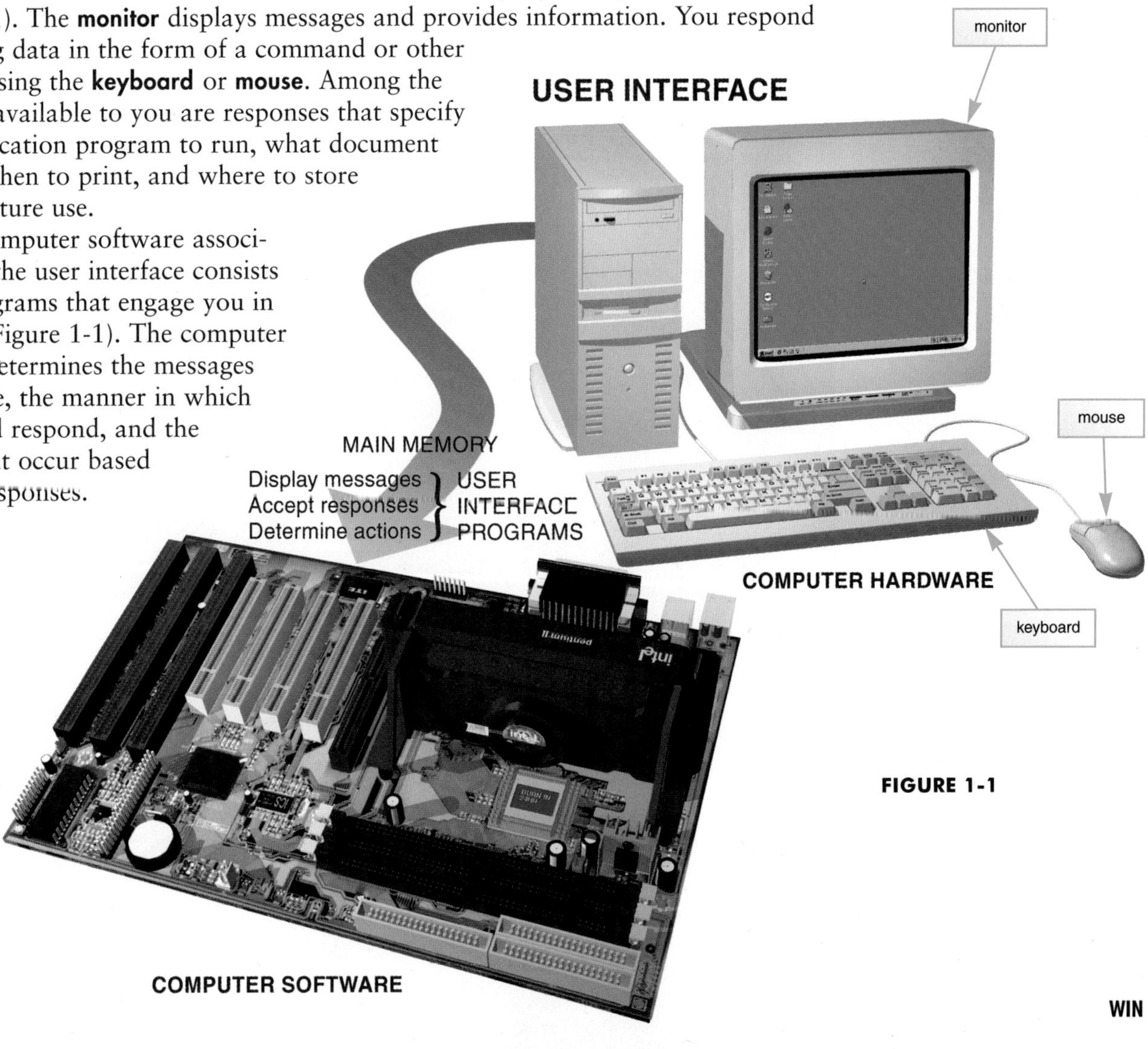

FIGURE 1-1

The Windows 98 Interface

The Windows 98 graphical user interface is similar to and an improvement of the Windows 95 graphical user interface. Thousands of hours were spent making improvements to Windows 95. Of tremendous importance were Microsoft's usability labs, where everyone from raw beginners to experts interacted with many different versions of the interface. The Quick Launch toolbar and other significant improvements of the Windows 98 interface emerged from the experiences in these labs.

The goal of an effective user interface is to be **user friendly**, meaning that the software can be used easily by individuals with limited training. Research studies have indicated that the use of graphics can play an important role in aiding users to interact effectively with a computer. A **graphical user interface**, or **GUI** (pronounced gooey), is a user interface that displays graphics in addition to text when it communicates with the user.

The Windows 98 graphical user interface was carefully designed to be easier to set up, simpler to learn, faster and more powerful, and better integrated with the Internet than previous versions of Microsoft Windows.

Launching Microsoft Windows 98

When you turn on your computer, an introductory screen consisting of the Windows logo and Windows 98 name displays on a blue sky and clouds background in the middle of the screen. The screen clears and several items display on a background called the **desktop.** The default color of the desktop background is green, but your computer may display a different color. Your screen will display as shown in Figure 1-2 or Figure 1-3 on page WIN 1.10, depending upon whether you have chosen to display the Welcome screen.

The Windows 98 Desktop

Because Windows 98 is easily customized, the desktop on your computer may not resemble the desktop in Figure 1-2. For example, the icon titles on the desktop may be underlined or objects not shown in Figure 1-2 may display on your desktop. If this is the case, refer to page viii of the Preface of this book for instructions for selecting the default desktop view settings or contact your instructor to change the desktop view.

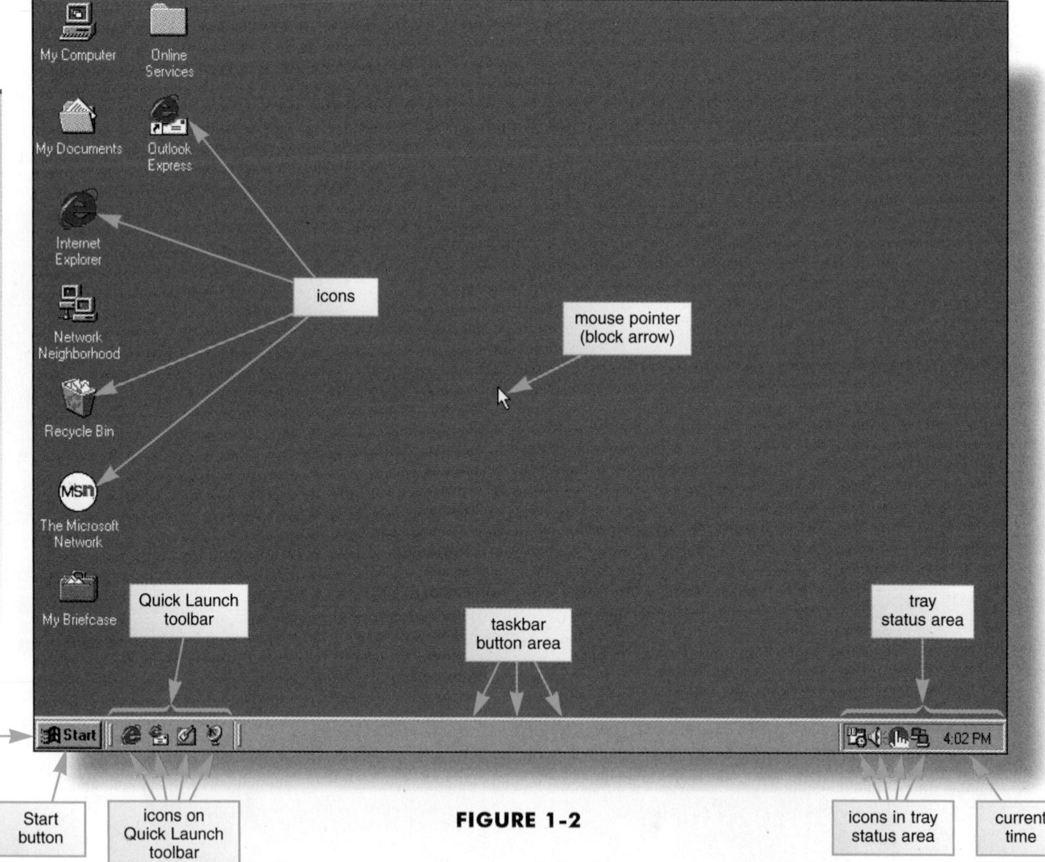

FIGURE 1-2

The items on the desktop shown in Figure 1-2 include nine icons and their titles on the left side of the desktop and the taskbar at the bottom of the desktop. Using the nine **icons**, you can view the contents of your computer (**My Computer**), store documents in one location (**My Documents**), connect to and browse the Internet (**Internet Explorer**), work with other computers connected to your computer (**Network Neighborhood**), discard unneeded objects (**Recycle Bin**), connect to the Microsoft Network online service (**The Microsoft Network**), transfer documents or folders to and from a portable computer (**My Briefcase**), investigate other online services (**Online Services**), and receive and send e-mail (**Outlook Express**). Your computer's desktop might contain more, fewer, or some different icons because the desktop of the computer can be customized.

The **taskbar** at the bottom of the screen in Figure 1-2 contains the Start button, Quick Launch toolbar, taskbar button area, and the tray status area. The **Start button** allows you to launch a program quickly, find or open a document, change your computer's settings, shut down the computer, and perform many more tasks. The **Quick Launch toolbar** contains four icons that allow you to launch Internet Explorer (**Launch Internet Explorer Browser**), launch Outlook Express (**Launch Outlook Express**), view an uncluttered desktop at any time (**Show Desktop**), and view a list of channels (**View Channels**).

The **taskbar button area** contains buttons to indicate which windows are open on the desktop. In Figure 1-2, no windows display on the desktop and no buttons display in the taskbar button area. The **tray status area** contains the **Task Scheduler icon** to schedule daily tasks, a **speaker icon** to adjust the computer's volume level, **The Microsoft Network icon** to connect to The Microsoft Network online service, the **Internet connection icon** to indicate a modem is being used to connect to the Internet, and the current time (4:02 PM). The tray status area on your desktop might contain more, fewer, or some different icons because the contents of the tray status area can be changed.

Nearly every item on the Windows 98 desktop is considered an object. Even the desktop itself is an object. Every **object** has properties. The **properties** of an object are unique to that specific object and may affect what can be done to the object or what the object does. For example, the properties of an object may be the color of the object, such as the color of the desktop. You will learn more about properties in Project 3 of this book.

In the middle of the screen is the mouse pointer. On the desktop, the **mouse pointer** is the shape of a block arrow. The mouse pointer allows you to point to objects on the desktop and may change shape when it points to different objects.

The Welcome to Windows 98 Screen

The Welcome to Windows 98 screen that may display on your desktop when you launch Windows 98 is shown in Figure 1-3 on the next page. The **title bar**, which is dark blue in color at the top of the screen, contains the Windows icon, identifies the name of the screen (Welcome to Windows 98), and contains the Close button, which can be used to close the Welcome to Windows 98 screen.

More *About*

Desktop Views

You can view the desktop in Classic style, Web style, or you can customize the desktop view by selecting features from both styles. You can choose to single-click or double-click icons, underline all icon titles or underline icon titles only when you point to them, and display the Classic Windows Desktop or the Active Desktop. When you customize the desktop view, the style is referred to as the Custom style.

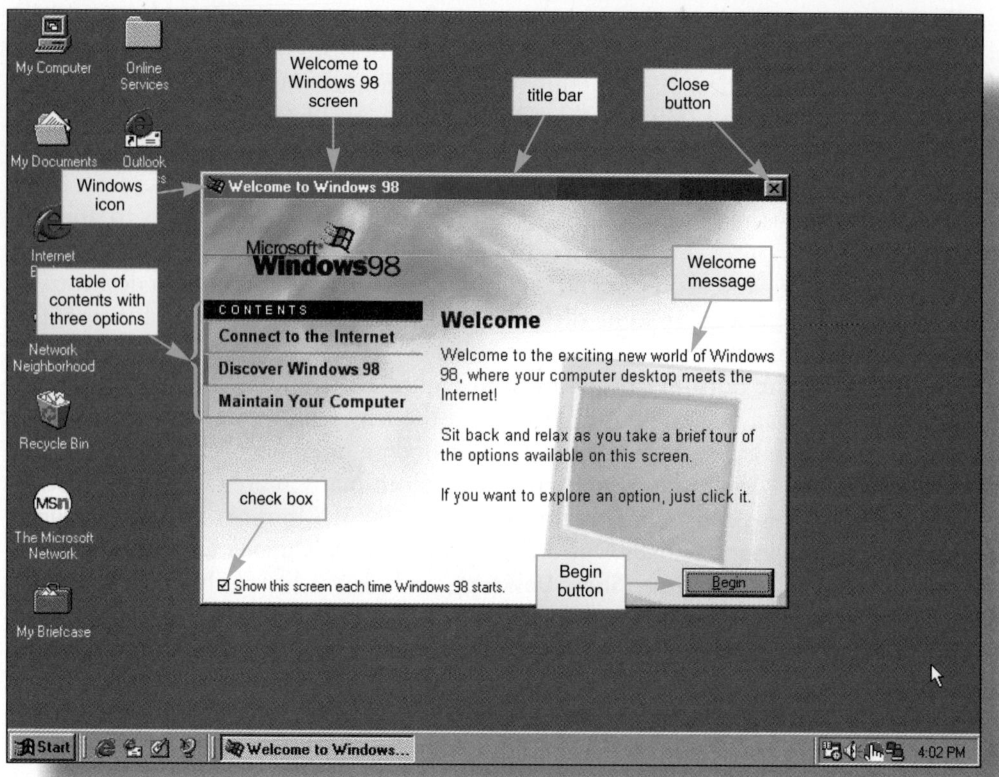

FIGURE 1-3

On the Welcome to Windows 98 screen, a table of contents contains three options (Connect to the Internet, Discover Windows 98, and Maintain Your Computer) and a welcome message (Welcome). The options in the table of contents allow you to perform different tasks such as connecting to the Internet, learning Windows 98 using the Discover Windows 98 tutorial, and improving the performance of your computer. A message to the right of the table of contents welcomes you to the world of Windows 98. Pointing to an option in the table of contents replaces the Welcome message with an explanation of the option. The **Begin button** in the lower-right corner begins the process of connecting to the Internet, and a check mark in the **check box** to the left of the Begin button indicates the Welcome to Windows 98 screen will display each time you start Windows 98.

Closing the Welcome Screen

As noted, the Welcome screen may display when you launch Windows 98. If the Welcome screen does display on the desktop, normally you should close it prior to beginning any other operations using Windows 98. To close the Welcome screen, complete the following step.

TO CLOSE THE WELCOME SCREEN

 Press and hold the ALT key on the keyboard and then press the F4 key on the keyboard. Release the ALT key.

The Welcome to Windows 98 screen closes and the desktop displays as shown in Figure 1-2 on page WIN 1.8.

The Desktop as a Work Area

The Windows 98 desktop and the objects on the desktop were designed to emulate a work area in an office or at home. The Windows desktop may be thought of as an electronic version of the top of your desk. You can move objects around on the desktop, look at them and then put them aside, and so on. In Project 1, you will learn how to interact with and communicate with the Windows 98 desktop.

More About

The Mouse

The mouse, though invented in the 1960s, was not used widely until the Apple Macintosh computer became available in 1984. Even then, some highbrows called mouse users "wimps." Today, the mouse is an indispensable tool for every computer user.

Communicating with Microsoft Windows 98

The Windows 98 interface provides the means for dialogue between you and your computer. Part of this dialogue involves your requesting information from your computer and responding to messages displayed by your computer. You can request information and respond to messages using either a mouse or a keyboard.

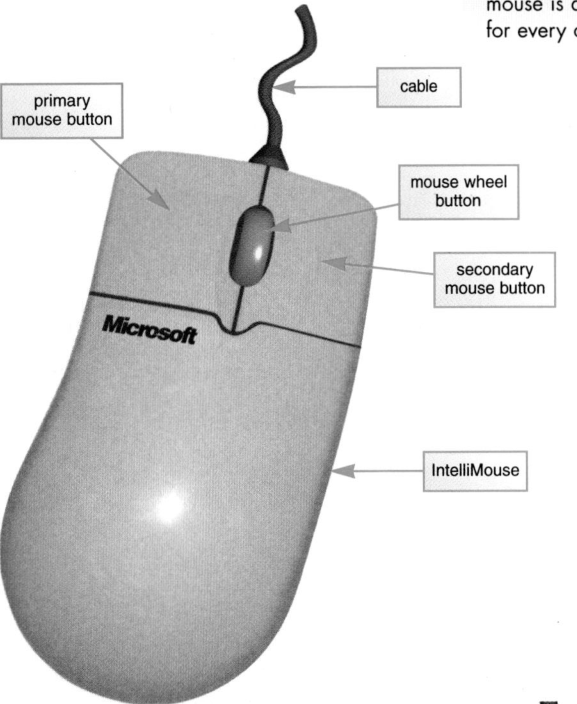

FIGURE 1-4

Mouse Operations

A **mouse** is a pointing device used with Windows 98 that is attached to the computer by a cable. Although not required to use Windows 98, Windows supports the use of the **Microsoft IntelliMouse** (Figure 1-4). The IntelliMouse contains three buttons, the primary mouse button, the secondary mouse button, and the wheel button between the primary and secondary mouse buttons. Typically, the **primary mouse button** is the left mouse button and the **secondary mouse button** is the right mouse button although Windows 98 allows you to switch them. In this book, the left mouse button is the primary mouse button and the right mouse button is the secondary mouse button. The function the **wheel button** and wheel perform depends on the software application being used. If the mouse connected to your computer is not an IntelliMouse, it will not have a wheel button between the primary and secondary mouse buttons.

Using the mouse, you can perform the following operations: (1) point; (2) click; (3) right-click; (4) double-click; (5) drag; and (6) right-drag. These operations are demonstrated on the following pages.

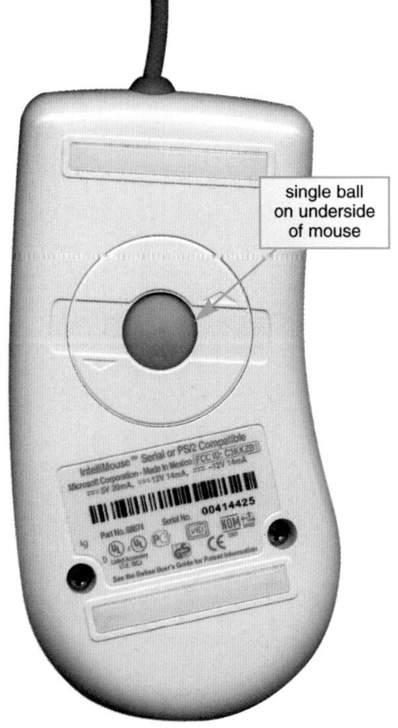

FIGURE 1-5

Point and Click

Point means you move the mouse across a flat surface until the mouse pointer rests on the item of choice on the desktop. As you move the mouse across a flat surface, the movement of a ball on the underside of the mouse (Figure 1-5) is sensed electronically, and the mouse pointer moves across the desktop in the same direction.

Click means you press and release the primary mouse button, which in this book is the left mouse button. In most cases, you must point to an item before you click. To become acquainted with the use of the mouse, perform the following steps to point to and click various objects on the desktop.

To Point and Click

1 Point to the Start button on the taskbar by moving the mouse across a flat surface until the mouse pointer rests on the Start button.

The mouse pointer on the Start button displays a ***ToolTip*** *(Click here to begin.) (Figure 1-6). The ToolTip, which provides instructions, displays on the desktop for approximately five seconds. Other ToolTips display on the screen until you move the mouse pointer off the object.*

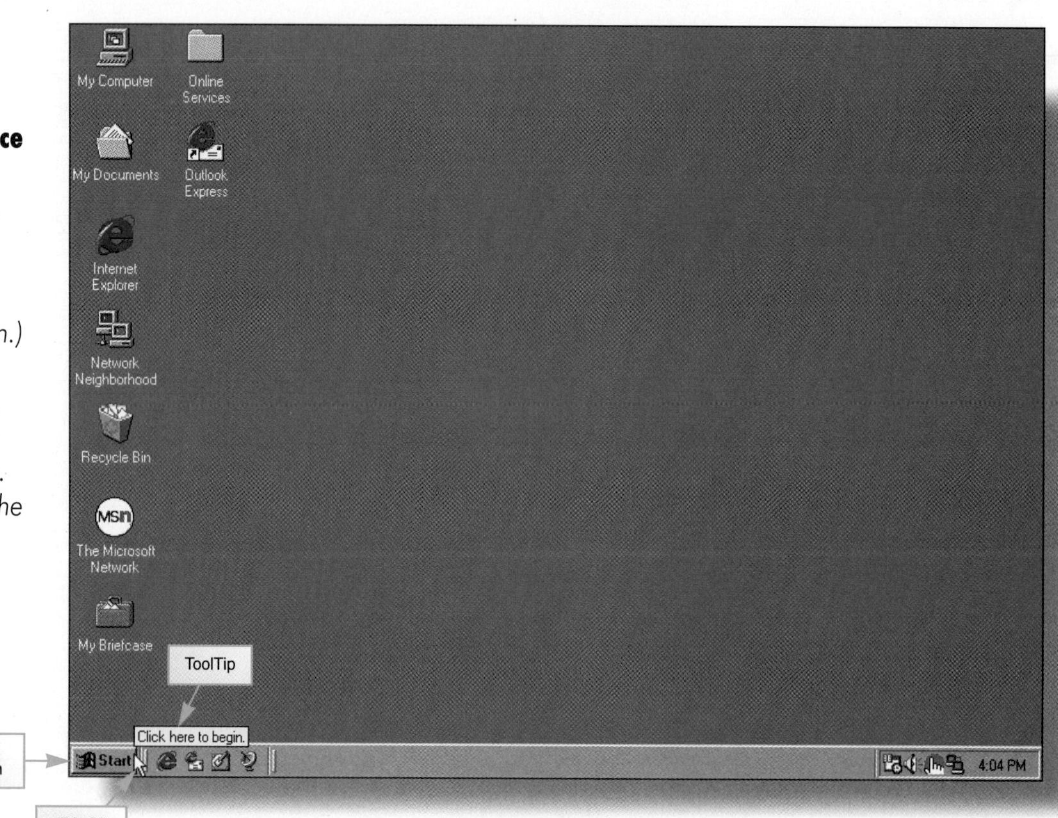

FIGURE 1-6

2 Click the Start button on the taskbar by pressing and releasing the left mouse button.

The ***Start menu*** *displays and the Start button is recessed on the taskbar (Figure 1-7). A* ***menu*** *is a list of related commands. A* ***command*** *directs Windows 98 to perform a specific action such as shutting down the operating system. Each command on the Start menu consists of an icon and a command name. A* ***right arrow*** *follows some commands to indicate pointing to the command will open a submenu. Three commands (Run, Log Off Steven Forsythe, and Shut Down) are followed by an* ***ellipsis*** *(...) to indicate more information is required to execute these commands.*

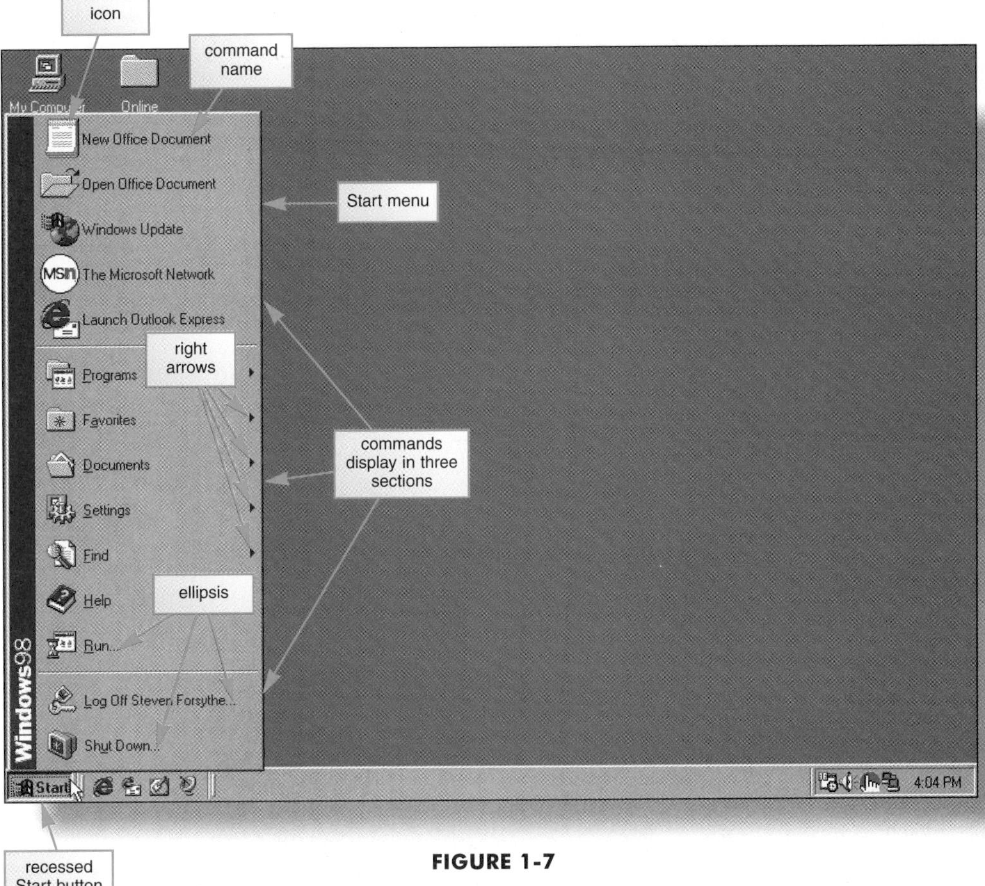

FIGURE 1-7

3 Point to Programs on the Start menu.

When you point to Programs, Windows 98 highlights the Programs command on the Start menu and the ***Programs submenu*** *displays (Figure 1-8). A* ***submenu, or cascading menu,*** *is a menu that displays when you point to a command that is followed by a right arrow. For example, pointing to the Accessories command on the Programs submenu will display another submenu. Whenever you point to a command on a menu, the command is highlighted.*

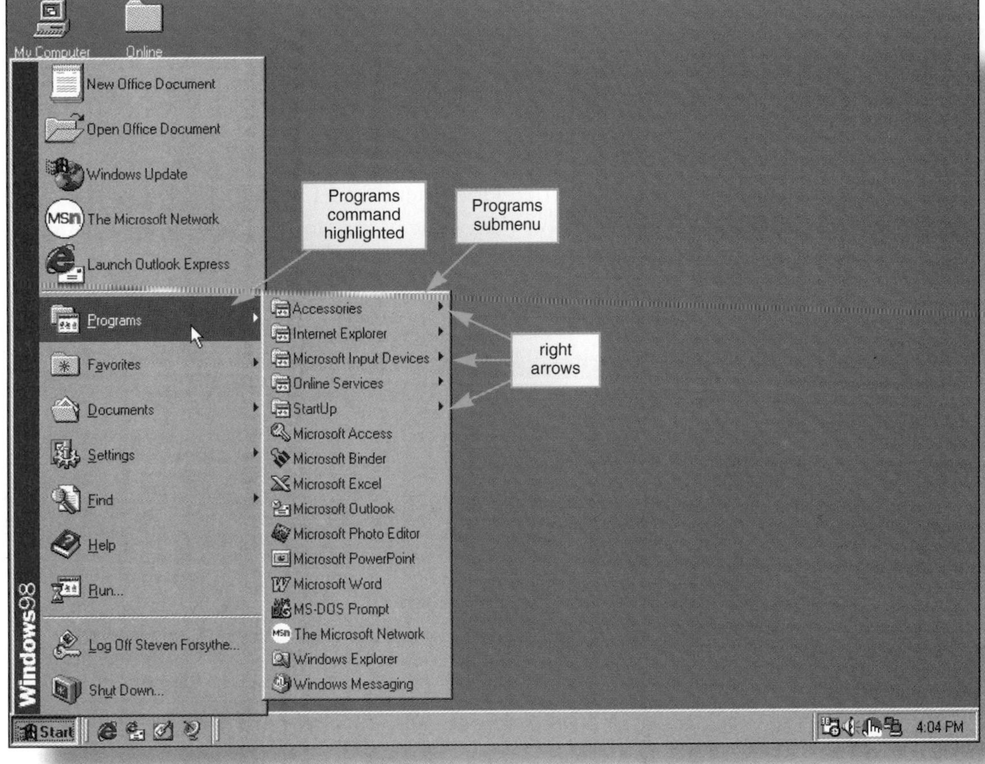

FIGURE 1-8

4 **Point to an open area of the desktop (Figure 1-9).**

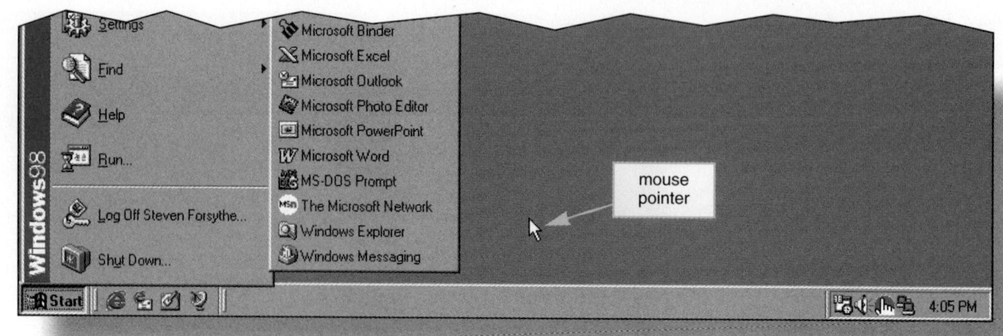

FIGURE 1-9

5 **Click the open area of the desktop.**

The Start menu and Programs submenu close (Figure 1-10). The mouse pointer points to the desktop. To close a menu anytime, click any open area of the desktop except on the menu itself. The Start button is no longer recessed.

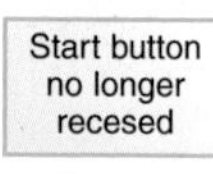

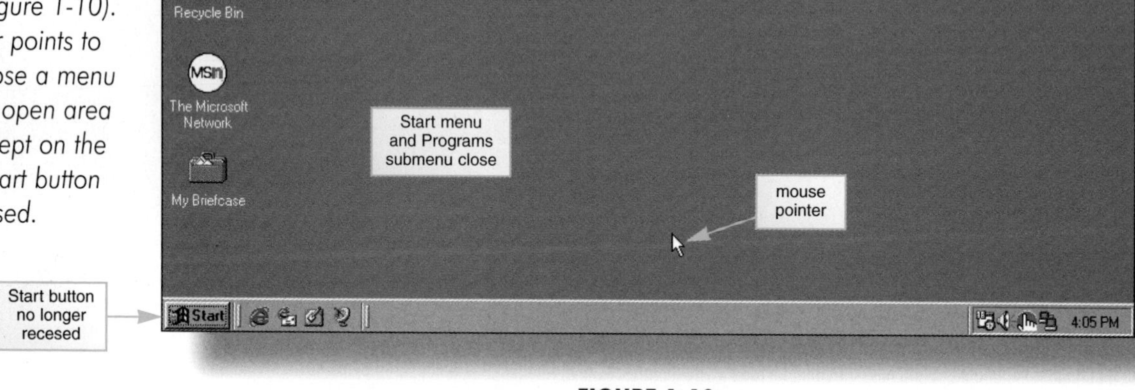

FIGURE 1-10

Buttons

Buttons on the desktop and in programs are an integral part of Windows 98. When you point to them, their function displays in a ToolTip. When you click them, they appear to indent on the screen to mimic what would happen if you pushed an actual button. All buttons in Windows 98 behave in the same manner.

The Right Mouse Button

Earlier versions of Microsoft Windows made little use of the right mouse button. In Windows 98, you will find using the right mouse button essential.

The Start menu in Figure 1-7 on the previous page is divided into three sections. The top section contains commands to create or open a Microsoft Office document (New Office Document and Open Office Document), launch the Windows Update application (Windows Update), connect to The Microsoft Network (The Microsoft Network), and launch the Outlook Express application (Launch Outlook Express); the middle section contains commands to launch an application, work with documents or Web sites, customize options, and search for files or Help (Programs, Favorites, Documents, Settings, Find, Help, and Run); and the bottom section contains basic operating tasks (Log Off Steven Forsythe and Shut Down).

When you click an object such as the Start button in Figure 1-7, you must point to the object before you click. In the steps that follow, the instruction that directs you to point to a particular item and then click is, Click the particular item. For example, Click the Start button means point to the Start button and then click.

Right-Click

Right-click means you press and release the secondary mouse button, which in this book is the right mouse button. As directed when using the primary mouse button for clicking an object, normally you will point to an object before you right-click it. Perform the following steps to right-click the desktop.

Steps To Right-Click

1 Point to an open area of the desktop and then press and release the right mouse button.

A shortcut menu displays (Figure 1-11). The shortcut menu in Figure 1-11 consists of nine commands. Right-clicking an object, such as the desktop, opens a ***shortcut menu*** *that contains a set of commands specifically for use with that object. When a command on a menu appears dimmed, such as the Paste Shortcut command, that command is unavailable.*

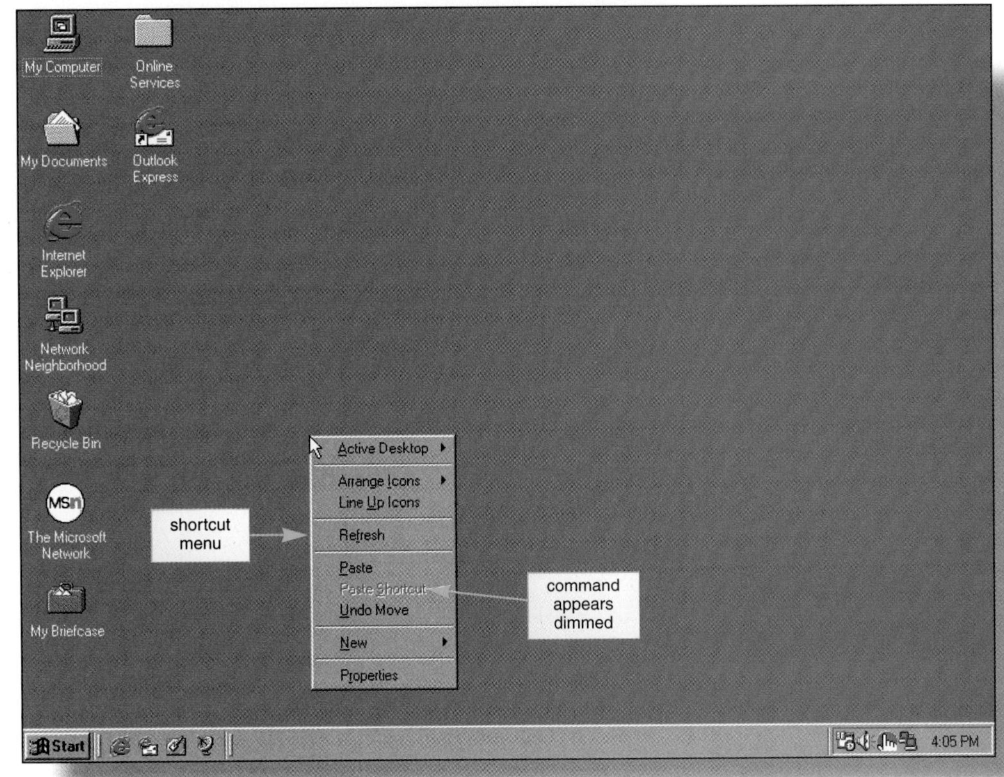

FIGURE 1-11

2 Point to New on the shortcut menu.

When you move the mouse pointer to the New command, Windows 98 highlights the New command and opens the New submenu (Figure 1-12). The New submenu contains a variety of commands. The number of commands and the actual commands that display on your computer may be different from those shown in Figure 1-12 because the New submenu lists some of the application programs available on your computer.

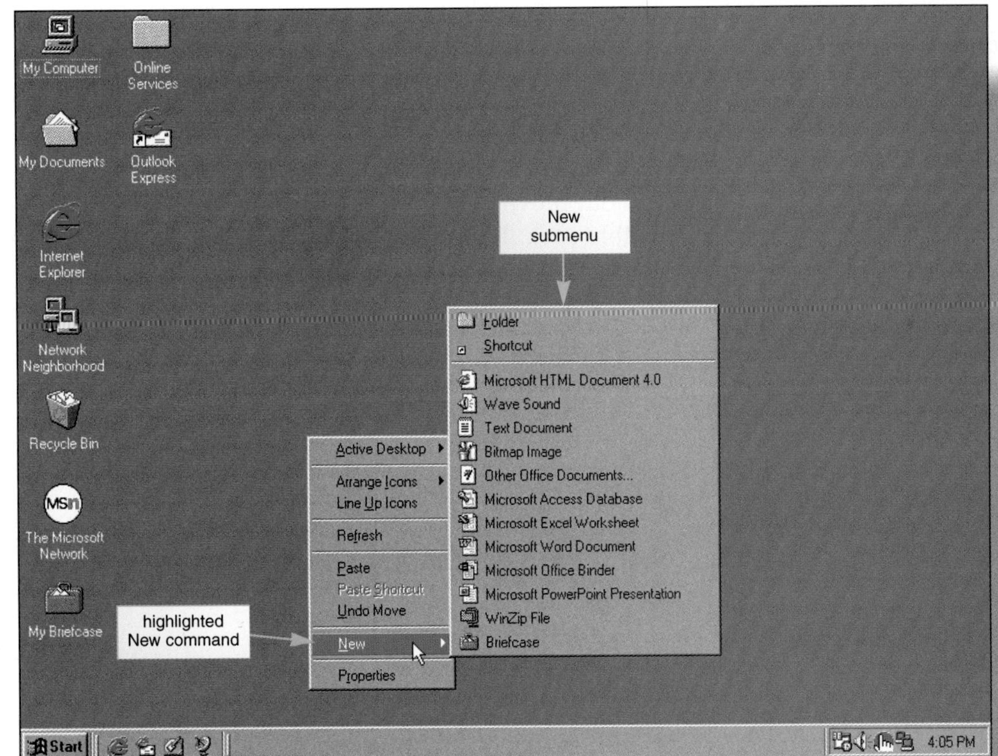

FIGURE 1-12

3 Click an open area of the desktop to remove the shortcut menu and the New submenu.

The shortcut menu and New submenu close (Figure 1-13). The mouse pointer remains on the desktop.

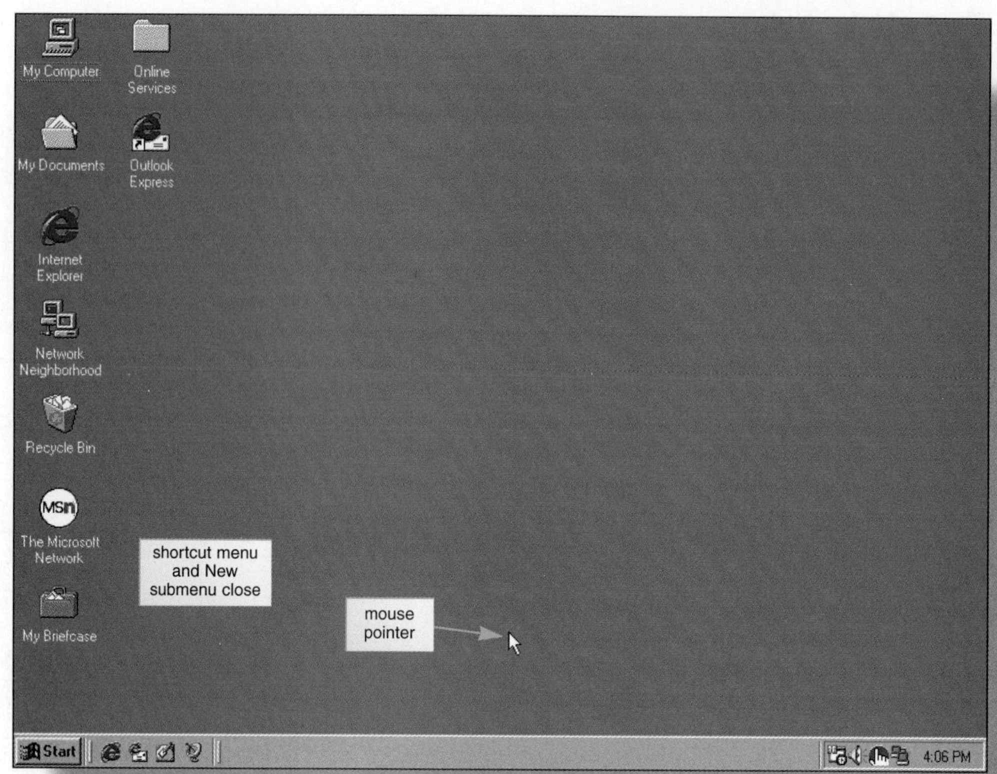

FIGURE 1-13

Right-Clicking

Right-clicking an object other than the desktop will display a different shortcut menu with commands useful to that object. Right-clicking an object is thought to be the fastest method of performing an operation on an object.

Whenever you right-click an object, a shortcut menu (also referred to as an object menu) will display. As you will see, the use of shortcut menus speeds up your work and adds flexibility to your interface with the computer.

Double-Click

Double-click means you quickly press and release the left mouse button twice without moving the mouse. In most cases, you must point to an item before you double-click. Perform the following step to open the My Computer window on the desktop by double-clicking the My Computer icon.

Double-Clicking

Double-clicking is the most difficult mouse skill to learn. Many people have a tendency to move the mouse before they click a second time, even when they do not want to move the mouse. You should find, however, that with a little practice, double-clicking becomes quite natural.

To Open a Window by Double-Clicking

1 Point to the My Computer icon on the desktop and then double-click by quickly pressing and releasing the left mouse button twice without moving the mouse.

The My Computer window opens (Figure 1-14). The recessed My Computer button is added to the taskbar button area.

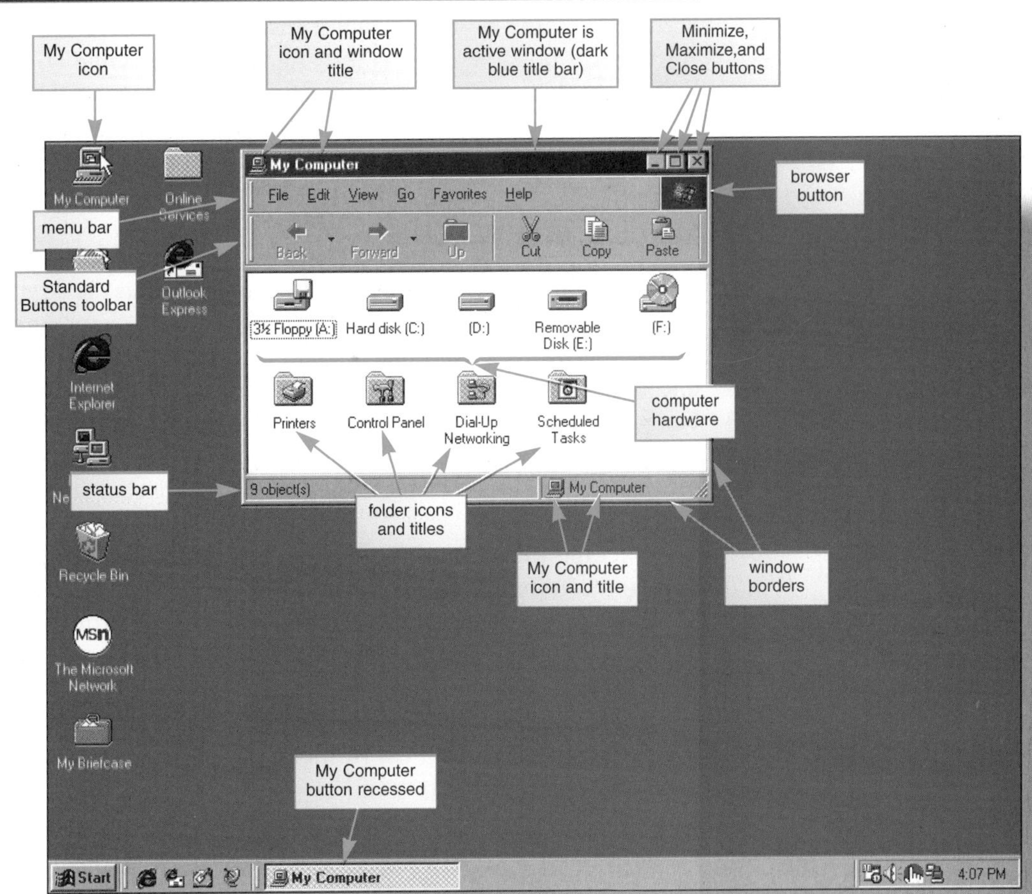

FIGURE 1-14

The My Computer window, the only open window, is the active window. The **active window** is the window currently being used. Whenever you click an object that can be opened, such as the My Computer icon, Windows 98 will open the object; and the open object will be identified by a recessed button in the taskbar button area. The recessed button identifies the active window.

The contents of the My Computer window on your computer may be different from the contents of the My Computer window in Figure 1-14.

Double-Clicking Errors

While double-clicking an object, you easily can click once instead of twice. When you click an object such as the My Computer icon once, the icon becomes the active icon and Windows 98 highlights the icon and its title. To open the My Computer window after clicking the My Computer icon once, double-click the My Computer icon as if you had not clicked the icon at all.

More About

The My Computer Window

Because Windows 98 is easily customized, the My Computer window on your computer may not resemble the window in Figure 1-14. If this is the case, check the commands on the View menu by clicking View on the menu bar. If a check mark precedes the as Web Page command, click the as Web Page command. If a large dot does not precede the Large Icons command, click the Large Icons command.

Another possible error is moving the mouse after you click the first time and before you click the second time. In most cases if you do this, the icon will be highlighted the same as if you click it just one time.

A third possible error is moving the mouse while you are pressing the mouse button. In this case, the icon might actually move on the screen because you have inadvertently dragged it. To open the My Computer window after dragging it accidentally, double-click the icon as if you had not clicked it at all.

More About

My Computer

The trade press and media have poked fun at the icon name, My Computer. One wag said no one should use Windows 98 for more than five minutes without changing the name (which is easily done). Microsoft responds that in their usability labs, beginning computer users found the name, My Computer, easier to understand.

My Computer Window

The thin line, or **window border**, surrounding the My Computer window in Figure 1-14 on the previous page determines its shape and size. The **title bar** at the top of the window contains a small icon that is the same as the icon on the desktop and the **window title** (My Computer) that identifies the window. The color of the title bar (dark blue) and the recessed My Computer button in the taskbar button area indicate the My Computer window is the active window. The color of the active window on your computer might be different from the dark blue color shown in Figure 1-14.

Clicking the icon at the left on the title bar will open the **System menu**, which contains commands to carry out the actions associated with the My Computer window. At the right on the title bar are three buttons, the Minimize button, the Maximize button, and the Close button, that can be used to specify the size of the window and close the window.

The **menu bar**, which is the horizontal bar below the title bar of a window (see Figure 1-14), contains a list of menu names for the My Computer window: File, Edit, View, Go, Favorites, and Help. One letter in each menu name is underlined. You can open a menu by clicking the menu name on the menu bar or by typing the corresponding underlined letter on the keyboard in combination with the ALT key. At the right end of the menu bar is a button containing the Windows logo. Clicking this button starts the Microsoft Internet Explorer Web browser and displays one of the Web pages in the Microsoft Web site in the browser window.

Below the menu bar is the **Standard Buttons toolbar** containing buttons that allow you to navigate through open windows on the desktop (Back, Forward, and Up) and copy and move text within a window or between windows (Cut, Copy, and Paste). Additional buttons display when the size of the window is increased. Each button contains a **text label** and an icon describing its function.

The area below the Standard Buttons toolbar contains nine icons. An underlined title below each icon identifies the icon. The five icons in the top row, called **drive icons**, represent a 3½ Floppy (A:) drive, a Hard disk (C:) drive, a different area on the same hard disk (D:), a Removable Disk (E:) drive, and a CD-ROM drive (F:).

The four icons in the second row are folders. A **folder** is an object created to contain related documents, applications, and other folders. A folder in Windows 98 contains items in much the same way a folder on your desk contains items.

The **Printers folder** (see Figure 1-14 on the previous page) allows you to add a new printer or change the settings for an existing printer. The **Control Panel folder** allows you to personalize your computer, such as specifying how you want your desktop to look. The **Dial-Up Networking folder** allows you to access information on other computers. The **Scheduled Tasks folder** allow you to schedule repetitive tasks, such as deleting all unnecessary files, when it is most convenient for you. If you double-click a drive or folder icon, the contents of the drive or folder display in place of the nine icons shown in Figure 1-14.

A message at the left on the **status bar** located at the bottom of the window indicates the right panel contains nine objects (see Figure 1-14). The My Computer icon and My Computer icon title display to the right of the message on the status bar.

Minimizing Windows

Windows management on the Windows 98 desktop is important in order to keep the desktop uncluttered. You will find yourself frequently minimizing windows and then later reopening them with a click of a button in the taskbar button area.

Minimize Button

Two buttons on the title bar of a window, the Minimize button and the Maximize button, allow you to control the way a window displays or does not display on the desktop. When you click the **Minimize button** (see Figure 1-14 on page WIN 1.17), the My Computer window no longer displays on the desktop and the recessed My Computer button in the taskbar button area changes to a non-recessed button. A minimized window is still open but it does not display on the screen. To minimize and then redisplay the My Computer window, complete these steps.

To Minimize and Redisplay a Window

1 Point to the Minimize button on the title bar of the My Computer window.

The mouse pointer points to the Minimize button on the My Computer window title bar (Figure 1-15). A ToolTip displays below the Minimize button and the My Computer button in the taskbar button area is recessed.

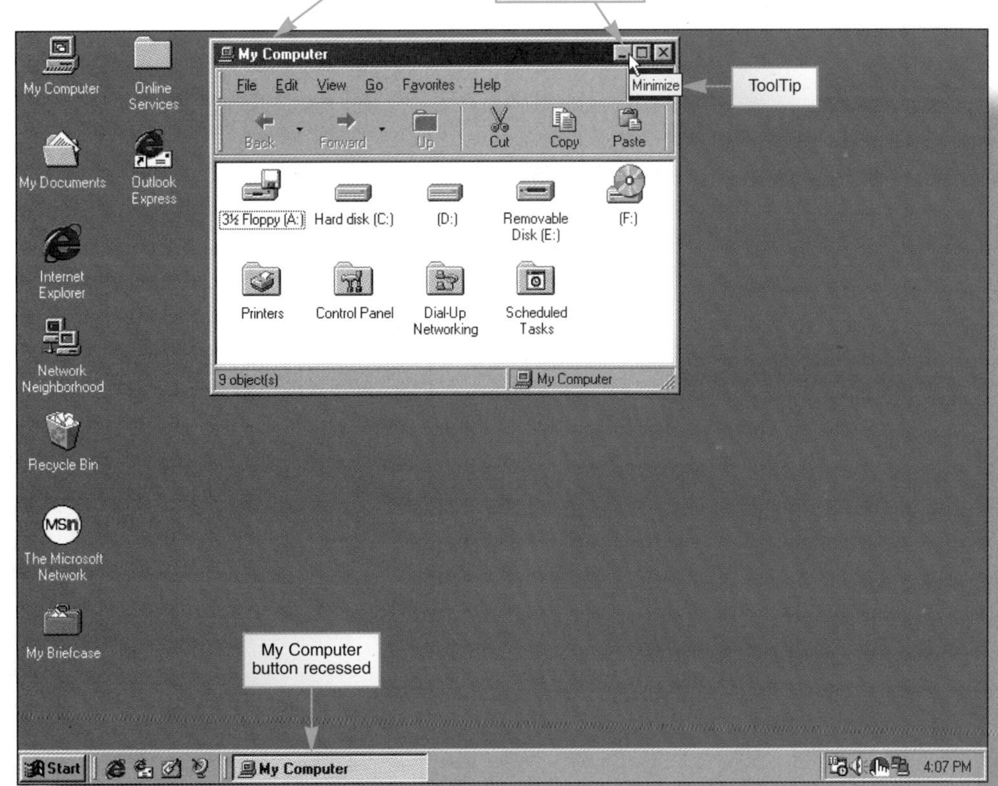

FIGURE 1-15

2 Click the Minimize button.

When you minimize the My Compuer window, Windows 98 removes the My Computer window from the desktop and the My Computer button changes to a non-recessed button (Figure 1-16).

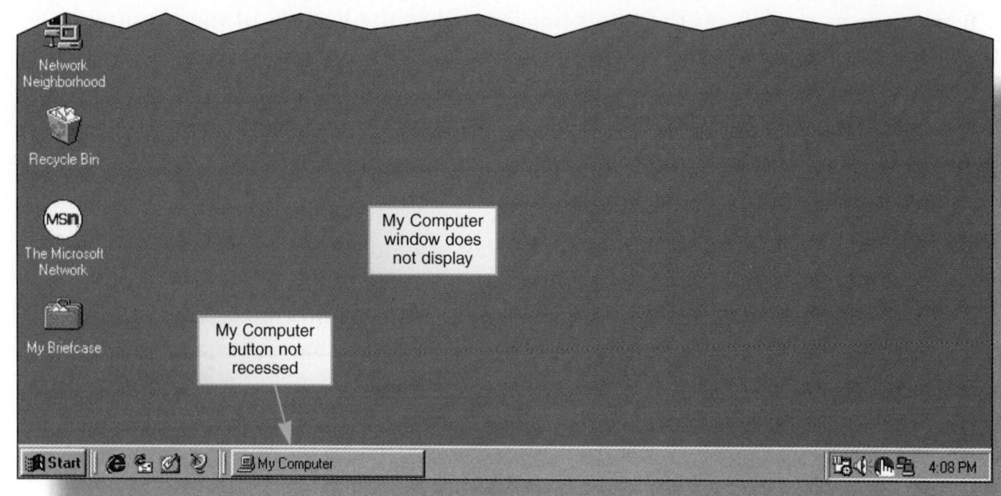

FIGURE 1-16

3 Click the My Computer button in the taskbar button area.

The My Computer window displays on the desktop in the same place and size as it was before being minimized (Figure 1-17). In addition, the My Computer window is the active window because it contains the dark blue title bar, and the My Computer button in the taskbar button area is recessed.

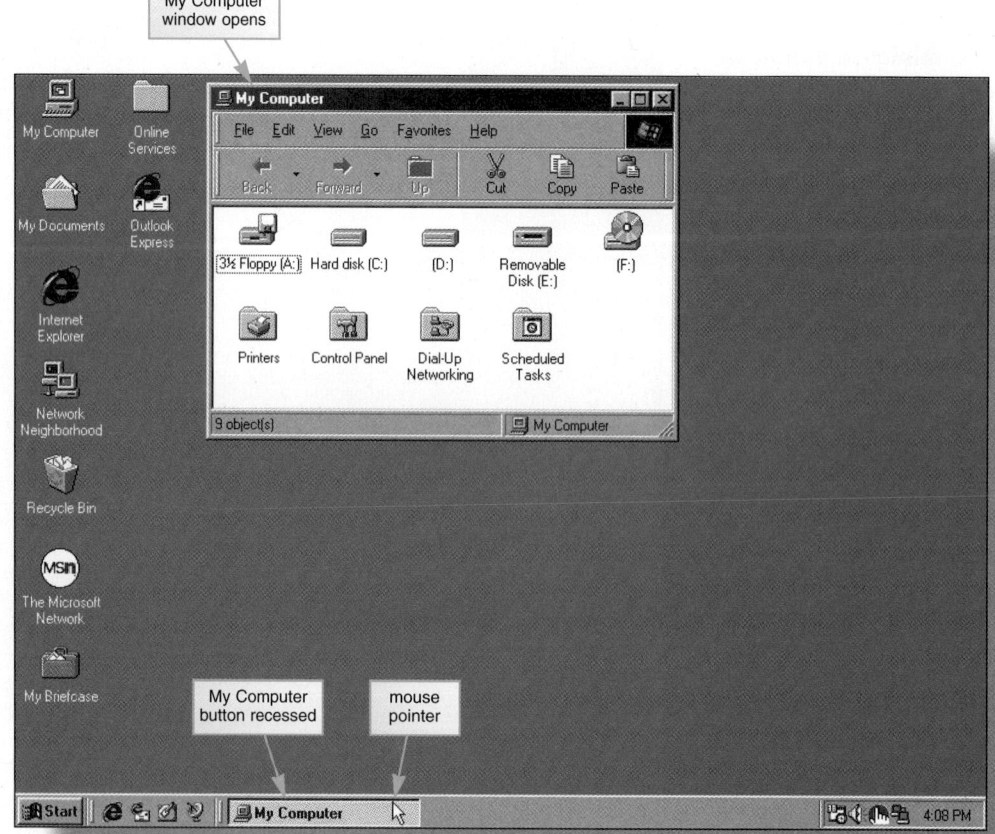

FIGURE 1-17

Whenever a window is minimized, it does not display on the desktop but a non-recessed button for the window does display in the taskbar button area. Whenever you want a minimized window to display and be the active window, click its button in the taskbar button area.

Maximize and Restore Buttons

Sometimes when information is displayed in a window, the information is not completely visible. One method to display the entire contents of a window is to enlarge the window using the **Maximize button**. The Maximize button maximizes a window so the window fills the entire screen, making it easier to see the contents of the window. When a window is maximized, the **Restore button** replaces the Maximize button on the title bar. Clicking the Restore button will return the window to its size before maximizing. To maximize and restore the My Computer window, complete the following steps.

Maximizing Windows

Many application programs run in a maximized window by default. Often you will find that you want to work with maximized windows.

To Maximize and Restore a Window

1 Point to the Maximize button on the title bar of the My Computer window (Figure 1-18).

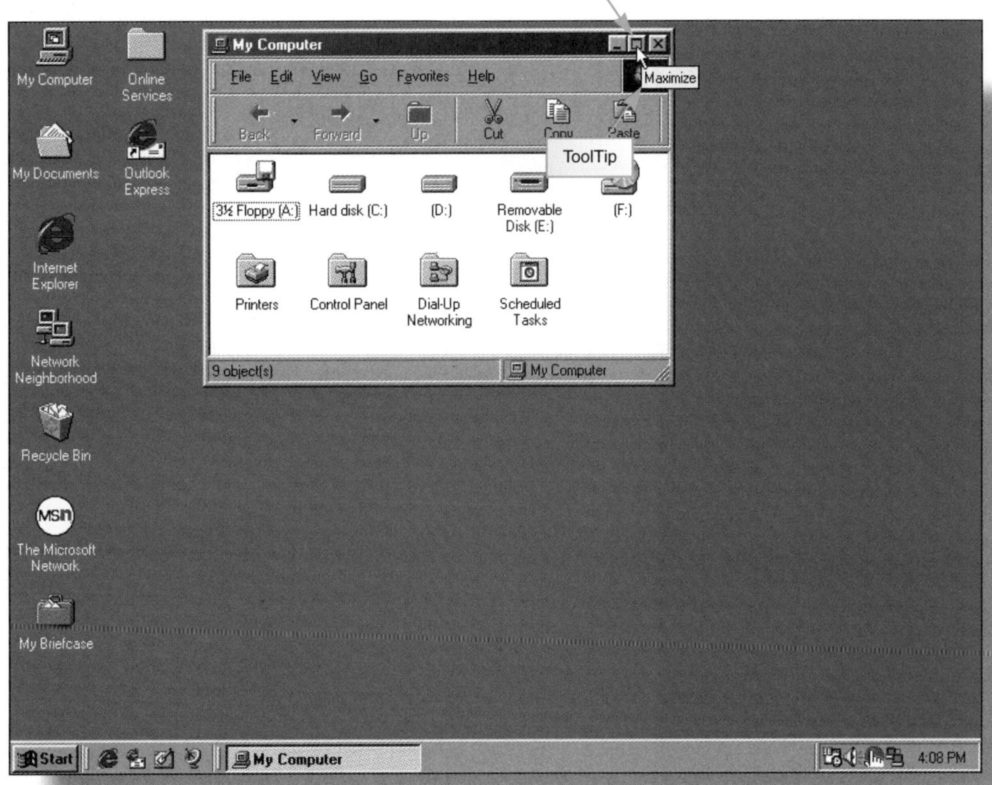

FIGURE 1-18

2 Click the Maximize button.

*The My Computer window expands so it and the taskbar fill the entire screen (Figure 1-19). The Restore button replaces the Maximize button and the My Computer button in the taskbar button area does not change. The My Computer window is still the active window and additional buttons display on the Standard Buttons toolbar that allow you to undo a previous action (**Undo**), delete text (**Delete**), display the properties of an object (**Properties**), and change the desktop view (Views).*

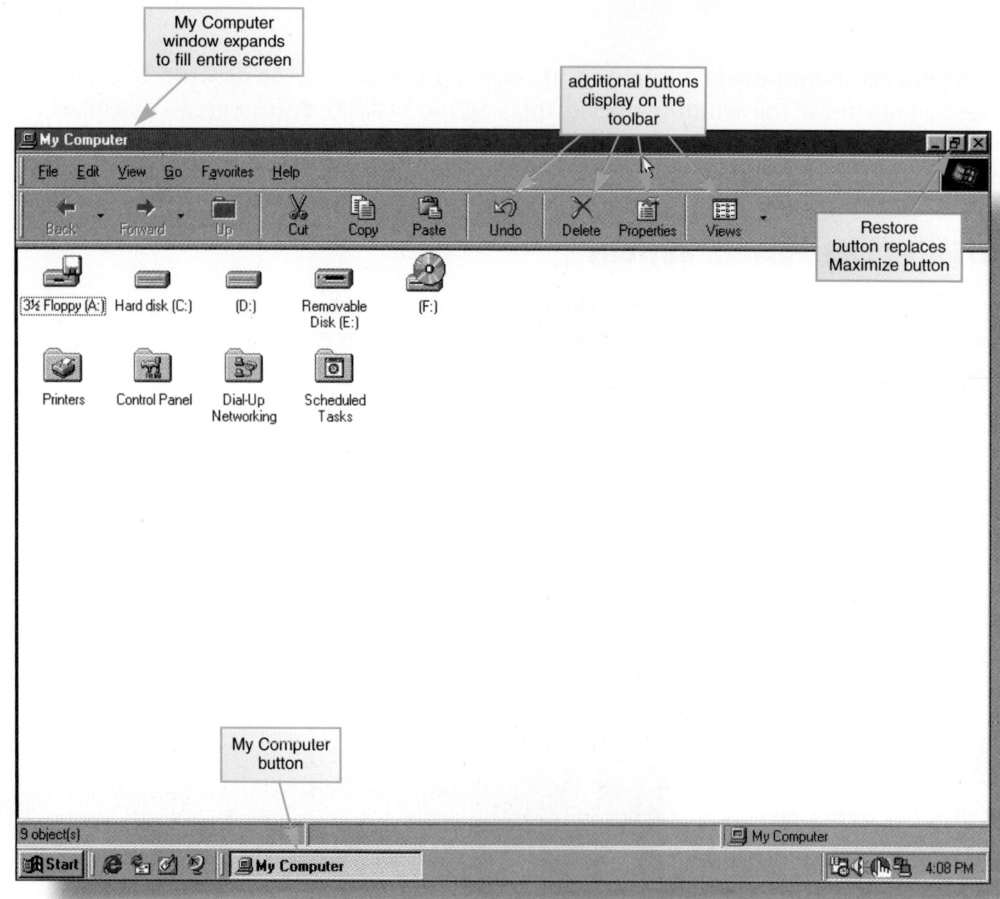

FIGURE 1-19

3 Point to the Restore button on the title bar of the My Computer window (Figure 1-20).

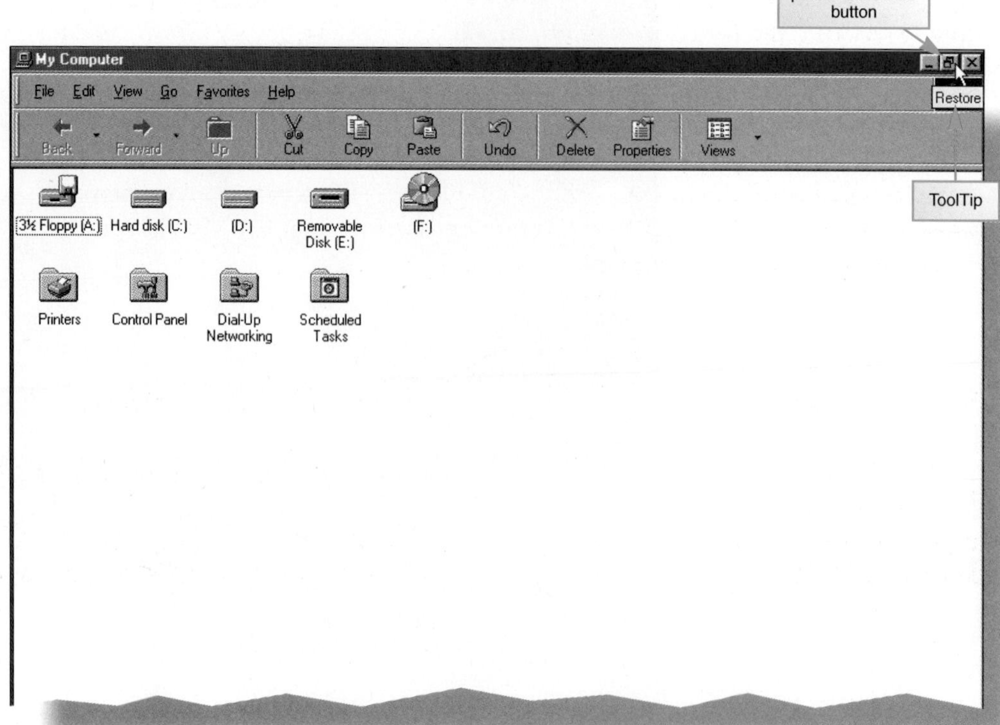

FIGURE 1-20

Click the Restore button.

The My Computer window returns to the size and position it occupied before being maximized (Figure 1-21). The My Computer button does not change. The Maximize button replaces the Restore button.

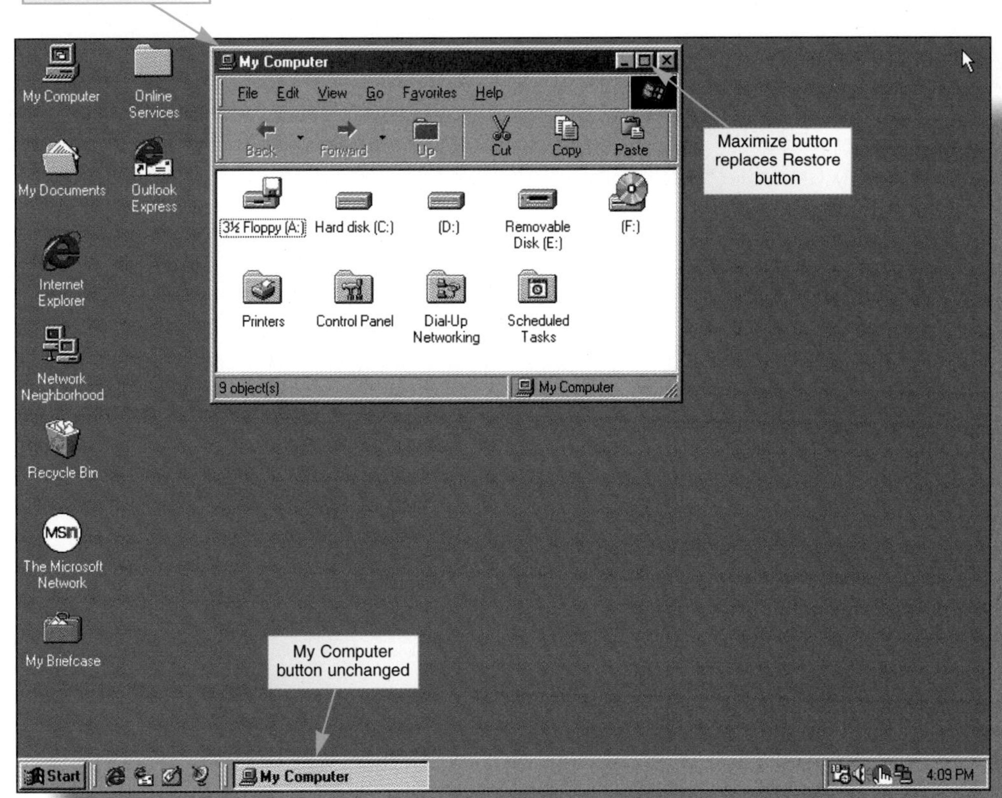

FIGURE 1-21

When a window is maximized, such as in Figure 1-19, you also can minimize the window by clicking the Minimize button. If, after minimizing the window, you click its button in the taskbar button area, the window will return to its maximized size.

Close Button

The **Close button** on the title bar of a window closes the window and removes the window button from the taskbar. To close and then reopen the My Computer window, complete the following steps.

The Close Button

The Close button was a new innovation in the Windows 95 operating system. Before Windows 95, the user either had to double-click a button or click a command on a menu to close the window. As always, the choice of how to perform an operation such as closing a window is a matter of personal preference. In most cases, you will want to choose the method that causes the least amount of work.

Steps To Close a Window and Reopen a Window

Point to the Close button on the title bar of the My Computer window (Figure 1-22).

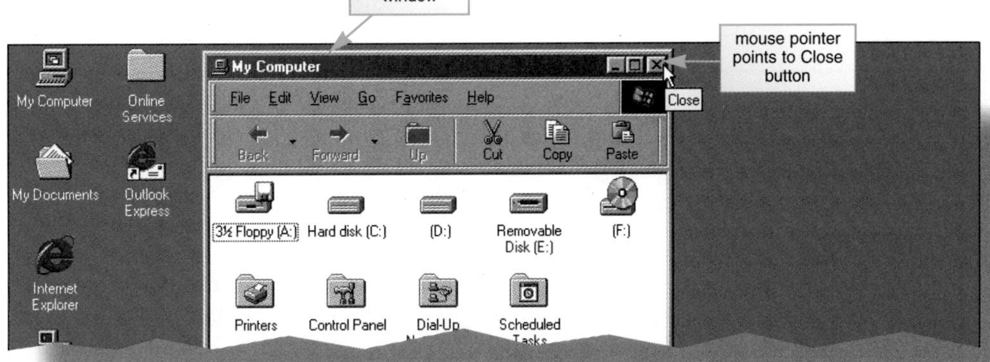

FIGURE 1-22

Click the Close button.

The My Computer window closes and the My Computer button no longer displays in the taskbar button area (Figure 1-23).

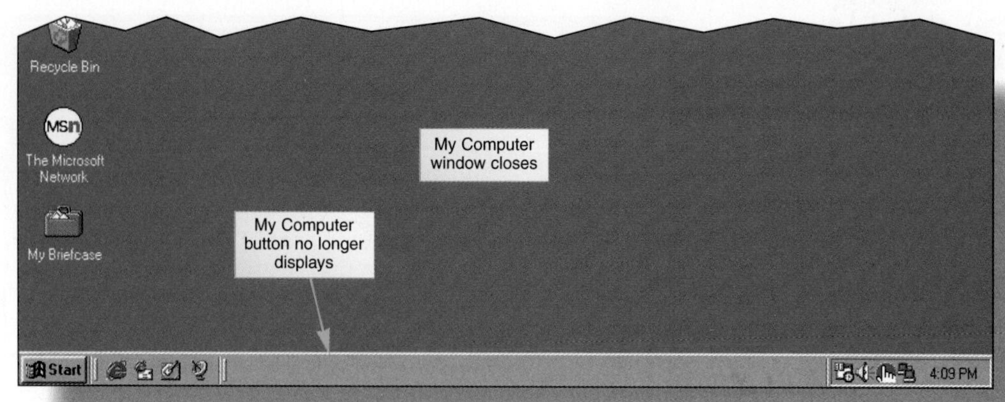

FIGURE 1-23

Double-click the My Computer icon on the desktop.

The My Computer window opens and displays on the screen (Figure 1-24). The My Computer button displays in the taskbar button area.

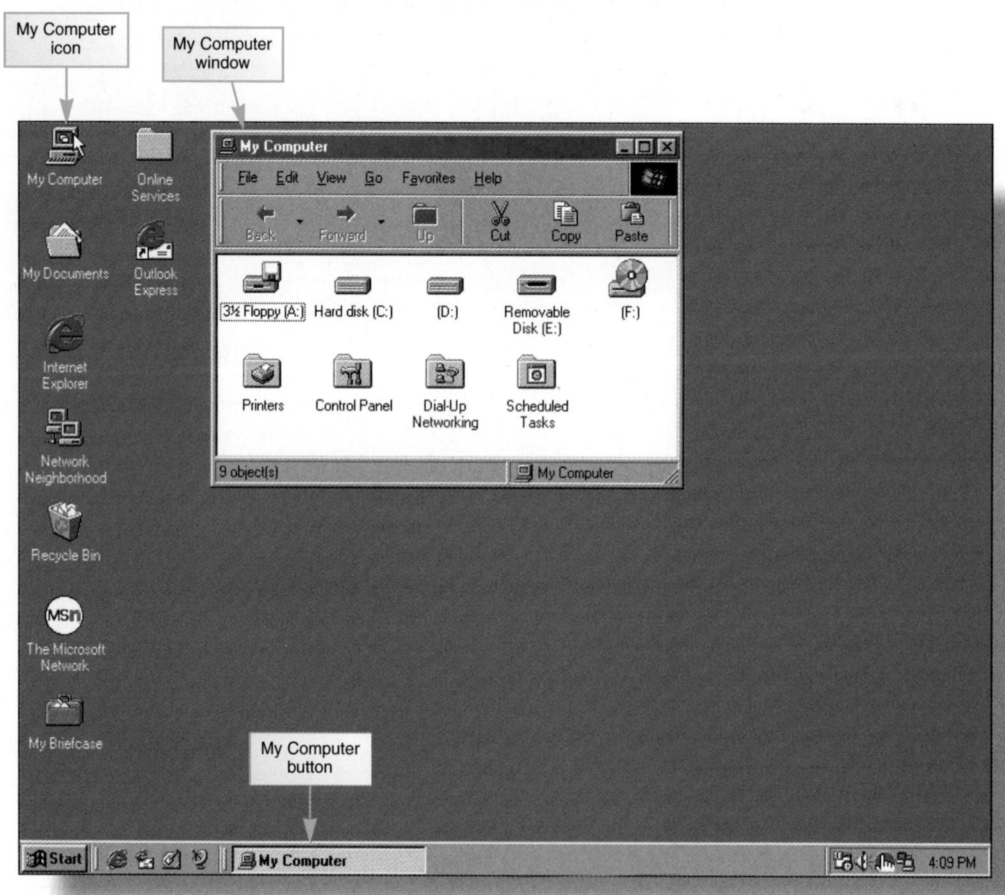

FIGURE 1-24

More About

Dragging

Dragging is the second-most difficult skill to learn with a mouse. You may want to practice dragging a few times so you are comfortable with it.

Drag

Drag means you point to an item, hold down the left mouse button, move the item to the desired location, and then release the left mouse button. You can move any open window to another location on the desktop by pointing to the title bar of the window and dragging the window. To drag the My Computer window to another location on the desktop, perform the following steps.

To Move an Object by Dragging

1 Point to the My Computer window title bar (Figure 1-25).

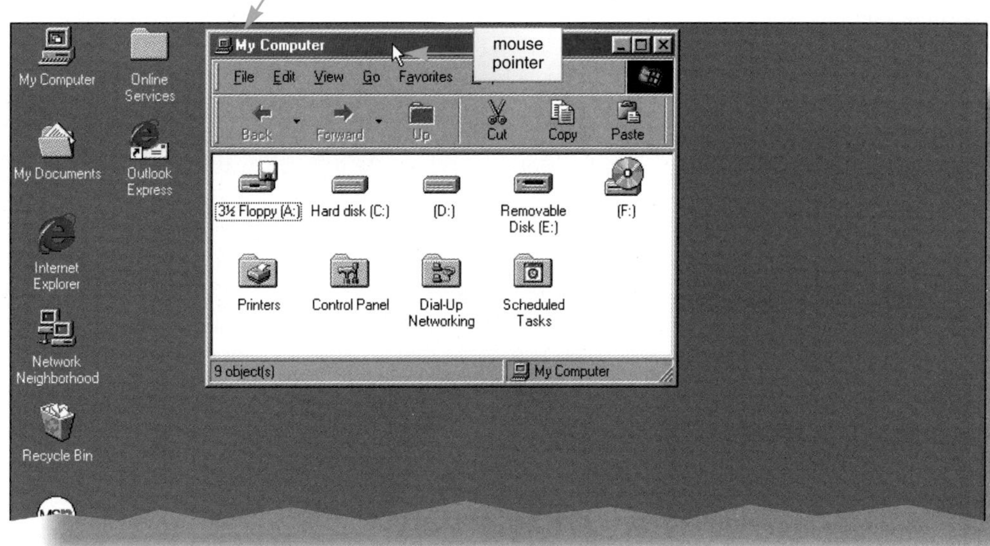

FIGURE 1-25

2 Hold down the left mouse button, move the mouse so the window moves to the center of the desktop, and release the left mouse button.

As you drag the My Computer window, the window moves across the desktop. When you release the left mouse button, the window displays in its new location on the desktop (Figure 1-26).

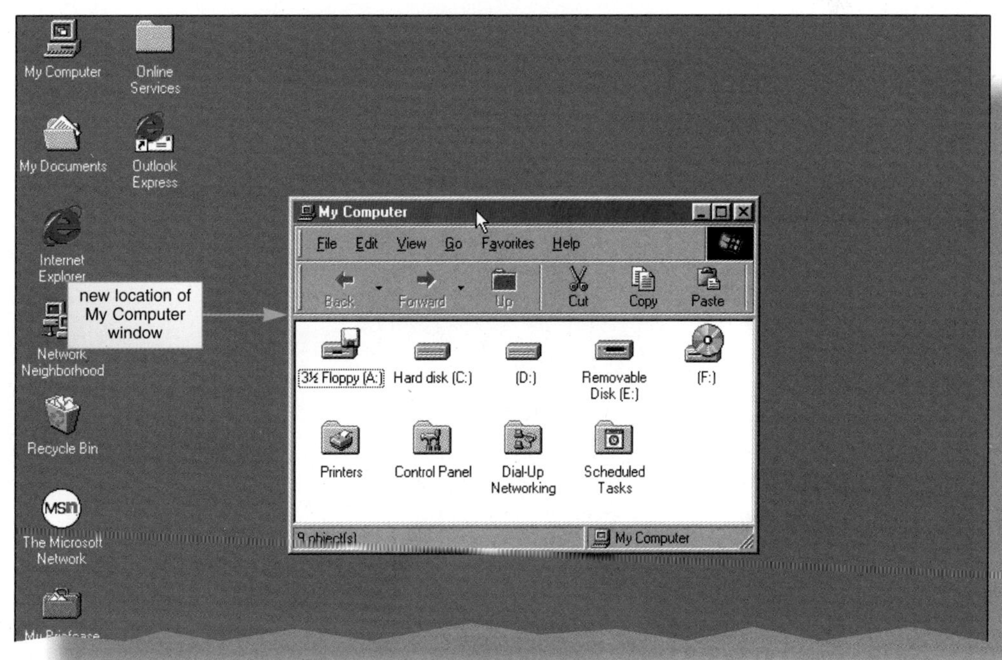

FIGURE 1-26

Sizing a Window by Dragging

As previously mentioned, sometimes when information is displayed in a window, the information is not completely visible. A second method to display information that is not visible is to enlarge the window by dragging the window. For example, you can drag the border of a window to change the size of the window. To change the size of the My Computer window, perform the steps on the next page

To Size a Window by Dragging

1 Position the mouse pointer over the lower-right corner of the My Computer window until the mouse pointer changes to a two-headed arrow.

When the mouse pointer is on top of the lower-right corner of the My Computer window, the pointer changes to a two-headed arrow (Figure 1-27).

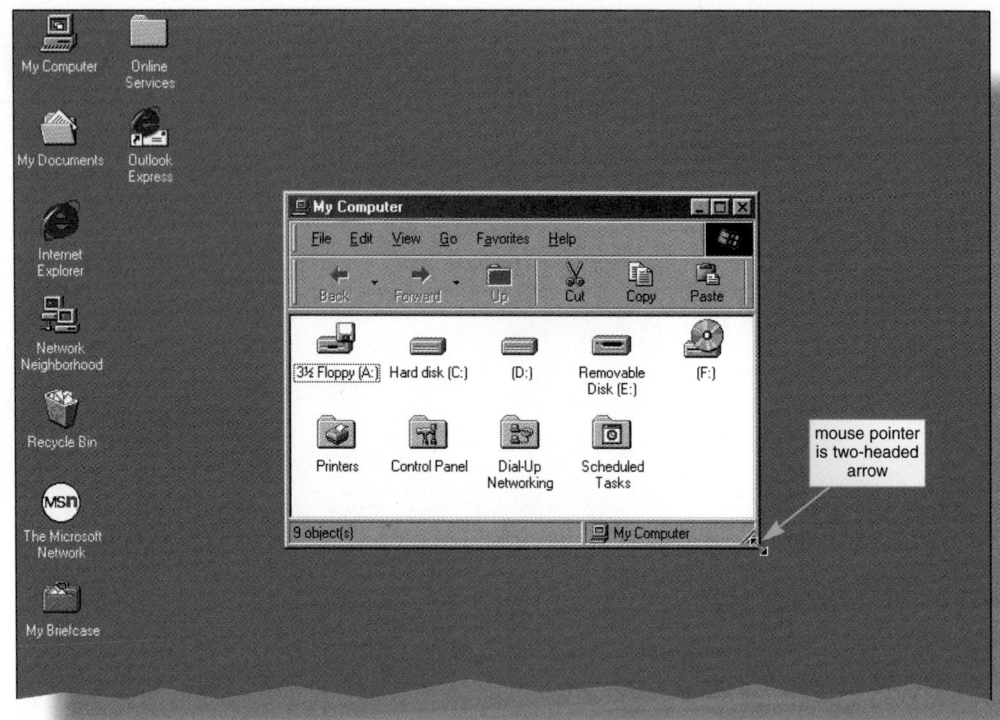

FIGURE 1-27

2 Drag the lower-right corner upward and to the left until the window on your desktop resembles the window shown in Figure 1-28.

As you drag the lower-right corner, the My Computer window changes size and a vertical scroll bar displays (Figure 1-28). Only five of the nine icons in the My Computer window are visible in the resized window in Figure 1-28.

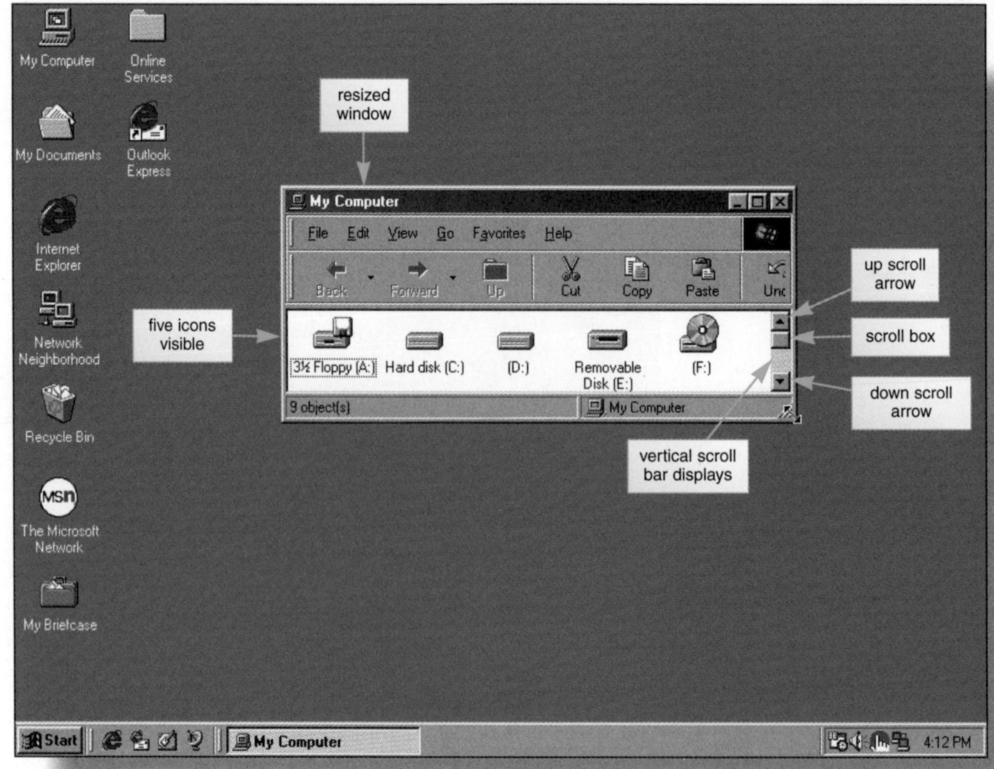

FIGURE 1-28

A scroll bar is a bar that displays at the right edge and/or bottom edge of a window when the window contents are not completely visible. A vertical scroll bar contains an **up scroll arrow**, a **down scroll arrow**, and a **scroll box** that enable you to view areas of the window not currently visible. A vertical scroll bar displays in the My Computer window shown in Figure 1-28.

The size of the scroll box in any window is dependent on the amount of the window that is not visible. The smaller the scroll box, the more of the window that is not visible. In Figure 1-28, the scroll box occupies approximately half of the scroll bar. This indicates that approximately half of the contents of the window are not visible. If the scroll box were a tiny rectangle, a large portion of the window would not be visible.

In addition to dragging a corner of a window, you also can drag any of the borders of a window. If you drag a vertical border, such as the right border, you can move the border left or right. If you drag a horizontal border, such as the bottom border, you can move the border of the window up or down.

> **More About**
> **Window Sizing**
> Windows 98 remembers the size of the window when you close the window. When you reopen the window, it will display in the same size as when you closed it.

Scrolling in a Window

Previously, two methods were shown to display information that was not completely visible in the My Computer window. These methods were maximizing the My Computer window and changing the size of the My Computer window. A third method uses the scroll bar in the window.

Scrolling can be accomplished in three ways: (1) click the scroll arrows; (2) click the scroll bar; and (3) drag the scroll box. On the following pages, you will use the scroll bar to scroll the contents of the My Computer window. Perform the following steps to scroll the My Computer window using the scroll arrows.

> **More About**
> **Scrolling**
> Most people will either maximize a window or size it so all the objects in the window are visible to avoid scrolling because scrolling takes time. It is more efficient not to have to scroll in a window.

To Scroll a Window Using Scroll Arrows

1 Point to the down scroll arrow on the vertical scroll bar (Figure 1-29).

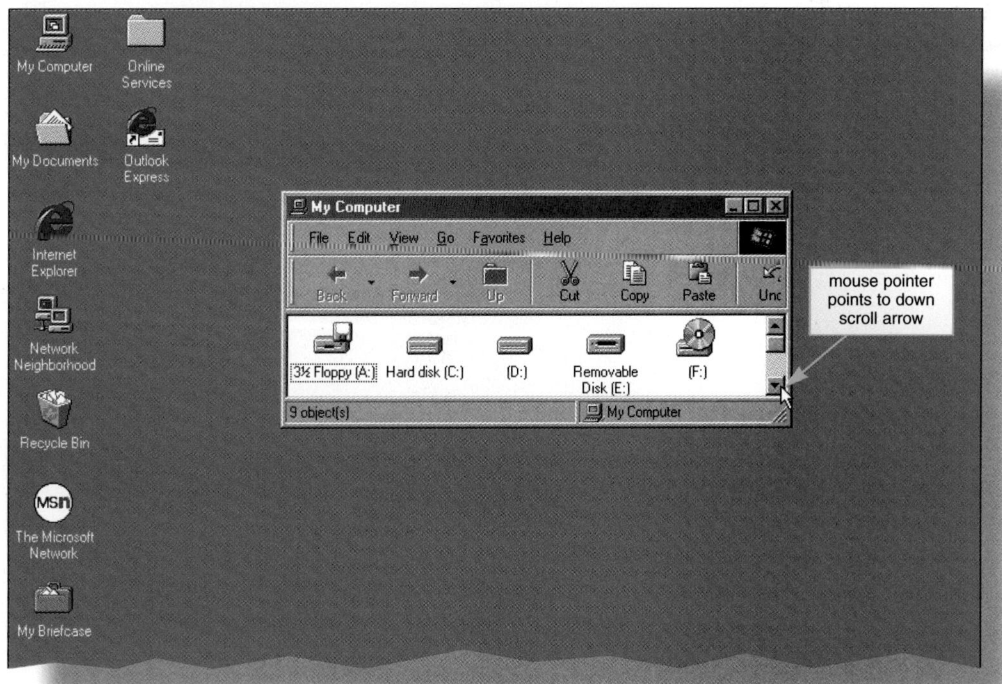

FIGURE 1-29

Click the down scroll arrow one time.

The window scrolls down (the icons move up in the window) and displays the tops of the icons previously not visible (Figure 1-30). Because the window size does not change when you scroll, the contents of the window will change, as seen in the difference between Figure 1-29 on the previous page and Figure 1-30.

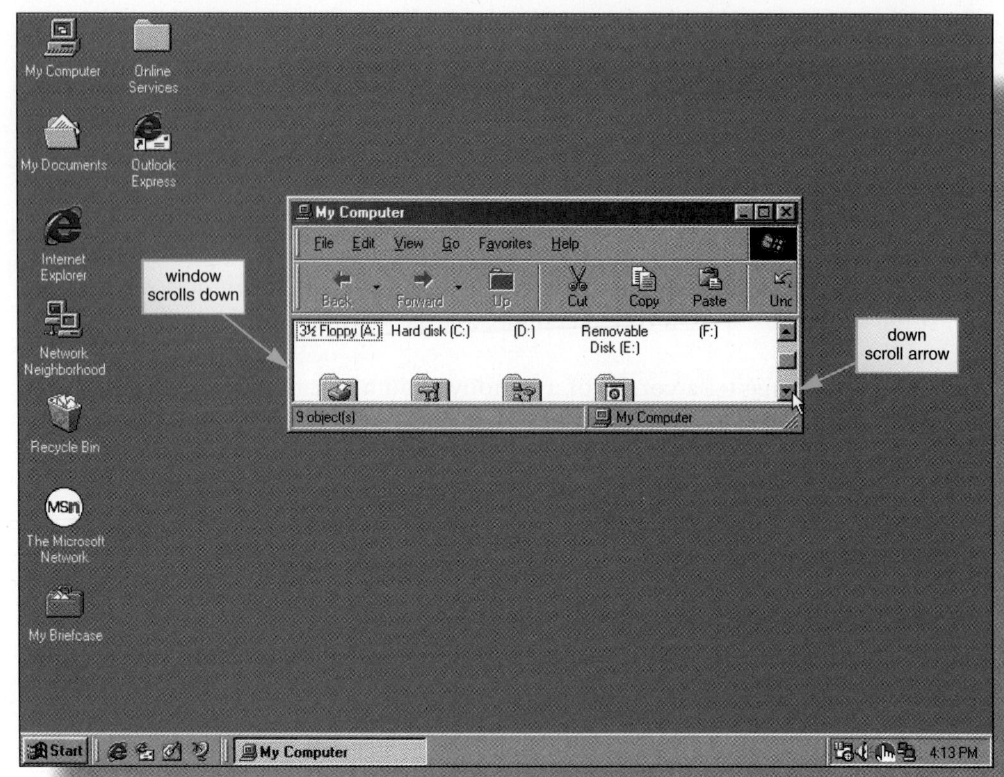

FIGURE 1-30

Click the down scroll arrow two more times.

The scroll box moves to the bottom of the scroll bar and the remaining icons in the window display (Figure 1-31).

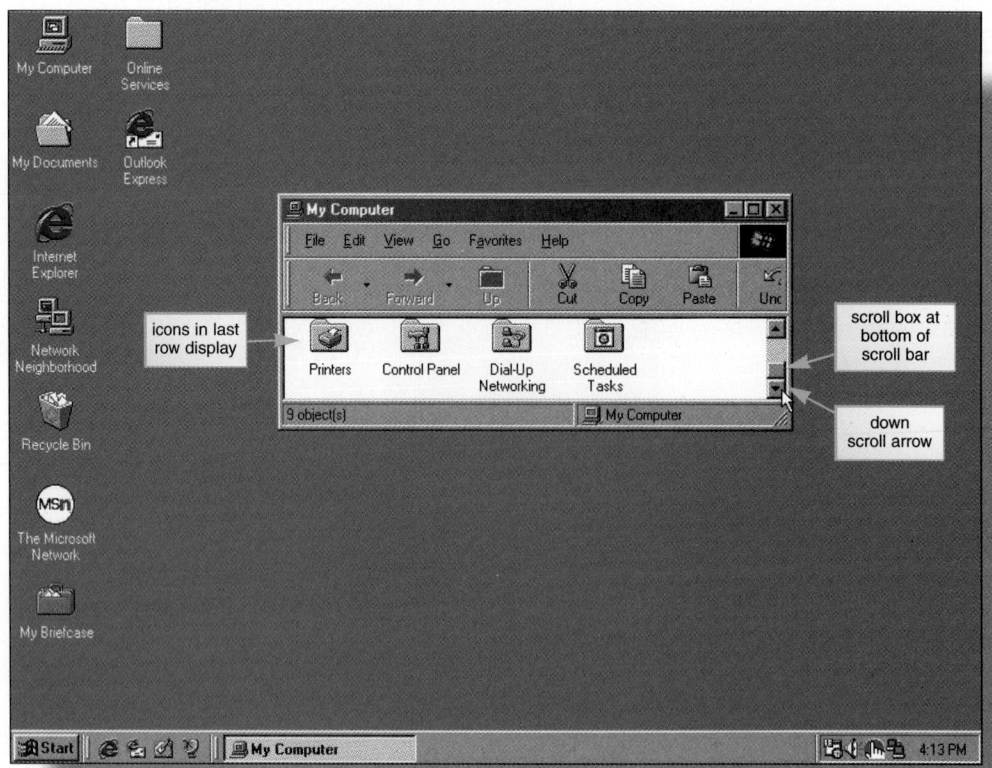

FIGURE 1-31

You can scroll continuously through a window using scroll arrows by pointing to the up or down scroll arrow and holding down the left mouse button. The window continues to scroll until you release the left mouse button or you reach the top or bottom of the window.

The Scroll Bar

In many application programs, clicking the scroll bar will move the window a full screen's worth of information up or down. You can step through a word processing document screen by screen, for example, by clicking the scroll bar.

Scrolling by Clicking the Scroll Bar

You can also scroll by clicking the scroll bar itself. To scroll to the top of the window by clicking the scroll bar, complete the following steps.

To Scroll a Window Using the Scroll Bar

1 Point to the scroll bar above the scroll box (Figure 1-32).

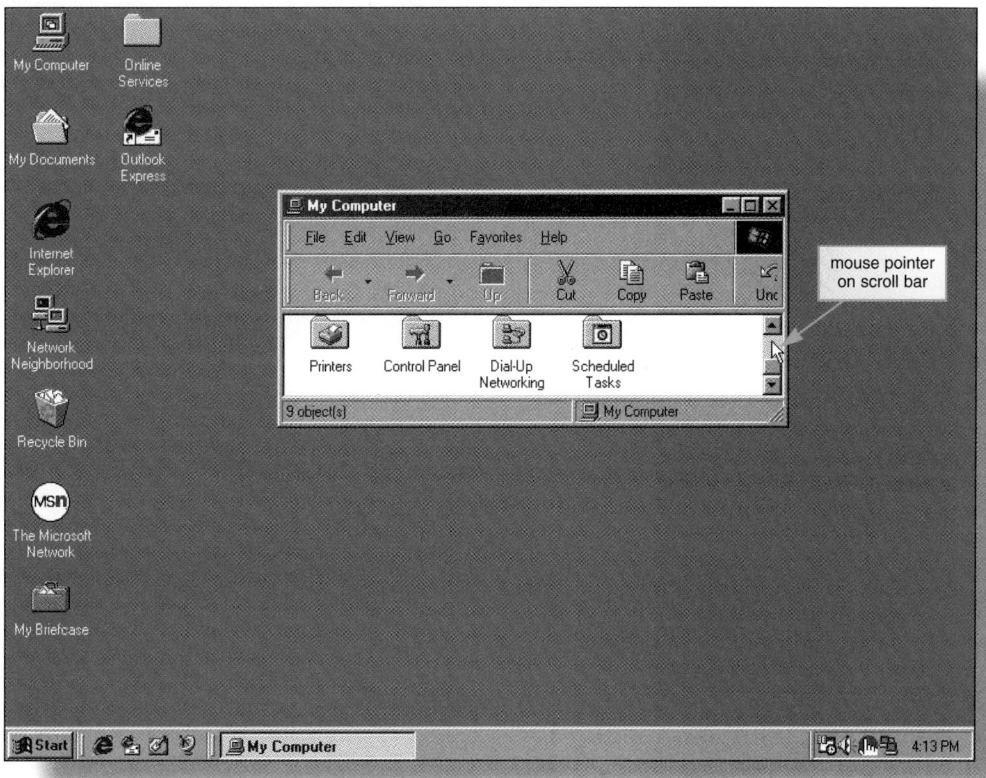

FIGURE 1-32

Click the scroll bar one time.

The scroll box moves toward the top of the scroll bar and a part of the icons at the top of the window display (Figure 1-33).

3 **Click the scroll bar one more time to display the top row of icons.**

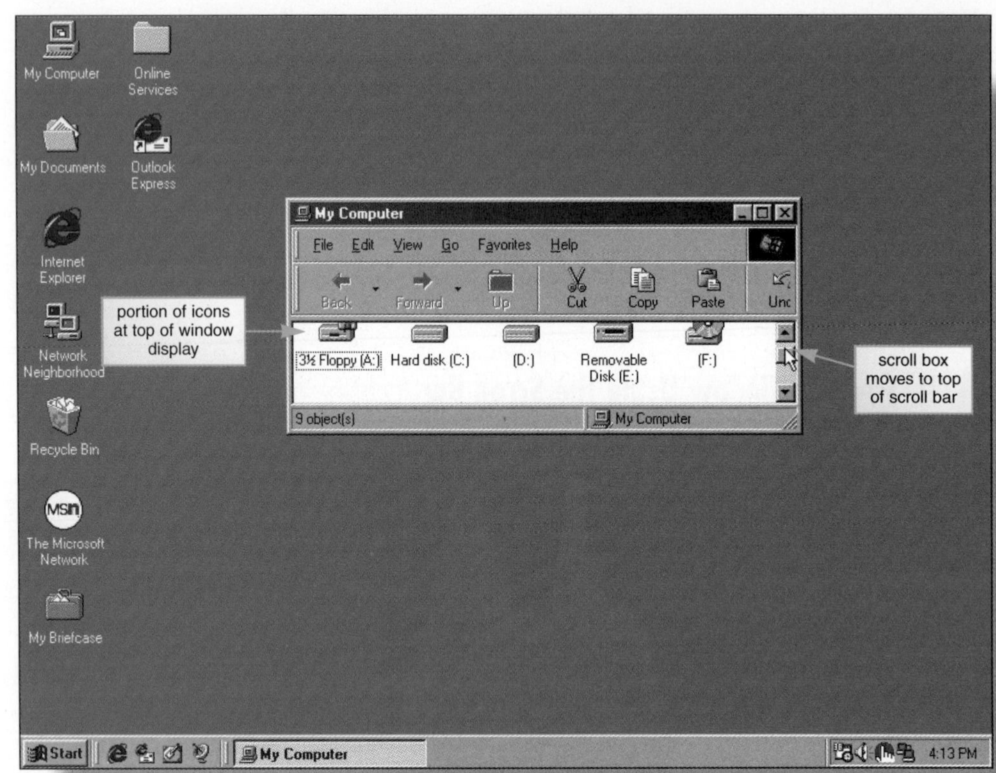

FIGURE 1-33

In the previous steps, you needed to click the scroll bar two times to move the scroll box to the top of the scroll bar and display the contents in the top of the window. In those cases where the scroll box is small and more contents of the window are not visible, you may have to click three or more times to scroll to the top.

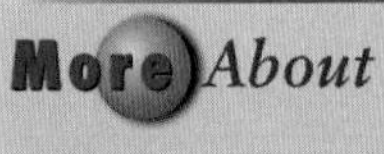

More About

The Scroll Box

Dragging the scroll box is the most efficient technique to scroll long distances. In many application programs, such as Microsoft Word, as you scroll using the scroll box, the page number of the document displays next to the scroll box.

Scrolling by Dragging the Scroll Box

The third way in which you can scroll through a window to view its contents is by dragging the scroll box. To view the contents of My Computer window by dragging the scroll box, complete the following step.

To Scroll a Window by Dragging the Scroll Box

1 With the mouse pointer pointing to the scroll box on the scroll bar, drag the scroll box down the scroll bar until the scroll box is about halfway down the scroll bar.

As you drag the scroll box down the vertical scroll bar, the icons move up in the window and additional icons become visible (Figure 1-34). Notice that the icons in the window move as you drag the scroll box.

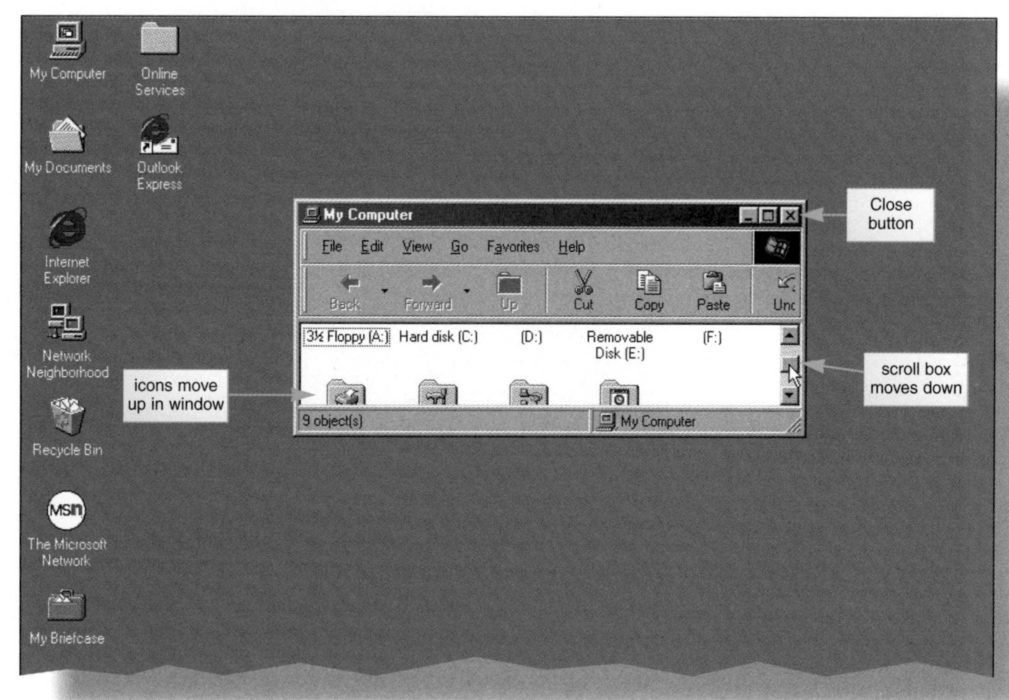

FIGURE 1-34

Being able to view the contents of a window by scrolling is an important Windows 98 skill because in many cases the entire contents of a window are not visible.

More About

Scrolling Guidelines

General scrolling guidelines: (1) To scroll short distances (line by line), click the scroll arrows; (2) To scroll one screen at a time, click the scroll bar; and (3) To scroll long distances, drag the scroll box.

Resizing a Window

After moving and resizing a window, you may wish to return the window to approximately its original size. To return the My Computer window to about its original size, complete the following steps.

TO RESIZE A WINDOW

 Position the mouse pointer over the lower-right corner of the My Computer window border until the mouse pointer changes to a two-headed arrow.

 Drag the lower-right corner of the My Computer window until the window is the same size as shown in Figure 1-27 on page WIN 1.26, and then release the mouse button.

The My Computer window is approximately the same size as before you made it smaller.

Closing a Window

After you have completed your work in a window, normally you will close the window. To close the My Computer window, complete the steps on the next page.

TO CLOSE A WINDOW

 Point to the Close button on the right of the title bar in the My Computer window (see Figure 1-34 on the previous page).

 Click the Close button.

The My Computer window closes and the desktop contains no open windows (Figure 1-35). Because the My Computer window is closed, the My Computer button no longer displays in the taskbar button area.

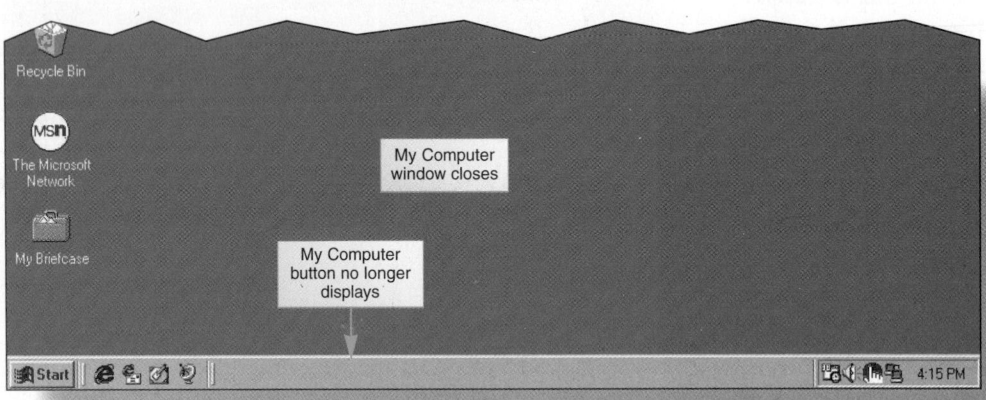

FIGURE 1-35

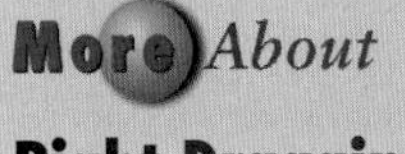

Right-Dragging

Right-dragging was not available on some earlier versions of Windows, so you might find people familiar with Windows not even considering right-dragging. Because it always produces a shortcut menu, however, right-dragging is the safest way to drag.

Right-Drag

Right-drag means you point to an item, hold down the right mouse button, move the item to the desired location, and then release the right mouse button. When you right-drag an object, a shortcut menu displays. The shortcut menu contains commands specifically for use with the object being dragged. To right-drag the My Briefcase icon to the right of its current position, perform the following steps. If the My Briefcase icon does not display on your desktop, you will be unable to perform Step 1 through Step 4 that follow.

To Right-Drag

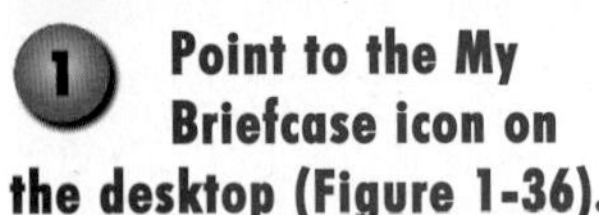

1 Point to the My Briefcase icon on the desktop (Figure 1-36).

FIGURE 1-36

2 Hold down the right mouse button, drag the icon to the right toward the middle of the desktop, and then release the right mouse button.

The dimmed My Briefcase icon and a shortcut menu display in the middle of the desktop (Figure 1-37). The My Briefcase icon remains at its original location on the left of the screen. The shortcut menu contains four commands: Move Here, Copy Here, Create Shortcut(s) Here, and Cancel. The Move Here command in bold (dark) type identifies what would happen if you were to drag the My Briefcase icon with the left mouse button.

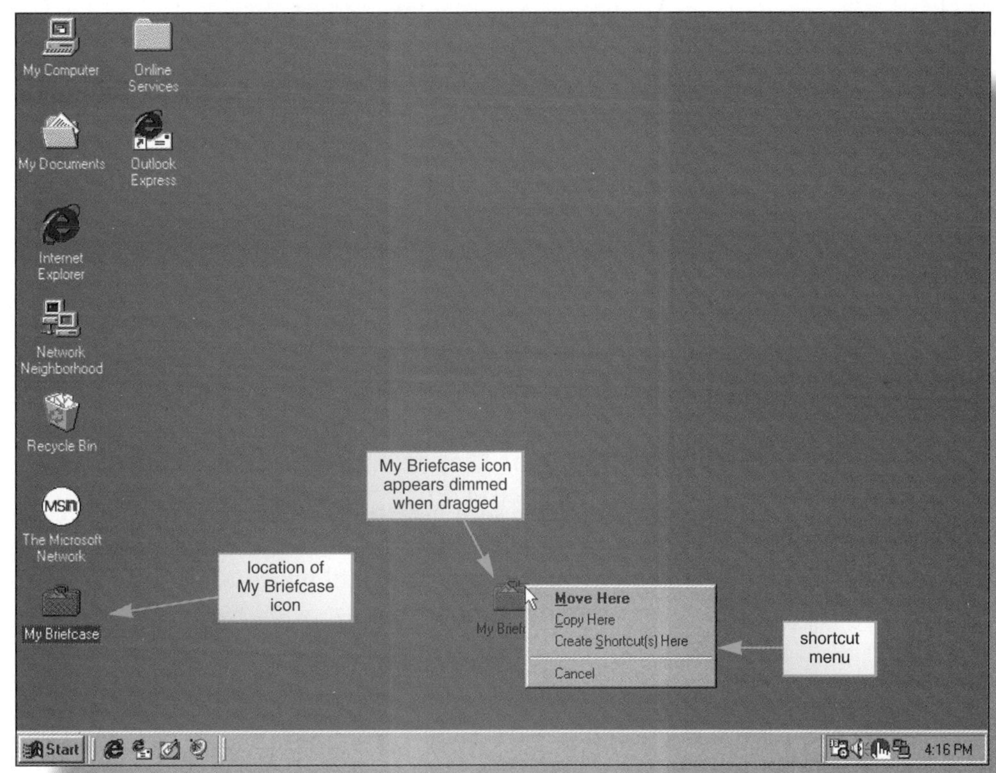

FIGURE 1-37

3 Point to Cancel on the shortcut menu.

The Cancel command is highlighted (Figure 1-38).

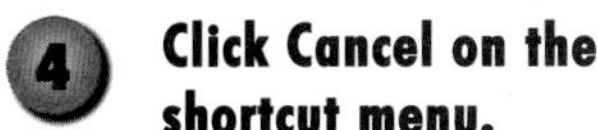

4 Click Cancel on the shortcut menu.

The shortcut menu and the dragged My Briefcase icon disappear from the screen.

FIGURE 1-38

Whenever you begin an operation but do not want to complete the operation, you can click Cancel on a shortcut menu or click the Cancel button in a dialog box. The **Cancel** command will reset anything you have done in the operation.

If you click **Move Here** on the shortcut menu shown in Figure 1-38 on the previous page, Windows 98 will move the icon from its current location to the new location. If you click **Copy Here**, the icon will be copied to the new location and two icons will display on the desktop. Windows 98 automatically will give the second icon a different title. If you click **Create Shortcut(s) Here**, a special object called a shortcut will be created. You will learn more about shortcuts in Project 2 of this book.

Although you can move icons by dragging with the primary (left) mouse button and by right-dragging with the secondary (right) mouse button, it is strongly suggested you right-drag because a menu displays and you can specify the exact operation you want to occur. When you drag using the left mouse button, a default operation takes place and the operation may not do what you want.

More About

The Microsoft Keyboard

The Microsoft keyboard in Figure 1-39(b) not only has special keys for Windows 98, but also is designed ergonomically so you type with your hands apart. It takes a little time to get used to, but several authors on the Shelly Cashman Series writing team report they type faster with more accuracy and less fatigue when using the keyboard.

Summary of Mouse and Windows Operations

You have seen how to use the mouse to point, click, right-click, double-click, drag, and right-drag in order to accomplish certain tasks on the desktop. The use of a mouse is an important skill when using Windows 98. In addition, you have learned how to move around and use windows on the Windows 98 desktop.

The Keyboard and Keyboard Shortcuts

The **keyboard** is an input device on which you manually key, or type, data. Figure 1-39a shows the enhanced IBM 101-key keyboard, and Figure 1-39b shows a Microsoft Natural keyboard designed specifically for use with Windows. Many tasks you accomplish with a mouse also can be accomplished using a keyboard.

To perform tasks using the keyboard, you must understand the notation used to identify which keys to press. This notation is used throughout Windows 98 to identify **keyboard shortcuts**.

FIGURE 1-39a

FIGURE 1-39b

Keyboard shortcuts consist of: (1) pressing a single key (example: press the ENTER key); or (2) pressing and holding down one key and pressing a second key, as shown by two key names separated by a plus sign (example: press CTRL+ESC). For example, to obtain Help about Windows 98, you can press the F1 key; to open the Start menu, hold down the CTRL key and then press the ESC key (press CTRL+ESC).

Often, computer users will use keyboard shortcuts for operations they perform frequently. For example, many users find pressing the F1 key to launch Windows 98 Help easier than using the Start menu as shown later in this project. As a user, you probably will find the combination of keyboard and mouse operations that particularly suit you, but it is strongly recommended that generally you use the mouse.

The Windows 98 Desktop Views

Windows 98 provides several ways to view your desktop and the windows that open on the desktop. The three desktop views include the Web style, Classic style, and Custom style. The desktop view you choose will affect the appearance of your desktop, how you open and work with windows on the desktop, and how you work with the files and folders on your computer.

The Classic Style

The **Classic style** causes the desktop and the objects on the desktop to display and function as they did in Windows 95, a previous version of Windows. When you choose the Classic style as your desktop view, the desktop is referred to as the **Classic Windows Desktop**. The Classic Windows Desktop is similar to the desktop shown in Figure 1-2 on page WIN 1.8 and is shown again in Figure 1-40.

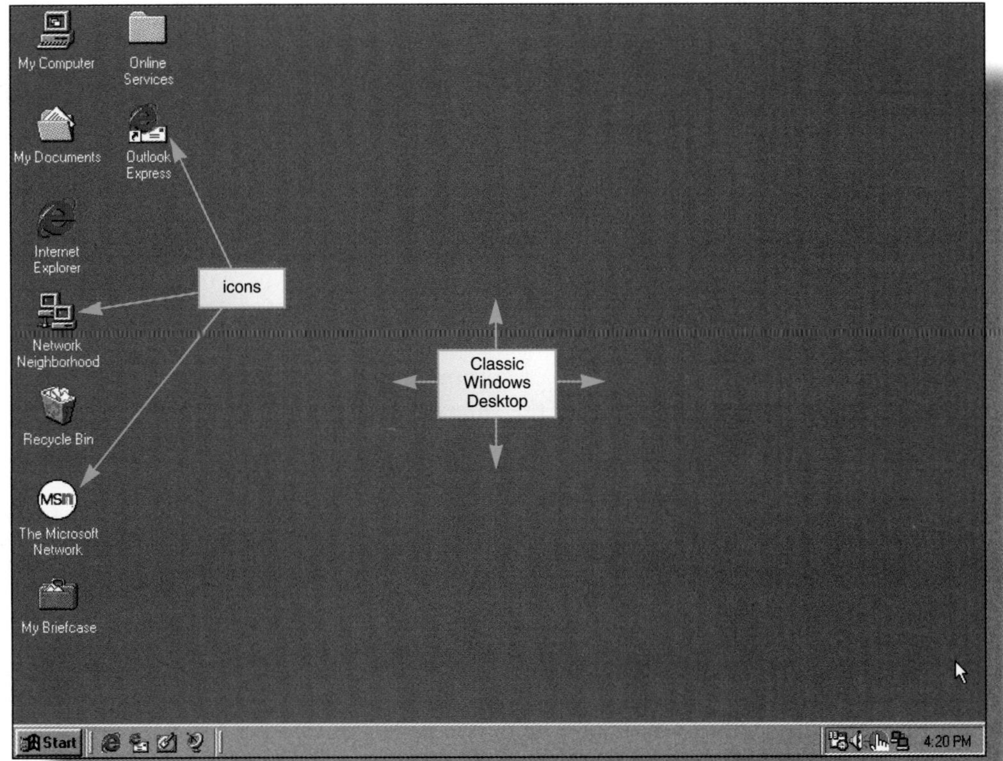

FIGURE 1-40

The icons on the desktop shown in Figure 1-40 on the previous page behave as they did in Windows 95. You double-click an icon to open its window and display its button in the taskbar button area. For example, double-clicking the My Computer icon on the desktop opens the My Computer window and displays the My Computer button in the taskbar button area (Figure 1-41).

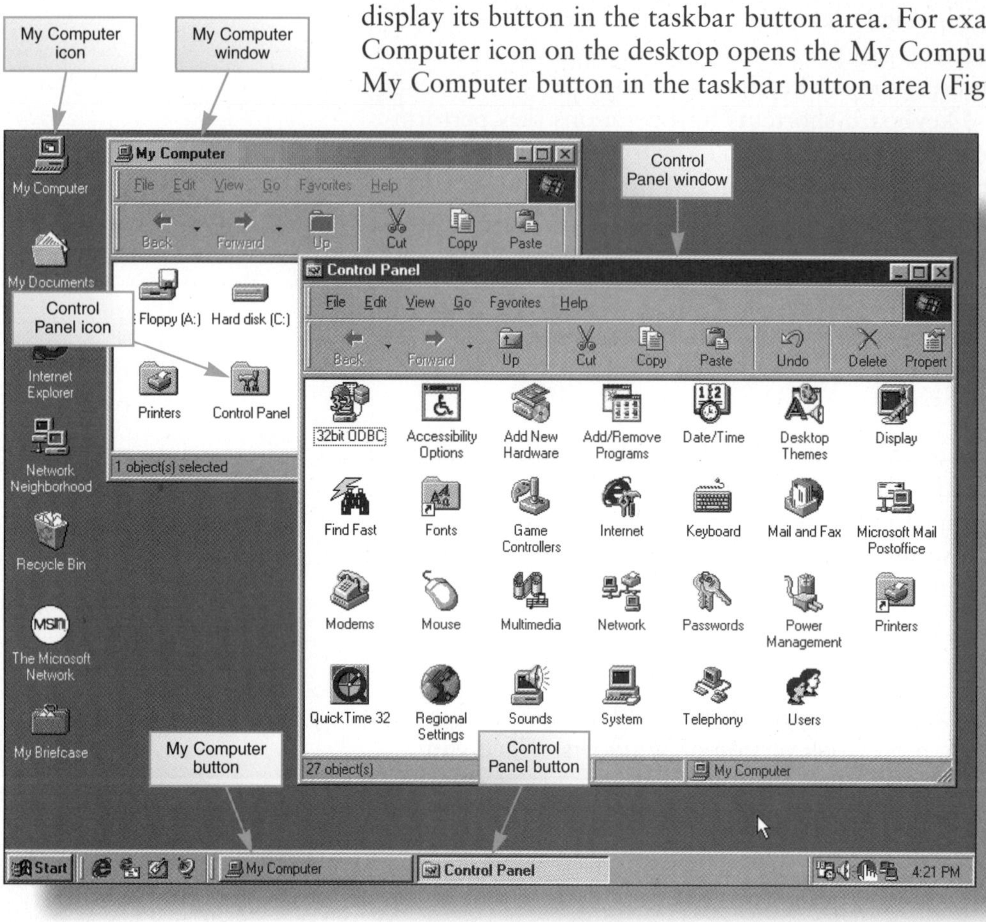

If, after opening the My Computer window, you want to display the contents of a drive or folder icon in the My Computer window, you double-click the drive or folder icon to open its window and display its taskbar button. For example, you might double-click the Control Panel icon in the My Computer window to open its window and display its taskbar button (Figure 1-41).

Double-clicking the Control Panel icon opens a second window on the desktop (Control Panel window) and places a second button (Control Panel button) in the taskbar button area.

FIGURE 1-41

The Internet and World Wide Web

The second desktop view available in Windows 98 is the Web style. The Web style uses the Internet and an area of the Internet called the World Wide Web to retrieve and display information on the desktop.

The **Internet** is a worldwide group of connected computer networks that allows public access to information on thousands of subjects and gives users the ability to send messages and obtain products and services. Computers connected to the Internet deliver information using a variety of computer media, including text, graphics, sound, video clips, and animation. On the Internet, this multimedia capability is called **hypermedia**, which is any variety of computer media. Underlined text, a picture, or an icon used to access hypermedia is called a **hyperlink**, or simply a **link**. Clicking a hyperlink on a computer in Los Angeles could cause a picture stored on a computer in Germany to display on the desktop of the computer in Los Angeles.

The collection of hyperlinks throughout the Internet creates an interconnected network of links called the **World Wide Web**, also referred to as the **Web**. Each computer within the Web that can be referenced by a hyperlink is called a **Web site**. Hundreds of thousands of Web sites around the world can be accessed through the Internet. Graphics, text, and other hypermedia are stored in files called **hypertext documents**, or **Web pages**. Figure 1-42 illustrates one of several Web pages in the Web site operated by ESPN, a popular sports broadcasting company.

FIGURE 1-42

The Web page shown in Figure 1-42 contains a variety of multimedia (text, graphics, and animation) and hyperlinks. A unique address, called a **Uniform Resource Locator (URL)**, identifies each Web page in a Web site. The URL for the ESPN Web page shown in Figure 1-42, http://espn.sportszone.com, displays in the Address bar at the top of the http://espn.sportszone.com/ – Microsoft Internet Explorer window.

A software tool, called a **Web browser**, allows you to locate a Web page if you know the URL for the Web page. The **Microsoft Internet Explorer 4 Web browser** included with Windows 98 displays the Web page shown in Figure 1-42. Clicking a hyperlink on the Web page causes the browser to locate the associated Web page and display its contents in the same window.

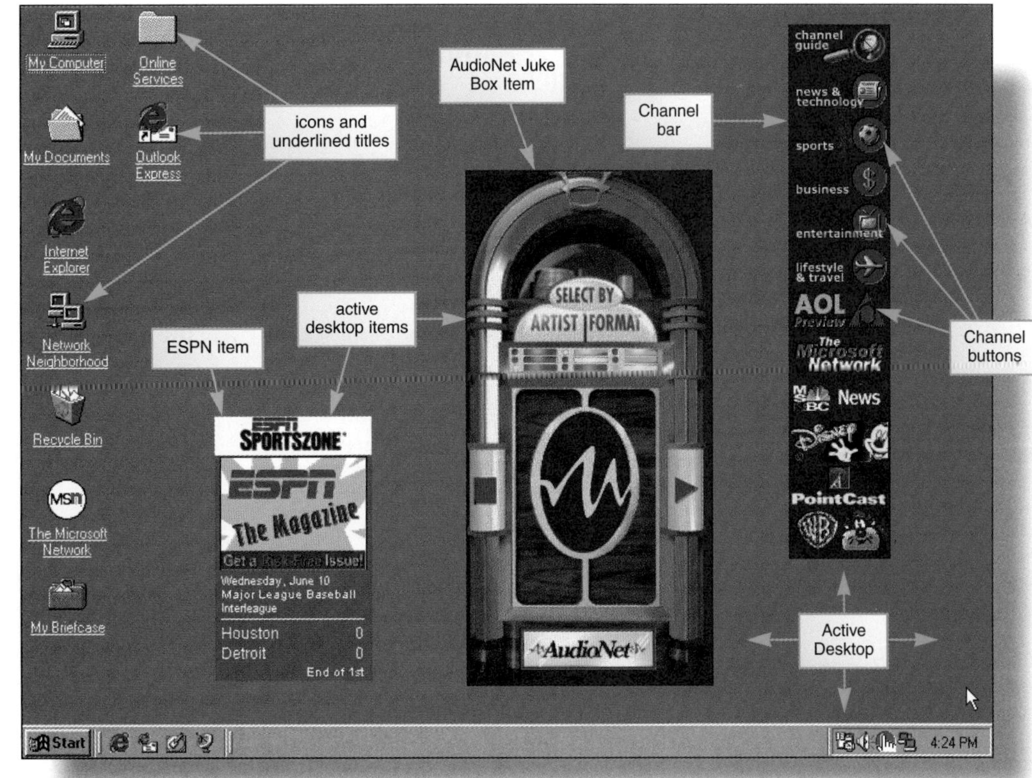

FIGURE 1-43

The Web Style

In **Web style**, the icon titles on the desktop are underlined similarly to the hyperlinks in a Web page, and the desktop is referred to as the **Active Desktop™** (Figure 1-43).

Desktop Views

The Classic style was included in the Windows 98 operating system to allow Windows 95 users to upgrade easily to the newer Windows 98 operating system. Responses from people in the Beta Test program, which is a program designed to test software prior to the public sale of the software, indicated that most Windows 95 users had little difficulty switching to Windows 98, and experienced users liked the Web style and Active Desktop.

The Web style causes the Channel bar to display on the desktop and allows you to place other objects, called **active desktop items**, on the desktop (see Figure 1-43 on the previous page). The **Channel bar** contains twelve **Channel buttons** (channel guide, news & technology, sports, business, entertainment, lifestyle & travel, AOL Preview, The Microsoft Network, MSNBC News, Disney, PointCast, and WB) that assist you in placing desktop items on the Active Desktop.

Two active desktop items (ESPN SportsZone™ and AudioNet Juke Box) display on the desktop shown in Figure 1-43. The **ESPN SportsZone™ item** displays the lastest sports scores from the ESPN SportsZone™ Web site shown in Figure 1-42 on the previous page and updates the scores periodically. The **AudioNet Juke Box item** allows you to select and listen to hundreds of audio CDs from the AudioNet Web site on the Internet.

Unlike the Classic style, the icon titles on the desktop are underlined and you click an icon to open its window and display its taskbar button. When you click an icon on the desktop, such as the My Computer icon, the My Computer window opens on the desktop with a different look and feel than the My Computer window that opens when you double-click its icon in Classic style (Figure 1-44). In Windows terminology, this look and feel is referred to as **displaying a folder as a Web page**.

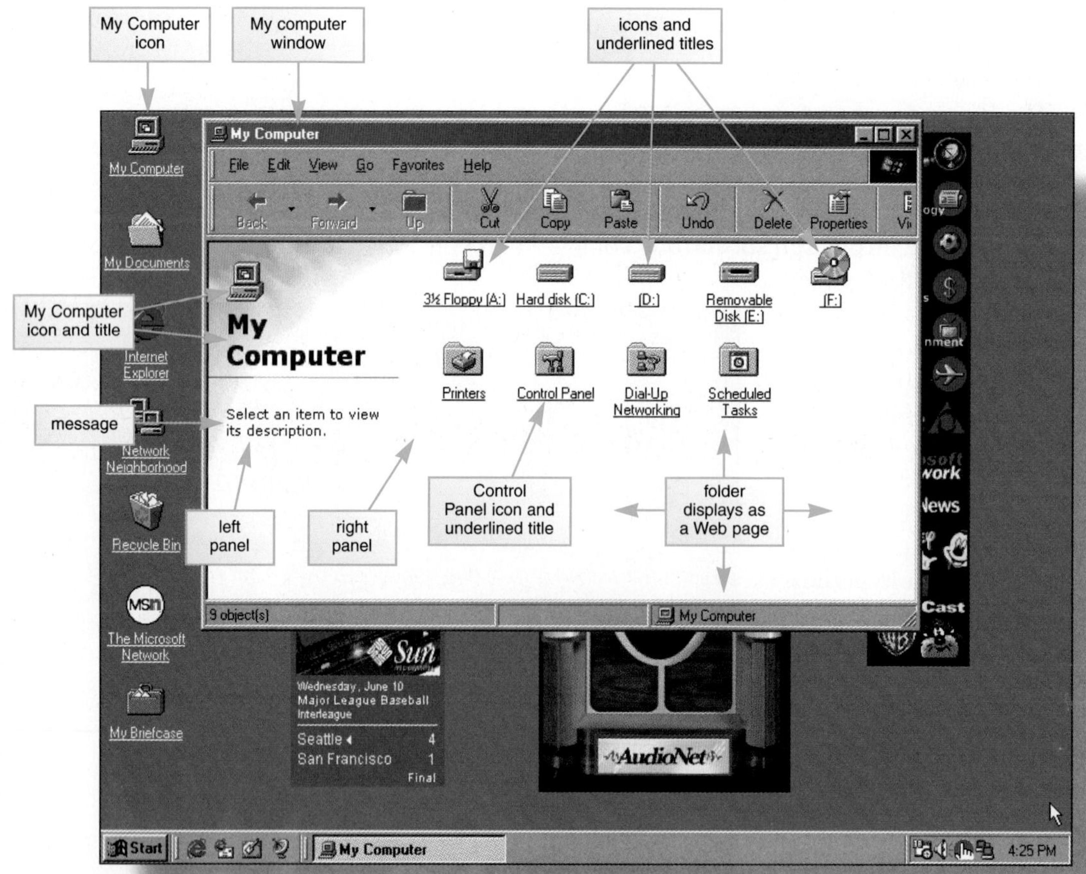

FIGURE 1-44

The My Computer window displays as a Web page with the area below the Standard Buttons toolbar divided into two panels. The My Computer icon and its icon title, My Computer, display at the top of the left panel. The text, Select an item to view its description, displays below the icon and title in the left panel. The right panel of the My Computer window contains nine icons and their underlined titles.

In Classic style, double-clicking the Control Panel icon in the My Computer window opened a second window on the desktop and displayed a second taskbar button (see Figure 1-41 on page WIN 1.36). In Web style, you click instead of double-click a drive or folder icon in the My Computer window to display the contents of the drive or folder. To display the contents of the Control Panel folder, you click the Control Panel icon in the My Computer window (Figure 1-45).

The Control Panel window opens in the same window in which the My Computer window was displayed, and the Control Panel button replaces the My Computer button in the taskbar button area. The Control Panel displays as a Web page with the left panel containing information about the Control Panel and the right panel containing the icons in the Control Panel folder.

If, after displaying the Control Panel window, you again want to display the My Computer window, you can click the Back button on the Standard Buttons toolbar to replace the Control Panel window and taskbar button with the My Computer window and taskbar button.

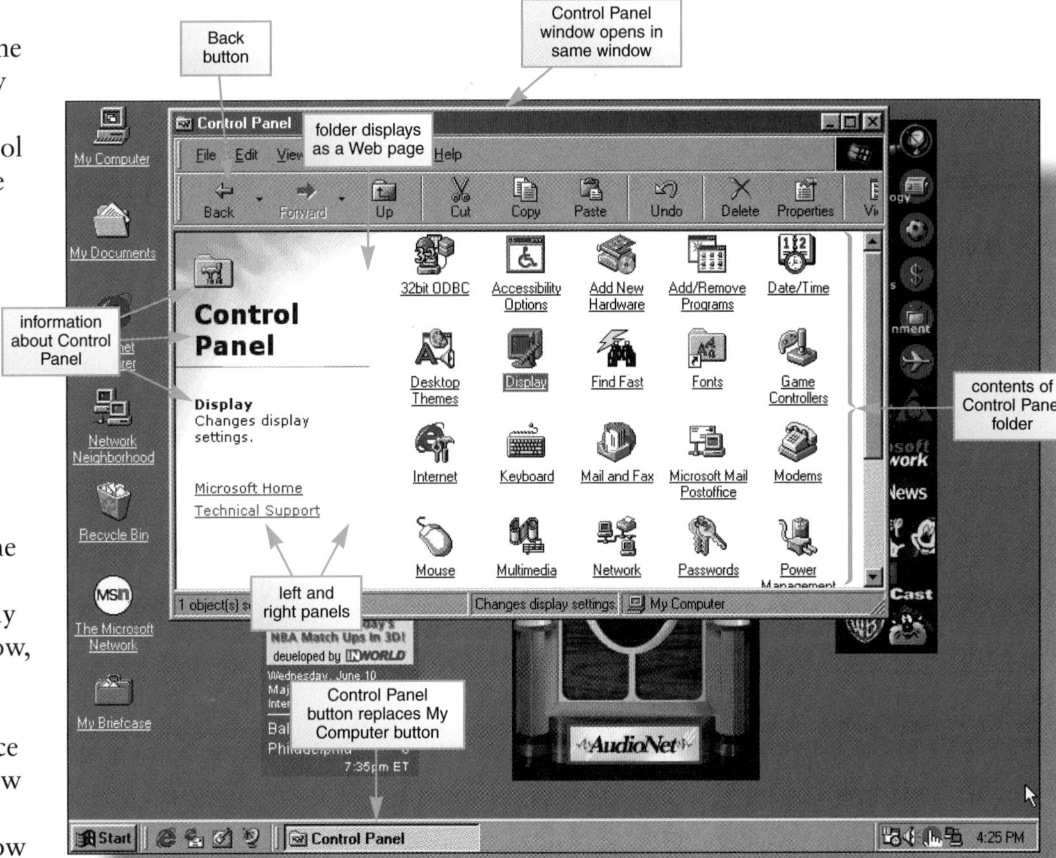

FIGURE 1-45

The Custom Style

The third desktop view available in Windows 98 is the Custom style. The **Custom style** allows you to pick and choose the options you prefer, including a combination of Classic style and Web-style settings. The options include being able to: (1) view the Active Desktop™ or the Classic Windows Desktop; (2) open a folder in the same window or its own window; (3) view Web content in all folders or only in folders you select; and (4) single-click or double-click to open an item.

When Windows 98 is installed on a computer, the desktop view that displays when you launch Windows 98 is the Custom style. The settings that were chosen by Microsoft, referred to as **default settings**, include: (1) viewing the Classic Windows Desktop; (2) opening a folder in the same window; (3) viewing Web content only in folders you select; and (4) double-clicking to open an item. As a result, you view the Classic Windows Desktop on the desktop, folders open in the same window on the desktop, left and right panels do not display in a window, and you double-click an icon to open its window.

The steps and screens you see in this book assume the default settings of the Custom style, as chosen by Microsoft Corporation, are installed on your computer. If you find this not to be the case, refer to the Preface of this book for instructions to switch the desktop view to the default desktop view or contact your instructor to change the desktop view.

More About

Application Programs

Some application programs, such as Internet Explorer, are part of Windows 98. Most application programs, however, such as Microsoft Office, Lotus SmartSuite, and others must be purchased separately from Windows 98.

Launching an Application Program

One of the basic tasks you can perform using Windows 98 is to launch an application program. A **program** is a set of computer instructions that carries out a task on your computer. An **application program** is a program that allows you to accomplish a specific task for which that program is designed. For example, a **word processing program** is an application program that allows you to create written documents; a **presentation graphics program** is an application program that allows you to create graphic presentations for display on a computer; and a **Web browser program** is an application program that allows you to search for and display Web pages.

The most common activity on a computer is to run an application program to accomplish tasks using the computer. You can launch an application program in a variety of ways. When several methods are available to accomplish a task, a computer user has the opportunity to try various methods and select the method that best fits his or her needs.

To illustrate the variety of methods available to launch an application program, three methods will be shown to launch the Internet Explorer Web browser program. These methods include using the Start button; using the Quick Launch toolbar; and using an icon on the desktop.

Launching an Application Using the Start Button

The first method to launch an application program is to use the Start menu. Perform the following steps to launch Internet Explorer using the Start menu and Internet Explorer command.

To Launch a Program Using the Start Menu

1 Click the Start button on the taskbar. Point to Programs on the Start menu. Point to Internet Explorer on the Programs submenu. Point to Internet Explorer on the Internet Explorer submenu.

The Start menu, Programs submenu, and Internet Explorer submenu display (Figure 1-46). The Internet Explorer submenu contains the **Internet Explorer command** *to launch the Internet Explorer program. You might find more, fewer, or different commands on the submenus on your computer than those shown in Figure 1-46 because different computers can contain different application programs.*

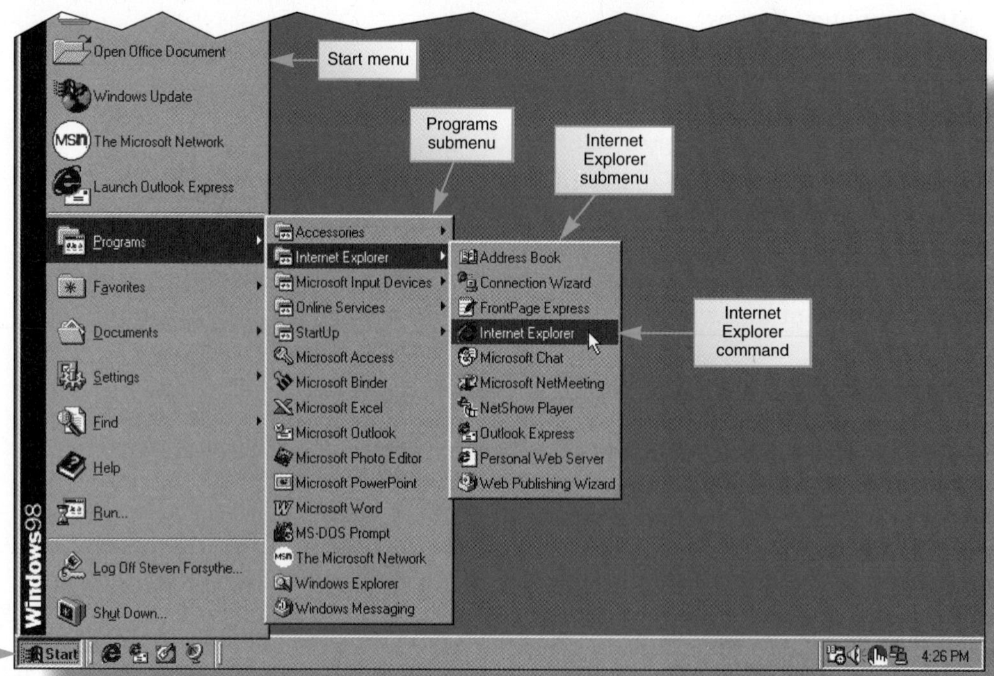

FIGURE 1-46

2 Click Internet Explorer.

Windows 98 launches the Internet Explorer program by opening the MSN.COM, Welcome Page – Microsoft Internet Explorer window on the desktop, displaying the Welcome to MSN.COM Web page in the window, and adding a recessed button to the taskbar button area (Figure 1-47). The URL for the Web page displays on the Address bar. Because Web pages are modified frequently, the Web page that displays on your desktop may be different from the Web page in Figure 1-47.

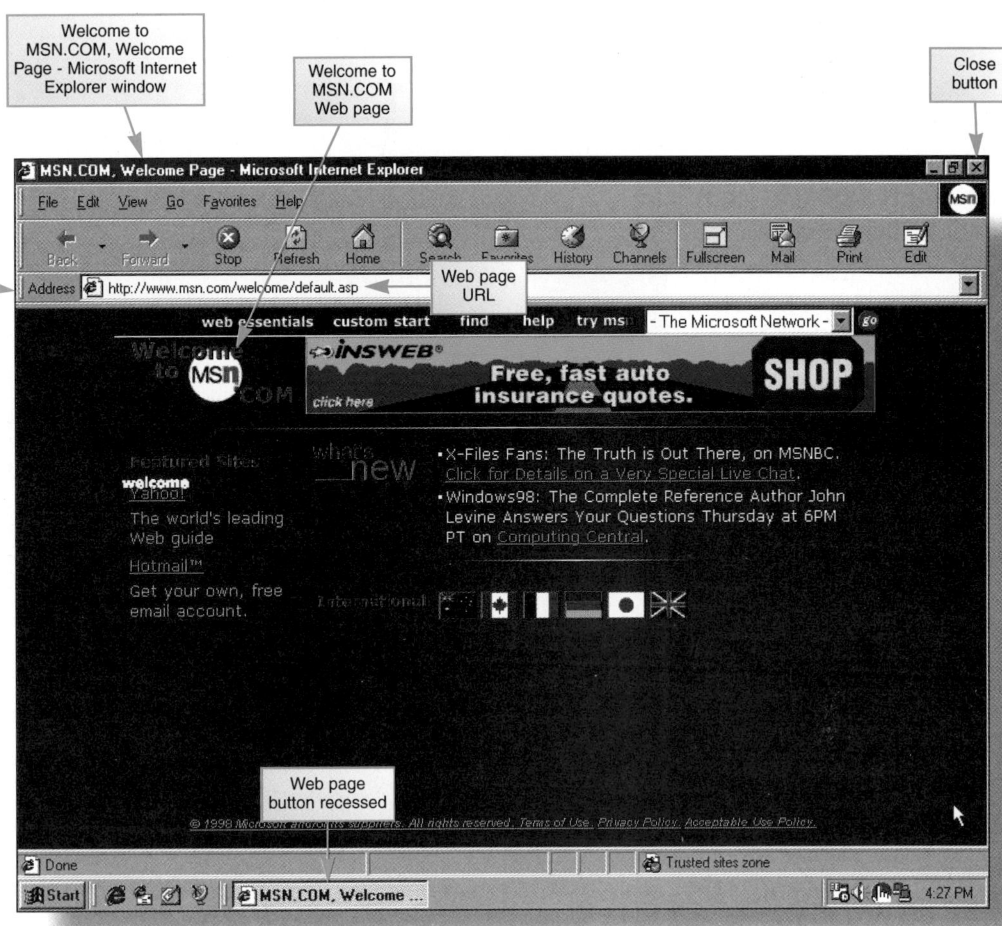

FIGURE 1-47

3 Click the Close button in the Internet Explorer window.

The Microsoft Internet Explorer window closes.

After you have launched Internet Explorer, you can use the program to search for and display different Web pages.

Launching an Application Using the Quick Launch Toolbar

The second method to launch an application is to use an icon on the Quick Launch toolbar. Currently, the Quick Launch toolbar contains four icons that allow you to launch Internet Explorer, launch Outlook Express, view an uncluttered desktop at any time, and view a list of channels (see Figure 1-48 on the next page). Perform the steps on the next page to launch the Internet Explorer program using the Launch Internet Explorer Browser icon on the Quick Launch toolbar.

To Launch a Program Using the Quick Launch Toolbar

1 Point to the Launch Internet Explorer Browser icon on the Quick Launch toolbar (Figure 1-48).

2 Click the Launch Internet Explorer Browser icon.

Windows 98 launches the Internet Explorer program as shown in Figure 1-47 on the previous page.

3 Click the Close button in the Internet Explorer window.

Windows 98 closes the Microsoft Internet Explorer window.

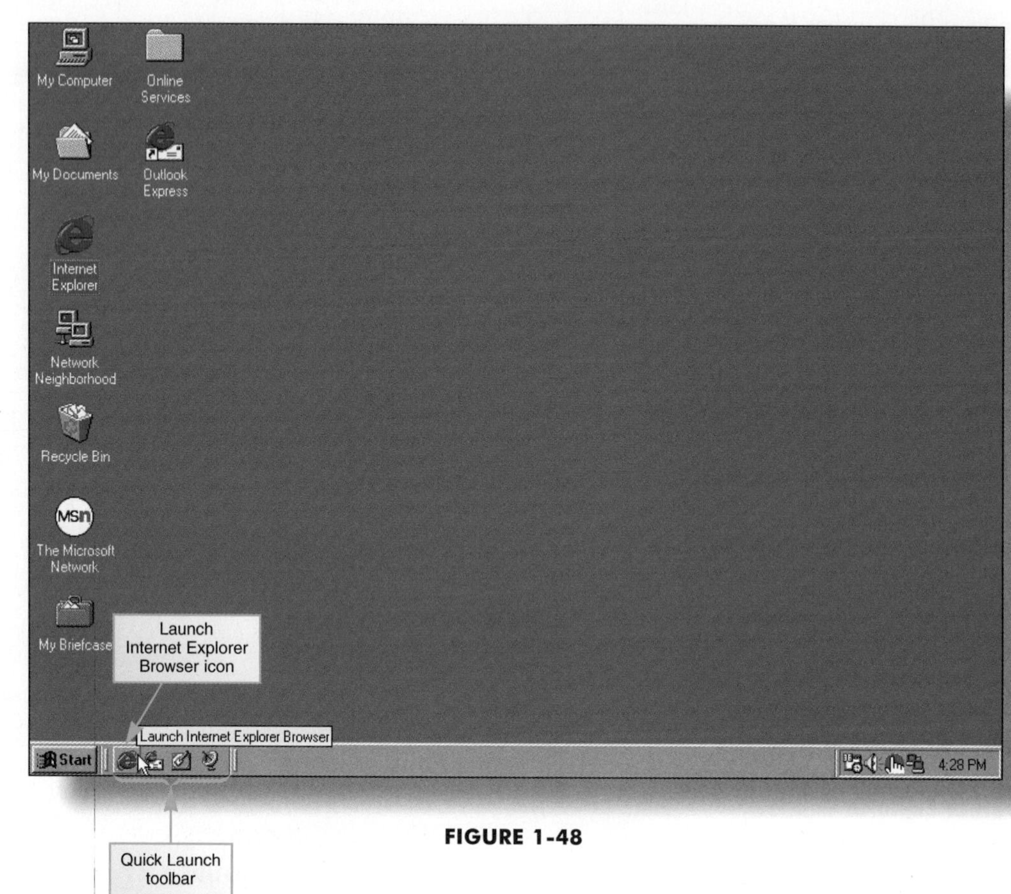

FIGURE 1-48

Launching an Application Using an Icon on the Desktop

The third method to launch an application is to use an icon on the desktop. Perform the following steps to launch the Internet Explorer program using the Internet Explorer icon on the desktop.

To Launch a Program Using an Icon on the Desktop

1 Point to the Internet Explorer icon on the desktop (Figure 1-49).

2 Double-click the Internet Explorer icon.

Windows 98 launches the Internet Explorer program as shown in Figure 1-47 on page WIN 1.41.

3 Click the Close button in the Internet Explorer window.

The Microsoft Internet Explorer window closes.

FIGURE 1-49

Other Ways

1. In open window, click button at right end of menu bar
2. Click Start button, click Run, type `iexplore`, click OK button

Windows 98 provides a number of ways in which to accomplish a particular task. Previously, three methods to launch the Internet Explorer program were illustrated. In the remainder of this book, a single set of steps will illustrate how to accomplish a task. Those steps may not be the only way in which the task can be completed. If you can perform the same task using other methods, the Other Ways box specifies the other methods. In each case, the method shown in the steps is the preferred method, but it is important for you to be aware of all the techniques you can use.

More About

Windows 98 Help

If you purchased an operating system or application program five years ago, you received at least one, and more often several, thick and heavy technical manuals that explained the software. With Windows 98, you receive a skinny manual less than 100 pages in length. The online Help feature of Windows 98 replaces reams and reams of printed pages in hard-to-understand technical manuals.

Using Windows Help

One of the more powerful application programs for use in Windows 98 is Windows Help. Windows Help is available when using Windows 98, or when using any application program running under Windows 98, to assist you in using Windows 98 and the various application programs. It contains answers to many questions you can ask with respect to Windows 98.

Contents Sheet

Windows Help provides a variety of ways in which to obtain information. One method to find a Help topic involves using the **Contents sheet** to browse through Help topics by category. To illustrate this method, you will use Windows Help to determine how to find a topic in Help. To launch Help, complete the following steps.

To Launch Windows Help

1 Click the Start button on the taskbar. Point to Help on the Start menu (Figure 1-50).

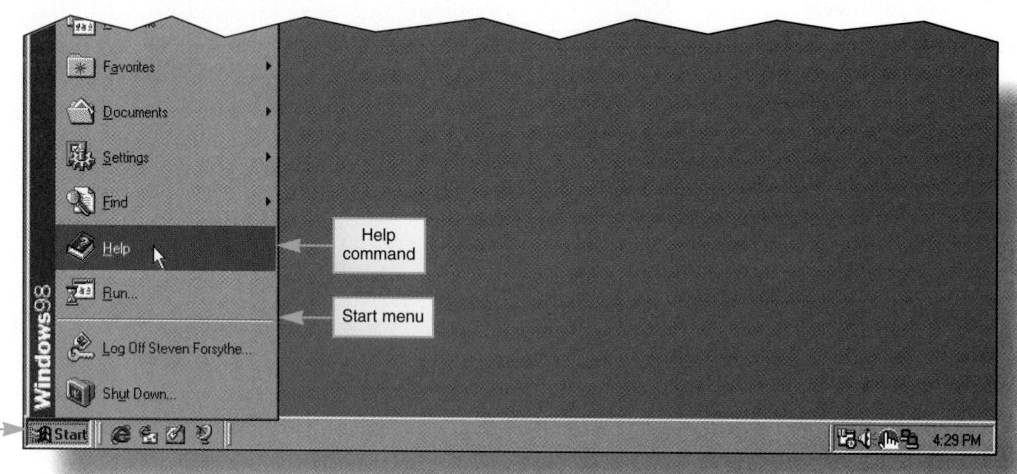

FIGURE 1-50

2 Click Help. Click the Maximize button on the Windows Help title bar. If the Contents sheet does not display, click the Contents tab.

*The Windows Help window opens and maximizes (Figure 1-51). The window contains the Help toolbar and two frames. The left frame contains three **tabs** (Contents, Index, and Search). The Contents sheet is visible in the left frame. The right frame contains information about the Welcome to Help topic.*

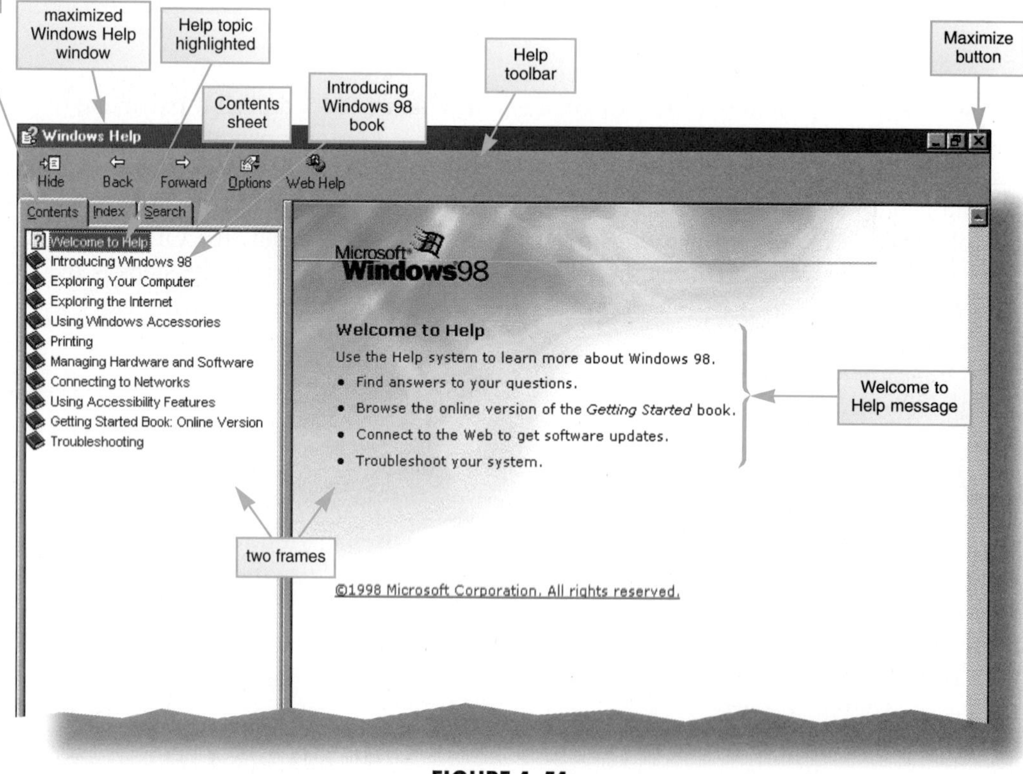

FIGURE 1-51

Other Ways

1. Press F1
2. Press WINDOWS+H (WINDOWS key on Microsoft Natural keyboard)

The Contents sheet contains a **Help topic** preceded by a question mark icon and followed by ten books. Each book consists of a closed book icon followed by a book name. The Help topic, Welcome to Help, is highlighted. In the left frame, the closed book icon indicates that Help topics or more books are contained in the book. The question mark icon indicates a Help topic without any further subdivisions. Clicking either the Index tab or the Search tab in the left frame opens the Index or Search sheet, respectively.

In addition to launching Help by using the Start button, you also can launch Help by pressing the F1 key.

After launching Help, the next step is to find the topic in which you are interested. To find the topic that describes how to find a topic in Help, complete the following steps.

To Use Help to Find a Topic in Help

1 Point to the Introducing Windows 98 closed book icon.

The mouse pointer changes to a hand when positioned on the icon and the Introducing Windows 98 book name displays in blue font and underlined (Figure 1-52).

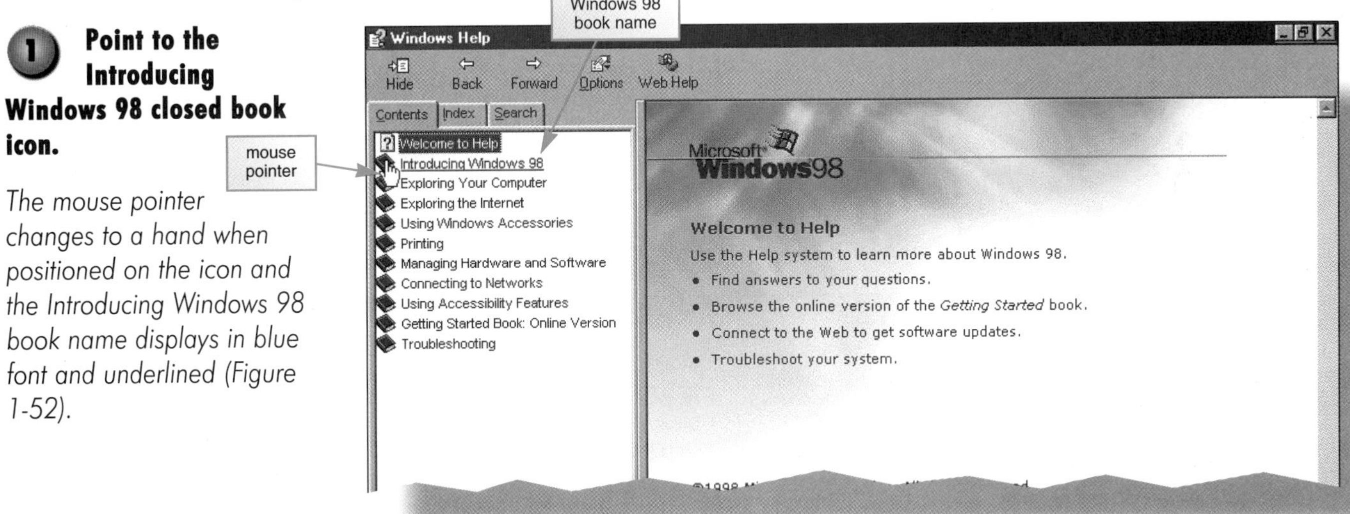

FIGURE 1-52

2 Click the Introducing Windows 98 closed book icon and then point to the How to Use Help closed book icon.

Windows 98 opens the Introducing Windows 98 book, changes the closed book icon to an open book icon, highlights the Introducing Windows 98 book name, underlines the How to Use Help book name, and displays the name and underline in blue font (Figure 1-53).

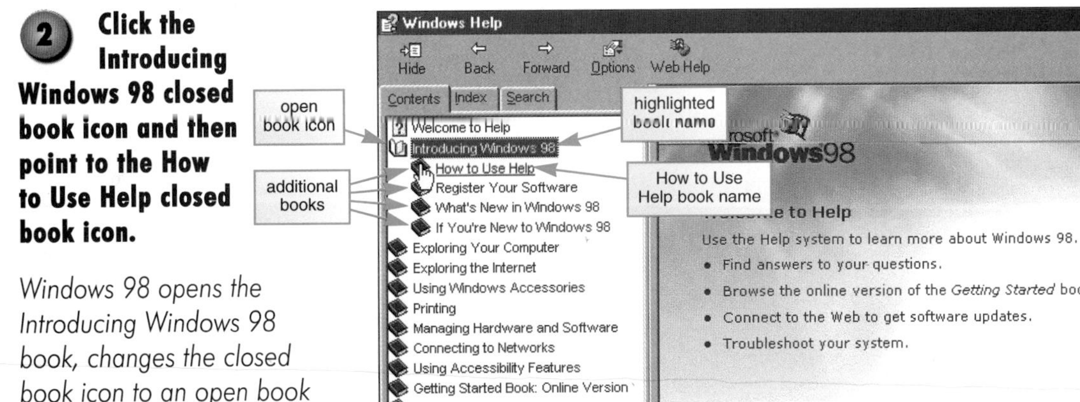

FIGURE 1-53

3 Click the How to Use Help closed book icon and then point to Find a topic in the opened How to Use Help book.

Windows 98 opens the How to Use Help book and displays several Help topics in the book, changes the closed book icon to an open book icon, highlights the How to Use Help book name, underlines the Find a topic Help topic name, and displays the topic name and underline in blue font (Figure 1-54).

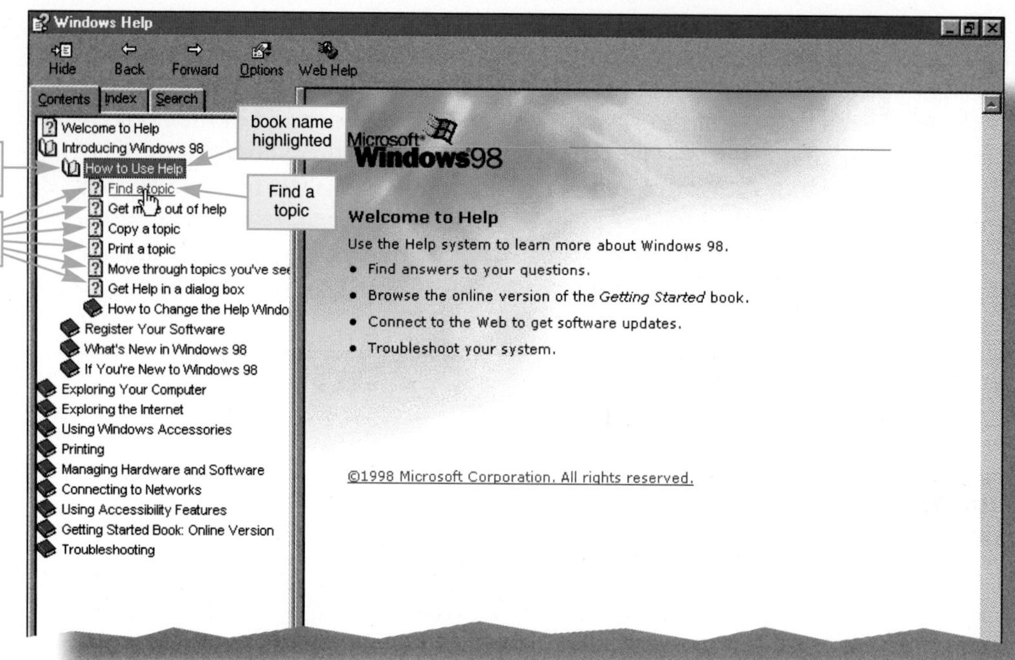

FIGURE 1-54

4 Click Find a topic. Read the information about finding a Help topic in the right frame of the Windows Help window.

Windows 98 highlights the Finding a topic Help topic and displays information about finding a Help topic in the right frame of the Windows Help window (Figure 1-55).

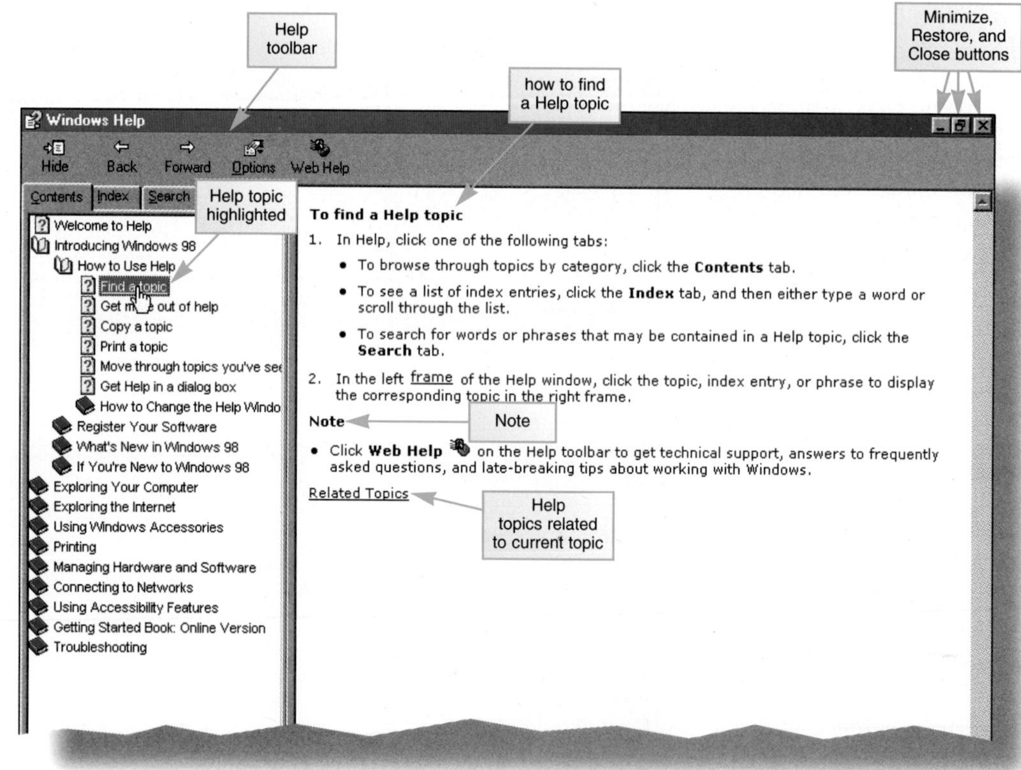

FIGURE 1-55

Other Ways

1. Press DOWN ARROW key until book or topic is highlighted, press ENTER, continue until Help topic displays, read Help topic

In Figure 1-55, if you click the **Hide button** on the Help toolbar, Windows 98 hides the tabs in the left frame and displays only the right frame in the Windows Help window. Clicking the **Back button** or **Forward button** displays a previously displayed Help topic in the right frame. Clicking the **Options button** allows you to hide or display the tabs in the left frame, display previously displayed Help topics in the right frame, stop the display of a Help topic, refresh the currently displayed Help topic, access Web Help, and print a Help topic. The **Web Help command** on the Options menu and the **Web Help button** on the Help toolbar allow you to use the Internet to obtain technical support, answers to frequently asked questions, and tips about working with Windows 98. Web Help will be explained in Project 2.

Notice also in Figure 1-55 that the Windows Help title bar contains a Minimize button, Restore button, and Close button. You can minimize or restore the Windows Help window as needed and also close the Windows Help window.

> **More About**
>
> **The Index Sheet**
>
> The Index sheet probably is the best source of information in Windows Help because you can enter the subject you are interested in. Sometimes, however, you will have to be creative to discover the index entry that answers your question because the most obvious entry will not always lead to your answer.

Index Sheet

A second method to find answers to your questions about Windows 98 or application programs running under Windows 98 is the Index sheet. The **Index sheet** lists a large number of index entries, each of which references one or more Help screens. To learn more about the Classic style, complete the following steps.

To Use the Help Index Sheet

1 **Click the Index tab. Type** classic style **(the flashing insertion point is positioned in the text box) in the text box. Point to the Display button at the bottom of the left frame.**

The Index sheet displays in the left frame and includes a list of entries that can be referenced (Figure 1-56). When you type an entry, the list automatically scrolls and the entry you type, such as classic style, is highlighted. To see additional entries, use the scroll bar at the right of the list. To highlight an entry in the list, click the entry.

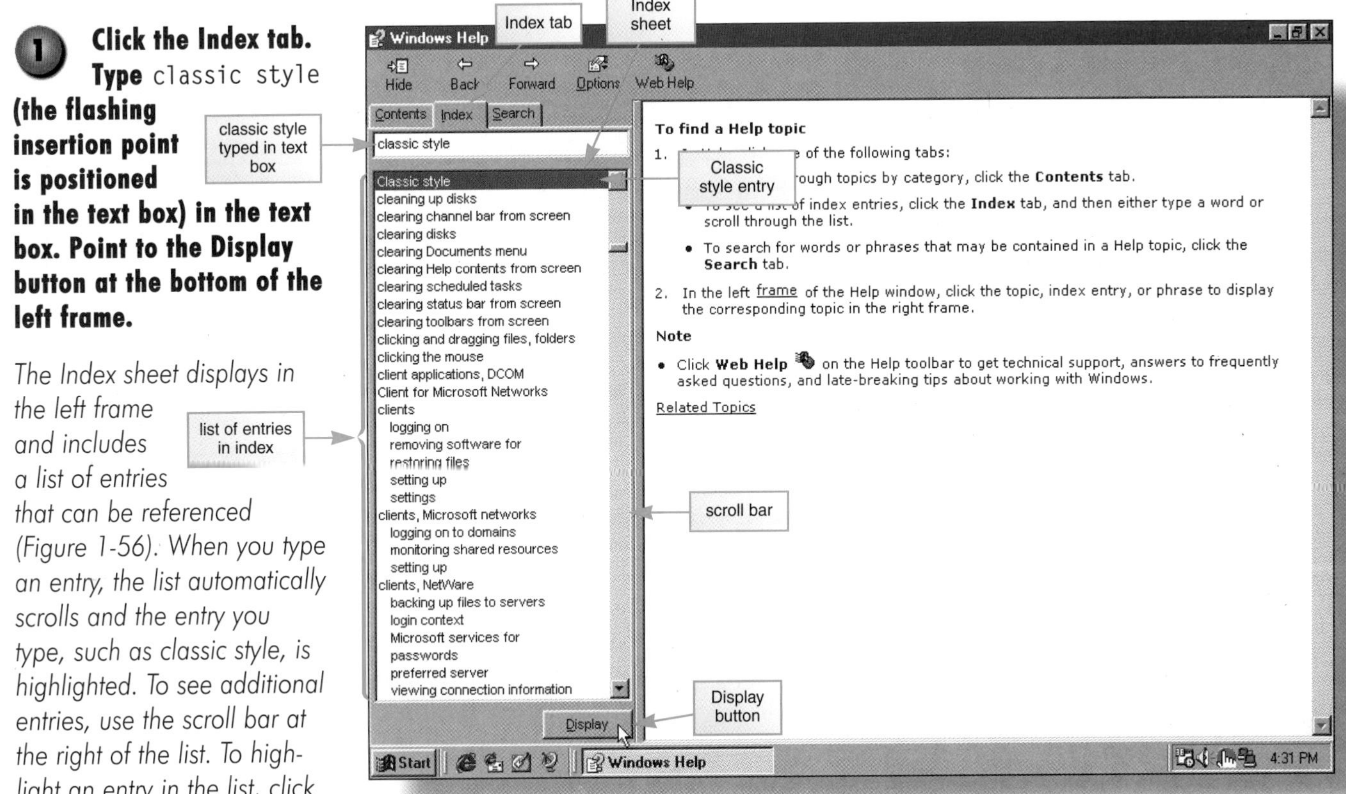

FIGURE 1-56

2 Click the Display button in the Windows Help window. Point to the Display button in the Topics Found dialog box.

The Topics Found dialog box displays on top of the Windows Help window and two Help topics display in the dialog box (Figure 1-57). The first topic, choosing Web or Classic style for folders, is highlighted. This topic contains information about the Web and Classic styles.

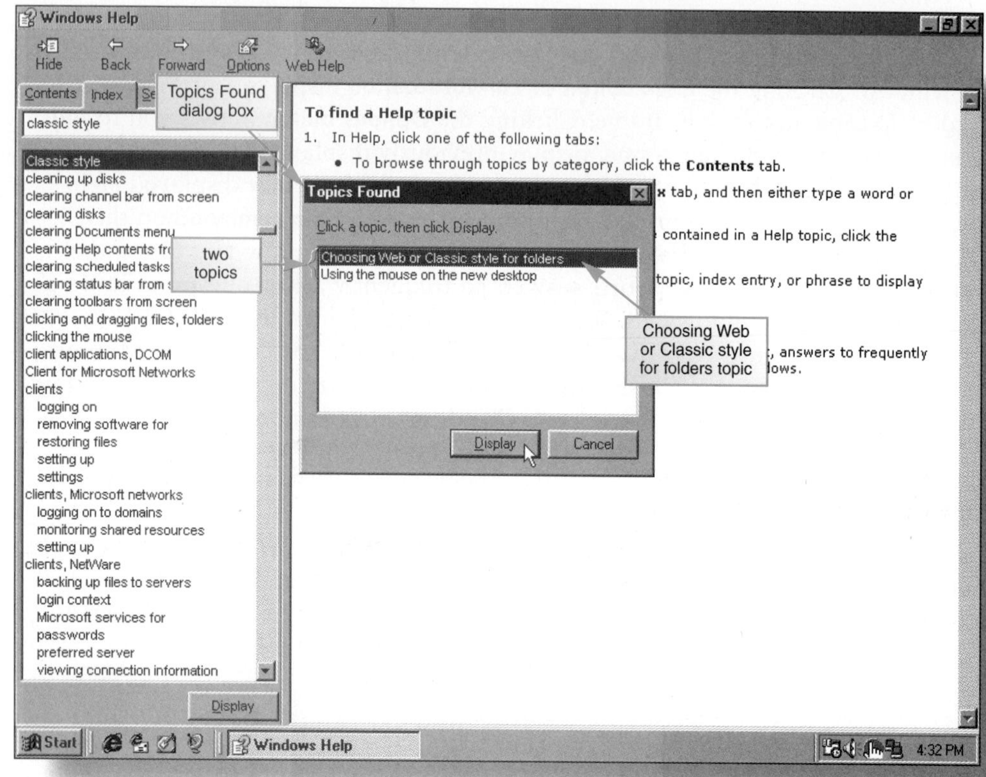

FIGURE 1-57

3 Click the Display button.

Information about the Web and Classic style, several hyperlinks, and one related topic displays in the right frame of the Windows Help window (Figure 1-58).

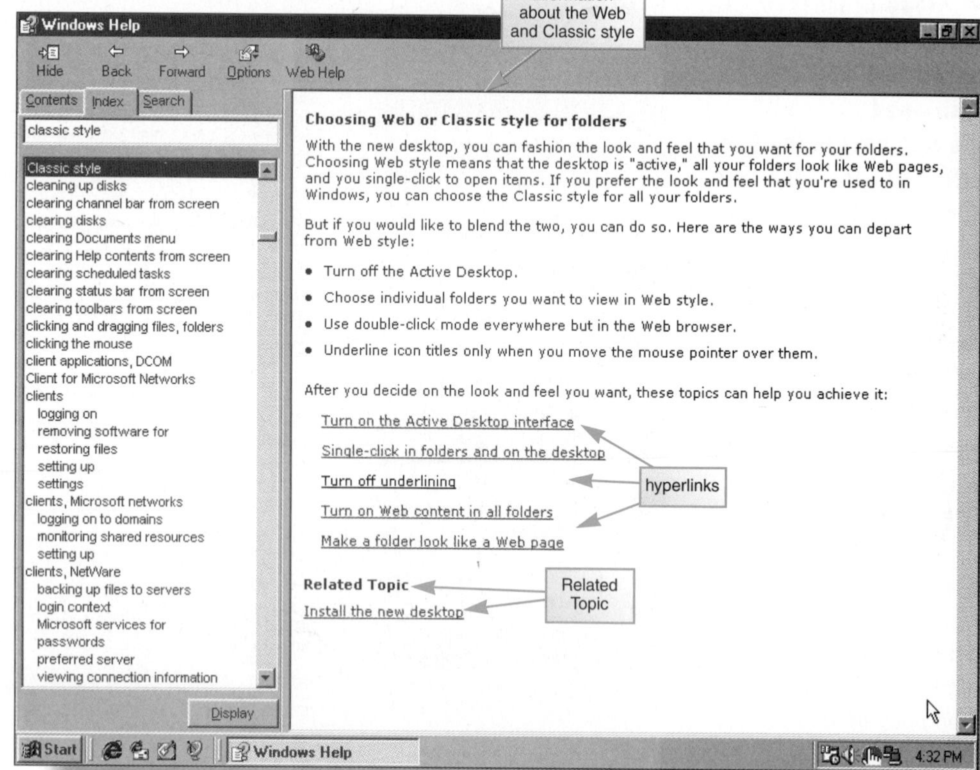

FIGURE 1-58

After viewing the index entries, normally you will close Windows Help. To close Windows Help, complete the following step.

TO CLOSE WINDOWS HELP

 Click the Close button on the title bar of the Windows Help window.

Windows 98 closes the Windows Help window.

Shut Down Procedures

Some users of Windows 98 have turned off their computers without following the shut down procedure only to find data they thought they had stored on disk was lost. Because of the way Windows 98 writes data on the disk, it is important you shut down Windows properly so you do not lose your work.

Shutting Down Windows 98

After completing your work with Windows 98, you may want to shut down Windows 98 using the **Shut Down command** on the Start menu. If you are sure you want to shut down Windows 98, perform the following steps. If you are not sure about shutting down Windows 98, read the following steps without actually performing them.

To Shut Down Windows 98

1 Click the Start button on the taskbar and then point to Shut Down on the Start menu (Figure 1-59).

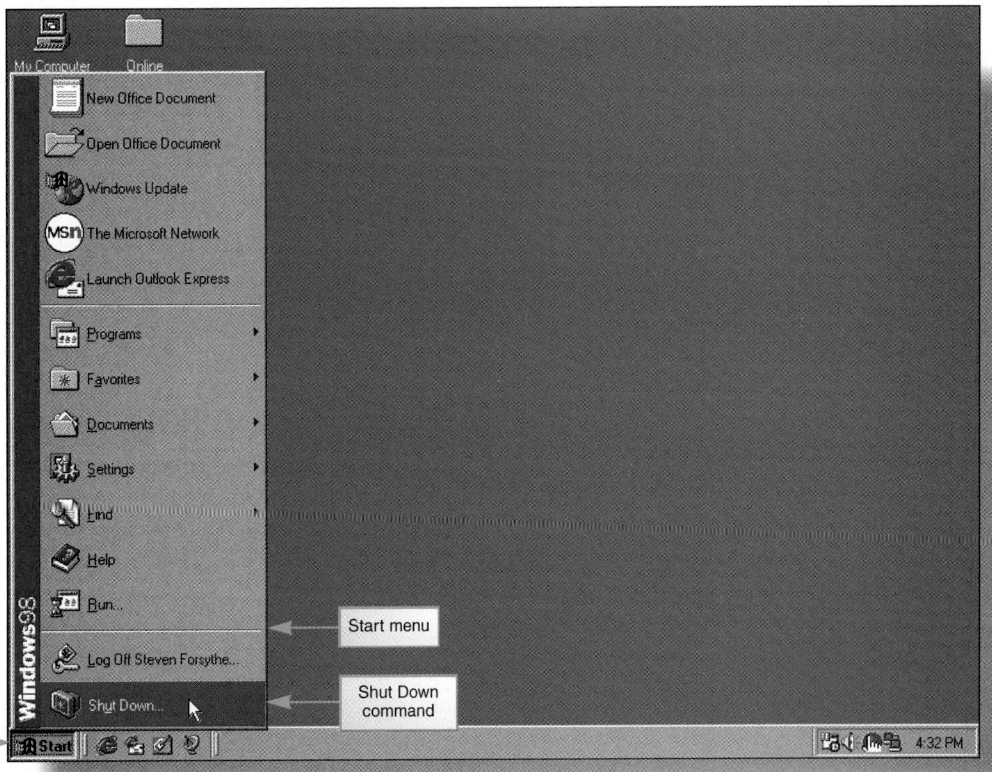

FIGURE 1-59

Click Shut Down. Point to the OK button in the Shut Down Windows dialog box.

The desktop darkens and the Shut Down Windows dialog box displays (Figure 1-60). A ***dialog box*** *displays whenever Windows 98 needs to supply information to you or requires you to enter information or select among several options. The dialog box contains three option buttons. The selected option button, Shut down, indicates that clicking the OK button will shut down Windows 98.*

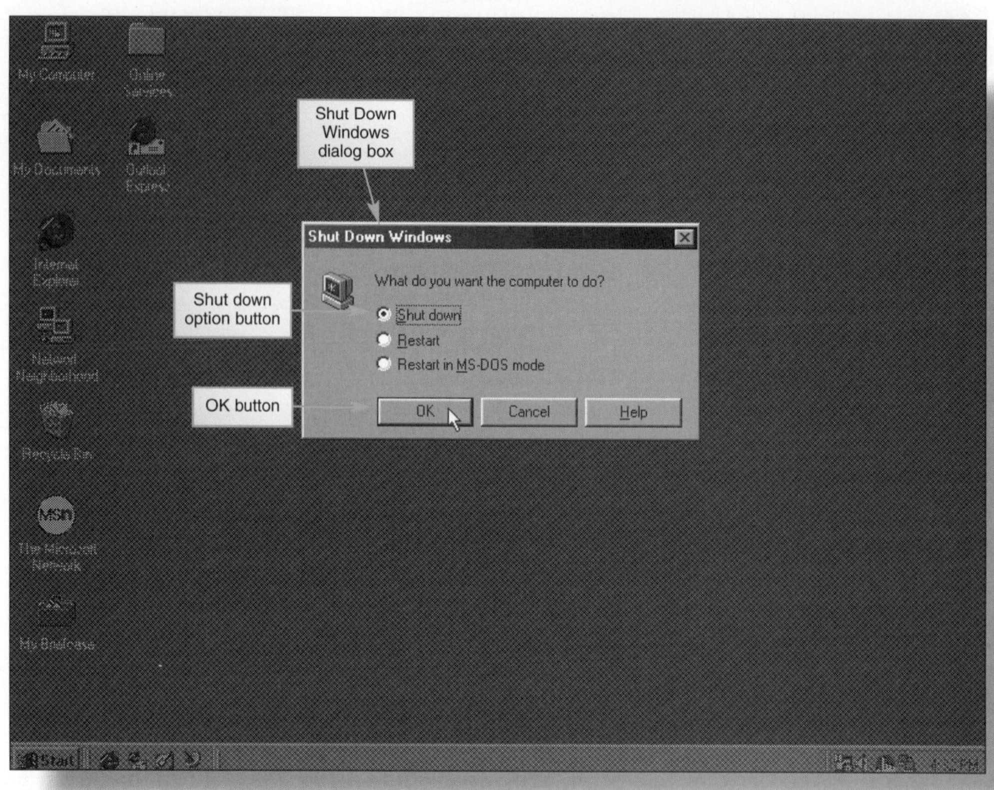

FIGURE 1-60

3 Click the OK button.

Windows 98 is shut down.

Other Ways

1. Press CTRL+ESC, press U, Press UP ARROW or DOWN ARROW key to select Shut down option button, press ENTER
2. Press ALT+F4, press UP ARROW or DOWN ARROW key to select Shut down option button, press ENTER

Two screens display while Windows 98 is shutting down. The first screen containing the Windows logo, Windows 98 name, and the text, Windows is shutting down, displays momentarily while Windows 98 is being shut down. Then, a second screen containing the text, It's now safe to turn off your computer, displays. At this point you can turn off your computer. When shutting down Windows 98, you should never turn off your computer before these two screens display.

If you accidentally click Shut Down on the Start menu and you do not want to shut down Windows 98, click the Cancel button in the Shut Down Windows dialog box to return to normal Windows 98 operation.

Project Summary

Project 1 illustrated the Microsoft Windows 98 graphical user interface. You started Windows 98, learned the parts of the desktop, and learned to point, click, right-click, double-click, drag, and right-drag. You learned about the Internet World Wide Web, the three desktop views (Classic, Web, and Custom), and launched an application. Using both the Help Content and the Help Index sheets you obtained Help about Microsoft Windows 98. You shut down Windows 98 using the Shut Down command on the Start menu.

What You Should Know

Having completed this project, you now should be able to perform the following tasks:

- Close a Window *(WIN 1.32)*
- Close a Window and Reopen a Window *(WIN 1.23)*
- Close the Welcome Screen *(WIN 1.10)*
- Close Windows Help *(WIN 1.49)*
- Launch a Program Using an Icon on the Desktop *(WIN 1.43)*
- Launch a Program Using the Quick Launch Toolbar *(WIN 1.42)*
- Launch a Program Using the Start Menu *(WIN 1.40)*
- Launch Windows Help *(WIN 1.44)*
- Maximize and Restore a Window *(WIN 1.21)*
- Minimize and Redisplay a Window *(WIN 1.19)*
- Move an Object by Dragging *(WIN 1.25)*
- Open a Window by Double-Clicking *(WIN 1.17)*
- Point and Click *(WIN 1.12)*
- Resize a Window *(WIN 1.31)*
- Right-Click *(WIN 1.15)*
- Right-Drag *(WIN 1.32)*
- Scroll a Window by Dragging the Scroll Box *(WIN 1.31)*
- Scroll a Window Using Scroll Arrows *(WIN 1.27)*
- Scroll a Window Using the Scroll Bar *(WIN 1.29)*
- Shut Down Windows 98 *(WIN 1.49)*
- Size a Window by Dragging *(WIN 1.26)*
- Use Help to Find a Topic in Help *(WIN 1.45)*
- Use the Help Index Sheet *(WIN 1.47)*

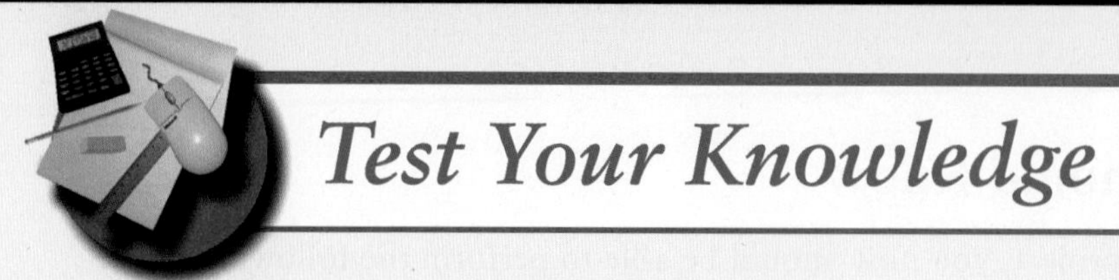

Test Your Knowledge

1 True/False

Instructions: Circle T if the statement is true or F if the statement is false.

T F 1. A user interface is a combination of computer hardware and computer software.

T F 2. The Quick Launch toolbar displays on the taskbar at the bottom of the desktop.

T F 3. Click means press the right mouse button.

T F 4. When you drag an object on the desktop, Windows 98 displays a shortcut menu.

T F 5. Double-clicking the My Computer icon on the desktop opens a window.

T F 6. You can maximize a window by dragging the title bar of the window.

T F 7. Viewing the desktop in Web style causes the desktop and the objects on the desktop to display and function as they did in Windows 95.

T F 8. One of the basic tasks you can perform using the Windows 98 operating system is to launch an application program.

T F 9. You can launch Windows Help by clicking the Start button and then clicking Help on the Start menu.

T F 10. To find an entry in the Windows Help Index, type the first few characters of the entry in the text box in the Contents sheet.

2 Multiple Choice

Instructions: Circle the correct response.

1. Through a user interface, the user is able to __________.
   a. control the computer
   b. request information from the computer
   c. respond to messages displayed by the computer
   d. all of the above
2. A shortcut menu opens when you __________ a(n) __________.
   a. right-click, object
   b. click, menu name on the menu bar
   c. click, submenu
   d. click, recessed button in the taskbar button area
3. In this book, a dark blue title bar and a recessed button in the taskbar button area indicate a window is __________.
   a. inactive
   b. minimized
   c. closed
   d. active

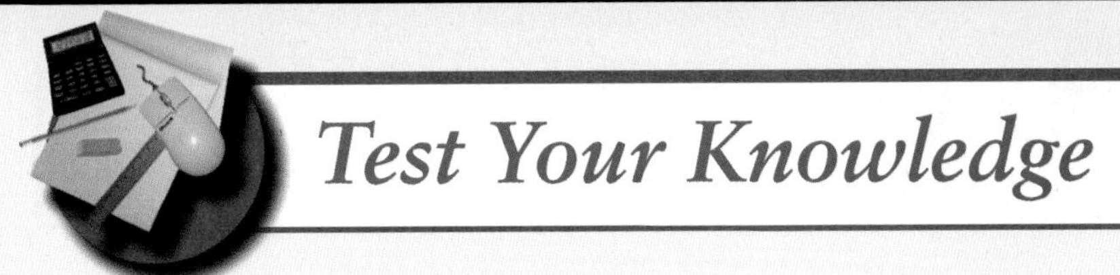

Test Your Knowledge

4. To view the contents of a window that are not currently visible in the window, use the __________.
   a. title bar
   b. scroll bar
   c. menu bar
   d. Restore button
5. __________ is holding down the right mouse button, moving an item to the desired location, and then releasing the right mouse button.
   a. Double-clicking
   b. Right-clicking
   c. Right-dragging
   d. Pointing
6. Text that is underlined in a browser window is called a(n) __________.
   a. uniform resource locator
   b. hyperlink
   c. hypertext document
   d. Web page
7. When the desktop is viewed in Web style, the icons on the desktop are __________ and the __________ Desktop displays.
   a. underlined, Active
   b. not underlined, Active
   c. underlined, Classic Windows
   d. not underlined, Classic Windows
8. Which method cannot be used to launch the Internet Explorer application?
   a. Click the Start button, point to Programs, point to Internet Explorer, and click Internet Explorer.
   b. Click the Launch Internet Explorer Browser icon on the Quick Launch toolbar.
   c. Click the Internet Explorer channel button on the Internet Explorer Channel bar.
   d. Click the Internet Explorer icon on the desktop.
9. For information about an index entry on the Index sheet of the Windows Help window, click the Help topic and __________.
   a. press the F1 key
   b. click the Forward button on the toolbar
   c. click the Search tab
   d. click the Display button
10. To shut down Windows 98, __________.
    a. click the Start button, click Shut Down, and click the OK button
    b. click File on the menu bar and then click Shut Down
    c. right-click the taskbar, click Shut down on the shortcut menu, and click the OK button
    d. press the F10 key and then click the OK button

Test Your Knowledge

3 Identifying the Objects on the Desktop

Instructions: On the desktop shown in Figure 1-61, arrows point to several items or objects on the desktop. Identify the items or objects in the spaces provided.

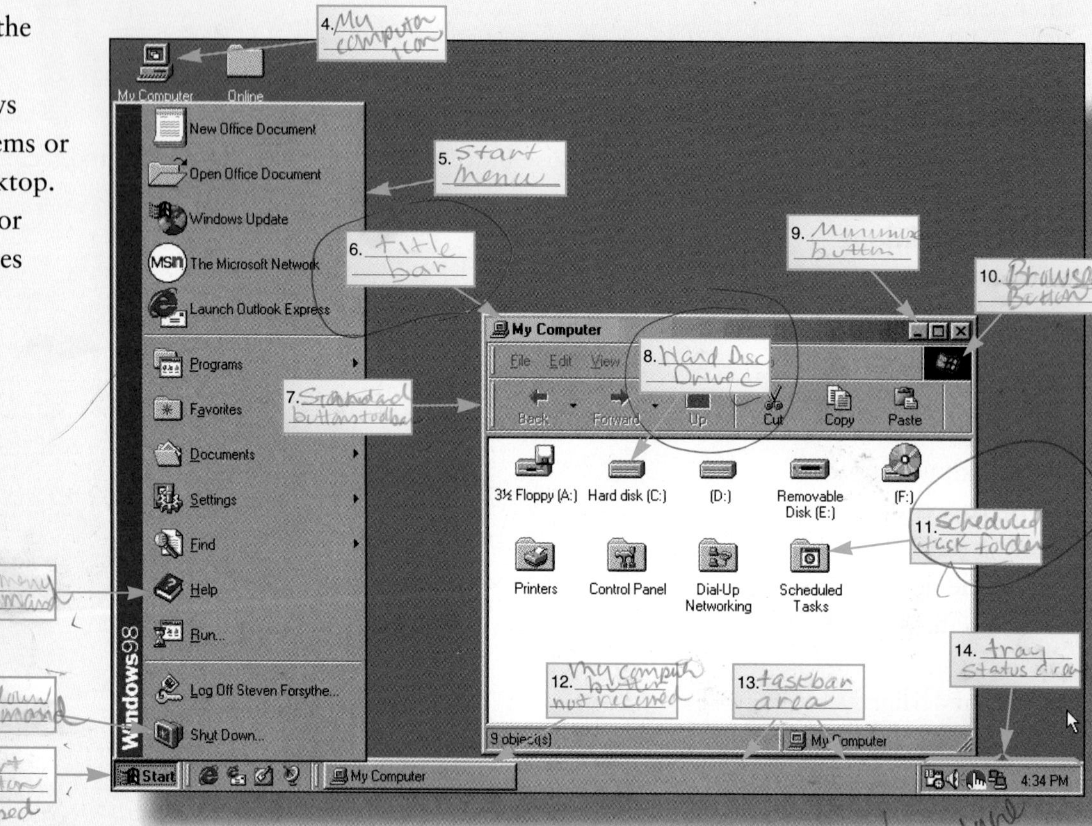

FIGURE 1-61

4 Launching the Internet Explorer Browser

Instructions: In the space provided, list the steps for the three methods used in this project to launch the Internet Explorer browser.

Method 1:

Step 1: ______________________________

Step 2: ______________________________

Step 3: ______________________________

Step 4: ______________________________

Method 2:

Step 1: ______________________________

Method 3:

Step 1: ______________________________

1 Using Windows Help

Instructions: Use Windows Help and a computer to perform the following tasks.

Part 1: Using the Question Mark Button

1. If necessary, start Microsoft Windows 98.
2. Click the Start button on the taskbar.
3. Point to Settings on the Start menu.
4. Click Folder Options on the Settings submenu.
5. Click the General tab in the Folder Options dialog box. A dialog box displays whenever Windows 98 needs to supply information to you or requires you to enter information or select among several options.
6. Click the question mark button on the title bar. The mouse pointer changes to a block arrow with question mark (Figure 1-62).
7. Click the preview monitor in the General sheet. A pop-up window displays explaining the contents of the preview monitor. Read the information in the pop-up window.
8. Click an open area of the General sheet to remove the pop-up window.
9. Click the question mark button on the title bar and then click the Web style option button. A pop-up window displays explaining what happens when you select this option. Read the information in the pop-up window.
10. Click the question mark button on the title bar and then click the Classic style option button. A pop-up window displays explaining what happens when you select this option. Read the information in the pop-up window.
11. Click the question mark button on the title bar and then click the Custom style option button. A pop-up window displays explaining what happens when you select this option. Read the information in the pop-up window.
12. Click the question mark button on the title bar and then click the Settings button. A pop-up window displays explaining the function of the button. Read the information in the pop-up window.
13. Click an open area of the General sheet to remove the pop-up window.
14. Summarize the function of the question mark button. ______________________________
15. Click the Close button in the Folder Options dialog box.

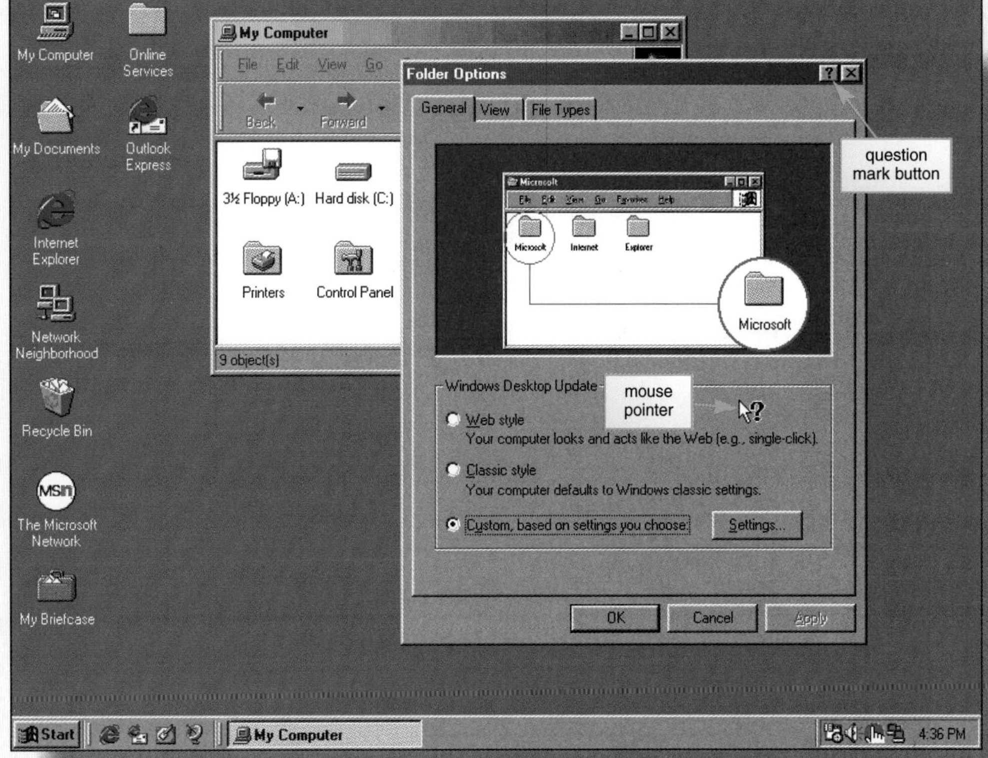

FIGURE 1-62

(continued)

Using Windows Help *(continued)*

Part 2: ***Finding What's New in Windows 98***

1. Click the Start button and then click Help on the Start menu.
2. Click the Maximize button on Windows Help title bar.
3. If the Contents sheet does not display, click the Contents tab. Click the Introducing Windows 98 closed book icon.
4. Click the What's New in Windows 98 closed book icon.
5. Click the True Web integration Help topic. Seven hyperlinks display in the right frame (Figure 1-63).

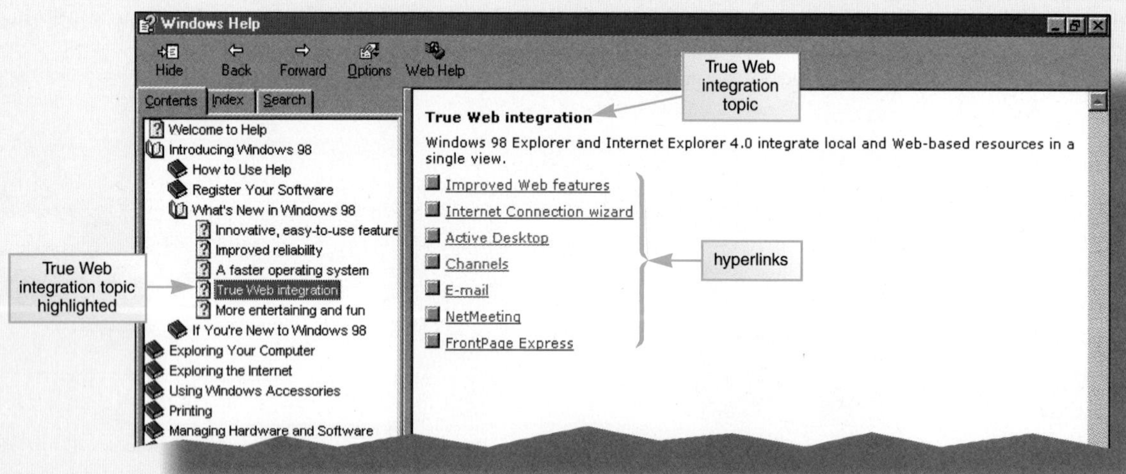

FIGURE 1-63

6. Click the Active Desktop hyperlink in the right frame and read the information about the Active Desktop.
7. Click the Channels hyperlink and read the information about channels.
8. Click the Options button on the Help toolbar to display the Options menu and then click Print.
9. Click the OK button in the Print dialog box to print the True Web integration screen.

Part 3: ***Reading About the Online Getting Started Manual***

1. Click the Getting Started Book: Online Version closed book icon in the left frame.
2. Click the Microsoft Windows 98 Getting Started Book Help topic. Read the information Windows 98 displays about the Getting Started Book in the right frame. The *Getting Started Book* is the printed manual for Windows 98.
3. Click the Click here hyperlink in the right frame to open the Getting Started window.
4. If the Contents sheet does not display, click the Contents tab. Click the Introducing Getting Started closed book icon. Click and read each of the four Help topics that display.
5. Click the Welcome closed book icon. Three Help topics and two closed book icons display in the open book. Click and read the Overview, Windows 98 at a Glance, and If You're New to Windows topics.

6. Click the Where to Find Information closed book icon.
7. Click the Resources Included with Windows 98 closed book icon. Click and read the Overview topic.
8. Click the Online Tutorial: Discover Windows 98 topic. Read the information about the topic.
9. Click the Troubleshooters topic. Read the information about the topic.
10. Click the Back button on the Help toolbar to display the previous screen (Online Tutorial: Discover Windows 98) in the right frame.
11. Click the Options button on the Help toolbar, click Print, and click the OK button to print the Help topic.
12. Click the Close button in the Getting Started window.
13. Click the Close button in the Windows Help window.

2 Using Windows Help to Obtain Help

Instructions: Use Windows Help and a computer to perform the following tasks.

1. Find Help about viewing the Welcome to Windows 98 screen that displays when you launch Windows 98. Use the search word, welcome, and the Index sheet. Answer the following questions in the spaces provided.
   a. How can you open the Welcome to Windows 98 screen? ______________________
   b. Open the Welcome to Windows 98 screen. How many entries does the Contents menu contain?
   ____
   c. Point to Discover Windows 98 on the Contents menu. What are the three choices available in Discover Windows 98? ______________________
   d. Point to Maintain Your Computer on the Contents menu. How can using Maintain Your Computer benefit your computer? ______________________
   e. Close the Welcome to Windows 98 screen.
2. Find Help about keyboard shortcuts by looking in the Exploring Your Computer book. Answer the following questions in the spaces provided.
   a. What keyboard shortcut is used to close the current window or quit a program?
   ____
   b. What keyboard shortcut is used to display the Start menu? ______________________
   c. What keyboard shortcut is used to display the shortcut menu for a selected item?
   ____
   d. What keyboard shortcut is used to rename an item? ______________________
   e. What keyboard shortcut is used to view an item's properties? ______________________
3. Find Help about changing the Windows Help window by looking in the Introducing Windows 98 book. Answer the following questions in the spaces provided.
   a. How do you hide the Contents, Index, and Search tabs? ______________________
   b. How do you make the left frame larger? ______________________
   c. Which software application do you use to change the color or fonts in the Help window?
   ____

(continued)

Using Windows Help to Obtain Help *(continued)*

4. Find Help about the desktop by looking in the Windows Desktop book in the Exploring Your Computer book. Answer the following questions in the spaces provided.
   a. What does the Active Desktop allow you to do? ____________________
   b. What does the Address toolbar enable you do? ____________________
   c. What commands do you use to find a person on the Internet? ____________________
5. Find Help about what to do if you have a problem in Windows 98. The process of solving such a problem is called ____________________. Answer the following questions in the spaces provided.
   a. What should you check if only part of a document prints on your printer?
   ____
   b. What could the problem be if Windows 98 does not detect that you have a modem connected to your computer?" ____________________
   c. What could the problem be if the computer restarts each time a sound is played?
   ____
6. Using the Index sheet in the Windows Help window, answer the following questions in the space provided.
   a. How do you get Help in a dialog box? ____________________
   b. What dialog box do you use to change the appearance of the mouse pointer?
   ____
   c. How do you minimize all open windows? ____________________
   d. How do you hide the Internet Explorer Channel bar? ____________________
7. Obtain information on software licensing by answering the following questions. Find and then print information from Windows Help that supports your answers.
   a. How does the law protect computer software? ____________________
   b. What is software piracy? ____________________ Why should I be concerned about it?
   ____
   c. What is an EULA (end user licensing agreement)?
   d. Can you use your own software on both your desktop and your laptop computers?
   ____
   e. How can you identify illegal software? ____________________
8. Your best friend just bought a new computer. Among the software packages she obtained when she received the computer was a NHL hockey game from Microsoft. She has no interest in hockey but she knows you are an avid hockey fan. Answer the following questions and then print the information supporting your answers from Windows Help. Can she legally give this software to you? ____________________
   Can she legally sell this software to you to help recover some of her costs? ____________________
   Can she give you the software and still keep the hockey game on her computer for use by another member of her family? ____________________
9. Close all open windows.

1 Improving Your Mouse Skills

Instructions: Use a computer to perform the following tasks:

1. Start Microsoft Windows 98 if necessary.
2. Click the Start button on the taskbar, point to Programs on the Start menu, point to Accessories on the Programs submenu, point to Games on the Accessories submenu, and click Solitaire on the Games submenu.
3. Click the Maximize button in the Solitaire window (Figure 1-64).

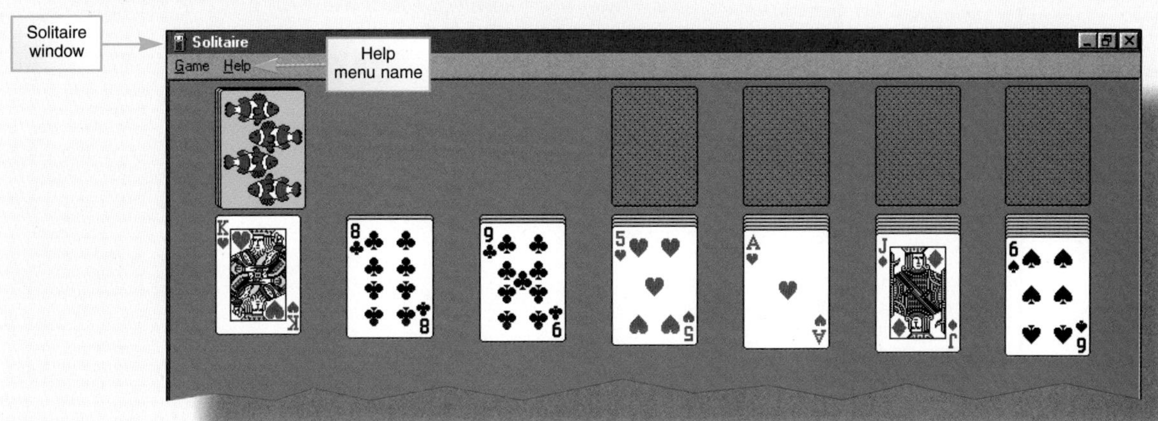

FIGURE 1-64

4. Click Help on the Solitaire menu bar and then click Help Topics.
5. If the Contents sheet does not display, click the Contents tab.
6. Review the Playing Solitaire and Choosing a scoring system topics in the Contents sheet.
7. After reviewing the Help topics, close all Help windows.
8. Play the game of Solitaire.
9. Click the Close button on the Solitaire title bar to close the game.

2 Using the Discover Windows 98 Tutorial

Instructions: To use the Discover Windows 98 tutorial you will need a copy of the Windows 98 CD-ROM. If this CD-ROM is not available, skip this lab assignment. Otherwise, use a computer and the CD-ROM to perform the following tasks:

1. Start Microsoft Windows 98 if necessary.
2. Insert the Windows 98 CD-ROM in your CD-ROM drive. If the Windows 98 CD-ROM window displays, click the Close button in the window to close the window.
3. Click the Start button on the taskbar, point to Programs on the Start menu, point to Accessories on the Programs submenu, point to System Tools on the Accessories submenu, and click Welcome to Windows on the System Tools submenu.
4. Click Discover Windows 98 in the Welcome to Windows 98 window to display the Discover Windows 98 Contents.

(continued)

Using the Discover Windows 98 Tutorial *(continued)*

5. Click the Computer Essentials title (hyperlink) in the right panel of the Discover Windows 98 Contents screen (Figure 1-65).

   The Computer Essentials tutorial starts and fills the desktop. The left panel contains a list of lessons. A left arrow to the right of a lesson indicates the current lesson.

FIGURE 1-65

   Pressing the RIGHT ARROW key on the keyboard displays the next screen in the lesson. Pressing the UP ARROW key quits the Computer Essentials tutorial. Clicking the Contents button displays the Table of Contents in the Discover Windows 98 Contents screen.
6. Press the RIGHT ARROW key to begin the Introduction.
7. When appropriate, press the number 1 key to begin the Meeting Your Computer section. Complete this lesson. This lesson takes approximately ten minutes.
8. Click the Contents button to display the Discover Windows 98 Contents screen.
9. If you have experience using Windows 3.0 or Windows 3.1 and are learning to use Windows 98, click the Windows 98 Overview title. Otherwise, go to Step 10. This lesson takes approximately ten minutes.
10. If you have experience using Windows 95 and are learning to use Windows 98, click the What's New title. Otherwise, go to Step 11. Press any key on the keyboard to begin the lesson. Features are organized into five groups. Click each feature (hyperlink) in each group to view a demonstration. When finished, click the Exit button. This lesson takes approximately twenty minutes.
11. If time permits, click the More Windows 98 Resources title. Click the Microsoft Windows 98 Starts Here title (1) and then click the Microsoft Press title (2) to view additional information about Windows 98. Click each the three hyperlinks below the Resources title to explore three Windows-related Web sites. When finished, click the Close button in the Microsoft Internet Explorer window and click the Contents button.
12. Click the Close button in the Discover Windows 98 Contents screen.
13. Click the Yes button in the Discover Windows 98 dialog box.
14. Click the Close button in the Welcome to Windows 98 window.
15. Remove the Windows 98 CD-ROM from your CD-ROM drive.

3 Launching and Using the Internet Explorer Application

Instructions: Perform the following steps to launch the Internet Explorer application.

Part 1: ***Launching the Internet Explorer Application***

1. Start Microsoft Windows 98 and, if necessary, connect to the Internet.
2. Click the Internet Explorer icon on the Quick Launch toolbar.
3. If the Address bar does not display below the Standard Buttons toolbar in the Microsoft Internet Explorer window, click View on the menu bar, point to Toolbars, and click Address Bar on the Toolbars submenu.

Part 2: ***Entering a URL in the Address Bar***

1. Click the URL in the Address bar to highlight the URL.
2. Type http://www.microsoft.com in the Address bar and press the ENTER key.
3. What URL displays in the Address bar? ____________________ What window title displays in the title bar? ____________________
4. Scroll the Web page to view the contents of the Web page. List two topics that are shown on this Web page. ____________________ List five hyperlinks (underlined text) that are shown on this Web page. ____________________
5. Click any hyperlink on the Web page. What hyperlink did you click? ____________________
6. Describe the Web page that displayed when you clicked the hyperlink? ____________________
7. Click the Print button on the Standard Buttons toolbar to print the Web page.

Part 3: ***Entering a URL in the Address Bar***

1. Click the URL in the Address bar to highlight the URL.
2. Type http://www.disney.com in the Address bar and press the ENTER key.
3. What window title displays in the title bar? ____________________
4. Scroll the Web page to view the contents of the Web page. Do any graphic images display on the Web page? ____________________ If so, describe two images. ____________________
5. Pointing to an image on a Web page and having the mouse pointer change to a hand indicates the image is a hyperlink. Does the Web page include an image that is a hyperlink? ____________________ If so, describe the image. ____________________
6. Click the hyperlink to display another Web page. What window title displays in the title bar? ____________________
7. Click the Print button on the Standard Buttons toolbar to print the Web page.

Part 4: ***Displaying Previously Displayed Web Pages***

1. Click the Back button on the Standard Buttons toolbar. What Web page displays? ____________________
2. Click the Back button on the Standard Buttons toolbar twice. What Web page displays? ____________________
3. Click the Forward button on the Standard Buttons toolbar bar. What Web page displays? ____________________

Part 5: ***Entering a URL in the Address Bar***

1. Click the URL in the Address bar to highlight the URL.
2. Type http://www.scsite.com/WIN98/ in the Address bar and press the ENTER key.
3. Click the Steve's Cool Sites hyperlink on the Web page.
4. Click any hyperlinks that are of interest to you. Which hyperlink did you like the best? ____________________
5. Use the Back or Forward button to display the Web site you like the best.
6. Click the Print button on the Standard Buttons toolbar to print the Web page.
7. Click the Close button on the Microsoft Internet Explorer title bar.

4 Launching an Application

Instructions: Perform the following steps to launch the Notepad application using the Start menu, and create the daily reminders list shown in Figure 1-66. **Notepad** is a popular application program available with Windows 98 that allows you to create, save, and print simple text documents.

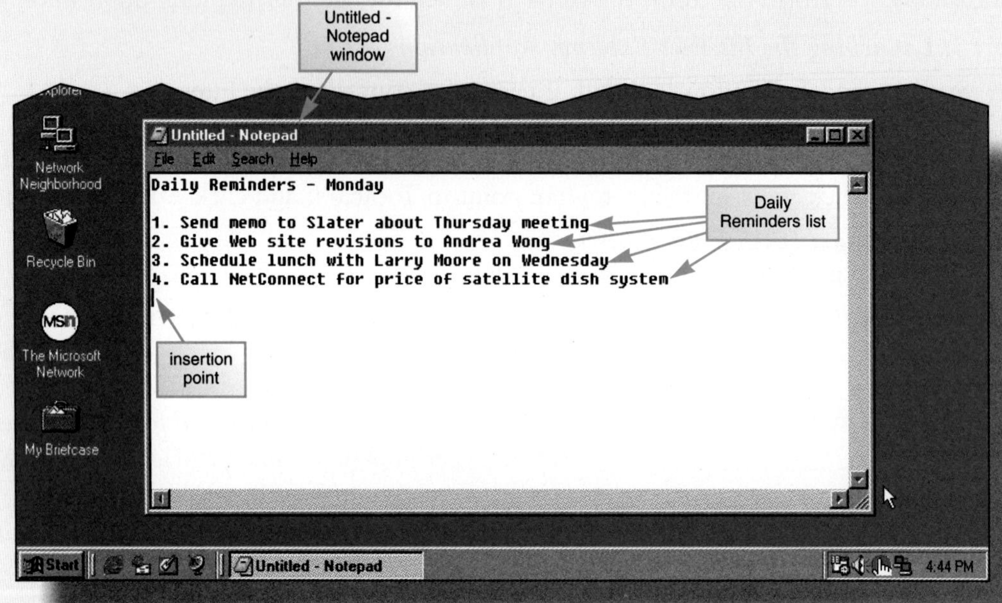

FIGURE 1-66

Part 1: ***Launching the Notepad Application***

1. Start Microsoft Windows 98 if necessary.
2. Click the Start button.
3. Point to Programs on the Start menu, point to Accessories on the Programs submenu, and click Notepad on the Accessories submenu. The Untitled - Notepad window displays and an insertion point (flashing vertical line) displays in the blank area below the menu bar.

Part 2: ***Creating a Document Using Notepad***

1. Type `Daily Reminders - Monday` and press the ENTER key twice.
2. Type `1. Send memo to Slater about Thursday meeting` and press the ENTER key.
3. Type `2. Give Web site revisions to Andrea Wong` and press the ENTER key.
4. Type `3. Schedule lunch with Larry Moore on Wednesday` and press the ENTER key.
5. Type `4. Call NetConnect about prices for satellite dish system` and press the ENTER key.

Part 3: ***Printing the Daily Reminders Document***

1. Click File on the menu bar and then click Print.
2. Retrieve the printed Daily Reminders list from the printer.

Part 4: ***Closing the Notepad Window***

1. Click the Close button on the Notepad title bar.
2. Click the No button in the Notepad dialog box to not save the Daily Reminders document.

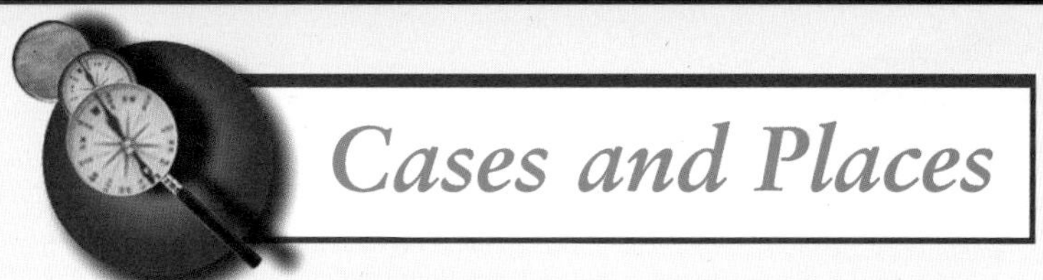

Cases and Places

The difficulty of these case studies varies:
◗ are the least difficult; ◗◗ are more difficult; and ◗◗◗ are the most difficult.

1 ◗ Using Windows Help, locate the Getting Started Online Manual. Using the Online Manual read about the following ten topics: Connecting to a Network, Customizing Your Desktop, Emergency Startup Disk, FAT32 File, System Explorer Bars, Microsoft NetMeeting, My Documents Folder, OnNow Power Management, TDD Service, and Watching TV. Select five of the ten topics. In a brief report, summarize the five topics you have selected.

2 ◗ Technical support is an important consideration when installing and using an operating system or an application software program. The ability to obtain a valid answer to your question at the moment you have the question can be the difference between a frustrating experience and a positive experience. Using Windows 98 Help, the Internet, or another research facility, write a brief report on the options that are available for obtaining help and technical support while using Windows 98.

3 ◗ Early personal computer operating systems were adequate, but they were not user-friendly and had few advanced features. Over the past several years, however, personal computer operating systems have become increasingly easy to use, and some now offer features once available only on mainframe computers. Using the Internet, a library, or other research facility, write a brief report on two personal computer operating systems. Describe the systems, pointing out their similarities and differences. Discuss the advantages and disadvantages of each. Finally, tell which operating system you would purchase for your personal computer and explain why.

4 ◗◗ Microsoft's decision to make the Internet Explorer 4 Web browser part of the Windows 98 operating system caused many legal problems for Microsoft. Using the Internet, computer magazines and newspapers, or other resources, prepare a brief report on these legal problems. Explain the arguments for and against combining the browser and operating system. Identify the key players on both sides of the legal battle and summarize the final decision. Did the legal process or final decision affect the release date and contents of Windows 98? Do you think computer users benefited from this decision? Explain your answers.

5 ◗◗◗ Software must be compatible with (capable of working with) the operating system of the computer on which it will be used. Visit a software vendor and find the five application packages (word processing, spreadsheet, games, and so on) you would most like to have. List the names of the packages and the operating system used by each. Make a second list of five similar packages that are compatible (meaning they use the same operating system). Using your two lists, write a brief report on how the need to purchase compatible software can affect buying application packages, and even the choice of an operating system.

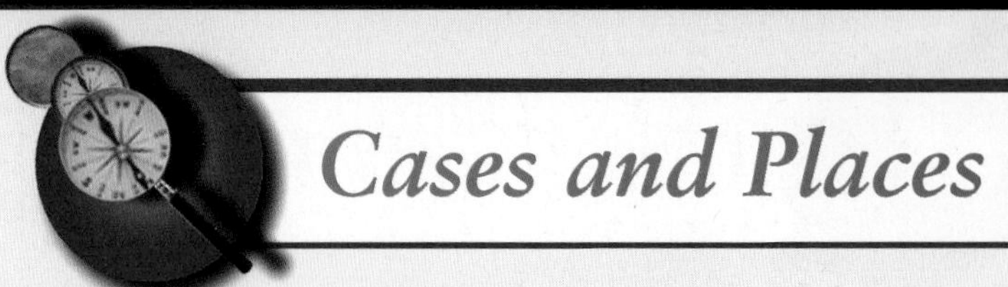

Cases and Places

6 ▶▶▶ Because of the many important tasks an operating system performs, most businesses put a great deal of thought into choosing an operating system for their personal computers. Interview a person at a local business on the operating system it uses with its personal computers. Based on your interview, write a brief report on why the business chose that operating system, how satisfied it is with it, and under what circumstances it might consider switching to a different operating system.

7 ▶▶▶ In addition to Windows 98, Microsoft also sells the Windows NT operating system. Some say Windows NT will replace Windows 98 in the future. Using the Internet, computer magazines, or other resources, prepare a brief report comparing and contrasting the operating systems. How do their graphical user interfaces compare? What features and commands are shared by both operating systems? Does either operating system have features or commands that the other operating system does not have? Explain whether you think Windows NT could replace Windows 98.

Microsoft Windows 98

Working on the Windows 98 Desktop

OBJECTIVES

You will have mastered the material in this project when you can:

- Launch an application, create a text document, and save the document on the desktop
- Create, name, and save a text document on the desktop
- Open and modify a document on the desktop
- Create a folder on the desktop
- Move documents to a folder on the desktop
- Display the contents of a folder
- Modify and print documents in a folder
- Open and modify multiple documents
- Copy a folder from the desktop onto a floppy disk
- Open a folder stored on a floppy disk
- Add and delete shortcuts on the Start menu
- Create and delete shortcuts on the desktop
- Open a document using a shortcut
- Delete shortcut icons and document icons from the desktop
- Turn on and turn off the Active Desktop
- Describe Active Web content and subscriptions
- Add and remove a desktop item from the desktop
- Use Windows Support Online

Doing Windows

Graphical Computing Clicks with Users

"Doing Windows" has an entirely new meaning since Bill Gates announced plans to add graphical capabilities to the IBM personal computer in 1983. The Microsoft CEO decided to take this step to help current personal computer users work more effectively and entice others to buy systems.

Up until this time, users were typing cumbersome disk operating system (DOS) commands to run their computers. When IBM decided to design a personal computer in 1980, corporate executives approached Gates to develop its new operating system. Gates declined the offer and suggested that IBM contact Gary Kildall at Digital Research, a leading microcomputer software developer.

Kildall had

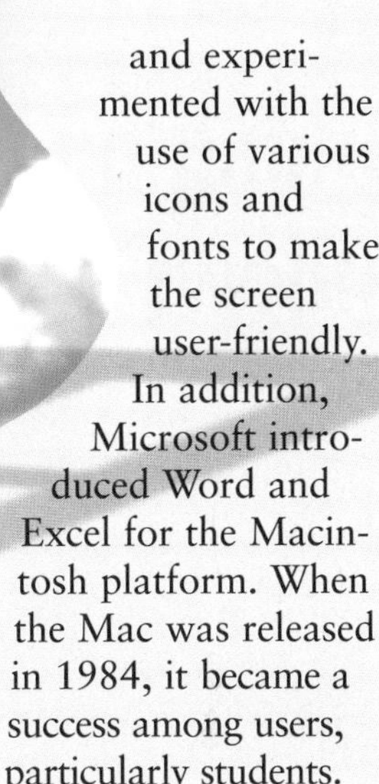

developed a widely used operating system called CP/M.

Kildall, however, decided not to attend the meeting at IBM headquarters. The frustrated IBM executives contacted Gates once again, and this time he reconsidered, even though he knew very little about operating systems. By chance, a neighboring company in Washington named Seattle Computer Products was developing an operating system it called QDOS (QDOS was an acronym for Quick and Dirty Operating System). Bill Gates made a proposal to the company, and in December 1980, Microsoft obtained nonexclusive rights to QDOS. Later, Microsoft acquired all rights for a total purchase price of $1 million, and renamed the system MS-DOS (an acronym for Microsoft Disk Operating System).

Microsoft modified the program, and then shipped it in the first IBM personal computer, the IBM PC, unveiled in August 1981. The sale of millions of IBM PCs and consequently millions of copies of the operating system, propelled Microsoft to the world's largest software company.

Gates's graphical intentions were fueled by work being done at Xerox's Palo Alto Research Center in California. He saw researchers there using an invention they called a mouse to move a pointer instead of using arrow keys on the keyboard to move a cursor.

Then, working with Apple, Microsoft developed software for the Macintosh computer. Combining its original innovations with those of Xerox, Microsoft created the graphical user interface and experimented with the use of various icons and fonts to make the screen user-friendly. In addition, Microsoft introduced Word and Excel for the Macintosh platform. When the Mac was released in 1984, it became a success among users, particularly students.

Microsoft's next step was to develop these applications for the IBM PC and IBM-compatible computers. The company's innovations resulted in the release of Windows 3.1 and Windows 95 prior to Windows 98. Currently more than 100 million computers worldwide use the Windows operating system.

Programmers at Microsoft use a process the corporation calls *continuous reinvention* to constantly add new features to enhance Windows performance. Microsoft also allows anyone to write programs for the Windows platform without requiring prior permission. Indeed, today many of the thousands of Windows-based programs compete with Microsoft's own programs.

Gates predicts his company will continue to release new Windows versions every two or three years. He is convinced that individuals will want to take advantage of user interface enhancements and innovations that make computing easier, more reliable, faster, and integrated with the Internet.

Working on the Windows 98 desktop in this project, you will find out for yourself how these features can help you launch an application, create folders and documents, use shortcuts, and access Windows Support Online.

Microsoft Windows 98

Working on the Windows 98 Desktop

CASE PERSPECTIVE

As you work with Windows 98, you will find one of its major features is the ease with which you can access documents and files you use constantly. You also will find that working with multiple documents at the same time is vital to working efficiently. The company where you work has placed you in charge of developing the text documents to keep track of the daily appointments. As you begin the assignment, you ascertain that daily appointments seem to change constantly. If you could work on the Windows 98 desktop, you would save a great deal of time. In this project, you will learn the skills that are essential to your success and gain the knowledge required to work efficiently on the Windows 98 desktop.

Introduction

In Project 1, you learned three methods to launch the Internet Explorer application. To launch Internet Explorer, you used the Start button and Start menu, an icon on the Quick Launch toolbar, and a shortcut icon on the desktop. The ability to accomplish a task, such as launching an application, in a variety of ways is one of Windows 98's most powerful features.

In Project 2, you will learn two methods to create documents on the desktop and discover the intuitive nature of the Windows 98 desktop by creating a folder on the desktop in which to store multiple documents, storing documents in the folder, and moving the folder from the desktop onto a disk. In addition, you will turn on the Active Desktop and add an Active Desktop item to the desktop. An **Active Desktop item** allows you to display the constantly changing content of a Web page directly on the Active Desktop and automatically update the content.

Assume each morning you create two daily appointments lists; one list for Mr. Lopez and a second list for Ms. Parks. Mr. Lopez and Ms. Parks use the lists to remind them of the appointments they have throughout the day. On occasion, you must update the lists as new appointments are made during the day. You decide to use **Notepad**, a popular application program available with Windows 98, to create the daily appointments lists. The finished documents are shown in Figure 2-1.

The name of each document displays at the top of the printed page, the text of the document (the daily appointments) displays below the document name, and a page number displays at the bottom of the page. The first printed document contains a list of Monday's appointments scheduled for Mr. Lopez. The second printed document contains a list of Monday's appointments scheduled for Ms. Parks. The following sections illustrate two methods to create these documents.

2 **Click Notepad. Type** `Lopez Appointments (Monday)` **and then press the ENTER key twice. Type** `9:00 Budget Meeting - Jim Branch's Office` **and then press the ENTER key. Type** `12:00 Lunch at Grant's Cafe - Angela Manning` **and then press the ENTER key. Type** `2:00 Department Meeting - Conference Room B` **and then press the ENTER key.**

The Notepad program starts, the text of the document is entered, and a recessed Notepad button displays in the taskbar button area (Figure 2-3).

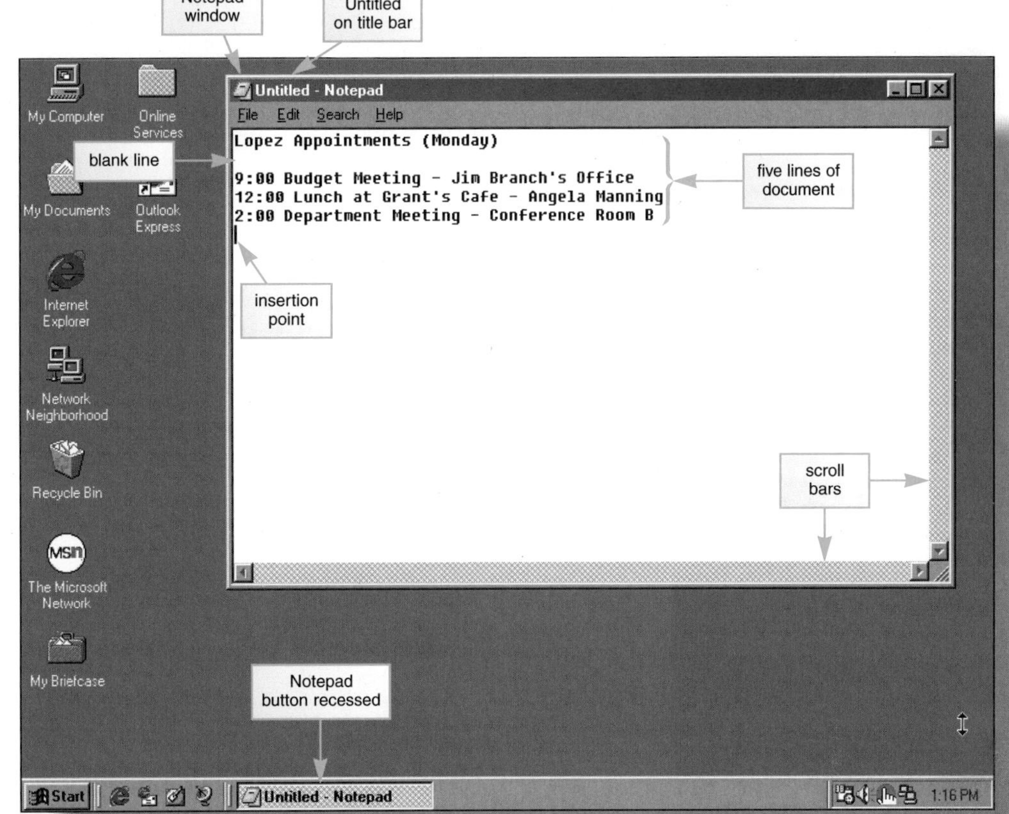

FIGURE 2-3

Other Ways

1. Right-click desktop, point to New, click Text Document, double-click New Text Document icon, enter text
2. Click Start button, click Run, type `Notepad`, click OK button, enter text
3. Press CTRL+ESC, press R, type `Notepad`, press ENTER key, enter text

In Figure 2-3, the word, Untitled, in the window title bar (Untitled - Notepad) and on the Notepad button indicates the document has not been saved on disk. The area below the menu bar contains the five lines of the document, a blank line, a line containing an insertion point, and two scroll bars. The **insertion point** is a flashing vertical line that indicates the point at which text typed on the keyboard will be displayed. The scroll bars do not contain scroll boxes, indicating the document is not large enough to allow scrolling.

Saving a Document on the Desktop

When you create a document using a program such as Notepad, the document is stored in the main memory (RAM) of your computer. If you close the program without saving the document or if your computer accidentally loses electrical power, the document will be lost. To protect against the accidental loss of a document and to allow you to modify the document easily in the future, you can save the document on a disk (hard disk or floppy disk) or on the desktop. When you save a document on the desktop, a document icon displays on the desktop and the document is stored on the hard disk.

More About

Saving a Document

Most people who have used a computer can tell at least one horror story of working on their computer for a long stretch of time and then losing the work because of some malfunction with the computer or even with the operating system or application program. *Be Warned:* Save and save often to protect the work you have completed on your computer.

File Names

Because of the restrictions with Microsoft DOS, some versions of Windows allowed file names of only eight or fewer characters. F56QPSLA and similar indecipherable names were common. When long file names were introduced in Windows 95, Microsoft touted the new feature as a significant breakthrough. Apple Macintosh users, however, shrug and ask, What's the big deal? They have used long file names for years.

When you save a document, you must assign a file name to the document. All documents are identified by a **file name**. A file name should be descriptive of the file you save. Typical file names are Lopez Appointments (Monday), Office Supplies List, and Automobile Maintenance. A file name can contain up to 255 characters, including spaces. Any uppercase or lowercase character is valid when creating a file name, except a backslash (\), slash (/), colon (:), asterisk (*), question mark (?), quotation mark ("), less than symbol (<), greater than symbol (>), or vertical bar (|). File names cannot be CON, AUX, COM1, COM2, COM3, COM4, LPT1, LPT2, LPT3, PRN, or NUL.

To associate a document with an application, Windows 98 assigns an extension of a period and up to three characters to each document. All documents created using the Notepad program are text documents and are saved with the .txt extension.

To save the document you created using Notepad on the desktop of your computer using the file name, Lopez Appointments (Monday), perform the following steps.

To Save a Document on the Desktop

1 Click File on the menu bar and then point to Save As.

The File menu opens in the Notepad window (Figure 2-4). The ellipsis (...) following the Save As command indicates Windows 98 requires more information to carry out the Save As command and will open a dialog box when you click Save As.

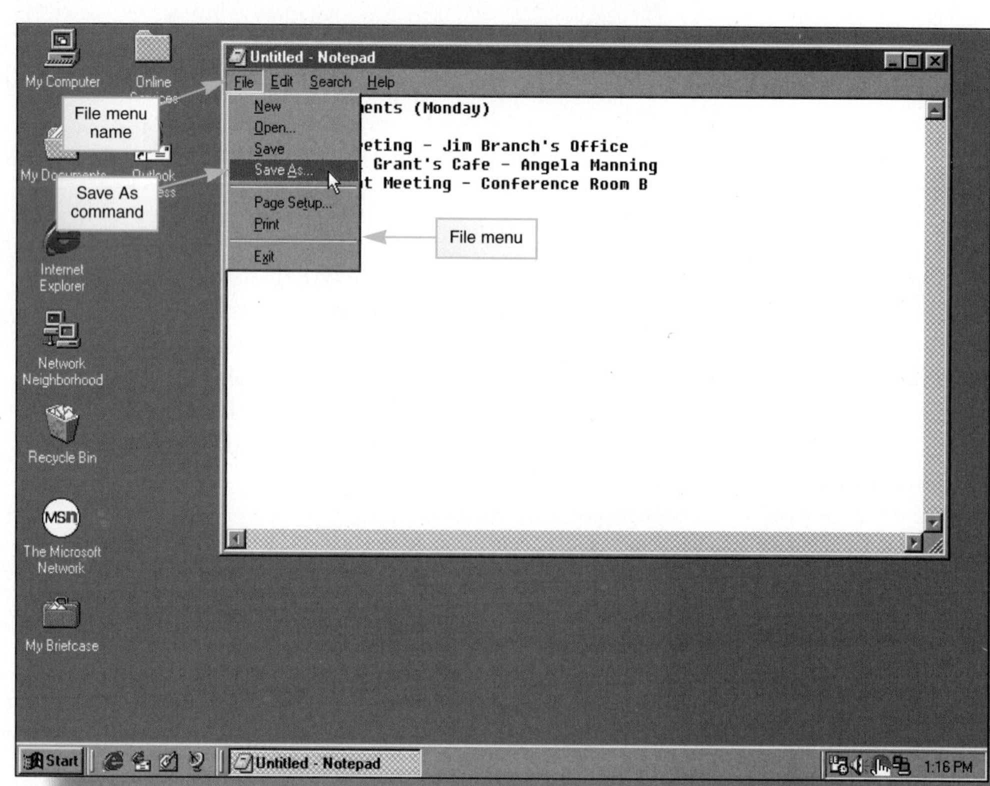

FIGURE 2-4

Click Save As. Type `Lopez Appointments (Monday)` **in the File name text box and then point to the Save in box arrow.**

The Save As dialog box displays (Figure 2-5). The Save in box contains the My Documents icon and icon title. This entry indicates where the file will be saved. The File name text box contains the document name (Lopez Appointments (Monday)) and the insertion point. When you save this document, Notepad will add the .txt extension to the file name automatically.

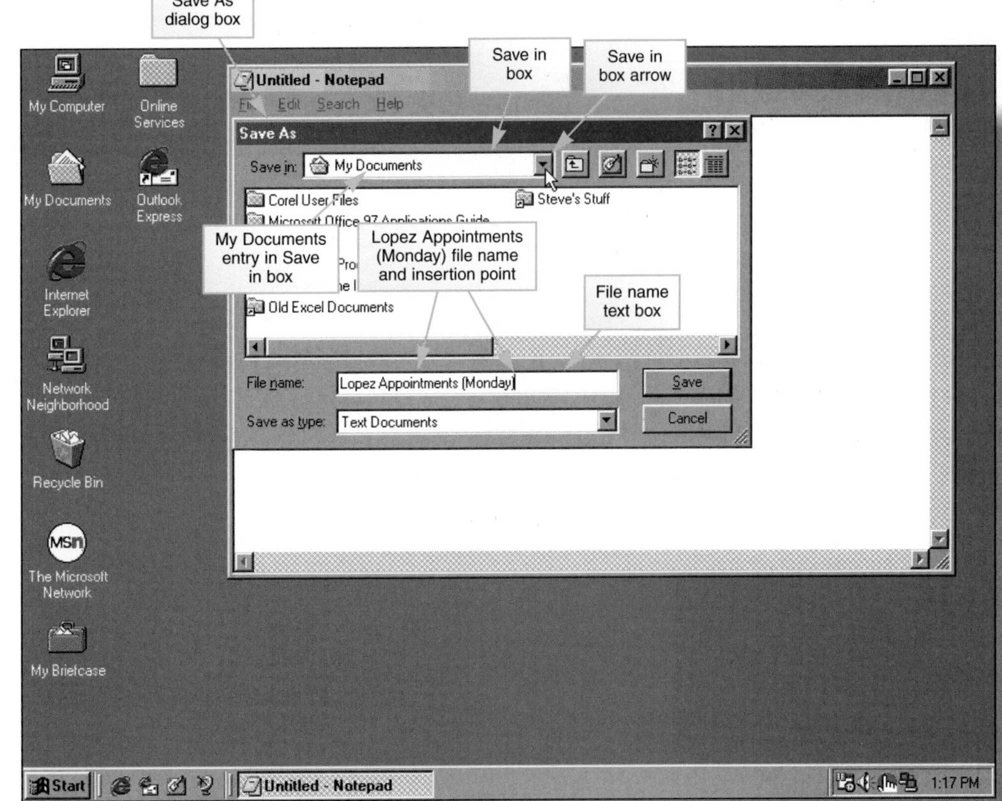

FIGURE 2-5

3 Click the Save in box arrow and then point to the Desktop icon.

The Save in list box displays (Figure 2-6). The list contains various elements of your computer, including the Desktop, My Documents, My Computer, Network Neighborhood, My Briefcase, and Online Services. Within My Computer are 3½ Floppy (A:), Hard disk (C:), (D:), Removable Disk (E:), and (F:). When you point to the Desktop icon, the entry in the list is highlighted. The entries in the Save In list may be different from those on your computer.

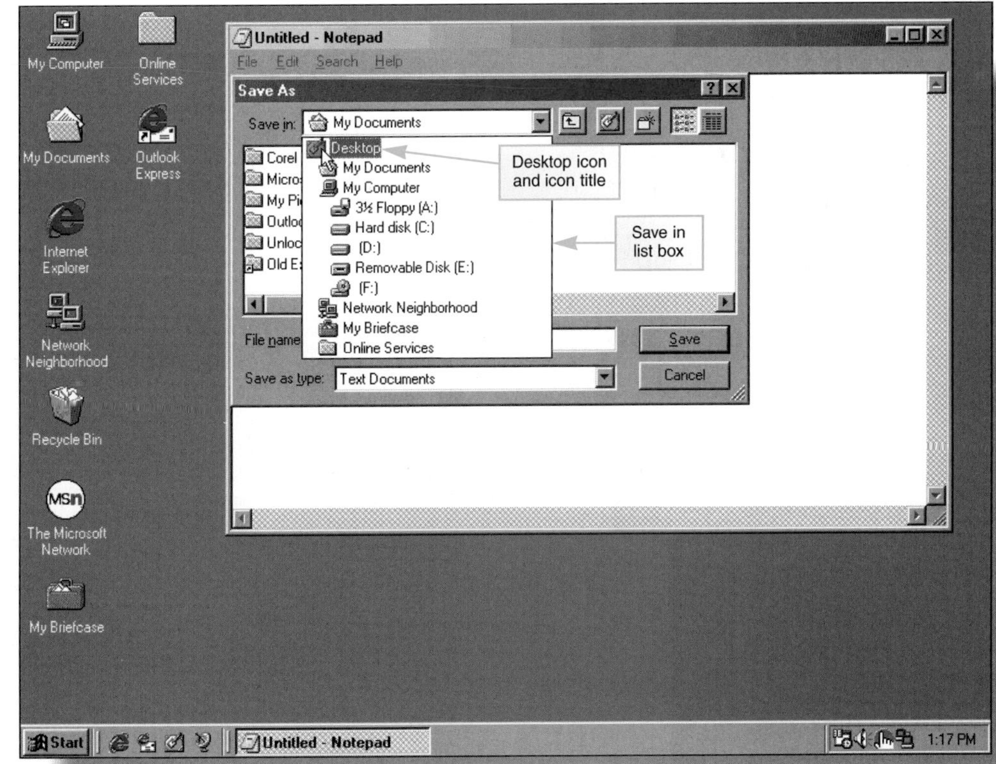

FIGURE 2-6

4 **Click the Desktop icon and then point to the Save button in the Save As dialog box.**

The Desktop entry displays in the Save in box (Figure 2-7). This specifies that the file will be saved on the desktop using the file name contained in the File name text box.

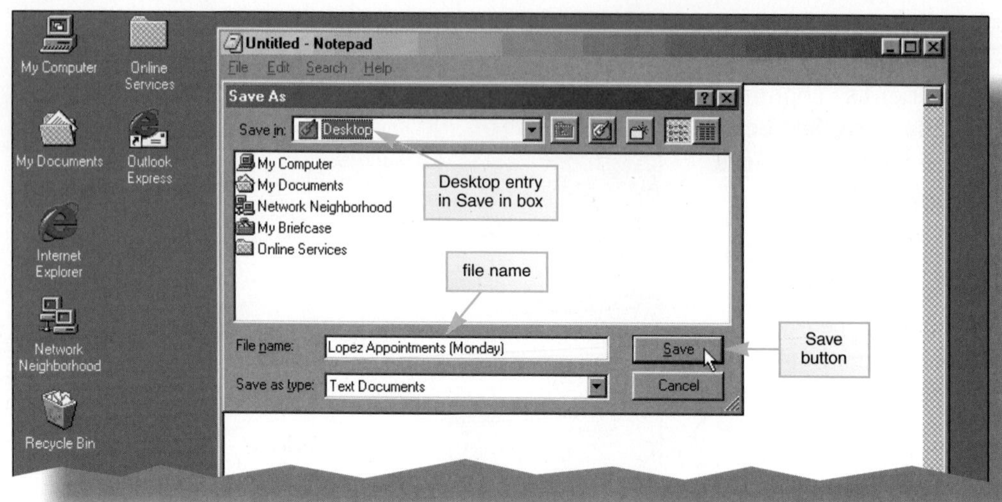

FIGURE 2-7

5 **Click the Save button.**

Windows 98 displays an ***hourglass icon*** *while saving the Lopez Appointments (Monday) document on the desktop. The Save As dialog box closes. The Lopez Appointments (Monday) document icon displays on the desktop, and the file name becomes part of the Notepad window title and button name in the taskbar button area (Figure 2-8).*

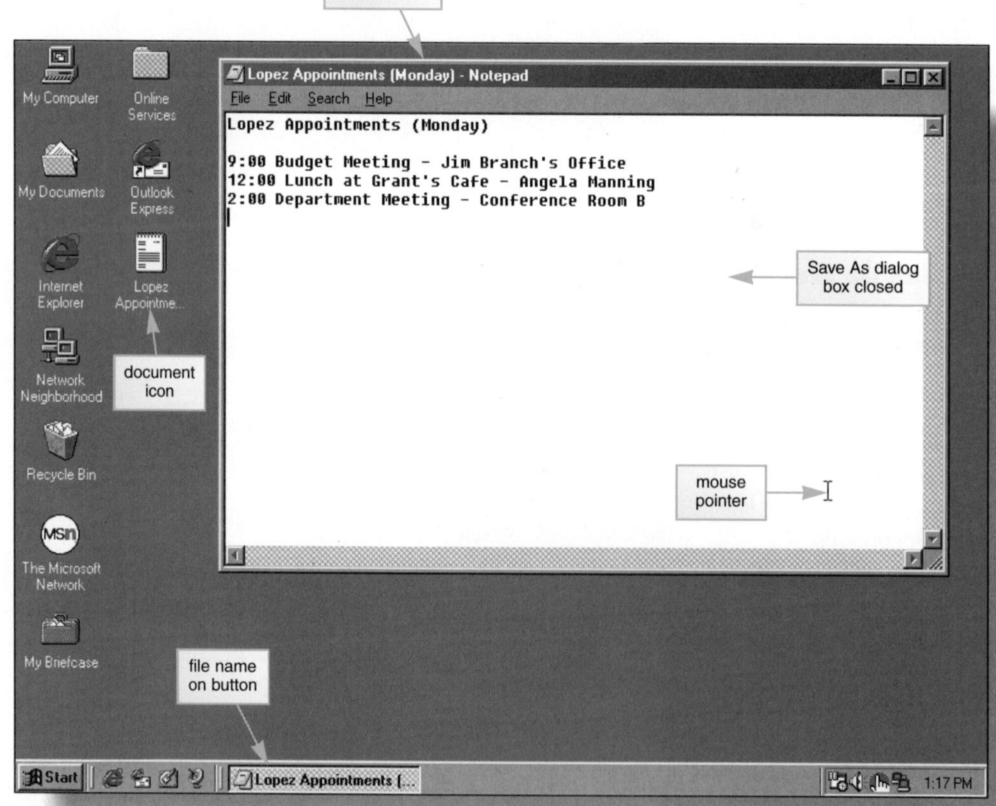

FIGURE 2-8

More About

Menus

Once you have clicked a menu name on the menu bar to open it, you need only point to another menu name on the menu bar to open that menu. To close a menu without carrying out a command, click anywhere on the desktop except on the menu.

Other Ways

1. On File menu click Save, type file name, select Desktop, click Save button
2. Press ALT+F, press A, type file name, select Desktop, click TAB repeatedly to select Save button, press S

In Figure 2-8, the file name on the button in the taskbar button area, (Lopez Appointments (...) contains an ellipsis to indicate the entire button name does not fit on the button. To display the entire button name for a button in the taskbar button area, point to the button. Notice that when the mouse pointer displays within the Notepad text area, it becomes an I-beam.

The method shown in the previous steps for saving a file on the desktop can be used to save a file on a floppy disk or on a hard disk by clicking 3½ Floppy (A:) or Hard disk (C:) in the Save in list.

Printing

Printing is and will remain important for documents. Many sophisticated application programs, however, are extending the printing capability to include transmitting faxes, sending e-mail, and even posting documents on Web pages of the World Wide Web.

Printing a Document

Quite often, after creating a document and saving it, you will want to print it. One method to print a document on the desktop is to print it directly from an application program. To print the Lopez Appointments (Monday) document, perform the following steps.

To Print a Document

1 Click File on the menu bar and point to Print (Figure 2-9).

2 Click Print.

A Notepad dialog box briefly displays with a message indicating the Lopez Appointments document is being printed. The document prints as shown in Figure 2-1 on page WIN 2.5.

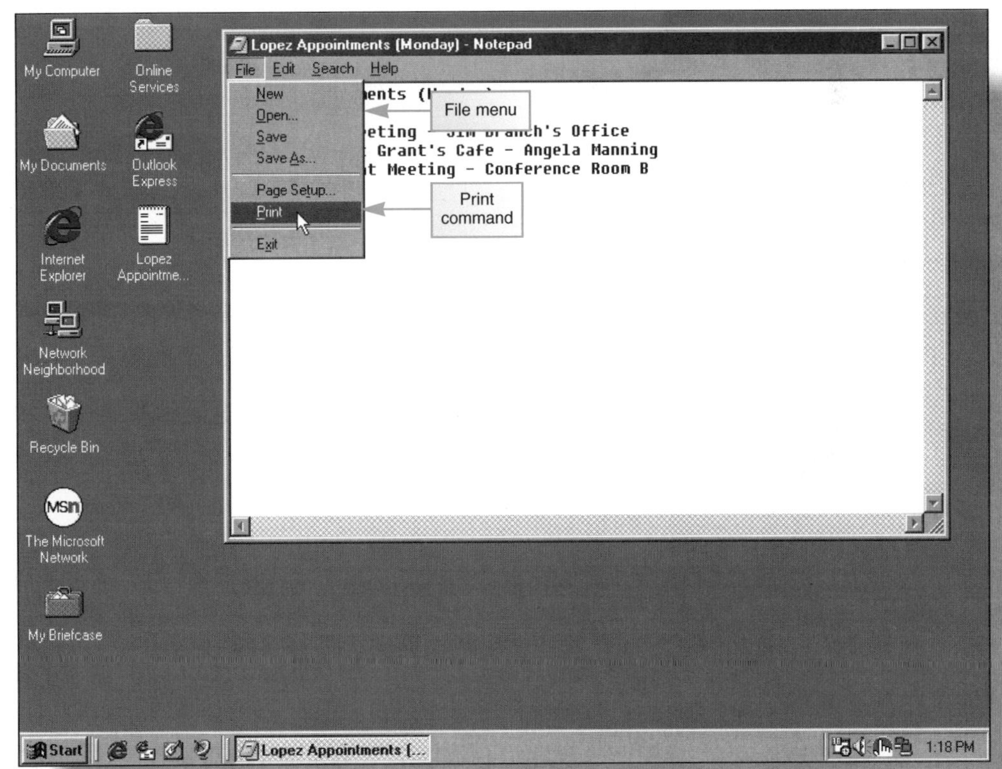

FIGURE 2-9

1. Right-click document icon on desktop, click Print
2. Press ALT+F, press P

Closing a Document

After creating the Lopez Appointments (Monday) document, saving the document, and printing it, your use of the document is complete. Perform the steps on the next page to close the Notepad window containing the document.

To Close a Document

1 Point to the Close button on the Notepad title bar (Figure 2-10).

2 Click the Close button.

The Lopez Appointments (Monday) - Notepad window closes and the Lopez Appointments (Monday) - Notepad button no longer displays.

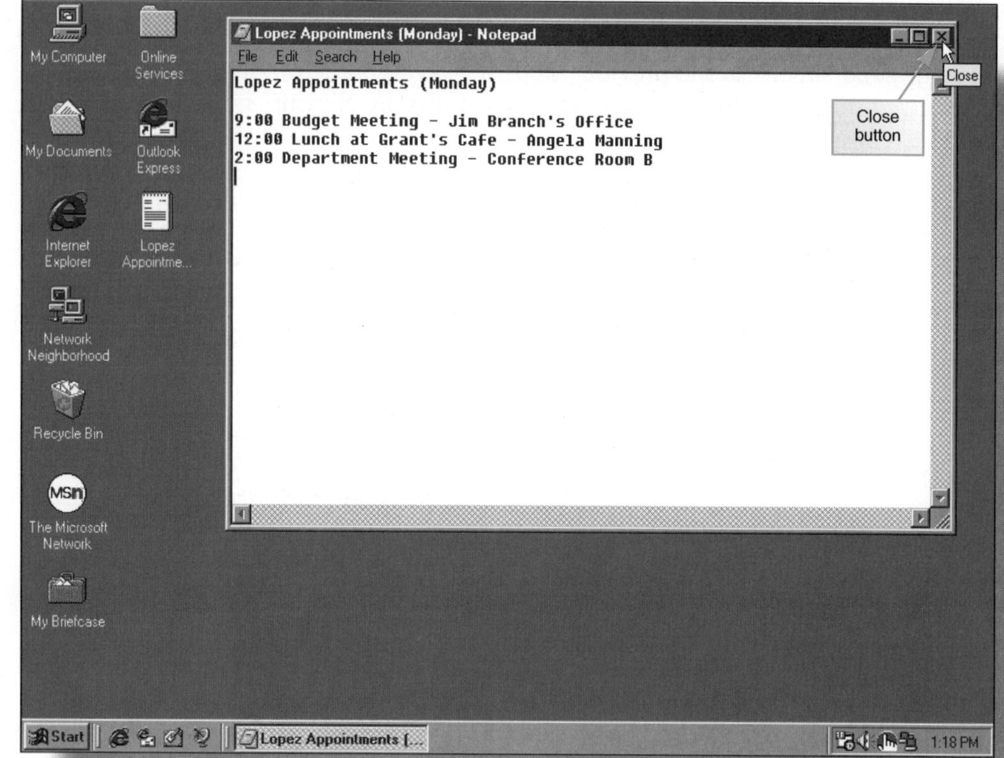

FIGURE 2-10

Other Ways

1. Double-click Notepad logo on title bar
2. Click Notepad logo on title bar, click Close
3. On File menu click Exit
4. Press ALT+F, press X; or press ALT+F4

More About

Document-Centric

The document-centric concept will progress ever further to the point where you neither know nor care what application was used to create a document. For example, when you include a Web page hyperlink in your word processing document, you will not care how the page was created. Only the content of the page is of interest.

After completing the appointments list for Mr. Lopez, the next step is to create a similar list for Ms. Parks.

Creating and Naming a Document on the Desktop

Opening an application program and then creating a document (application-centric approach) was the method you used to create the first document. Although the same method could be used to create the second document for Ms. Parks, another method and one that often will be easier and more straightforward, is to create the new document on the Windows 98 desktop without first starting an application program. Instead of launching a program to create and modify a document, you create a blank document directly on the desktop and then use the Notepad program to enter data into the document. This method, called the **document-centric approach**, will be used to create the document to contain the appointments for Ms. Parks.

To create a blank document directly on the desktop, perform the following steps.

More About

Creating Documents on the Desktop

The phrase, creating a document on the desktop, may be confusing. The document you create contains no data. It is blank. In effect you are placing a blank piece of paper with a name on your desktop. The document has little value until you add data.

To Create a Blank Document on the Desktop

1 Right-click an open area on the desktop, point to New on the shortcut menu, and then point to Text Document on the New submenu.

The shortcut menu and New submenu display (Figure 2-11).

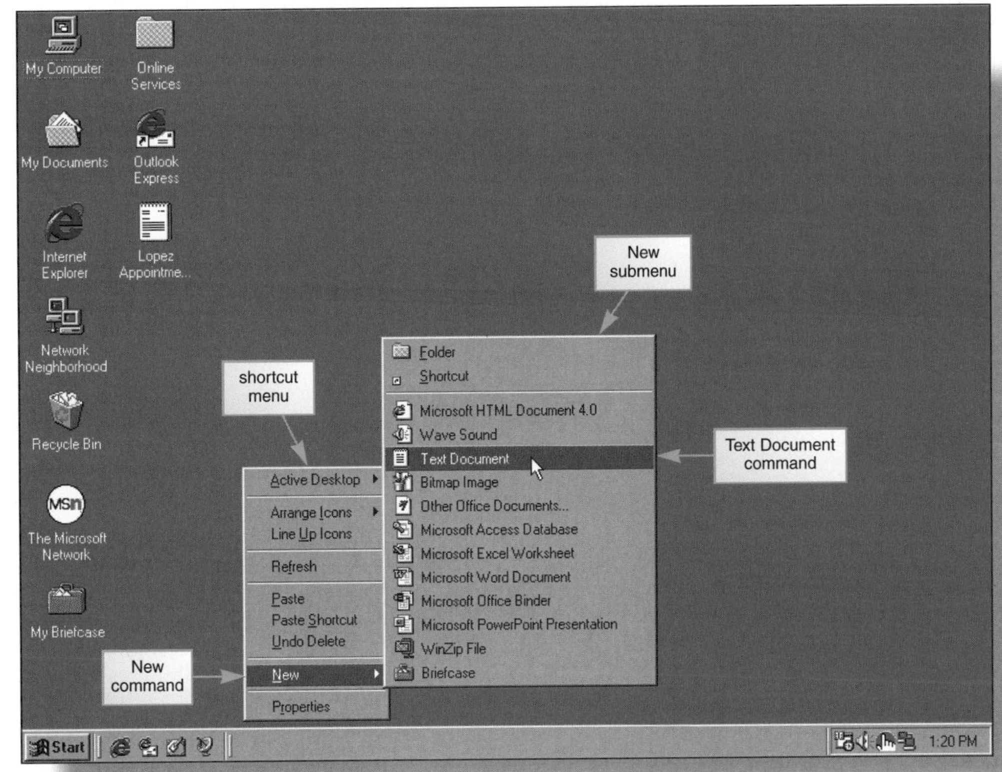

FIGURE 2-11

2 Click Text Document.

The shortcut menu and New submenu close, a blank text document with the default name, New Text Document, is created and its icon displays on the desktop (Figure 2-12). The **icon title text box** *below the icon contains the highlighted default file name followed by an insertion point. Whenever text is highlighted in a text box, any characters you type will replace the highlighted text.*

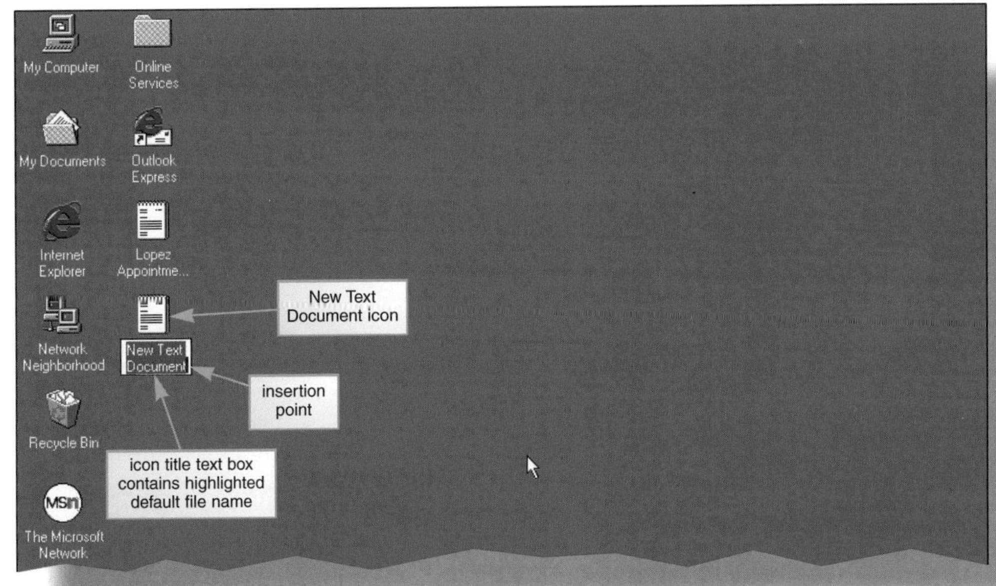

FIGURE 2-12

A blank document has been created on the desktop to contain the daily appointments for Ms. Parks.

Naming a Document

After you create a blank document on the desktop, normally you will name the document so it is easily identifiable. In Figure 2-12 on the previous page, the default file name (New Text Document) is highlighted and the insertion point is blinking, so you can type the new name. To give the name, Parks Appointments (Monday), to the document you just created, complete the step below.

To Name a Document on the Desktop

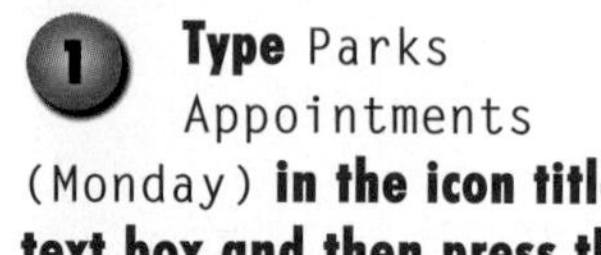

1 Type `Parks Appointments (Monday)` **in the icon title text box and then press the ENTER key.**

The file name, Parks Appointments (Monday), displays in the icon title text box, replacing the default name, and the Parks Appointments (Monday) icon is selected (Figure 2-13).

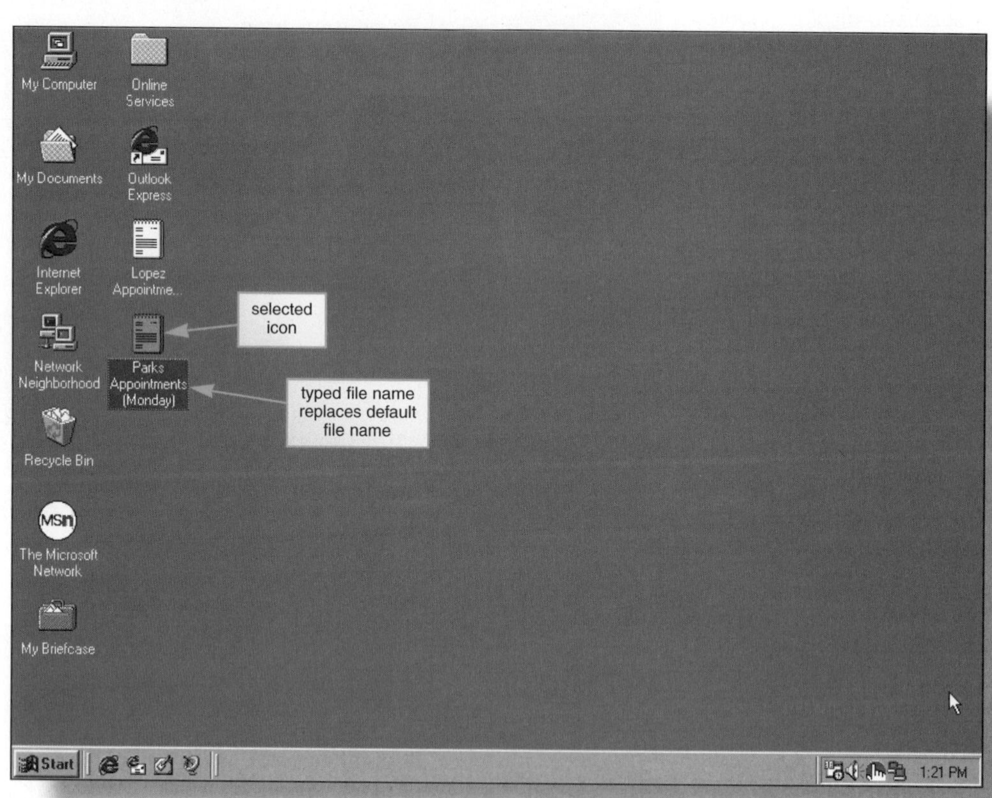

FIGURE 2-13

Other Ways

1. Right-click icon, click Rename, type name, press ENTER
2. Click icon to select icon, press F2, type name, press ENTER

Entering Data into a Blank Document on the Desktop

Although you have created the Parks Appointments (Monday) document, the document contains no data. To enter data into the blank document, you first must open the document. To open a document on the desktop, perform the following steps.

To Open a Document on the Desktop

1. **Point to the Parks Appointments (Monday) icon on the desktop (Figure 2-14).**

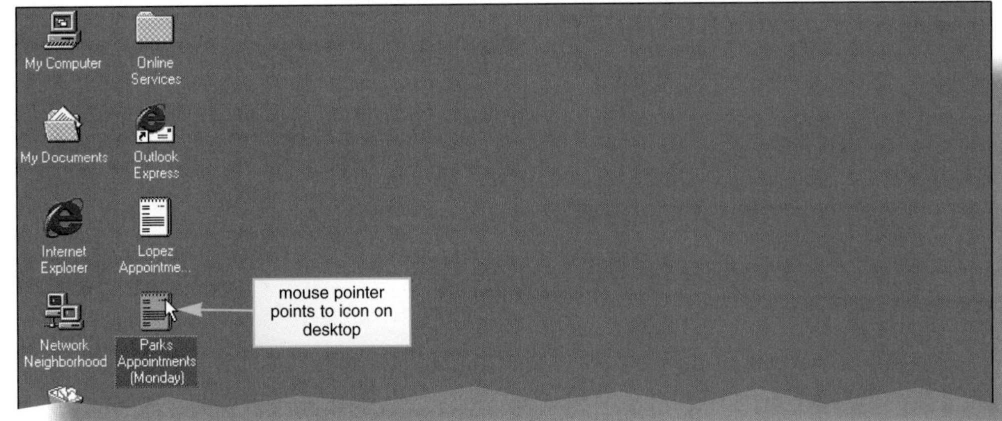

FIGURE 2-14

2. **Double-click the Parks Appointments (Monday) icon.**

The Notepad window opens and the Parks Appointments (Monday) document displays in the Notepad window (Figure 2-15). The document contains no text. The insertion point is located at the beginning of the first line of the document.

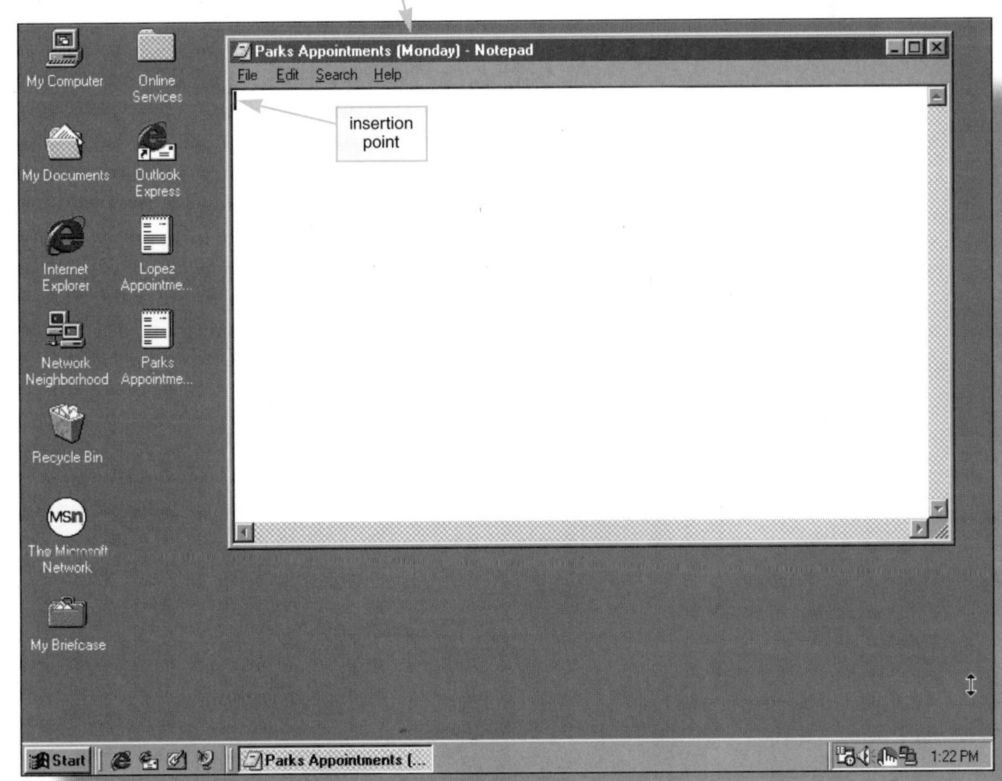

FIGURE 2-15

Other Ways

1. Right-click icon on desktop, click Open on shortcut menu
2. Click icon to select icon, press ENTER

After the document is open, you can enter the required data by typing the text (the daily appointments) you want in the document. To enter the text for the Parks Appointments (Monday) document, perform the step on the next page.

To Enter Data into a Blank Document

1 Type the text shown in Figure 2-16 for the Parks Appointments (Monday) document.

The text for Parks Appointments (Monday) displays in the document (Figure 2-16).

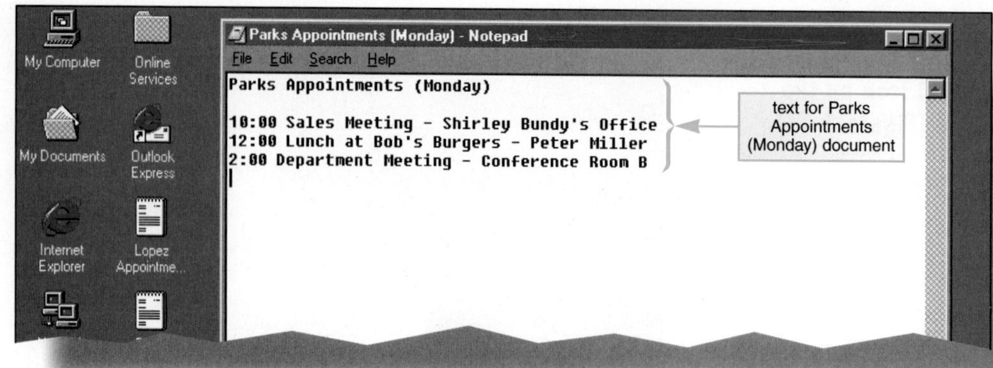

FIGURE 2-16

You can type as many words and lines as necessary for your document. The entry of the text into the Parks Appointments (Monday) document modifies the document resulting in the need to save the document.

More About

Saving a Document

If you make many changes to a document, you should save the document while you are working on it. To do so, click File on the menu bar and then click Save.

Closing and Saving a Document

After entering the text into the Parks Appointments (Monday) document, often you will close the document. You also must save the document so the text you entered will remain part of the document. You could accomplish this by using the Save As command on the File menu as shown earlier in this project. In Windows 98 applications, however, you can close and save a document in one set of steps. To close and save the Parks Appointments (Monday) document, complete the following steps.

To Close and Save a Modified Document on the Desktop

1 Click the Close button on the Notepad title bar. Point to the Yes button in the Notepad dialog box (Figure 2-18).

Because the Parks Appointments (Monday) document has been changed, Windows 98 displays the Notepad dialog box asking if you want to save the changes you made in the document (Figure 2-17).

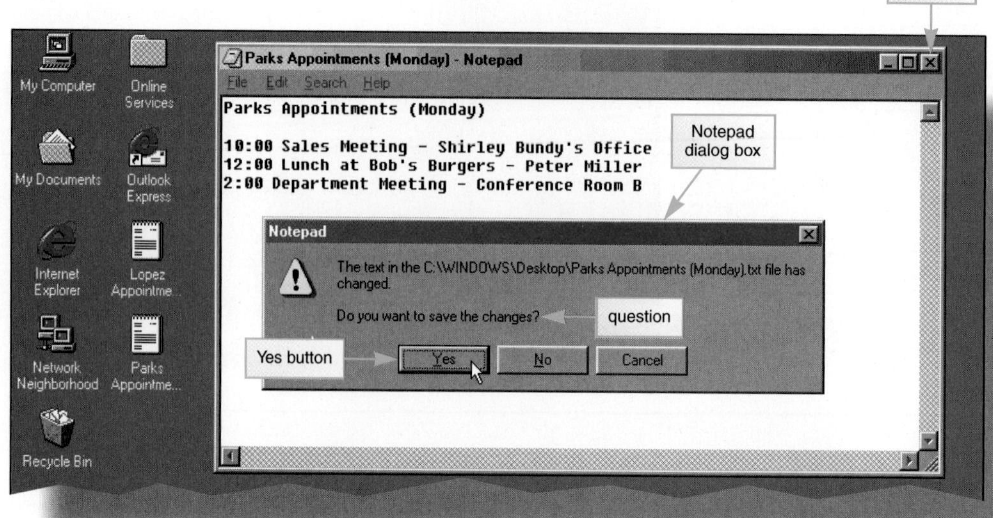

FIGURE 2-17

Click the Yes button.

The Notepad dialog box and Notepad window close and the modified Parks Appointments (Monday) document is saved on the desktop (Figure 2-18).

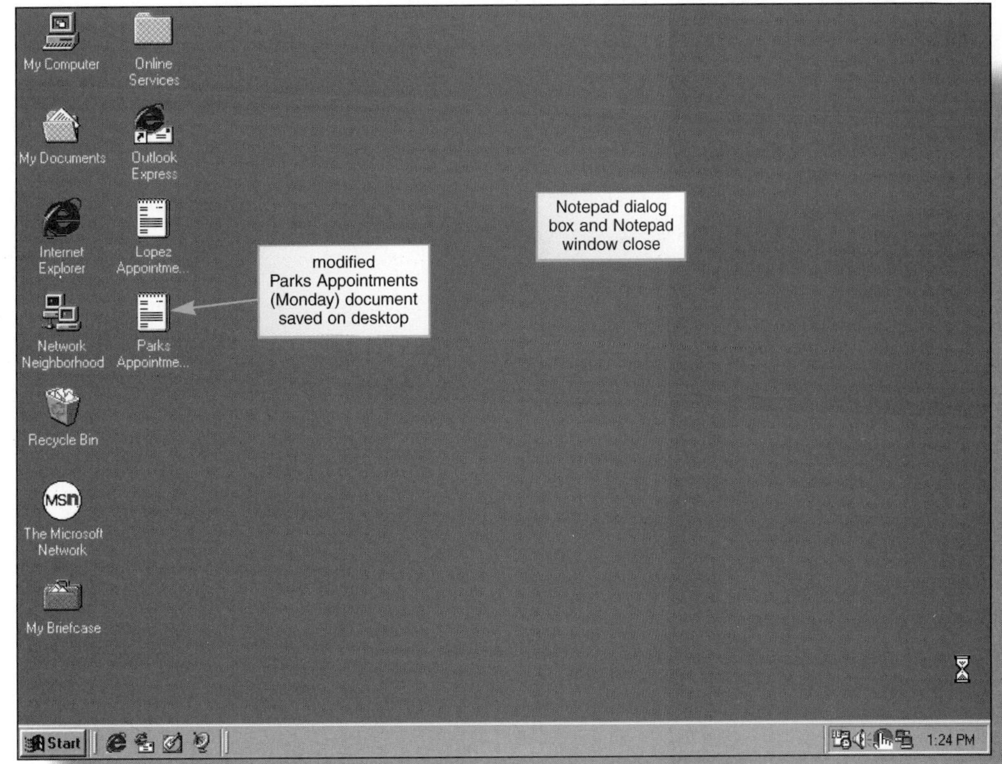

FIGURE 2-18

Other Ways

1. On File menu click Save As, click Save button, click Yes button in Save As dialog box, click Close button
2. Click Notepad icon on title bar, click Close, click Yes button
3. Double-click Notepad icon on title bar, click Yes button
4. Press ALT+F, press S , press ALT+F, press X

In most Windows 98 application programs, if you close the program and the document has not been saved since being changed, a dialog box displays asking if you want to save the document before closing the program. This is the way in which Windows 98 ensures you accidentally do not lose work you have completed for a document.

After saving and closing the Parks Appointments (Monday) document, the second document is complete.

Storing Documents in a Folder on the Desktop

When you have created one or more documents on the desktop, you often will want to keep them together so they can be found and referenced easily. Windows 98 allows you to place one or more documents into a folder in much the same manner as you might take a letter written on a piece of paper and place it in a file folder. To place a document in a folder, you must first create the folder. To create and name a folder on the desktop into which you can place the Lopez Appointments (Monday) and Parks Appointments (Monday) documents, complete the steps on the next page.

More About

The Desktop

The desktop model for interfacing with a computer is quite popular. Critics insist, however, that more efficient and effective models exist. Can you think of any model that would be more efficient for you? What about the interfaces you use for interactive games?

To Create and Name a Folder on the Desktop

1 Right-click an open area on the desktop, point to New on the shortcut menu, and then point to Folder on the New submenu.

The shortcut menu and New submenu display (Figure 2-19). Clicking Folder on the New submenu will create a folder using the default folder name, New Folder.

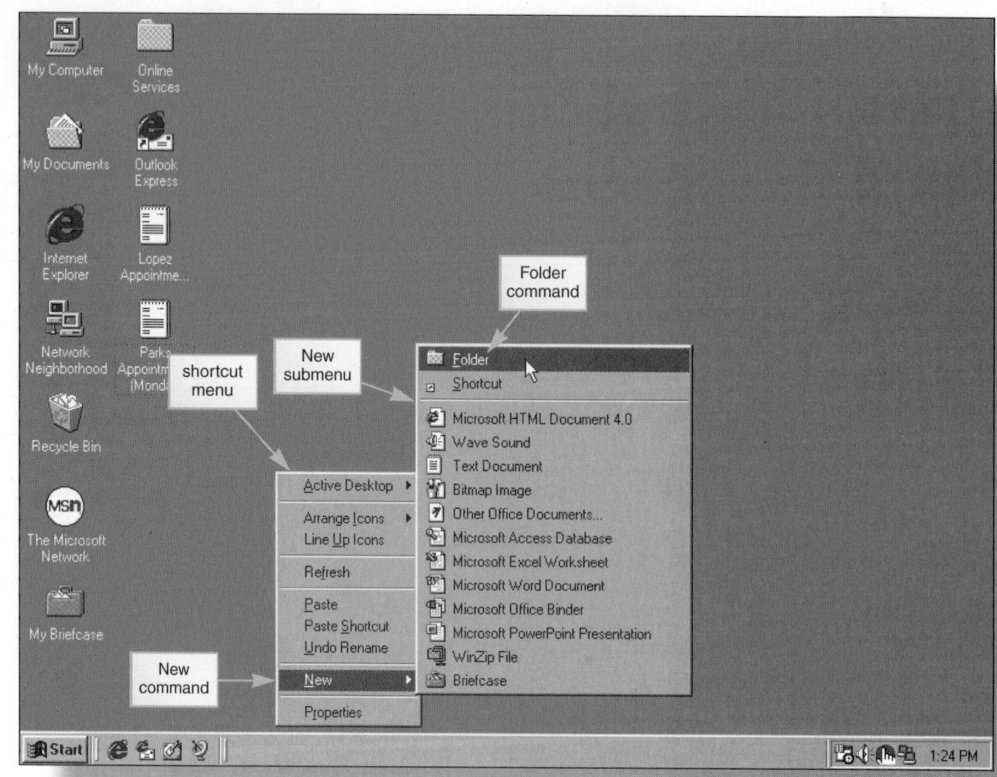

FIGURE 2-19

Click Folder, type `Daily Appointments` **in the icon title text box, and press the ENTER key.**

The selected Daily Appointments folder icon displays on the desktop (Figure 2-20). The folder name, Daily Appointments, displays in the icon title text box.

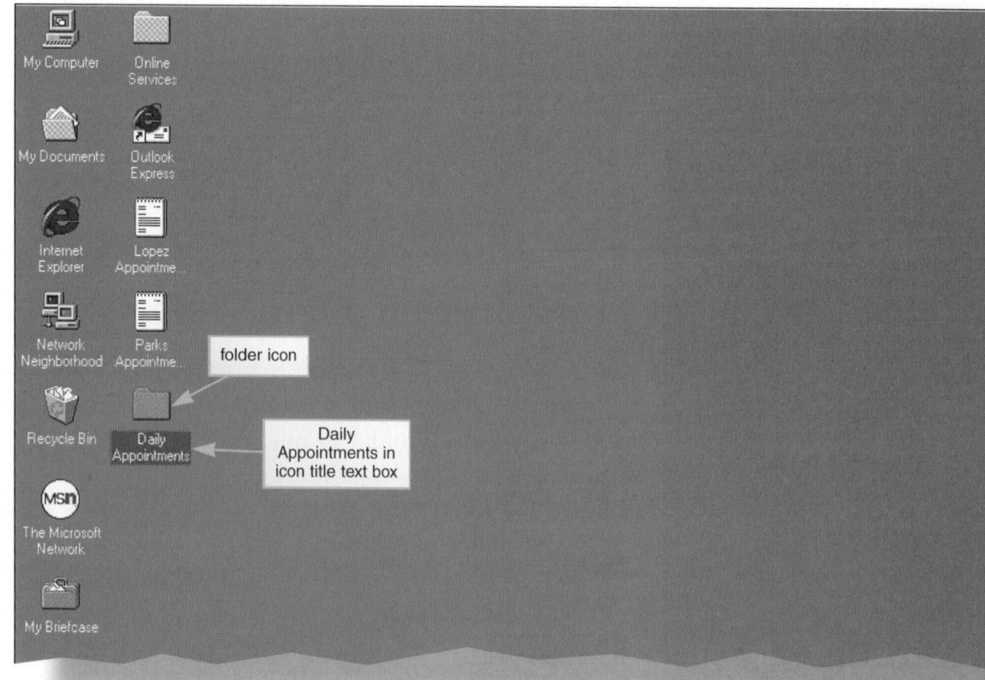

FIGURE 2-20

After you create a folder on the desktop, normally the next step is to move one or more documents into the folder. For the Daily Appointments folder, you should move the Parks Appointments (Monday) and the Lopez Appointments (Monday) documents into the folder. To accomplish this task, complete the following steps.

Steps To Move a Document into a Folder

1 Right-drag the Parks Appointments (Monday) icon on top of the Daily Appointments folder icon and then point to Move Here on the shortcut menu.

The dimmed Parks Appointments (Monday) icon displays on top of the Daily Appointments folder icon, and a shortcut menu displays (Figure 2-21). The highlighted Parks Appointments (Monday) icon still displays on the desktop.

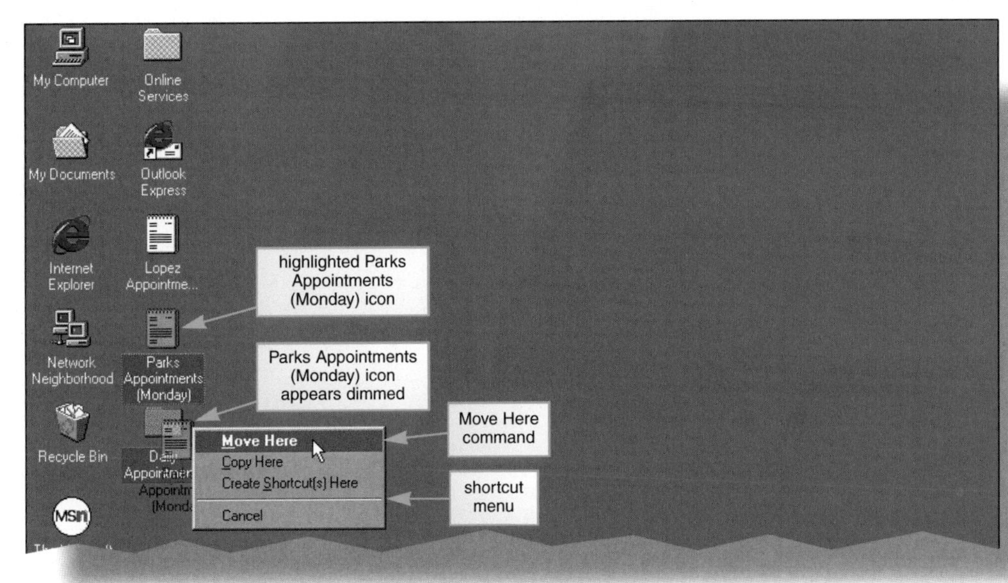

FIGURE 2-21

2 Click Move Here.

The Parks Appointments (Monday) document is moved into the Daily Appointments folder, and the Parks Appointments (Monday) icon no longer displays on the desktop (Figure 2-22). Windows 98 rearranges the desktop.

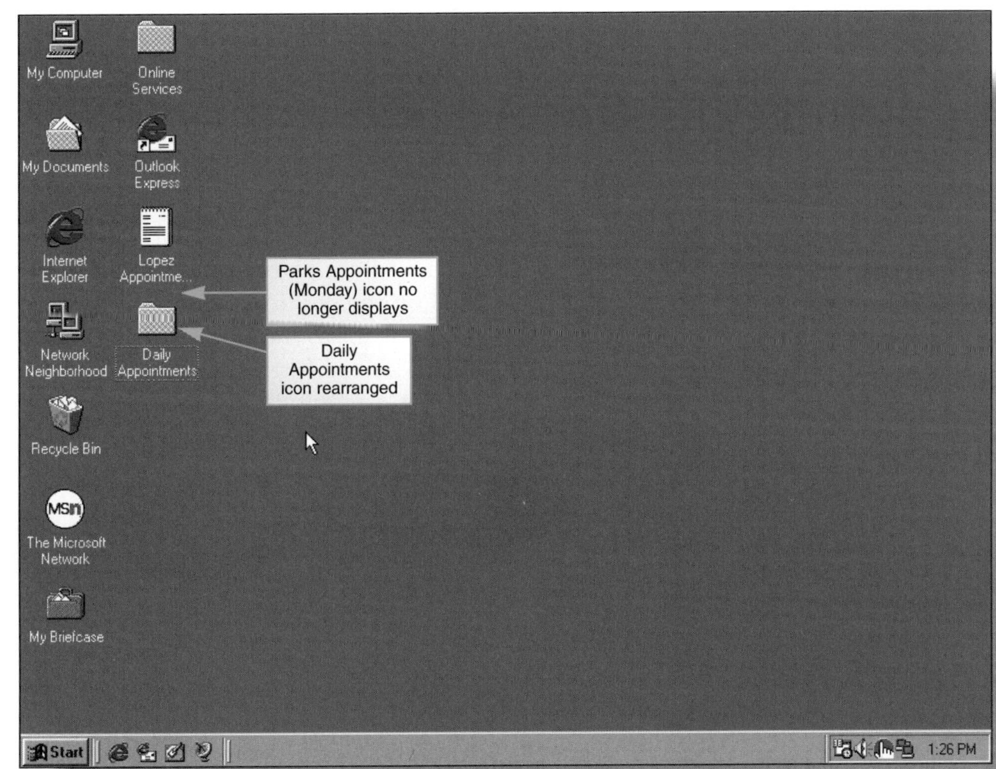

FIGURE 2-22

3 Right-drag the Lopez Appointments (Monday) icon on top of the Daily Appointments icon. Click Move Here on the shortcut menu.

The Lopez Appointments (Monday) document is moved into the Daily Appointments folder, and the Lopez Appointments (Monday) icon no longer displays on the desktop (Figure 2-23). Windows 98 rearranges the icons on the desktop.

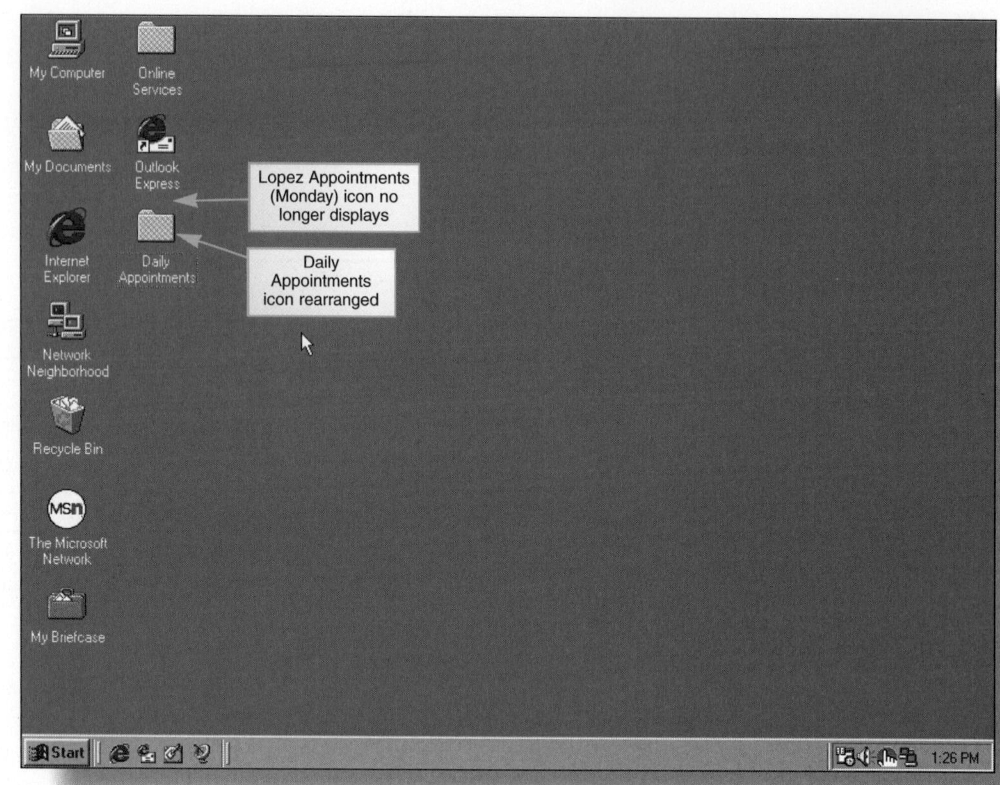

FIGURE 2-23

Other Ways

1. Right-click document icon, click Cut, right-click folder icon, click Paste
2. Drag document icon on top of folder icon

The capability of organizing documents and files within a folder allows you to keep your desktop organized when using Windows 98. Project 3 will discuss the manner in which you can organize your files on your floppy and hard drives.

Opening and Modifying Documents Within a Folder

Documents stored in a folder on the desktop can be modified in much the same way as documents stored on the desktop. First, you must open the folder and then you must open the file you want to modify.

Assume that you received further information about the daily appointments for Mr. Lopez. An Internet meeting with Gary Carney in the Eastern United States has been scheduled at 4:00 p.m. To add this item to the schedule, first you must open the Daily Appointments folder that contains the Lopez Appointments (Monday) document. To do so, complete the following step.

To Open a Folder

1 Double-click the Daily Appointments folder icon on the desktop. Move and resize the Daily Appointments window to resemble the window shown in Figure 2-24.

The Daily Appointments window opens and the recessed Daily Appointments button displays in the taskbar button area (Figure 2-24). The Daily Appointments folder icon remains on the desktop. Each of the document icons display within the folder window, indicating they are contained within the folder.

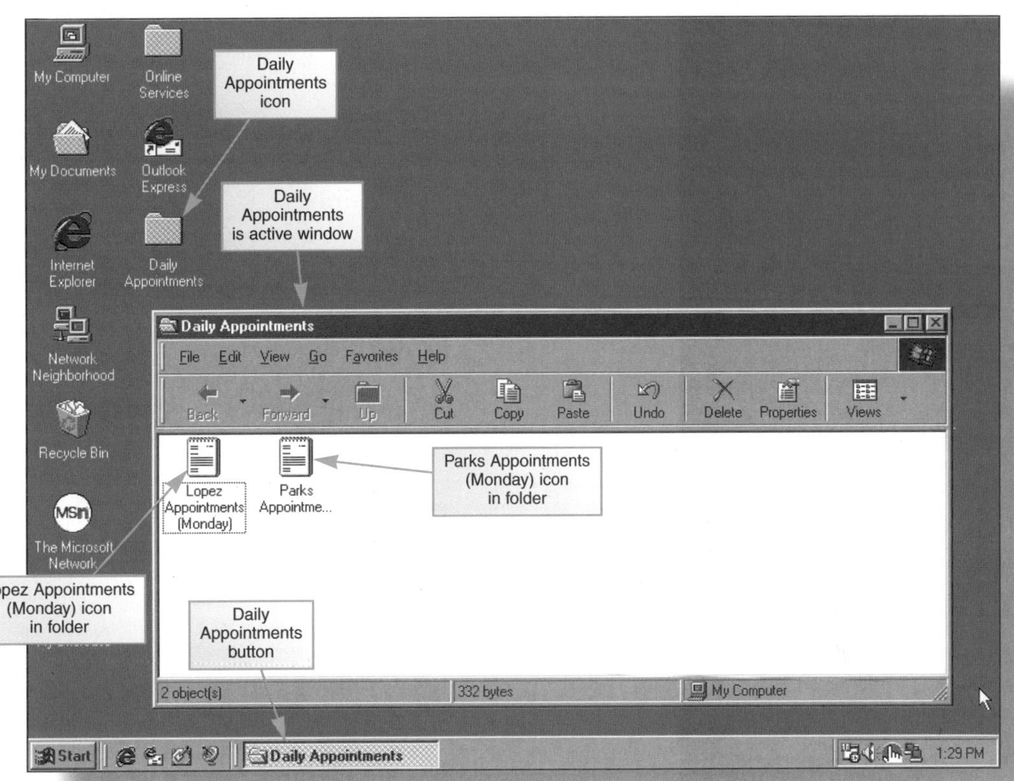

FIGURE 2-24

Other Ways

1. Right-click folder icon, click Open
2. Click folder icon to select icon, press ENTER key

In Figure 2-24, the color of the Daily Appointments title bar (dark blue) and the recessed button in the taskbar button area indicate the Daily Appointments window is the active window.

Opening and Modifying a Document Stored in a Folder

After opening the folder, you must open the document you want to modify. To open the Lopez Appointments (Monday) document in the Daily Appointments folder and then enter the text about the Internet meeting, complete the steps on the next page.

More About

Working with Documents

To modify your document, you are opening the document rather than starting an application program and then opening the document as you did previously in this project. Does this feel more natural? Research has indicated that people feel more at home dealing with documents instead of dealing with application programs and then documents.

To Open and Modify a Document in a Folder

1 Double-click the Lopez Appointments (Monday) icon in the Daily Appointments window.

Notepad starts and the Lopez Appointments (Monday) document displays in the Notepad window. The Lopez Appointments (Monday) - Notepad button is added to the taskbar button area (Figure 2-25). The active Notepad window and the inactive folder window now are open and the Daily Appointments folder button is no longer recessed.

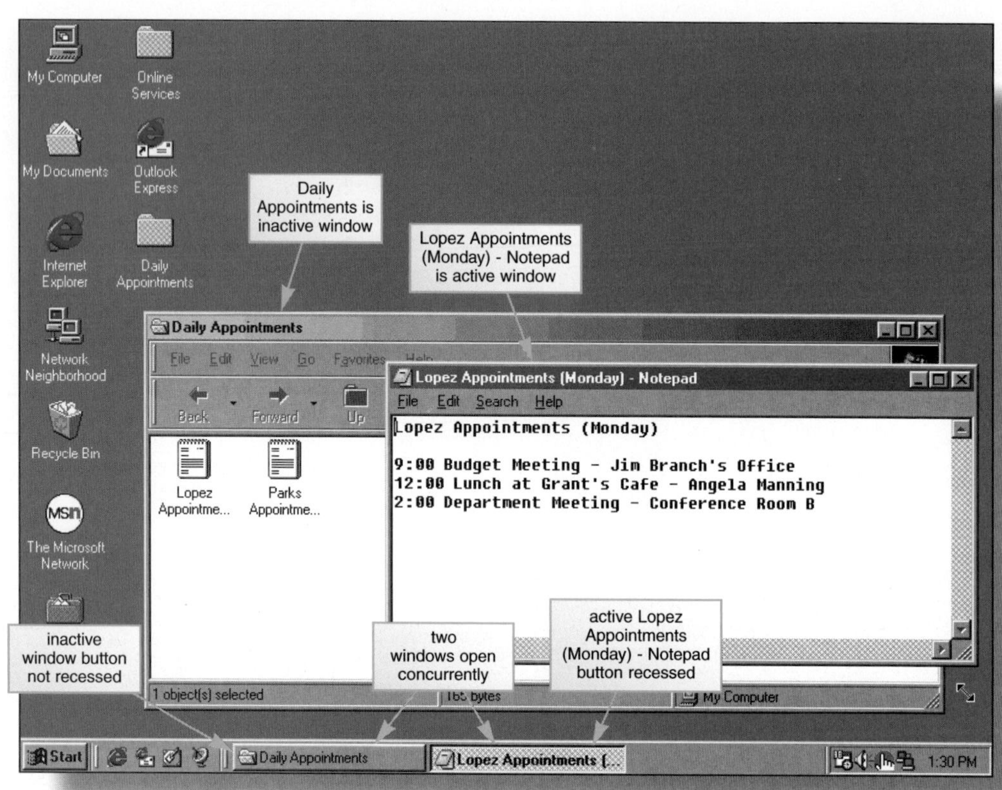

FIGURE 2-25

2 Press the DOWN ARROW key five times to move the insertion point to the end of the document. Type `4:00 NetMeeting - Gary Carney` **and then press the ENTER key.**

The insertion point moves to the end of the document and the entry is added to the document (Figure 2-26).

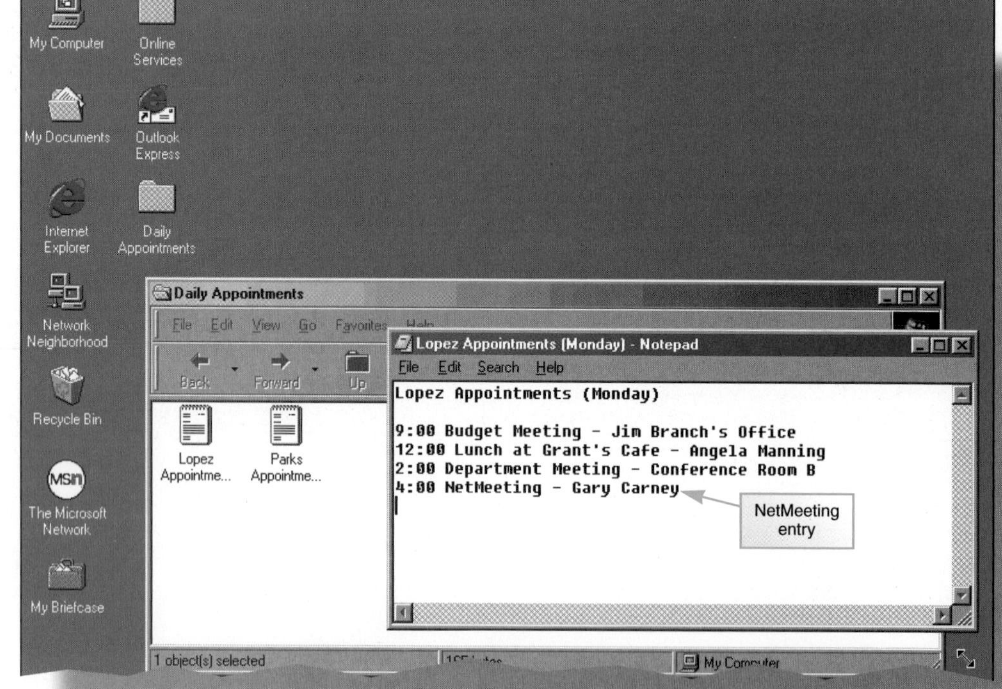

FIGURE 2-26

Other Ways

1. Right-click document icon, click Open on shortcut menu
2. Click document icon to select icon, press ENTER key

As you can see, it is just as easy to modify a document stored in a folder as it is to modify a document stored on the desktop. The method for opening and modifying a document, regardless of where the document is stored, is the same.

Opening Multiple Documents

Windows 98 allows you to open more than one document and application program at the same time. You then can work on any desired document. The concept of multiple programs running at the same time is called **multitasking**. To illustrate two documents and an application program open at the same time, assume you need to make a change to the Parks Appointments (Monday) document to include a three-way conference call with Brandy Schiller that is scheduled for 4:30 p.m. You do not have to close the Lopez Appointments (Monday) document to do this. Complete the following steps to open the Parks Appointments (Monday) document and make the changes.

To Open and Modify Multiple Documents

1 Click the Daily Appointments button in the taskbar button area and then point to the Parks Appointments (Monday) icon in the Daily Appointments window.

The Daily Appointments window moves on top of the Lopez Appointments document (Figure 2-27). The Daily Appointments window becomes the active window (dark blue title bar) and the inactive Lopez Appointments window is partially visible behind the Daily Appointments window. The Daily Appointments button is recessed, and the Lopez Appointments (Monday) - Notepad button is not recessed.

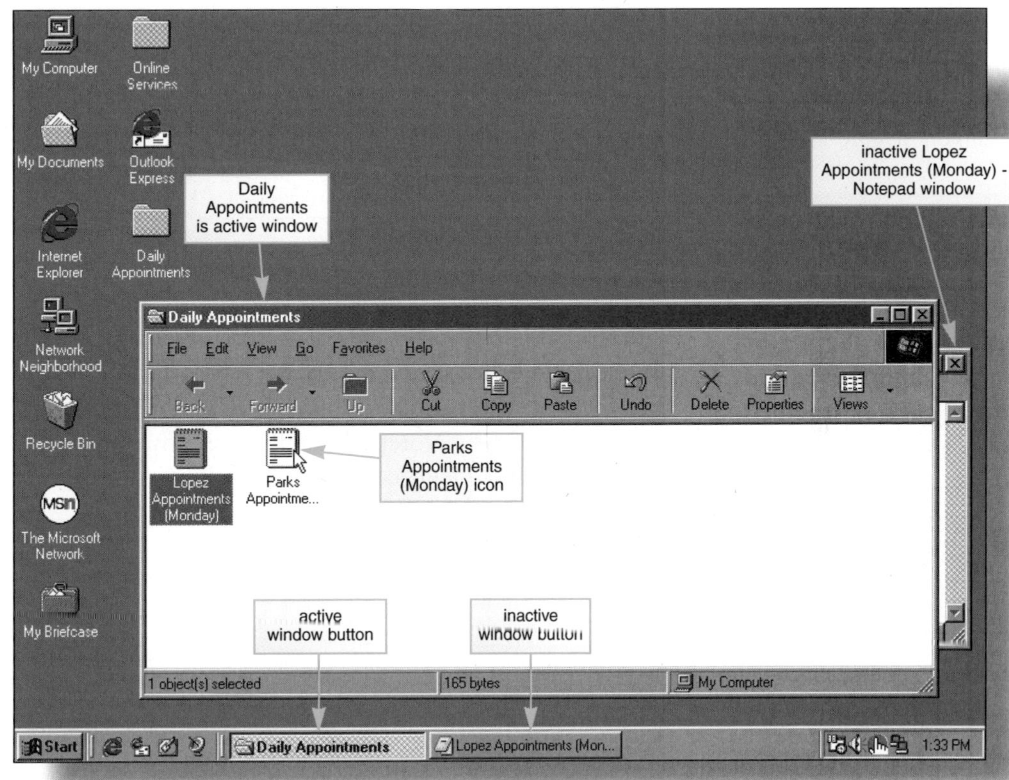

FIGURE 2-27

2 **Double-click the Parks Appointments (Monday) icon in the Daily Appointments window. Press the DOWN ARROW key five times to move the insertion point to the end of the document in the Notepad window. Type** `4:30 Conference Call - Brandy Schiller` **and then press the ENTER key.**

The Parks Appointments (Monday) - Notepad window opens on top of the other two open windows, the recessed Parks Appointments (Monday) - Notepad button is added to the taskbar button area, and the insertion point moves to the end of the document (Figure 2-28).

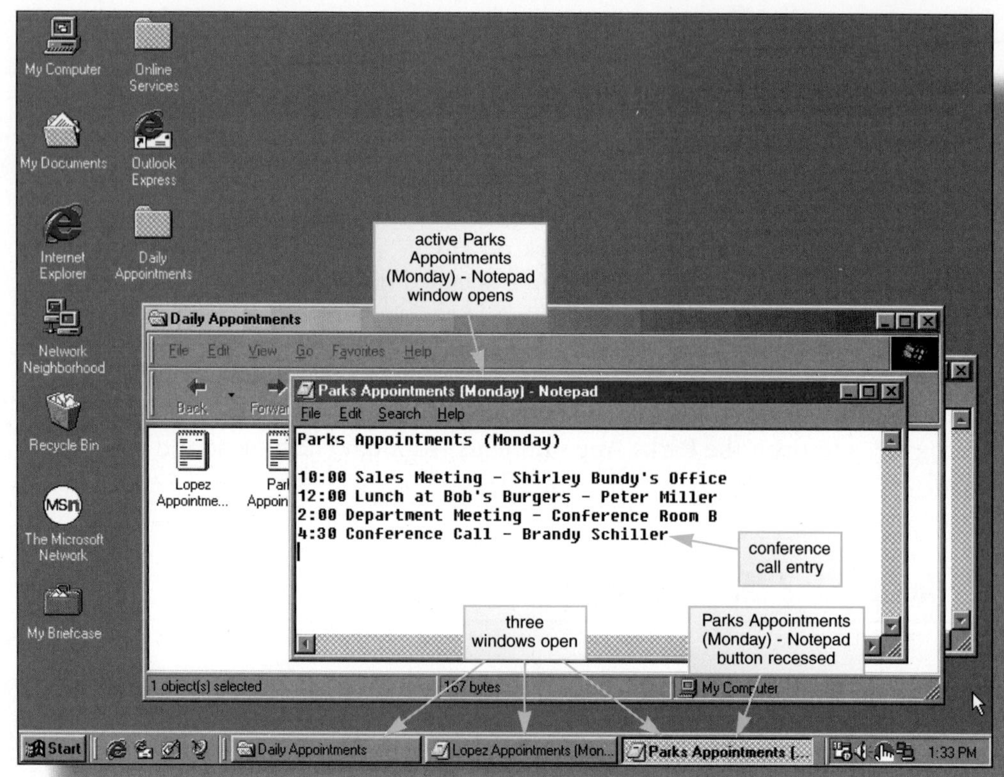

FIGURE 2-28

1. Right-click document icon, click Open on shortcut menu
2. Click to document icon to select icon, press ENTER

Opening Windows

In addition to clicking the taskbar button of an inactive window to make that window the active window, you also may click any open area of the window. Many people routinely click the title bar of a window to activate the window.

After you have modified the Parks Appointments (Monday) document, assume you receive information that a dinner engagement with Sam Goebel has been scheduled for Mr. Lopez at 6:00 p.m. at the London House. You are directed to add this entry to Mr. Lopez's appointments. To do this, you must open the Lopez Appointments (Monday) - Notepad inactive window. To open an inactive window and modify the document, complete the following step.

To Open an Inactive Window

1 Click the Lopez Appointments (Monday) - Notepad button in the taskbar button area. When the window opens, type `6:00 Dinner at London House - Sam Goebel` **and then press the ENTER key.**

The Lopez Appointments (Monday) - Notepad window displays on top of the other windows on the desktop, and the dinner entry is added to the document (Figure 2-29).

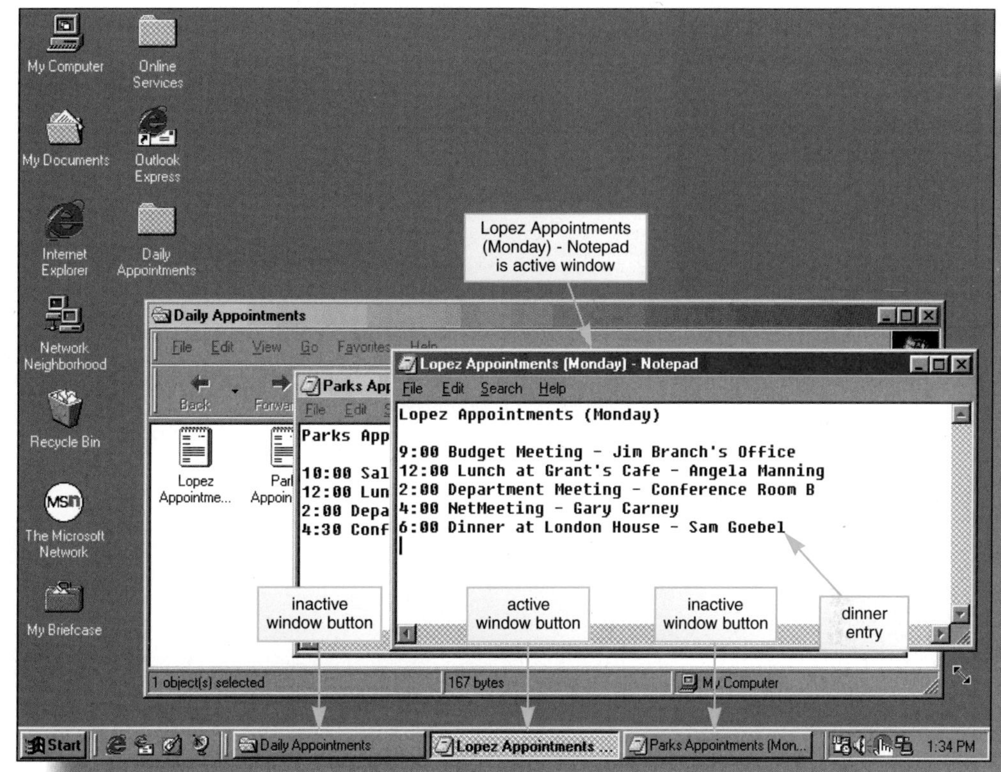

FIGURE 2-29

Other Ways

1. Press ALT+TAB until name of window displays, release keys
2. If visible, click title bar of window

Minimizing All Open Windows

As mentioned earlier, Windows 98 allows you to open multiple windows on the desktop and work within any of the windows by clicking the window button in the taskbar button area. As convenient as it may be to have multiple windows open on the desktop, too many windows or a single maximized window can limit or block your view of the objects on the desktop. To allow you to view the desktop easily without closing all or some of the windows on the desktop, the Quick Launch tool bar contains the Show Desktop icon. The **Show Desktop icon** makes the desktop visible by minimizing all open windows on the desktop.

Currently, the Lopez Appointments (Monday) - Notepad window, Daily Appointments window, and Parks Appointments (Monday) - Notepad window display on the desktop, and a button for each window displays in the taskbar button area (see Figure 2-29). A recessed button displays for the active Lopez Appointments (Monday) - Notepad window and non-recessed buttons for the inactive windows. To minimize the open windows and view the objects on the desktop, perform the steps on the next page.

To Minimize All Open Windows

1 Point to the Show Desktop icon on the Quick Launch toolbar on the taskbar (Figure 2-30).

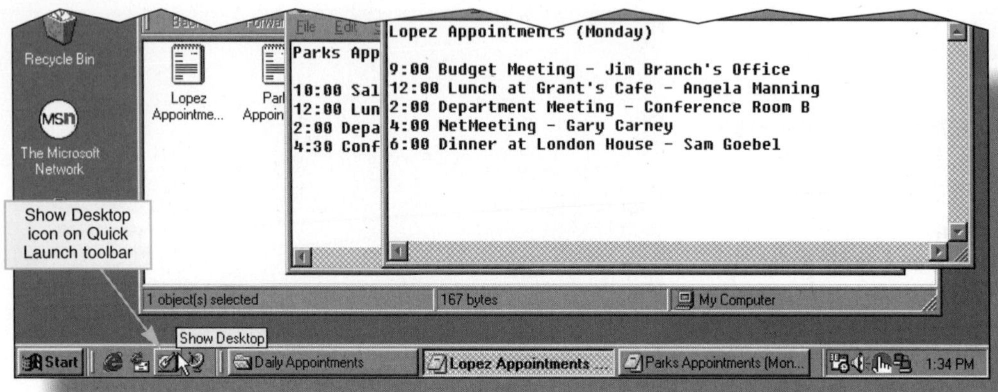

FIGURE 2-30

2 Click the Show Desktop icon.

Windows 98 minimizes all three open windows (Figure 2-31). A button for each minimized window displays in the taskbar button area.

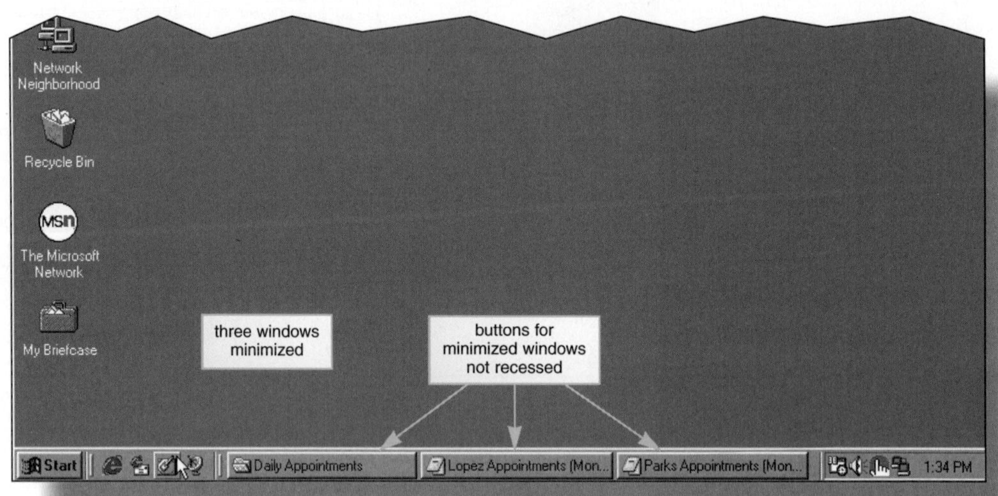

FIGURE 2-31

1. Right-click taskbar, click Minimize All Windows
2. Click the Minimize button on each window

To open one of the three minimized windows and be able to work in that window, click the corresponding button in the taskbar button area. To open all three windows and return the desktop to the way it looked before clicking the Show Desktop icon (see Figure 2-29 on the previous page), click the Show Desktop button a second time.

Closing Windows

The choice of how to close windows is yours. In most cases, you will want to choose the method that causes the least amount of work.

Closing Multiple Windows

When you are finished working with multiple windows, normally you will close them. If the windows are open on the desktop, you can click the Close button on the title bar of each open window to close the windows, as you have done in previous examples. Regardless of whether the windows are open on the desktop or the windows have been minimized using the Show Desktop icon, you also can close the windows using the buttons in the taskbar button area. To close the Lopez Appointments (Monday) - Notepad and Parks Appointments (Monday) - Notepad windows from the taskbar, complete the following steps.

To Close and Save Open Windows from the Taskbar

1 Right-click the Lopez Appointments (Monday) - Notepad button in the taskbar button area. Point to Close on the shortcut menu.

A shortcut menu displays containing a variety of commands for the window associated with the button that was clicked (Figure 2-32).

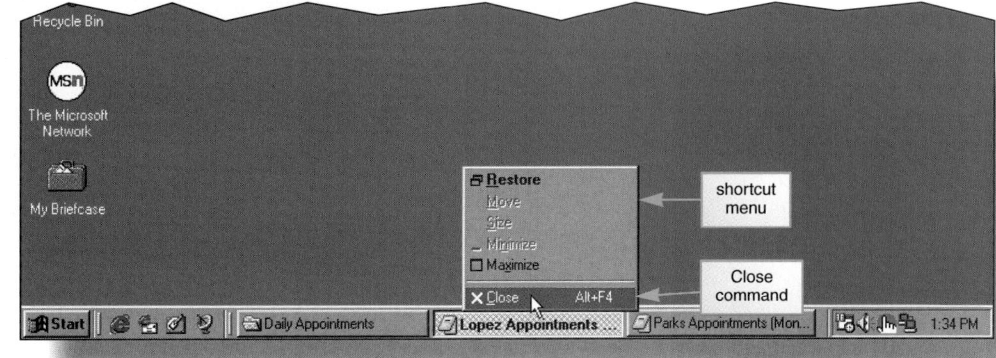

FIGURE 2-32

2 Click Close. Point to the Yes button.

The Notepad dialog box displays asking if you want to save the changes (Figure 2-33).

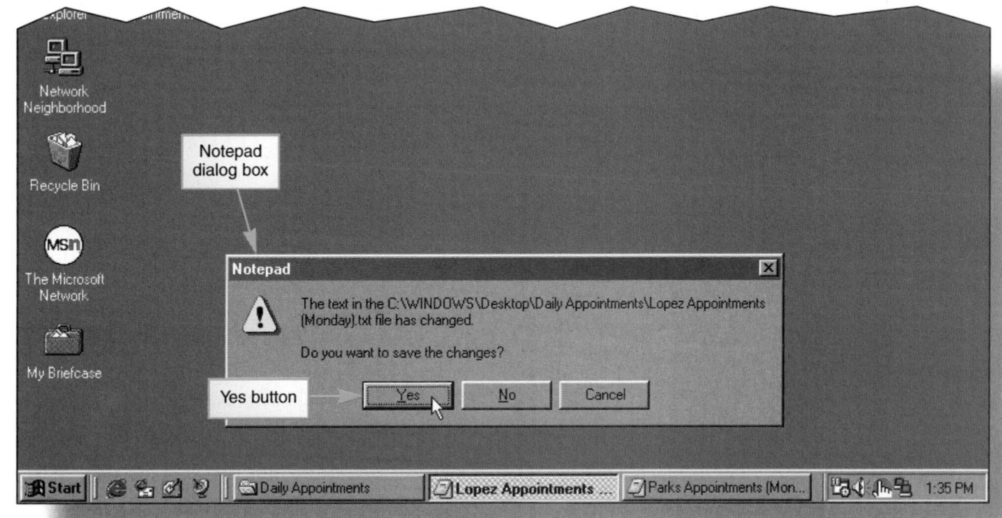

FIGURE 2-33

3 Click the Yes button. Right-click the Parks Appointments (Monday) - Notepad button in the taskbar button area. Point to Close on the shortcut menu.

A shortcut menu displays (Figure 2-34). The modified Lopez Appointments (Monday) document is saved in the Daily Appointments folder and its button no longer displays in the taskbar button area.

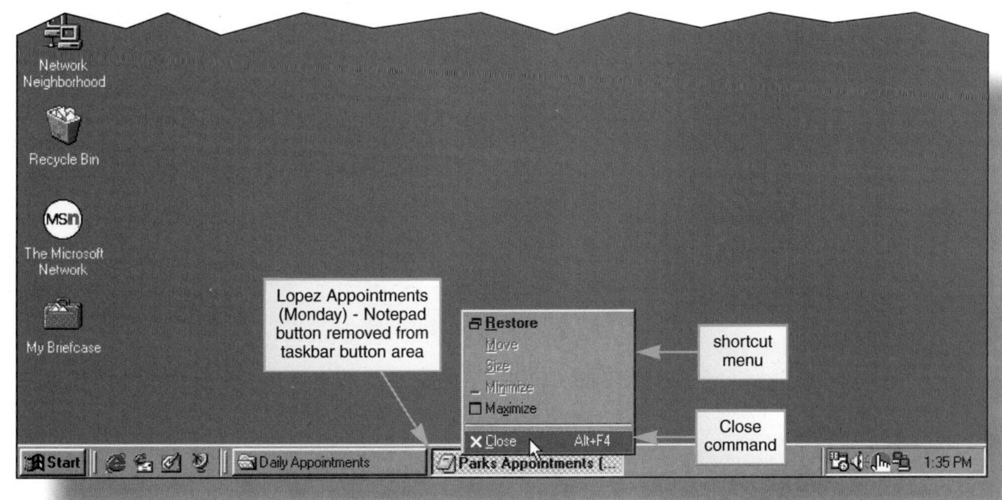

FIGURE 2-34

Click Close on the shortcut menu. When the Notepad dialog box displays asking if you want to save the changes, click the Yes button.

Only the Daily Appointments button remains in the taskbar button area (Figure 2-35).

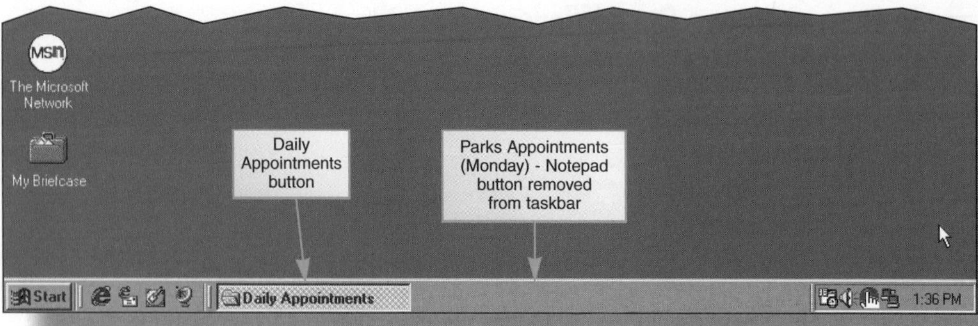

FIGURE 2-35

Other Ways

1. Click taskbar button, on File menu click Save, click Close button
2. Click taskbar button, click Close button on title bar, click Yes button
3. Click taskbar button, on File menu click Exit, click Yes button

The capability of Windows 98 to process multiple documents at the same time and perform multitasking with multiple programs running at the same time is one of the primary features of the operating system.

More About

Printing

Normally it is more efficient to print directly from the document within a folder or on the desktop than to open the document first.

Printing a Document from Within a Folder

After documents are modified and saved on the desktop, you may wish to print them so you have an updated printed version of the Lopez Appointments (Monday) and the Parks Appointments (Monday) documents. Earlier in this project, you used the Print command from the File menu to print an open document. You also can print documents from a folder without opening the documents, and you can print multiple documents at the same time. To print both the Lopez Appointments (Monday) and the Parks Appointments (Monday) documents from the Daily Appointments folder, perform the following steps.

Steps To Print Multiple Documents from Within a Folder

1 Click the Daily Appointments button in the taskbar button area. Click the Lopez Appointments (Monday) icon in the Daily Appointments folder to select the icon, hold down the SHIFT key, and click the Parks Appointments (Monday) icon. Release the SHIFT key.

Both icons become selected (Figure 2-36).

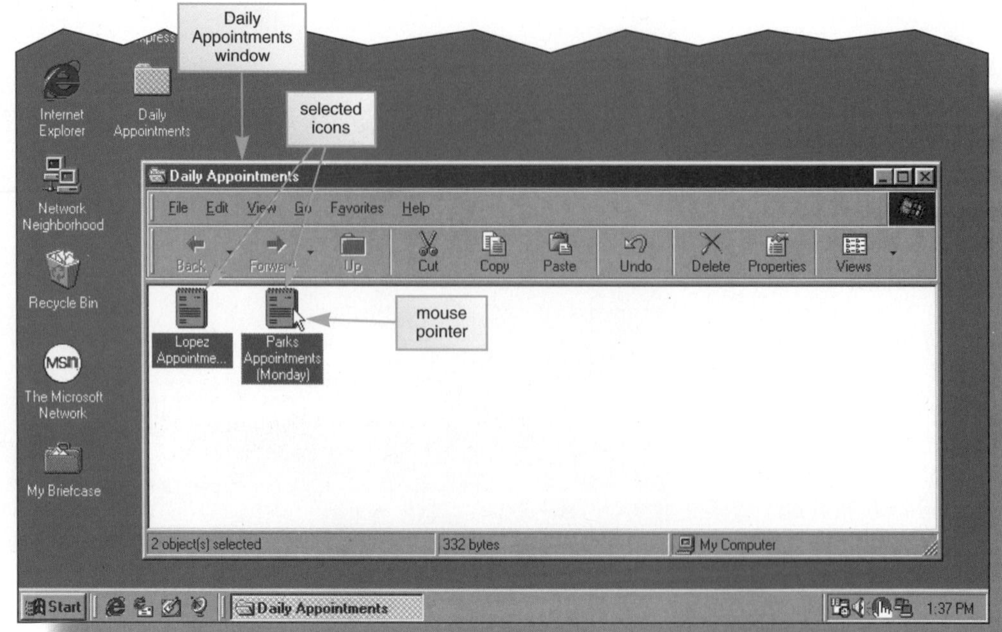

FIGURE 2-36

2 **Right-click the Parks Appointments (Monday) icon and then point to Print on the shortcut menu (Figure 2-37).**

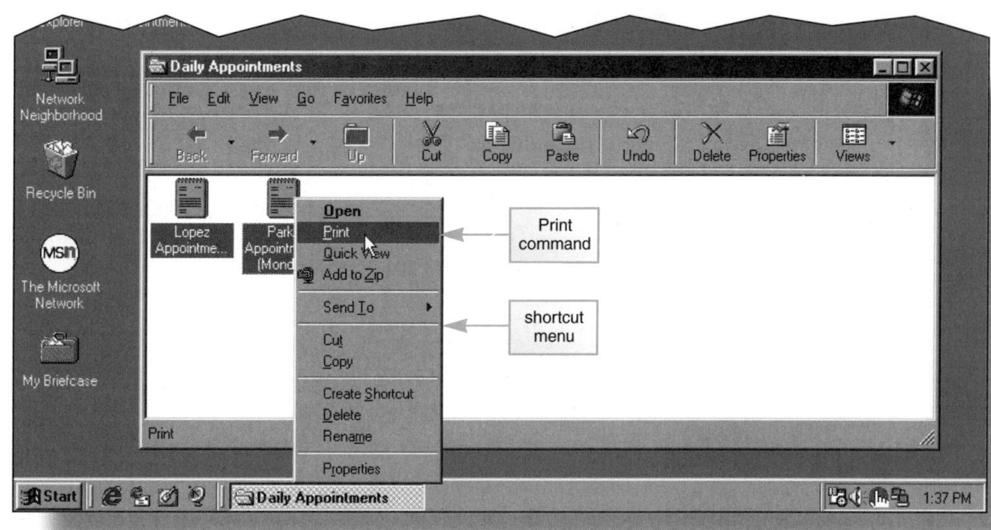

FIGURE 2-37

3 **Click Print.**

The modified documents print as shown in Figure 2-38.

4 **Click the Close button on the Daily Appointments title bar.**

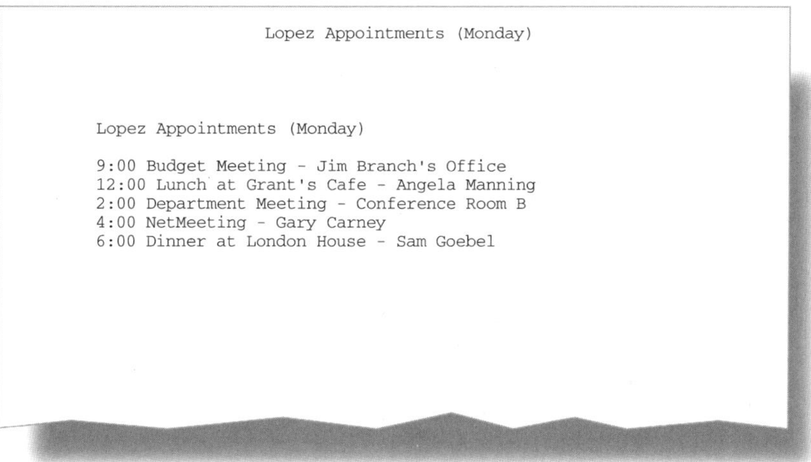

Lopez Appointments (Monday)

Lopez Appointments (Monday)

9:00 Budget Meeting - Jim Branch's Office
12:00 Lunch at Grant's Cafe - Angela Manning
2:00 Department Meeting - Conference Room B
4:00 NetMeeting - Gary Carney
6:00 Dinner at London House - Sam Goebel

Parks Appointments (Monday)

Parks Appointments (Monday)

10:00 Sales Meeting - Shirley Bundy's Office
12:00 Lunch at Bob's Burgers - Peter Miller
2:00 Department Meeting - Conference Room B
4:30 Conference Call - Brandy Schiller

FIGURE 2-38

1. Select document icons, on File menu click Print

Copying a Folder onto a Disk

A folder on the desktop is useful when you are using one or more documents within the folder frequently. It is a good policy, however, to make a copy of a folder and documents within the folder so that in case the folder or its contents are accidentally lost or damaged, you do not lose all your work. This often is called making a **backup** of your folders and files. To make a backup of the Daily Appointments folder on a floppy disk in drive A of your computer, complete the following steps.

To Copy a Folder on the Desktop onto a Floppy Disk

1 Insert a formatted floppy disk into drive A.

2 Right-click the Daily Appointments folder icon on the desktop. Point to Send To on the shortcut menu. Point to 3½ Floppy (A) on the Send To submenu.

The shortcut menu and Send To submenu display (Figure 2-39).

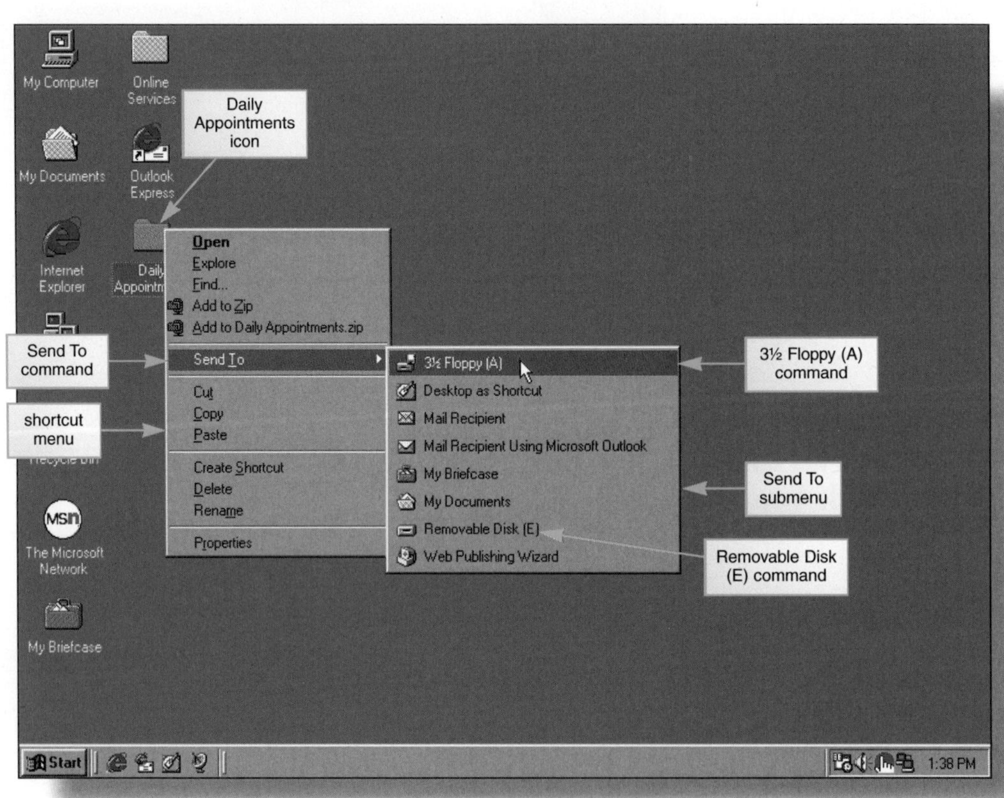

FIGURE 2-39

More About

The Send To Command

Commands can easily be added to and removed from the Send To submenu. Note the Removable Disk (E) command that has been added in Figure 2-39 to allow the user to back up files and folders to a removable disk.

Click 3½ Floppy (A).

While the Daily Appointments folder and the documents within the folder are being copied, the Copying dialog box displays (Figure 2-40).

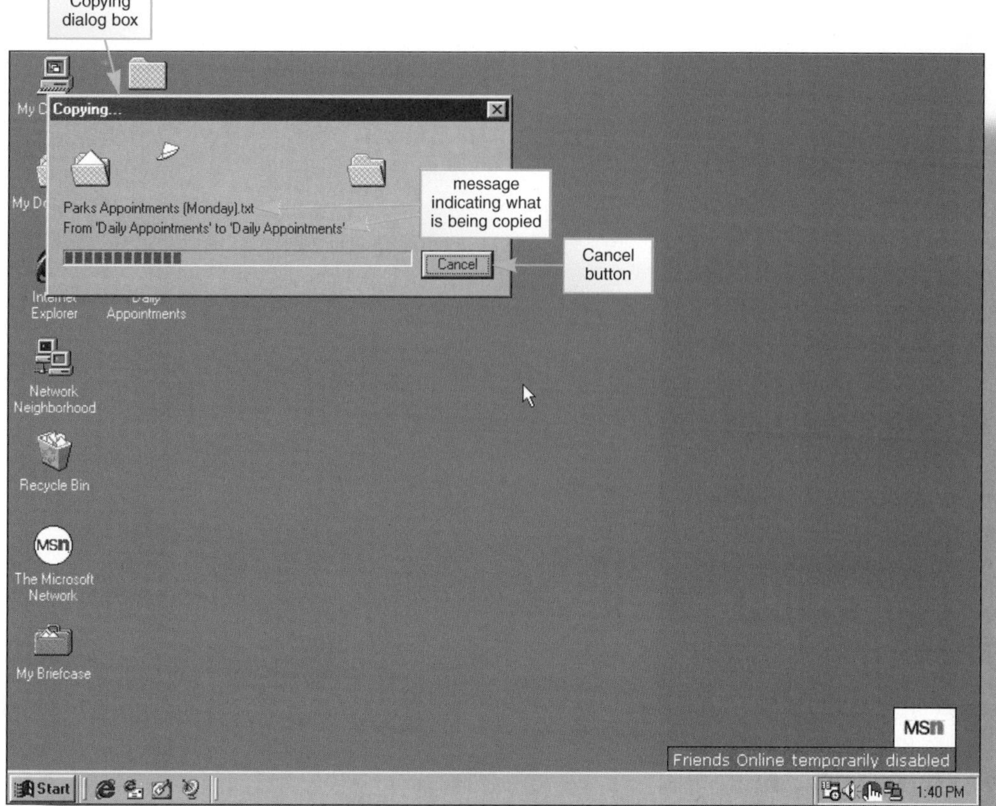

FIGURE 2-40

Other Ways

1. Double-click My Computer icon, right-drag folder icon to 3½ Floppy (A:) icon in My Computer window, click Copy Here
2. Double-click My Computer icon, drag folder icon to 3½ Floppy (A:) icon
3. Right-click the folder icon, click Copy, double-click My Computer icon, right-click 3½ Floppy (A:) icon, click Paste

In Figure 2-40, a message explains which folders and files are being copied, and animated pages fly from one folder to the other in the dialog box. After the folder and all documents have been copied, the Copying dialog box closes. At the conclusion of the copying process, the Daily Appointments folder and the documents in the folder are stored both on the desktop and on the floppy disk in drive A. If you want to stop the copying process, you can click the Cancel button in the Copying dialog box.

Opening a Folder on a Floppy Disk

After copying a folder onto a floppy disk, you may wish to verify that the folder has been copied properly onto the floppy disk; or, you may wish to open a document stored in the folder directly from the floppy disk. To open a folder stored on a floppy disk, complete the steps on the next two pages.

More About

Backups

Copying a file or folder to a floppy disk in drive A is one way to create a backup, but backing up files often is a much more elaborate process. Because floppy disks can contain only 1.44 megabytes of data, most backups are written on tape or portable hard disks that can contain hundreds of megabytes (millions of characters) and even gigabytes (billions of characters).

To Open a Folder Stored on a Floppy Disk

1 Double-click the My Computer icon. Move and resize the window to resemble the My Computer window shown in Figure 2-41. Point to the 3½ Floppy (A:) icon in the My Computer window.

The My Computer window opens and the My Computer button is recessed (Figure 2-41). Notice that the Back and Forward buttons on the toolbar appear dimmed and are unavailable. When the buttons are not dimmed, you can click the buttons to display previously displayed windows.

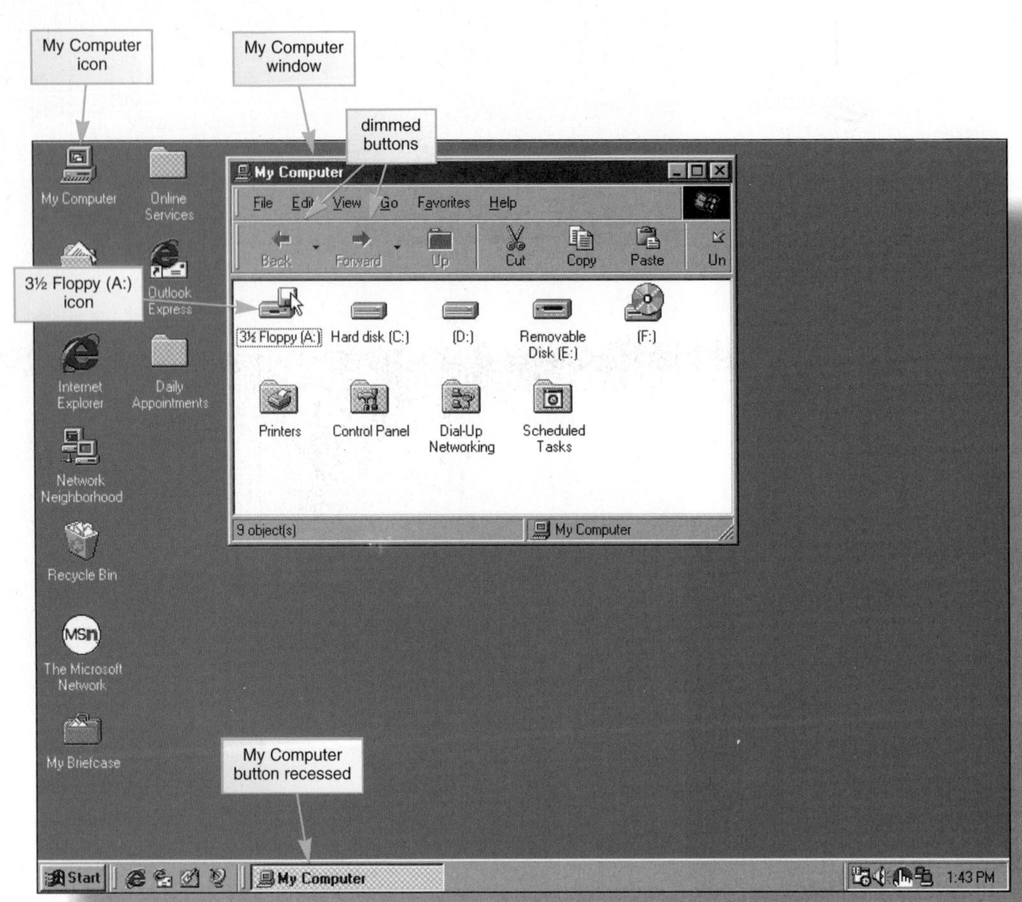

FIGURE 2-41

The Back and Forward Buttons

When the Back and Forward buttons are not dimmed, clicking the Back button displays the last window opened and clicking the Forward button displays the next window in a previously displayed sequence of windows.

2 **Double-click the 3½ Floppy (A:) icon and then point to the Daily Appointments icon in the 3½ Floppy (A:) window.**

The 3½ Floppy (A:) window opens in the same window in which the My Computer was displayed and the 3½ Floppy (A:) button replaces the My Computer button in the taskbar button area (Figure 2-42). Because the My Computer window was opened prior to opening the 3½ Floppy (A:) window, the Back button on the toolbar no longer is dimmed and is available. Clicking the ***Back button*** *displays the previously displayed window (My Computer window).*

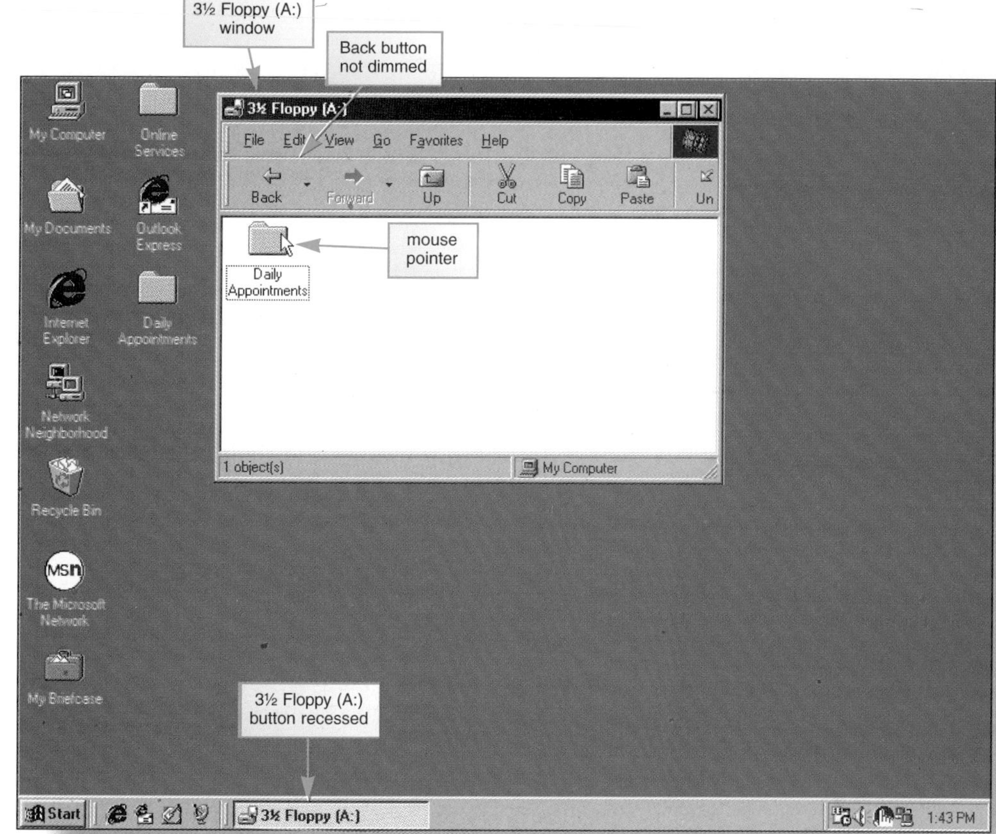

FIGURE 2-42

3 **Double-click the Daily Appointments icon. Point to the Close button on the Daily Appointments title bar.**

The Daily Appointments window opens in the same window in which 3½ Floppy (A:) was displayed and the Daily Appointments button replaces the 3½ Floppy (A:) button (Figure 2-43).

4 **Click the Close button and then remove the floppy disk from drive A.**

The Daily Appointments window closes and the Daily Appointments button no longer displays in the taskbar button area.

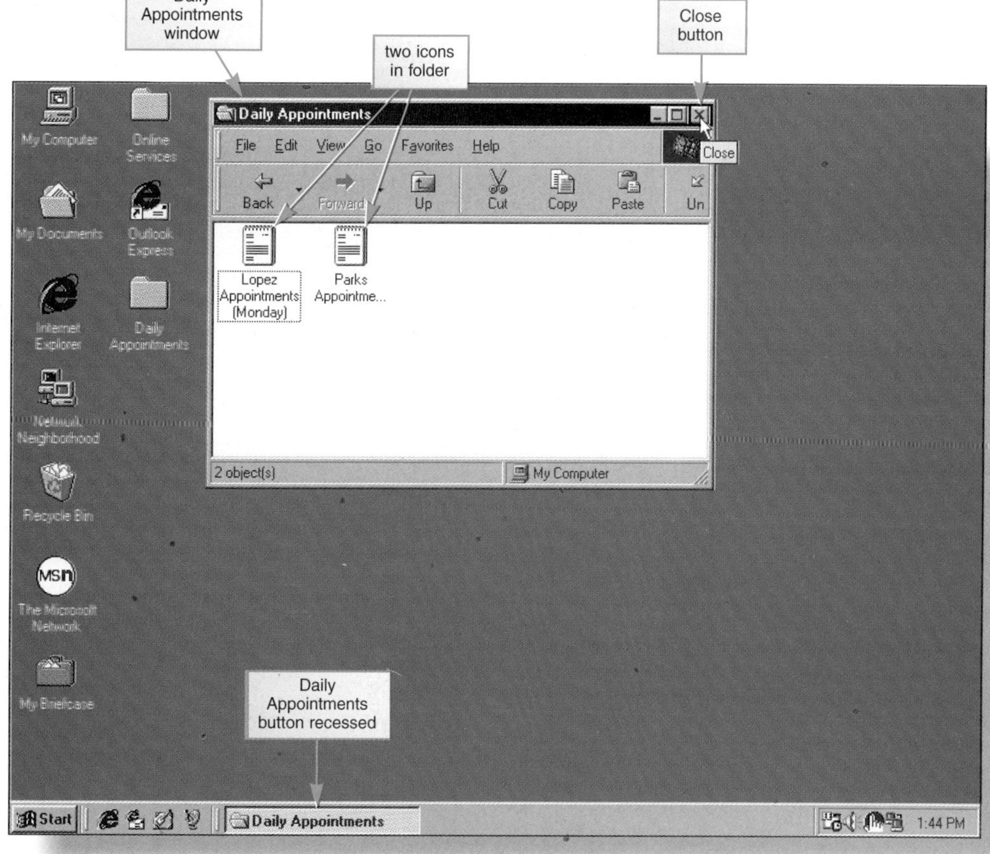

FIGURE 2-43

If you wish to open one of the documents in the folder stored on the floppy disk in drive A as shown in Figure 2-43 on the previous page, use the same procedure as when opening the document from the desktop; that is – double-click the document icon.

More About

Shortcuts

A shortcut icon is a pointer that references the location of a document or application on the hard drive. The shortcut icon is not the actual document or application. Thus, when you delete a shortcut icon, you are deleting the shortcut icon and its reference to the document or application. You are not deleting the document or the programs that comprise the application. They remain on the hard drive.

Creating Document Shortcuts

One of Windows 98's most powerful features is its capability of being easily customized. One of the many ways to customize Windows 98 is to use shortcuts to launch application programs and open documents. A **shortcut** is an icon that represents a document or an application program. Placing a shortcut to an application or document on the Start menu or on the desktop can make it easier to launch the application or open the document.

Placing a Shortcut on the Start Menu

One of the ways in which Windows 98 can be customized is to add an application shortcut or a document shortcut to the Start menu that displays when you click the Start button. You do not actually place the application or document on the menu, but instead, you place a shortcut to the document on the menu.

To illustrate this, assume you want to be able to open the Lopez Appointments (Monday) document from the Start menu. To place the Lopez Appointments (Monday) document shortcut on the Start menu, complete the following steps.

To Place a Document Shortcut on the Start Menu

1 Double-click the Daily Appointments icon to open the folder.

The Daily Appointments window opens (Figure 2-44). The Lopez Appointments (Monday) and Parks Appointments (Monday) document icons are contained in the folder.

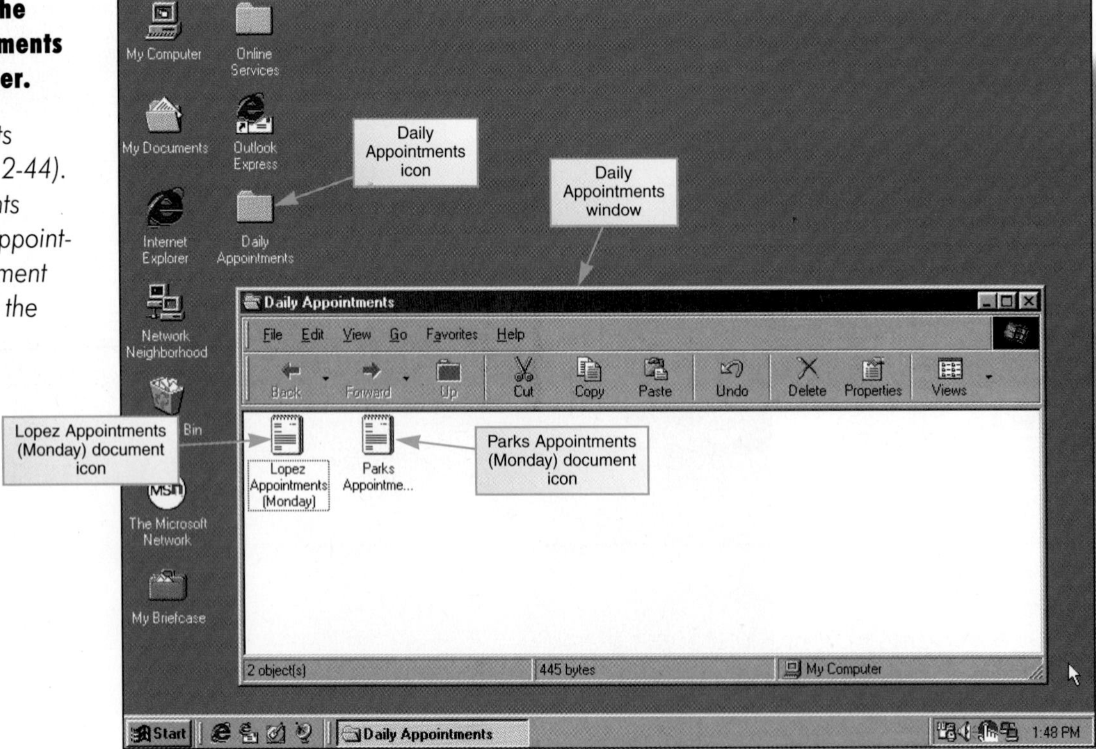

FIGURE 2-44

2 Drag the Lopez Appointments (Monday) icon on top of the Start button on the taskbar.

When you drag the icon on top of the Start button, the icon appears dimmed and the Start menu displays (Figure 2-45). When you release the mouse button, the Start menu remains on the desktop.

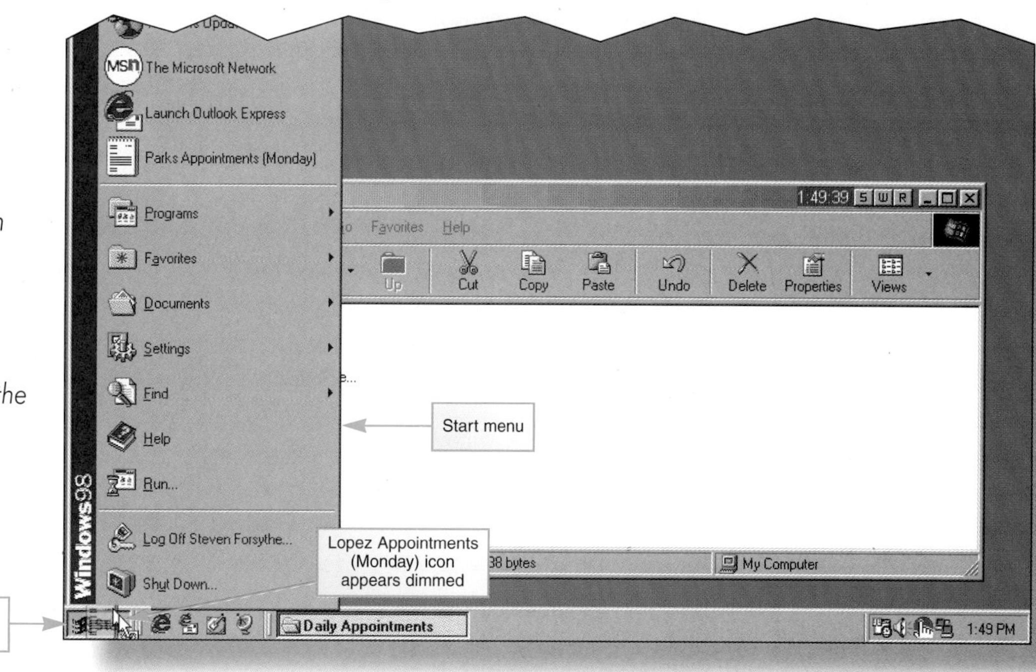

FIGURE 2-45

3 Click the Start button.

The Start menu displays (Figure 2-46). The Lopez Appointments (Monday) shortcut displays in the section above the Programs command on the Start menu.

4 Click an open area of the Daily Appointments window to close the Start menu.

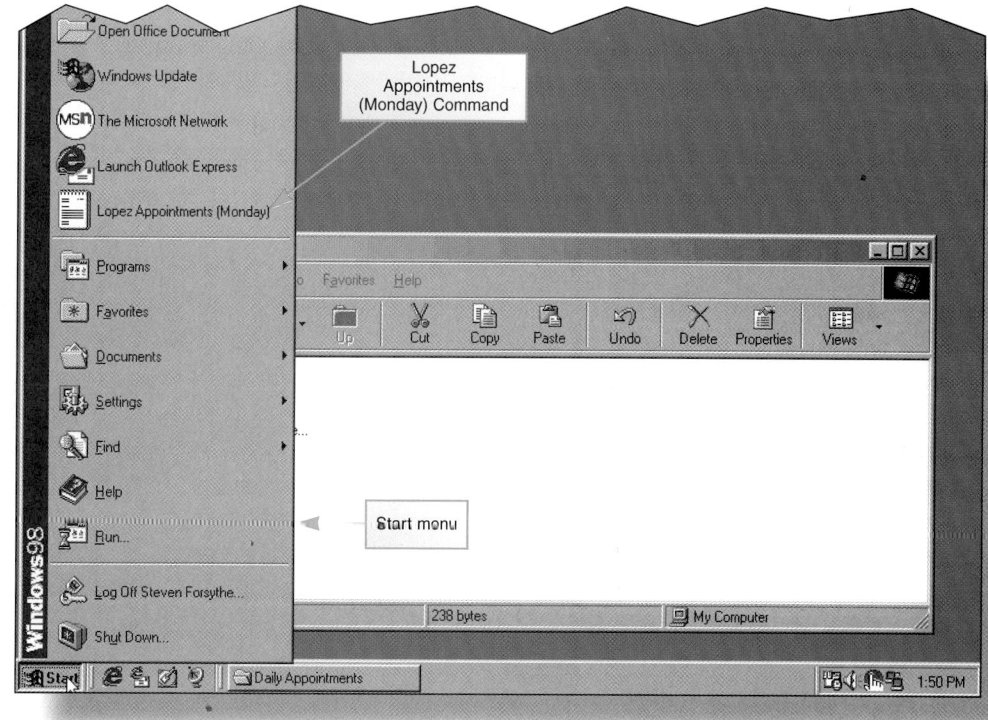

FIGURE 2-46

Opening a Document from the Start Menu

Once you have placed a document or application program shortcut on the Start menu, you can click the Start button and open the document or application program from the Start menu. To open the Lopez Appointments (Monday) document from the Start menu, complete the steps on the next page.

To Open a Document Using the Start Menu

1 Click the Start button on the taskbar. Point to Lopez Appointments (Monday) on the Start menu.

The Start menu displays (Figure 2-47).

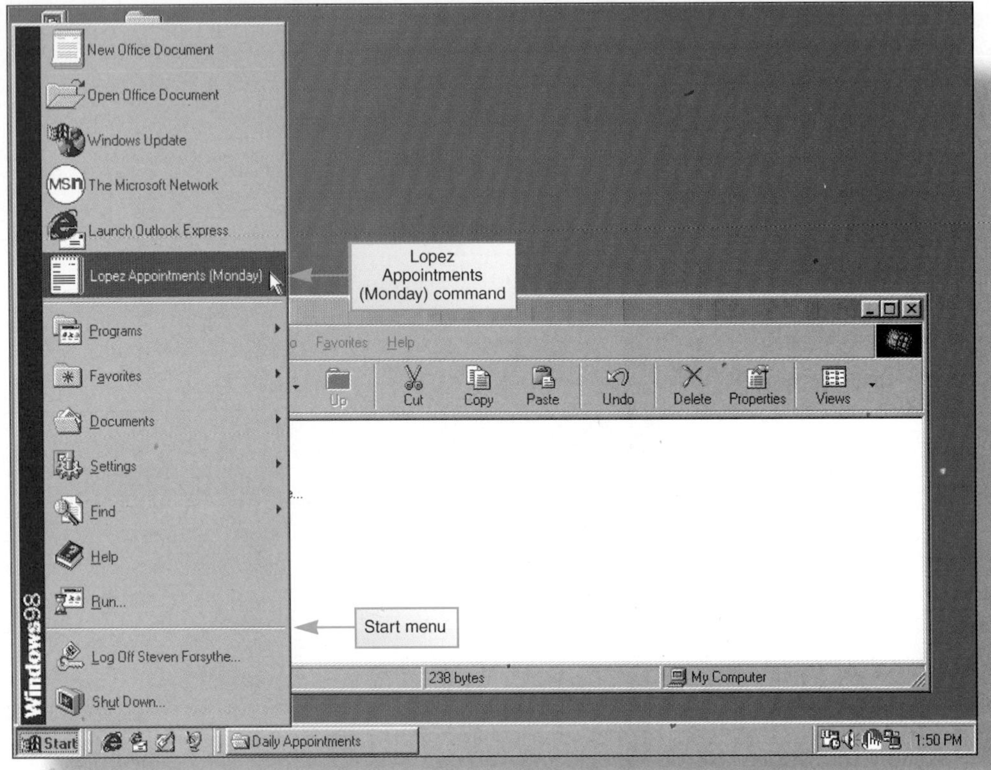

FIGURE 2-47

2 Click Lopez Appointments (Monday).

Notepad opens and the Lopez Appointments (Monday) document displays (Figure 2-48).

3 Click the Close button in the Lopez Appointments (Monday) - Notepad window. Click the Close button in the Daily Appointments window.

The two windows close.

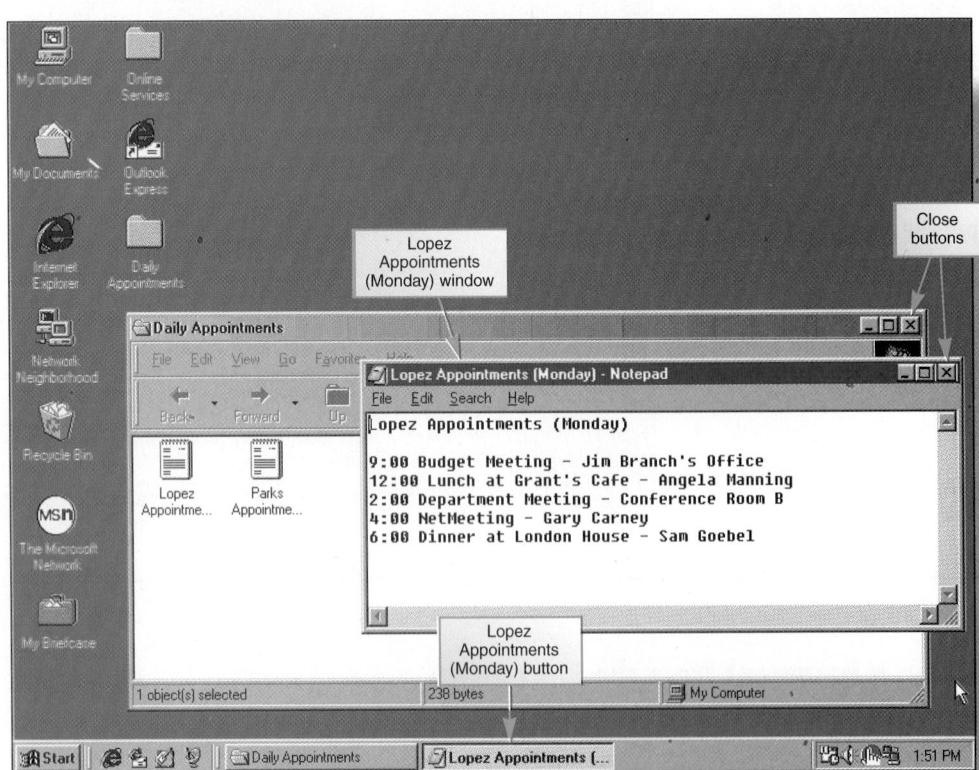

FIGURE 2-48

Removing a Shortcut from the Start Menu

Just as you can add document or application program shortcuts to the Start menu, you also can remove them from the Start menu. To remove the Lopez Appointments (Monday) shortcut from the Start menu, complete the following steps.

To Remove a Shortcut from the Start Menu

1 Click the Start button on the taskbar. Point to Lopez Appointments (Monday) on the Start menu (Figure 2-49).

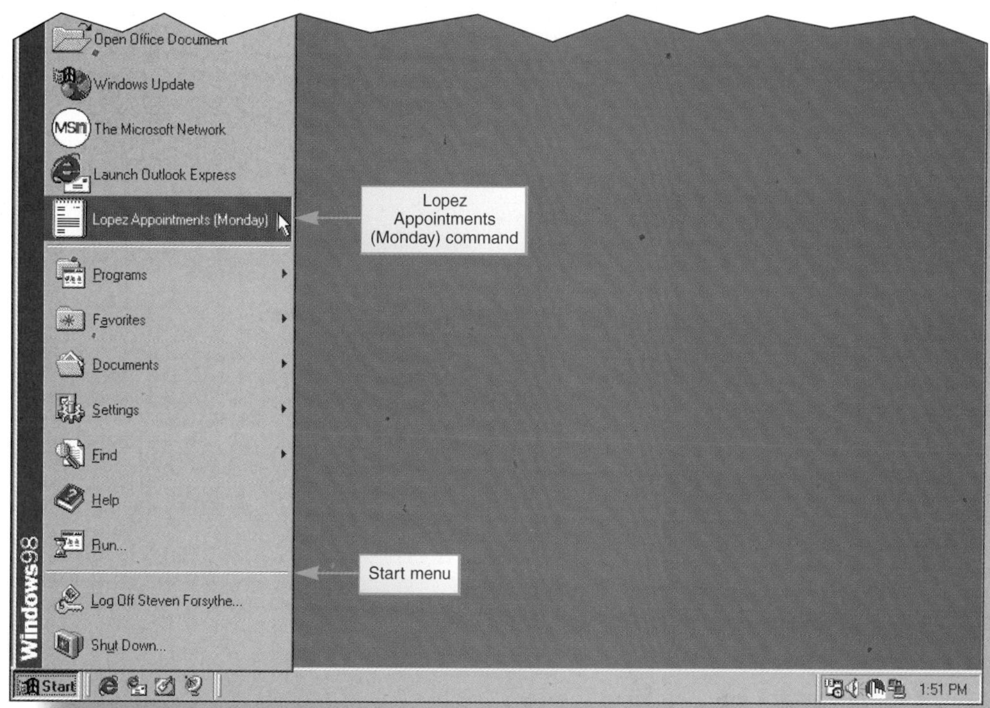

FIGURE 2-49

2 Right-click Lopez Appointments (Monday). Point to Delete on the shortcut menu (Figure 2-50).

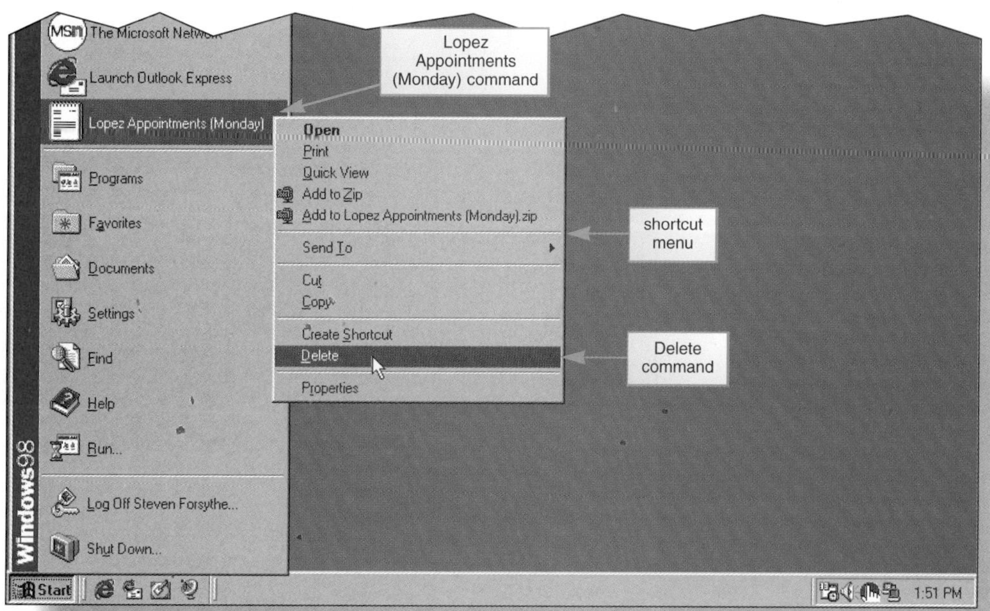

FIGURE 2-50

3 Click Delete. When the Confirm File Delete dialog box displays, point to the Yes button.

The Confirm File Delete dialog box displays (Figure 2-51).

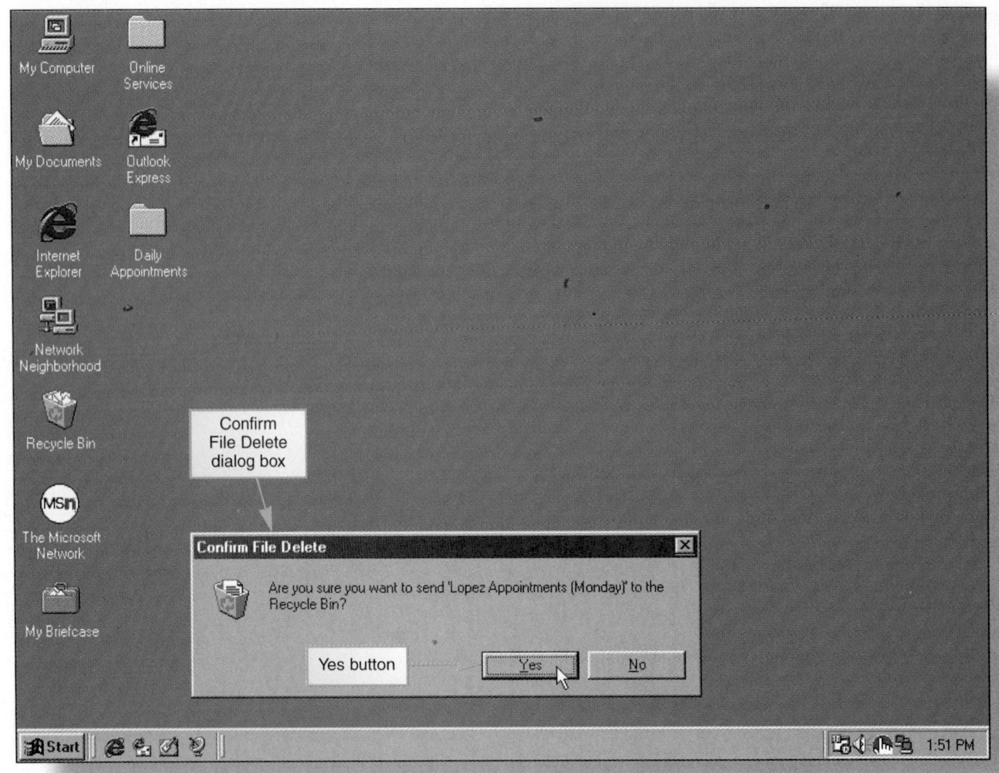

FIGURE 2-51

4 Click the Yes button. Click the Start button on the taskbar to view the Start menu.

The Lopez Appointments (Monday) shortcut is removed from the Start menu (Figure 2-52).

5 Click an open area of the desktop to close the Start menu.

The Start menu closes.

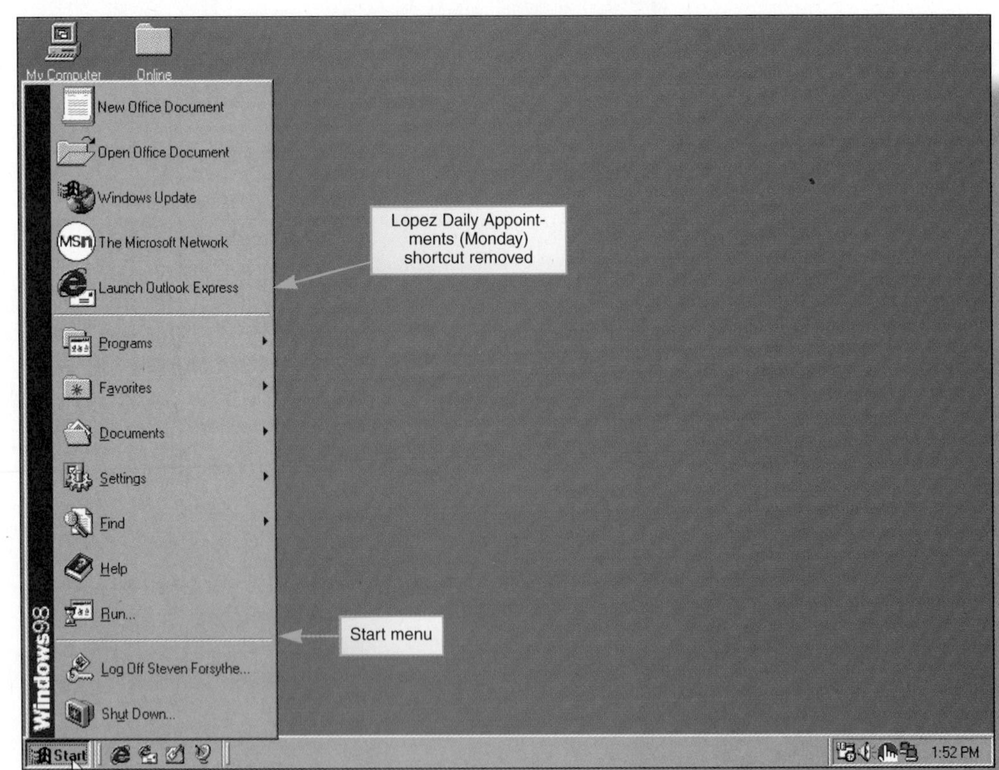

FIGURE 2-52

The capability of adding and removing shortcuts and folders on the Start menu provides great flexibility when customizing your computer.

Creating a Shortcut on the Desktop

You can create document and application program shortcuts directly on the desktop as well as on the Start menu. To create a shortcut for the Parks Appointments (Monday) document, complete the following steps.

To Create a Shortcut on the Desktop

1 Double-click the Daily Appointments icon to open the Daily Appointments window. Right-drag the Parks Appointments (Monday) icon from the Daily Appointments window to the desktop. Point to Create Shortcut(s) Here on the shortcut menu.

The Daily Appointments window, a dimmed icon, and a shortcut menu display on the desktop (Figure 2-53).

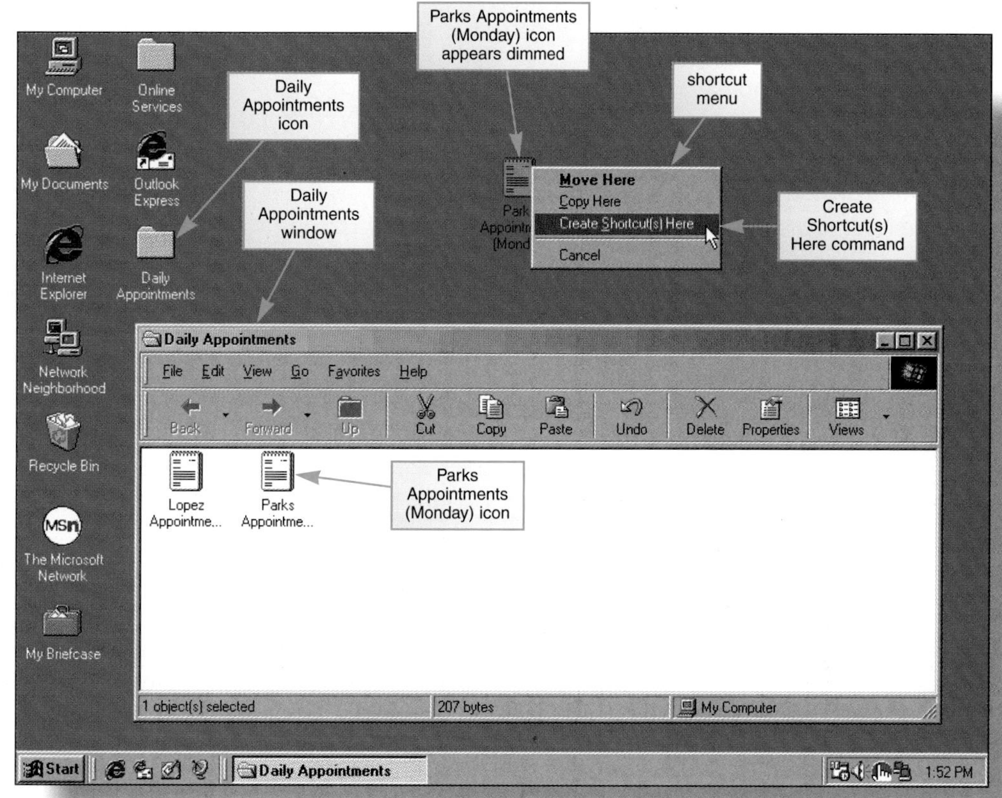

FIGURE 2-53

2 **Click Create Shortcut(s) Here. If the shortcut does not display on your desktop, move and resize the Daily Appointments window until the shortcut is visible.**

Windows 98 creates a shortcut on the desktop (Figure 2-54). The shortcut is identified with an icon title and a small arrow in the bottom-left corner of the icon. The shortcut might display on the desktop where you dragged it or it might display next in line in the columns of icons, depending your computer's settings.

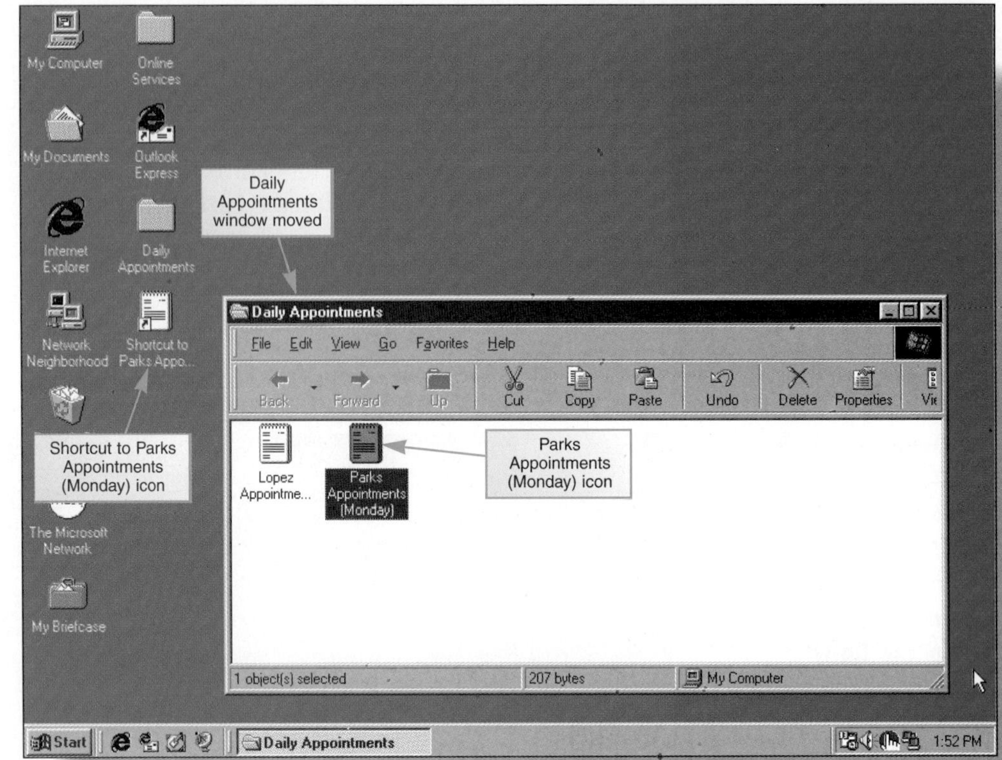

FIGURE 2-54

Other Ways

1. Press CTRL+SHIFT and drag icon to desktop, click Create Shortcut(s) Here

Opening a Document or Launching an Application Program Using a Shortcut on the Desktop

Once the shortcut has been placed on the desktop, you can open the document or launch the application program represented by the shortcut by double-clicking the shortcut. To open the Parks Appointments (Monday) document, complete the following steps.

To Open a Document Using a Shortcut on the Desktop

1 Double-click the Shortcut to Parks Appointments (Monday) icon.

Notepad launches and the Parks Appointments (Monday) document displays in the Notepad window (Figure 2-55).

2 Click the Close button on the Parks Appointments (Monday) - Notepad title bar to close the window. Click the Close button on the Daily Appointments title bar to close the window.

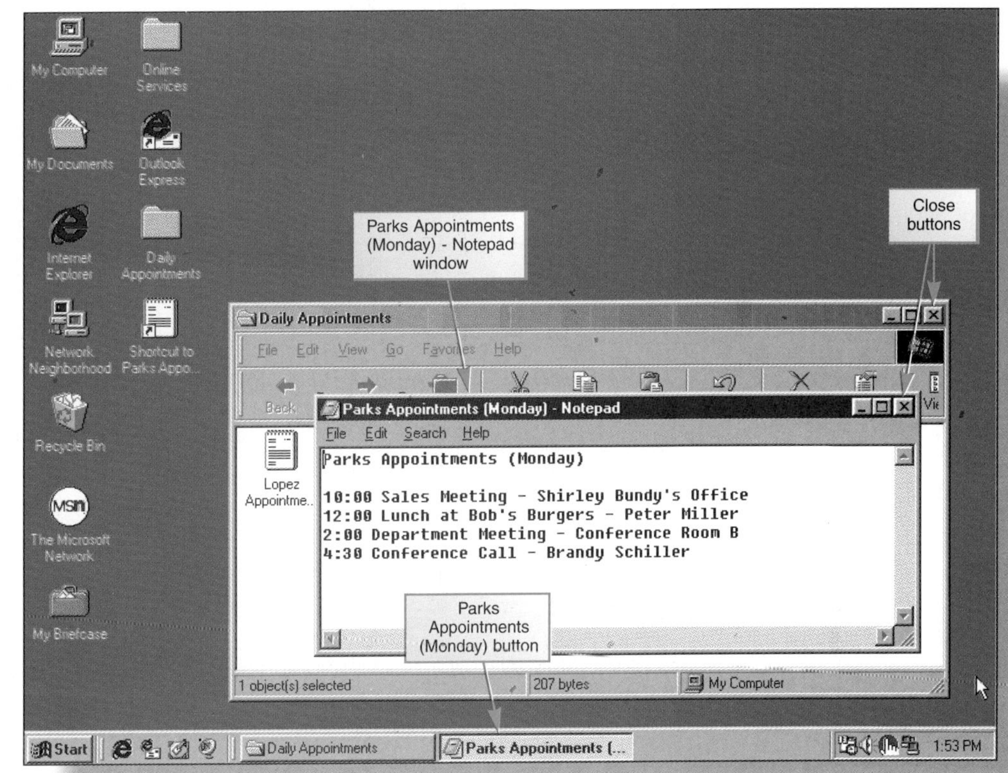

FIGURE 2-55

Other Ways

1. Right-click shortcut icon, click Open
2. Click shortcut icon, press ENTER

Shortcuts can be quite useful because they can reference application programs and documents stored on the hard disk. For instance, you can store a document in a folder on your computer's hard disk and create a shortcut to the folder on the desktop. In that manner, you can open the document from the desktop but the document remains stored in its logical place in a folder on your computer's hard disk.

Arranging Icons

In some instances you may want to control the sequence and arrangement of the icons on the desktop. To arrange the icons, you can use the shortcut menu that displays when you right-click the desktop. To display the shortcut menu and review your capability to arrange icons on the desktop, complete the steps on the next page.

To Display the Arrange Icons Submenu

1 Right-click an open area on the desktop and then point to Arrange Icons.

A shortcut menu and the Arrange Icons submenu display (Figure 2-56). A check mark precedes the Auto Arrange command to indicate the Auto Arrange command is selected and Windows 98 will automatically arrange the icons on the desktop.

2 Click an open area of the desktop.

The shortcut menu and Arrange Icons submenu no longer display on the desktop.

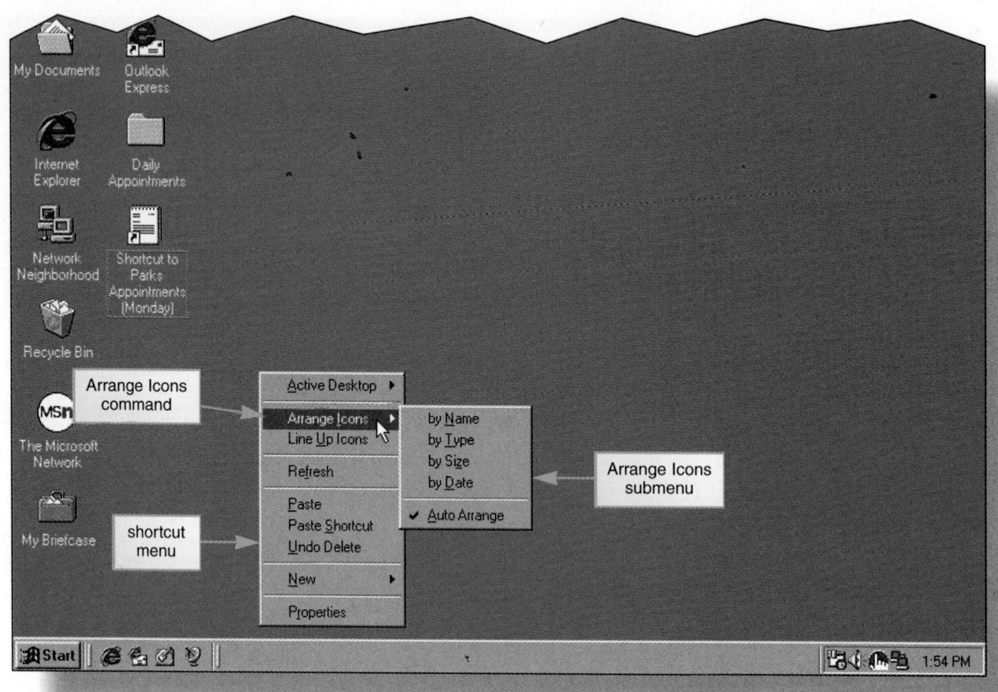

FIGURE 2-56

If the Auto Arrange command is selected, Windows 98 will automatically arrange all icons on the desktop. If an icon is added to the desktop, Windows 98 automatically will place the icon where it belongs in the columns of icons that display on the left side of the desktop. If the Auto Arrange command is not selected, you can place icons anywhere on the desktop you want.

If you click the **by Name command** on the Arrange Icons submenu, the icons you have created on your desktop will be arranged in ascending alphabetical order. The **by Type command** will arrange the icons by the type of file they represent. The **by Size command** arranges the icons from the smallest to the largest file, and the **by Date command** arranges the icons from the newest to the oldest based on when the files were created.

Deleting Shortcuts, Folders, and Documents on the Desktop

In many cases after you have worked with folders and documents on the desktop, at some time you will want to delete the folders and documents from the desktop. Windows 98 offers three different techniques to perform this operation: (1) right-click the object and then click Delete on the shortcut menu; (2) right-drag the object to the Recycle Bin; and (3) drag the object to the Recycle Bin. The steps in this section will demonstrate all three methods.

It is important you realize what you are doing when you delete a folder or document off the desktop, and always be extremely cautious when deleting anything. When you **delete a shortcut** from the desktop, you delete only the shortcut icon and its reference to the document or application program. The document or application program itself, which is stored elsewhere on your hard disk, is not deleted. When you **delete the icon** for a folder, document, or application program on the desktop that is not a shortcut, however, the actual folder, document, or application program is deleted. Therefore, whenever you delete from the desktop, you must be quite cautious and make sure you are deleting exactly what you want to delete.

When you delete a folder, document, or application program from the desktop, Windows 98 places these items in the **Recycle Bin**, which is an area on the hard disk that contains all the items you have deleted not only from the desktop but from the hard disk as well. When the Recycle Bin becomes full, you can empty it. Up until the time you empty the Recycle Bin, you can recover deleted files and application programs. Even though you have this safety net, you should be extremely cautious whenever deleting anything from your desktop or hard disk.

Assume at the end of the week you no longer have a need for the Lopez Appointments (Monday) and the Parks Appointments (Monday) documents. You decide, therefore, that you can delete them safely from the desktop. To accomplish this, you must delete the shortcut to the Parks Appointments (Monday) document, the two documents, and the folder in which the documents are stored. To delete the shortcut, complete the following steps.

To Delete a Shortcut from the Desktop

1 Right-drag the Shortcut to Parks Appointments (Monday) icon to the Recycle Bin icon on the desktop. Point to Move Here on the shortcut menu.

The Shortcut to Parks Appointments (Monday) icon appears dimmed on top of the Recycle Bin icon and a shortcut menu with two commands displays (Figure 2-57). The Shortcut to Parks Appointments (Monday) icon remains on the desktop.

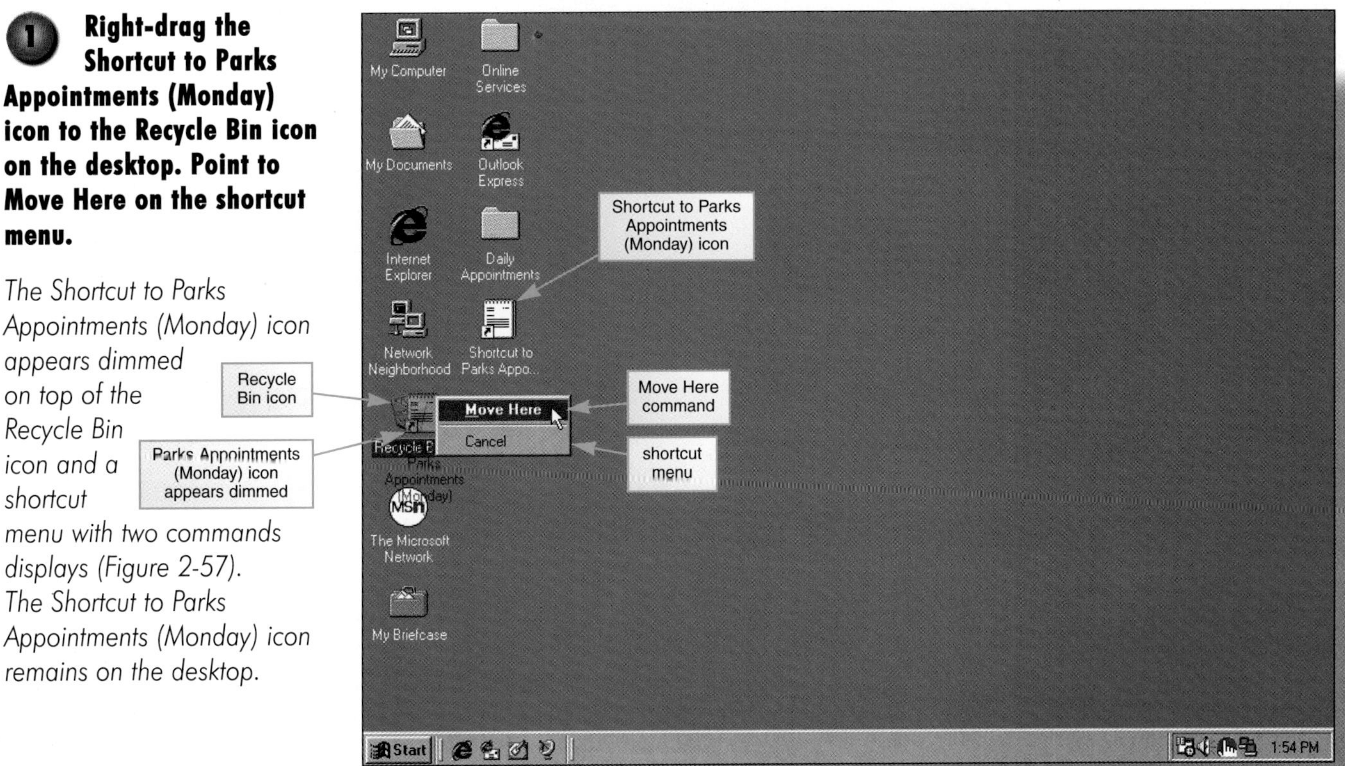

FIGURE 2-57

2 Click Move Here. When the Confirm File Delete dialog box displays, point to the Yes button.

The Confirm File Delete dialog box displays (Figure 2-58).

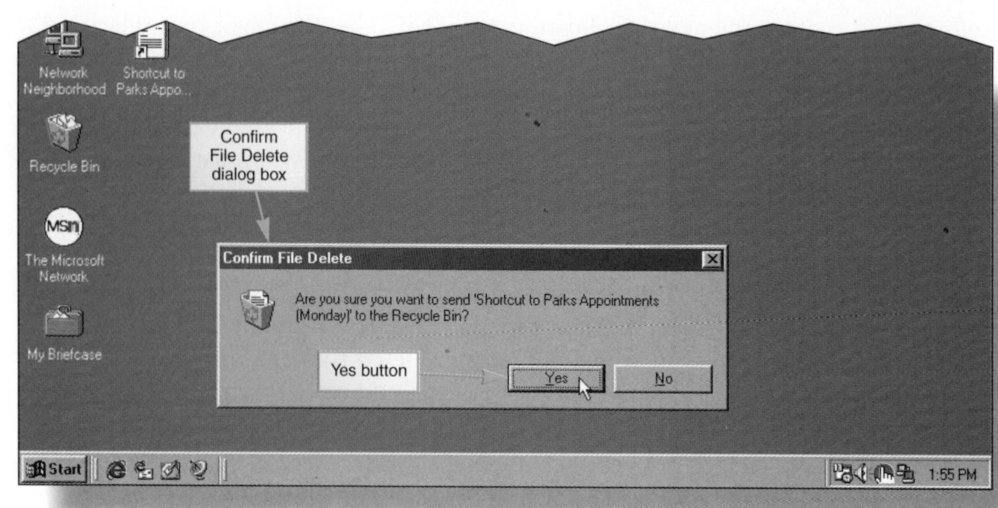

FIGURE 2-58

3 Click the Yes button.

The Shortcut to Parks Appointments (Monday) icon no longer displays on the desktop (Figure 2-59). The icon now is contained within the Recycle Bin.

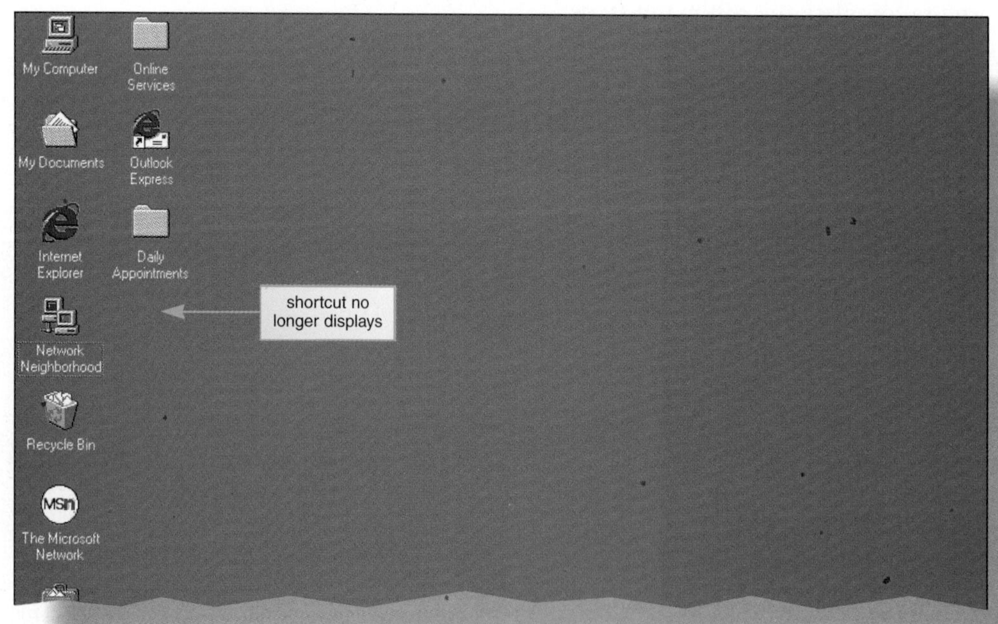

FIGURE 2-59

Other Ways

1. Drag shortcut icon to Recycle Bin, click Yes button
2. Right-click shortcut icon, click Delete, click Yes button

As noted previously, you can recover a shortcut, document, or application program you have moved to the Recycle Bin from the desktop or your hard disk. To do so, you double-click the Recycle Bin icon to open the Recycle Bin window, click the object you want to restore to the desktop, click File on the menu bar, and then click Restore.

Deleting Multiple Files

You can delete multiple files at the same time. Assume you want to delete both the Lopez Appointments (Monday) document and the Parks Appointments (Monday) document. To do so, complete the following steps.

To Delete Multiple Files

1 Double-click the Daily Appointments icon on the desktop. Place the mouse pointer below and to the right of the two document icons in the Daily Appointments window. Drag up and to the left until both icons are selected.

The Daily Appointments window opens, a dotted line surrounds the Lopez Appointments (Monday) and Parks Appointments (Monday) icons and the icons are selected (Figure 2-60).

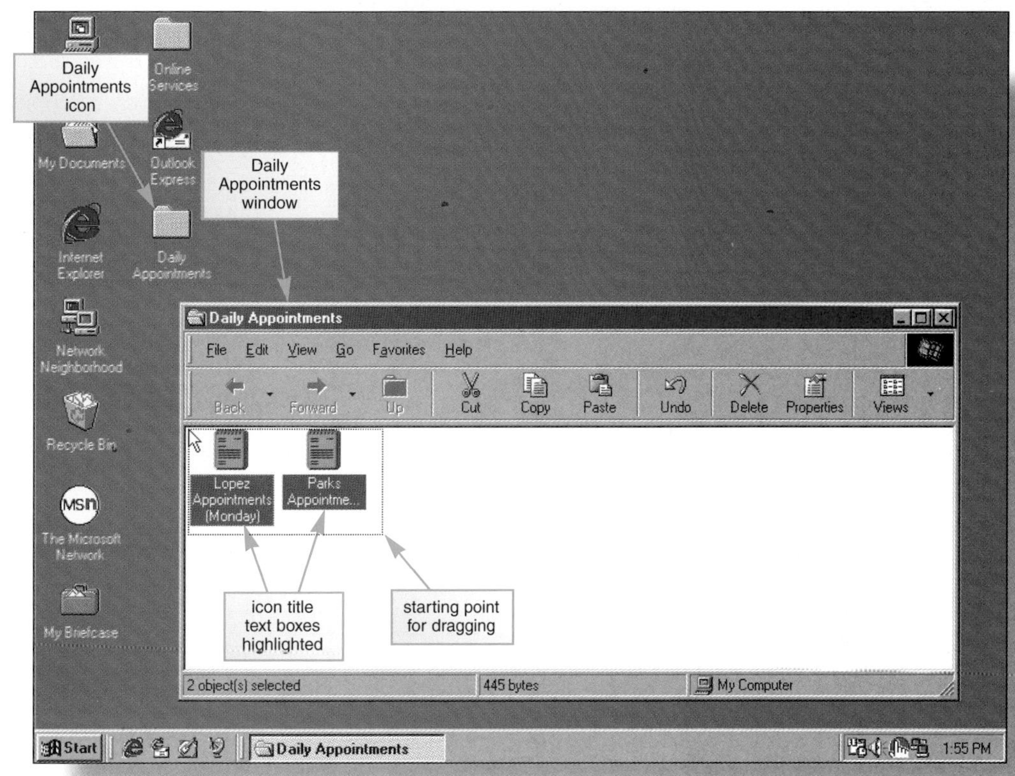

FIGURE 2-60

2 Right-click either icon. Point to Delete on the shortcut menu.

The Lopez Appointments (Monday) icon is right-clicked and a shortcut menu displays (Figure 2-61). Some of the commands on the shortcut menu might be different from those on your computer.

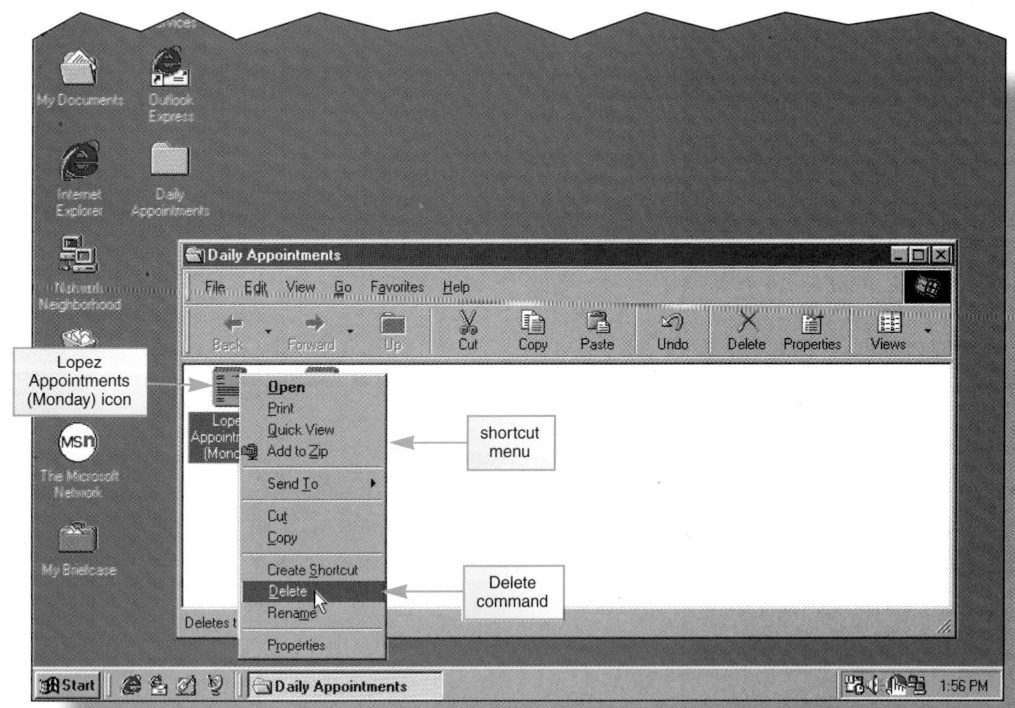

FIGURE 2-61

3 Click Delete. Point to the Yes button in the Confirm Multiple File Delete dialog box.

The Confirm Multiple File Delete dialog box displays (Figure 2-62). This dialog box ensures that you really want to delete the files. On some computers, this dialog box will not display because a special option has been chosen that specifies not to show this dialog box. If the dialog box does not display on your computer, the documents will be placed directly in the Recycle Bin.

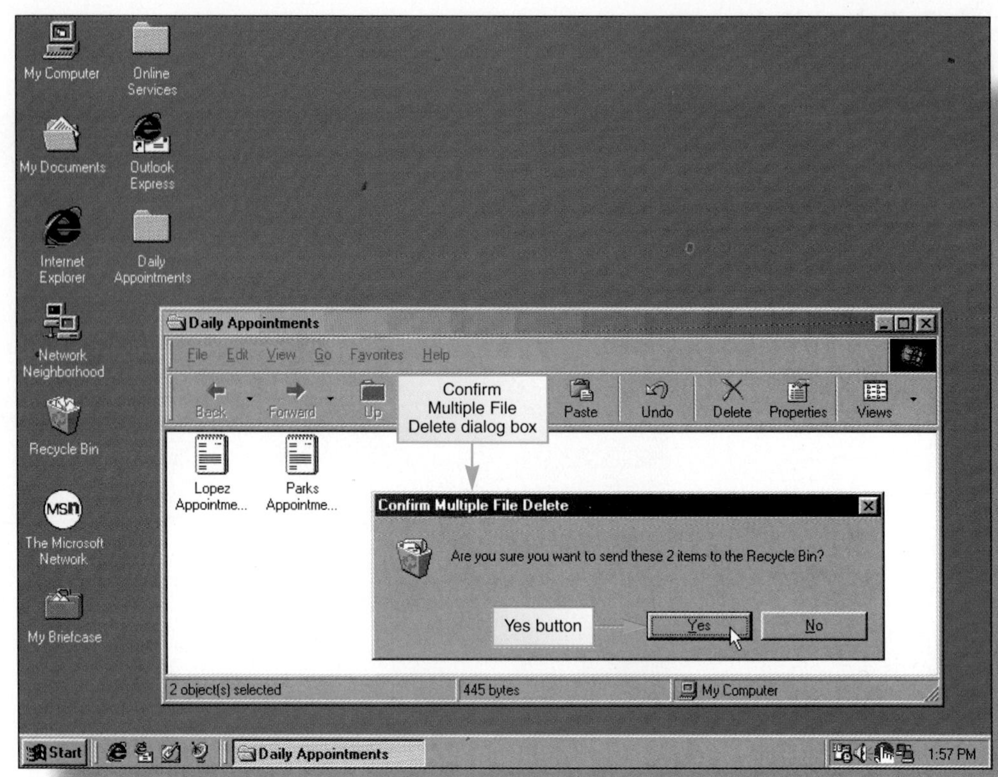

FIGURE 2-62

Click the Yes button.

The two files are removed from the Daily Appointments window and are placed in the Recycle Bin (Figure 2-63).

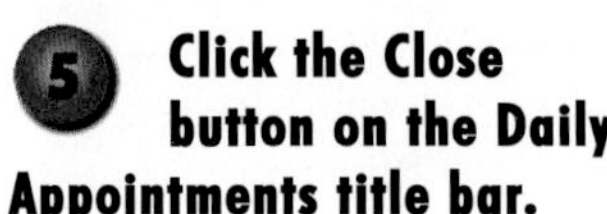

5 Click the Close button on the Daily Appointments title bar.

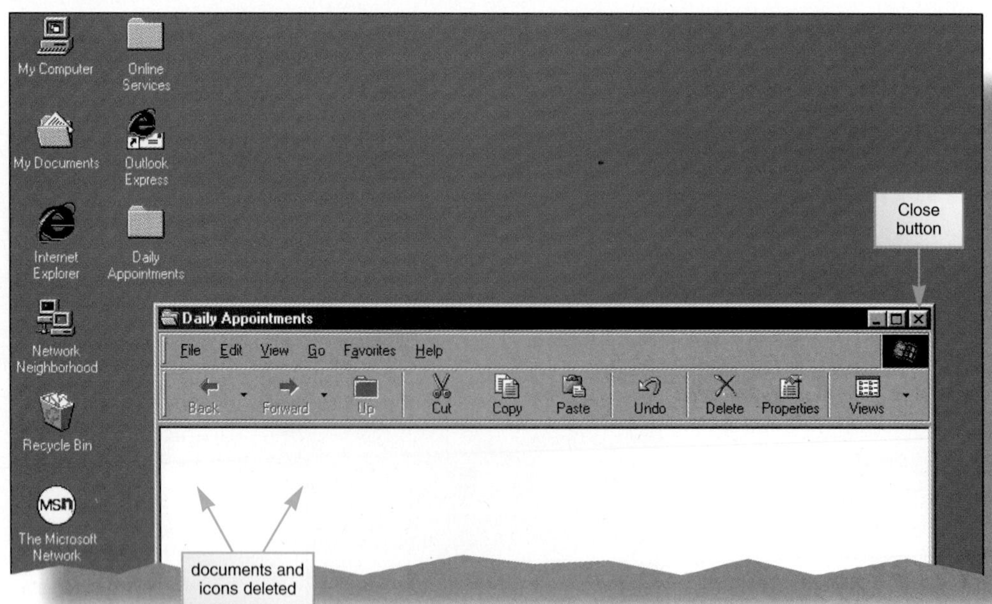

FIGURE 2-63

Other Ways

1. Click first document icon, hold down SHIFT key, click other icon, release SHIFT key, right-click either icon, click Delete, click Yes button

Deleting a Folder

Folders also can be deleted from the desktop. To delete the Daily Appointments folder from the desktop, complete the following steps.

To Delete a Folder from the Desktop

1 Drag the Daily Appointments icon to the Recycle Bin icon.

When you drag the icon over the Recycle Bin icon, a dimmed icon displays over the Recycle Bin icon (Figure 2-64). When you release the left mouse button, the dimmed icon no longer displays.

2 Click the Yes button in the Confirm Folder Delete dialog box.

When you click the Yes button in the dialog box, the folder no longer displays on the desktop.

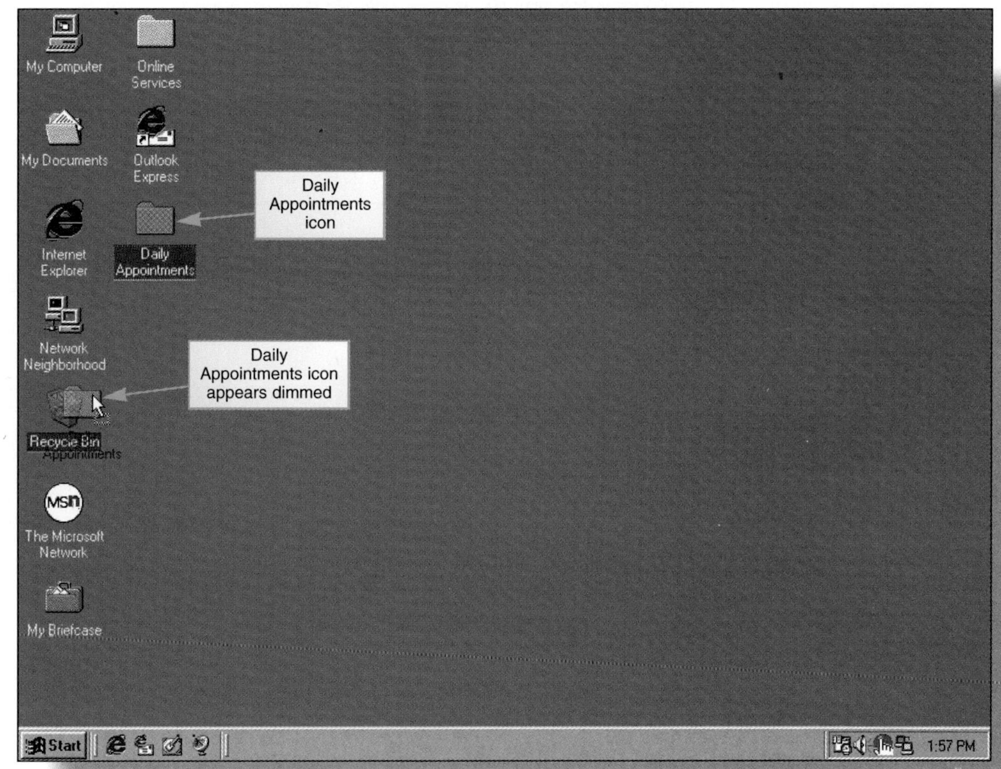

FIGURE 2-64

Other Ways

1. Right-drag folder icon to Recycle Bin, click Move Here, click Yes button
2. Right-click folder icon, click Delete on shortcut menu, click Yes button

In summary, you have used three different methods to delete an object from the desktop: (1) right-drag the object to the Recycle Bin; (2) right-click the object and then click Delete on the shortcut menu; and (3) drag the object to the Recycle Bin.

Again, it is important to understand that when you delete a folder icon, you are deleting the folder and its contents from your computer. Therefore, you must be extremely cautious when deleting files.

If after deleting an icon from the desktop, you want to return the icon immediately to the desktop after you delete the icon, you can right-click the desktop and then click the Undo Delete command on the shortcut menu. For example, if you delete the Daily Appointments icon from the desktop, right-click the desktop and click Undo Delete on the shortcut menu. The icon you deleted will be retrieved from the Recycle Bin and placed on the desktop. Multiple deleted icons also can be returned to the desktop in a similar fashion.

Working with the Windows 98 Active Desktop™

As mentioned in Project 1, the Active Desktop allows you to display the contents of a Web site located on a computer connected to the Internet on your desktop and update that content periodically. This constantly changing content, referred to as **Active Web content**, or **active content**, can be a weather map, a constantly updating stock market ticker of stock quotes, fast-breaking news stories from your favorite online newspaper, or the latest sports scores.

Turning On the Active Desktop™

Before you display active Web content on your desktop, you must turn on the Active Desktop. When the Active Desktop is turned on, the Internet Explorer Channel bar displays on the desktop and the desktop is active. Perform the following steps to turn on the Active Desktop.

To Turn On the Active Desktop

1 Right-click an open area of the desktop, point to Active Desktop on the shortcut menu, and then point to View As Web Page on the Active Desktop submenu.

A shortcut menu and the Active Desktop submenu display (Figure 2-65). The View As Web Page command on the Active Desktop submenu displays without a check mark preceding the command name to indicate the Active Desktop is turned off.

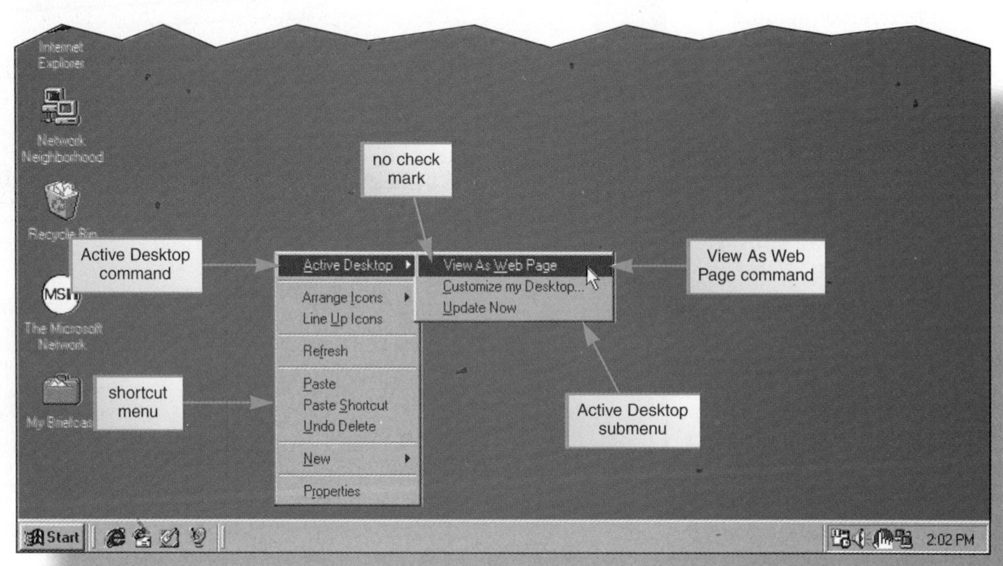

FIGURE 2-65

2 Click View As Web Page.

The Active Desktop is turned on, the Internet Channel bar displays on the desktop, and the shortcut menu and Active Desktop submenu no longer display on the desktop (Figure 2-66). Although not visible in Figure 2-66, a check mark precedes the View As Web Page command on the Active Desktop submenu.

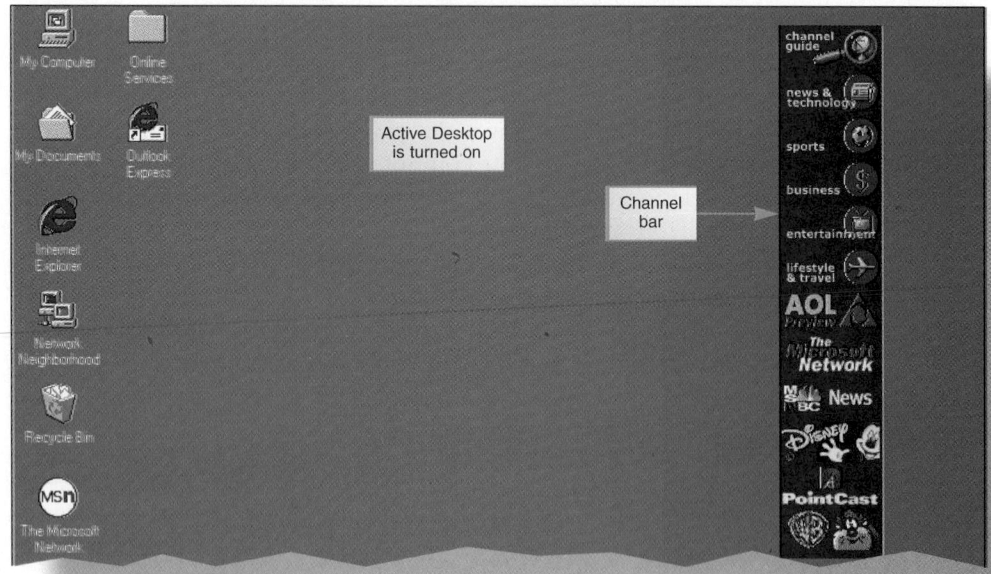

FIGURE 2-66

After turning on the Active Desktop, you can add active content to the Active Desktop.

Adding an Active Desktop Item to the Active Desktop

One method to display Active Web content of the desktop is to use the **Internet Explorer Channel bar** located on the right side of the Active Desktop. The Internet Explorer Channel bar contains **Channel buttons** that allow you to receive active content from Web pages and find new channels. The Channel buttons on the Channel bar in Figure 2-66 have been placed there by Microsoft Corporation to help you understand and use channels. You can customize the Channel bar by removing Channel buttons and adding new channels that are of interest to you.

Another method to display active content on the desktop is to add an Active Desktop item to the desktop. An **Active Desktop item** displays active content from a Web page directly on the Active Desktop and updates the content periodically. Once on the desktop, you can move and resize the item and specify how often you want the active content to be updated.

In the process of adding an Active Desktop item to the desktop, you create a subscription to the channel (Web site) containing the active content. A **subscription** allows the browser (Internet Explorer) to check the Web site to determine if the content has changed and deliver the new content to your desktop. When you **subscribe** to a channel, you have the choice of being notified when new content is available or having the updated content automatically delivered to your desktop. Subscriptions typically are free to the subscriber. Perform the following steps to subscribe to the ESPN SportsZone™ channel and add the ESPN SportsZone™ item to the Active Desktop.

Other Ways

1. Click Start button, point to Settings, point to Active Desktop, click View as Web Page
2. Click Start button, point to Settings, click Folder Options, click Settings button, click Enable all web-related content on my desktop, click OK button, click Close button

More About

The Active Desktop

Windows allows you to view the desktop in three views: Web style, Classic style, and Custom style. When you choose the Web style desktop view, the Active Desktop is automatically turned on, allowing you to view the Channel bar and active content.

Steps: To Subscribe to a Channel and Add an Item to the Active Desktop

1 Right-click an open area on the desktop. Point to Properties on the shortcut menu (Figure 2-67).

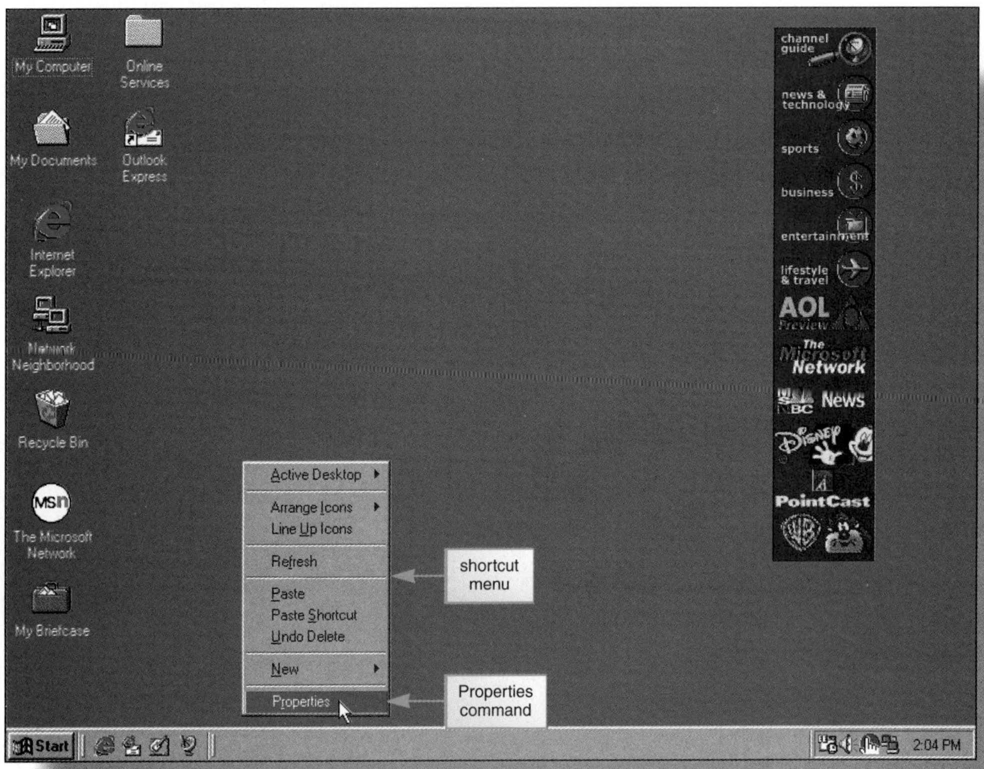

FIGURE 2-67

2 **Click Properties. Point to the Web tab in the Display Properties dialog box.**

The Display Properties dialog box displays (Figure 2-68). Seven tabs (Background, Screen Saver, Appearance, ScreenScan, Web, Effects, and Settings) display in the dialog box. Other tabs may display in the dialog box on your desktop. The Background sheet displays in the dialog box and contains a blank preview monitor, Wallpaper pane, and three command buttons (OK, Cancel, and Apply).

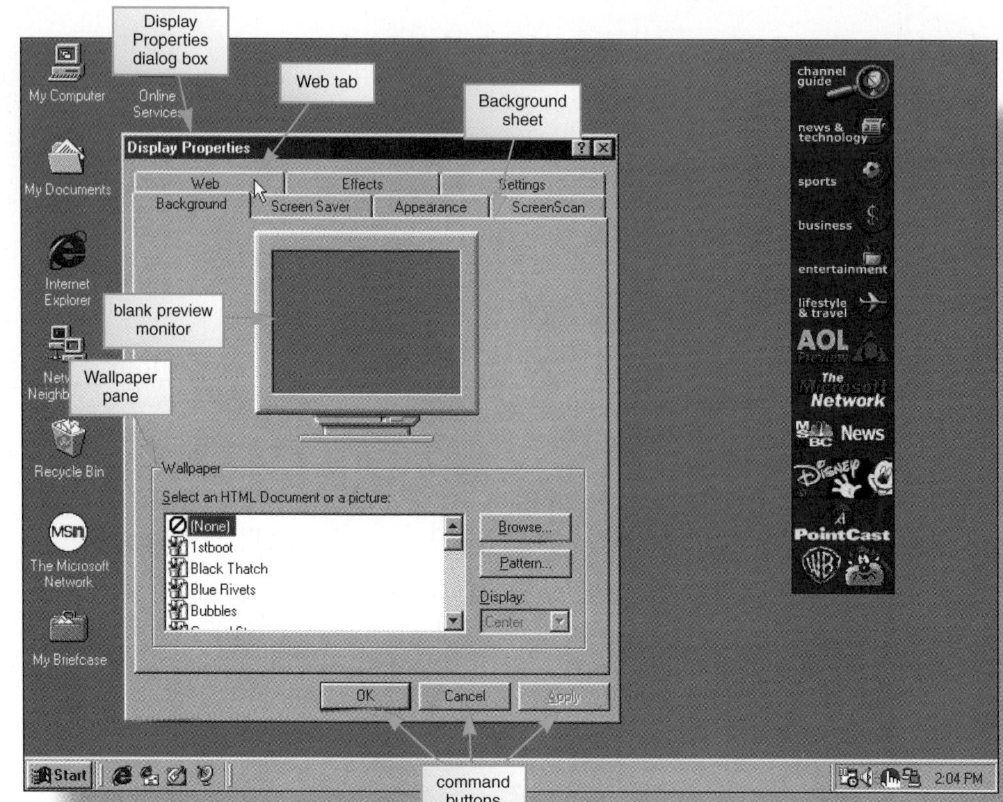

FIGURE 2-68

3 **Click the Web tab. Point to the New button on the Web sheet.**

The Web sheet displays (Figure 2-69). An object (dark blue rectangle) on the monitor illustrates the position of the Internet Explorer Channel bar on the desktop. Below the monitor, the View my Active Desktop as a web page check box is selected indicating the desktop is active. The Internet Explorer Channel bar check box is selected indicating the Channel bar displays on the Active Desktop.

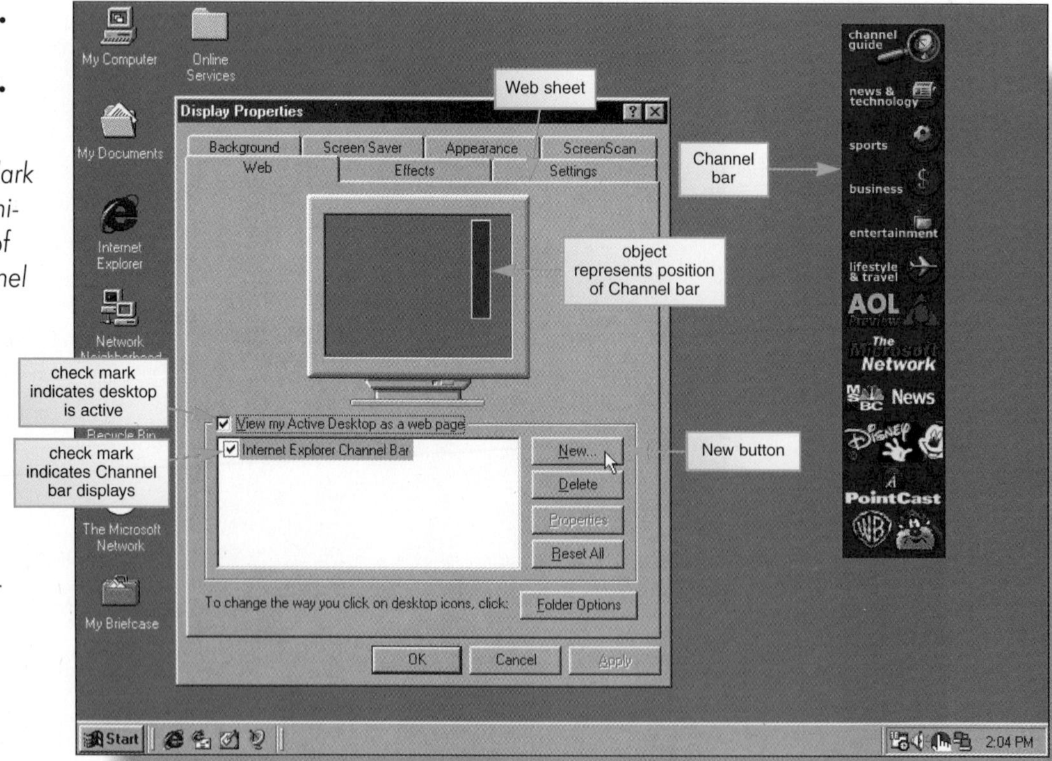

FIGURE 2-69

4 **Click the New button. Point to the Yes button in the New Active Desktop Item dialog box.**

The New Active Desktop Item dialog box displays (Figure 2-70). A message in the dialog box indicates you can visit the ***Active Desktop gallery*** *to preview and add new items to the desktop and you can save and close the Display Properties dialog box. If you click the check box, the dialog box will not display in the future.*

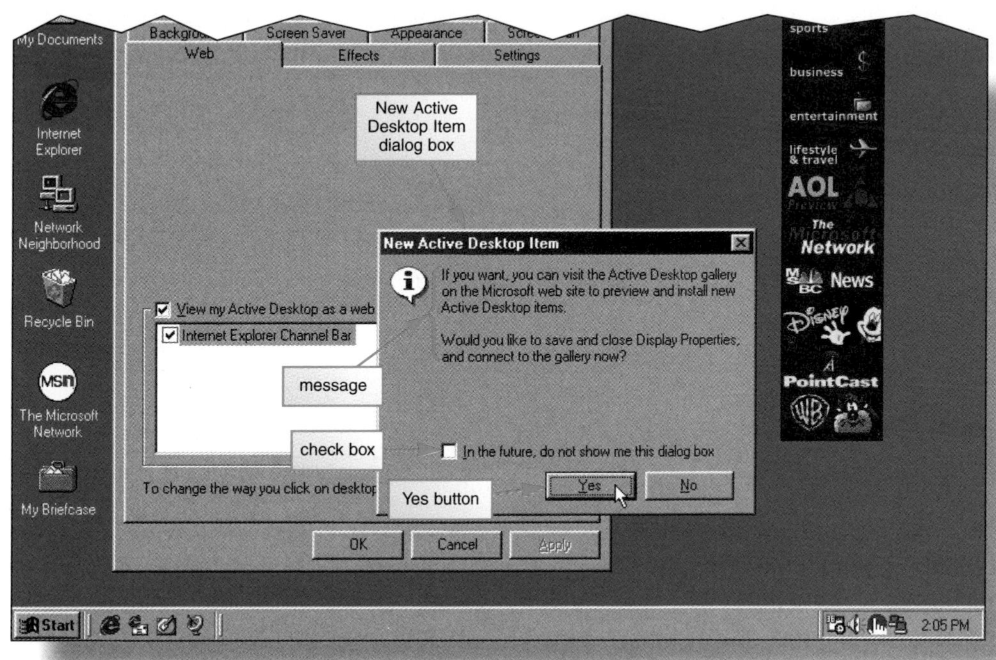

FIGURE 2-70

5 **Click the Yes button. Click the Maximize button in the Desktop Gallery - Microsoft Internet Explorer window. Point to the sports icon in the window.**

Windows 98 launches Microsoft Internet Explorer and displays the maximized Desktop Gallery window (Figure 2-71). The menu bar, Standard Buttons toolbar, and Address bar display at the top of the window. The icons shown in the window represent the categories that contain one or more channels. A message, the Microsoft Investor desktop item, and the Add to Active Desktop button display to the right of the icons.

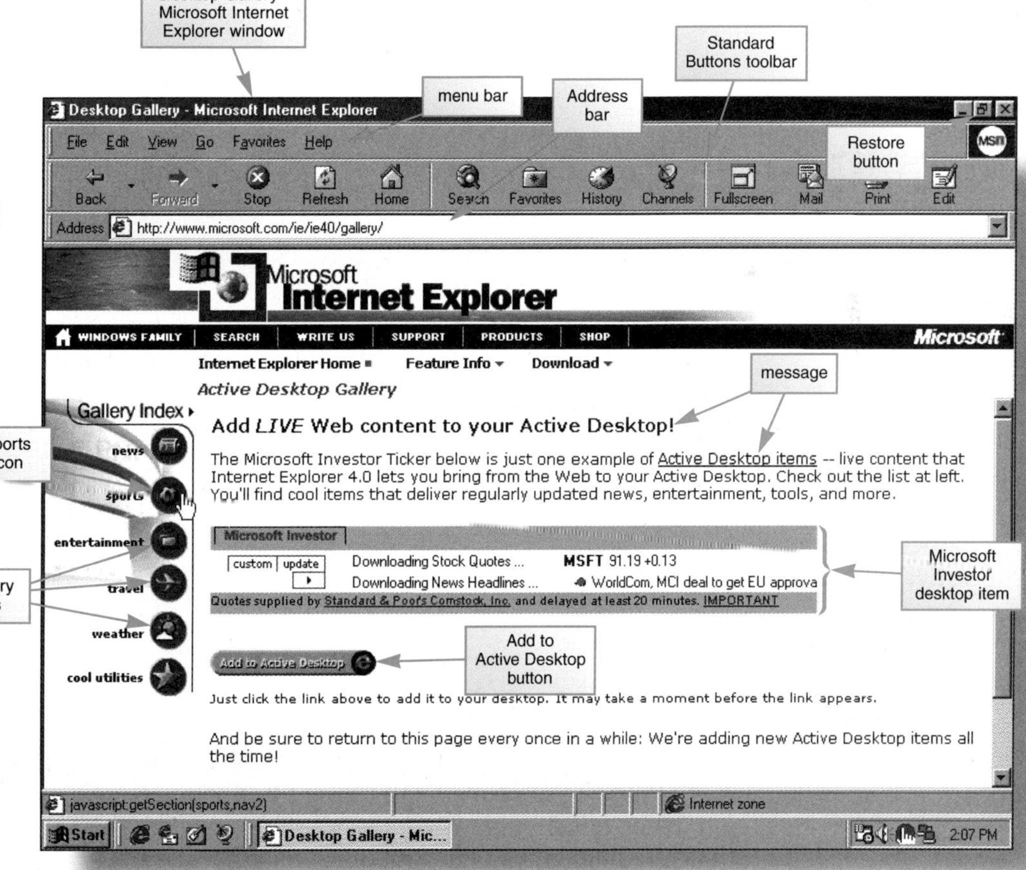

FIGURE 2-71

6 Click the sports icon. Point to the ESPN SportsZone™ channel name.

The sports icon is selected. The information that displayed to the right of the category icons has been replaced with the two channel names in the sports category (CBS Sportscenter and ESPN SportsZone™) (Figure 2-72). The ESPN SportsZone™ channel name displays in red text and the mouse pointer changes to a hand indicating it is positioned on a hyperlink.

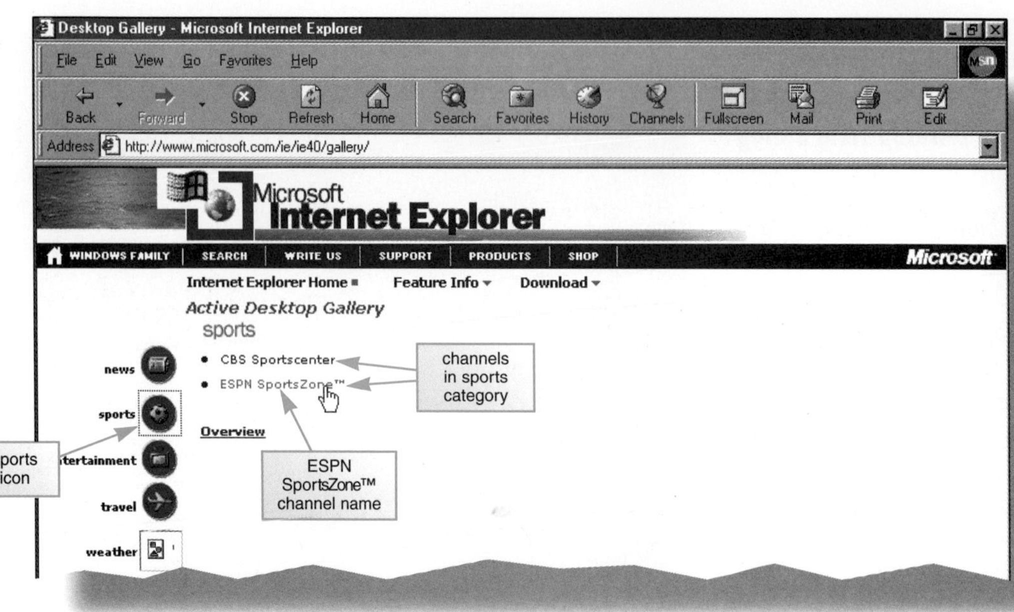

FIGURE 2-72

7 Click the ESPN SportsZone™ channel name. Point to the Add to Active Desktop button.

The ESPN SportsZone™ channel name is selected and a sample of the ESPN SportsZone™ desktop item displays (Figure 2-73).

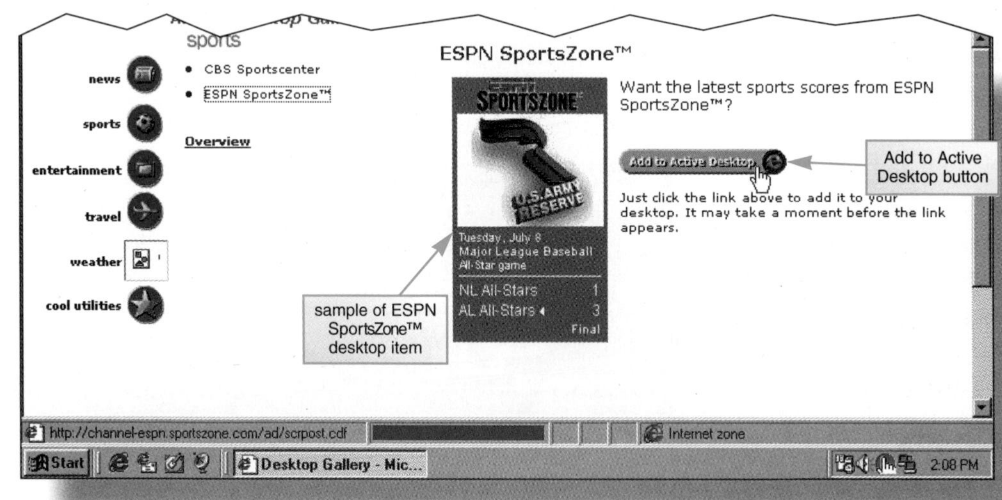

FIGURE 2-73

8 Click the Add to Active Desktop button. Point to the Yes button in the Security Alert dialog box.

The Security Alert dialog box displays (Figure 2-74). A question asks if you want to add a desktop item to the Active Desktop.

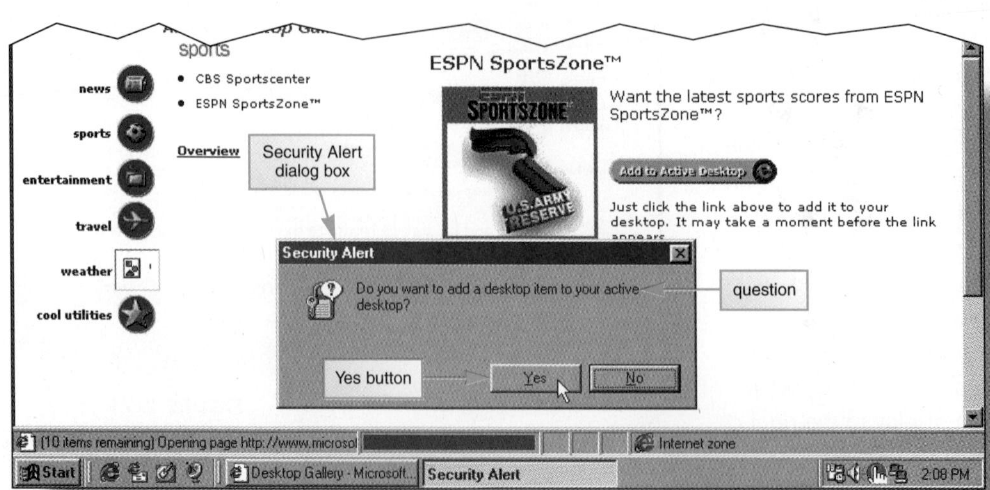

FIGURE 2-74

9 Click the Yes button. Point to the OK button in the Add item to Active Desktop(TM) dialog box.

The Add item to Active Desktop(TM) dialog box displays (Figure 2-75). The dialog box contains a message that indicates you are about to subscribe to a channel, the channel name (Scorepost: ESPN SportsZone), and the Web page URL of the channel.

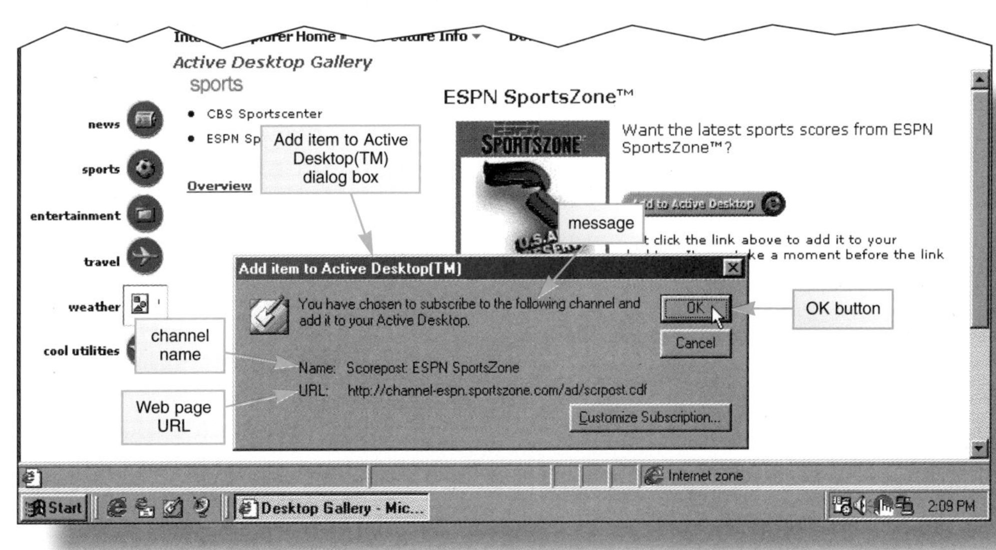

FIGURE 2-75

10 Click the OK button. Point to the Close button in the Desktop Gallery window.

The Downloading Subscriptions dialog box displays on top of the Desktop Gallery window while the connection is made to the Scorepost: ESPN SportsZone™ channel. After the connection is made, the dialog box closes and the desktop item can be viewed by clicking the Close button (Figure 2-76).

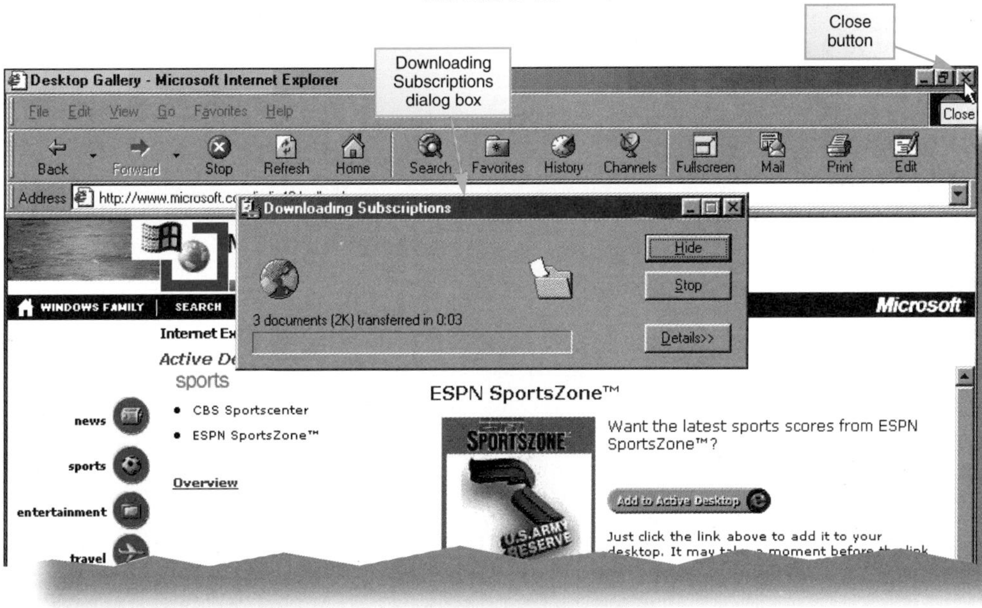

FIGURE 2-76

11 Click the Close button.

The Desktop Gallery window closes and the ESPN SportsZone™ item is visible on the desktop (Figure 2-77). The updated sports scores that display at the bottom of the item change approximately every four seconds.

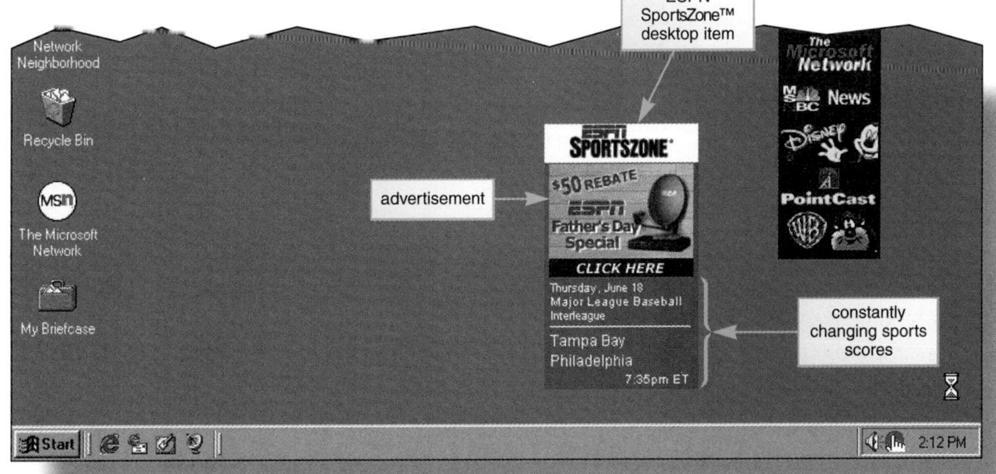

FIGURE 2-77

Other Ways

1. Click Channel button, click channel logo, click Add Active Channel button, click Add to Active Desktop button, click Yes option button, click OK button, click Close button
2. Right-drag sample desktop item from Desktop Gallery (Web page) to desktop, click Create Active Desktop item(s) Here, click Yes button, click OK button

A subscription to the Scorepost: ESPN SportsZone™ channel is established that allows you to view the changing scores of sporting events currently in progress, view the game times of sporting events yet to be played, and obtain additional information about the sporting event that currently displays on the desktop item. Unless changed, updates are performed according to the schedule set by the channel's publisher.

Displaying Additional Information About a Sporting Event

Sometimes, after adding the ESPN SportsZone™ desktop item to the Active Desktop, you may want to display additional information about a sporting event that displays at the bottom of the desktop item. Perform the following steps to display the additional information about a sporting event.

To Display Additional Information About a Sporting Event

1 Point to a score summary at the bottom of the ESPN SportsZone™ desktop item.

The mouse pointer points to the score summary of a baseball game (Figure 2-78).

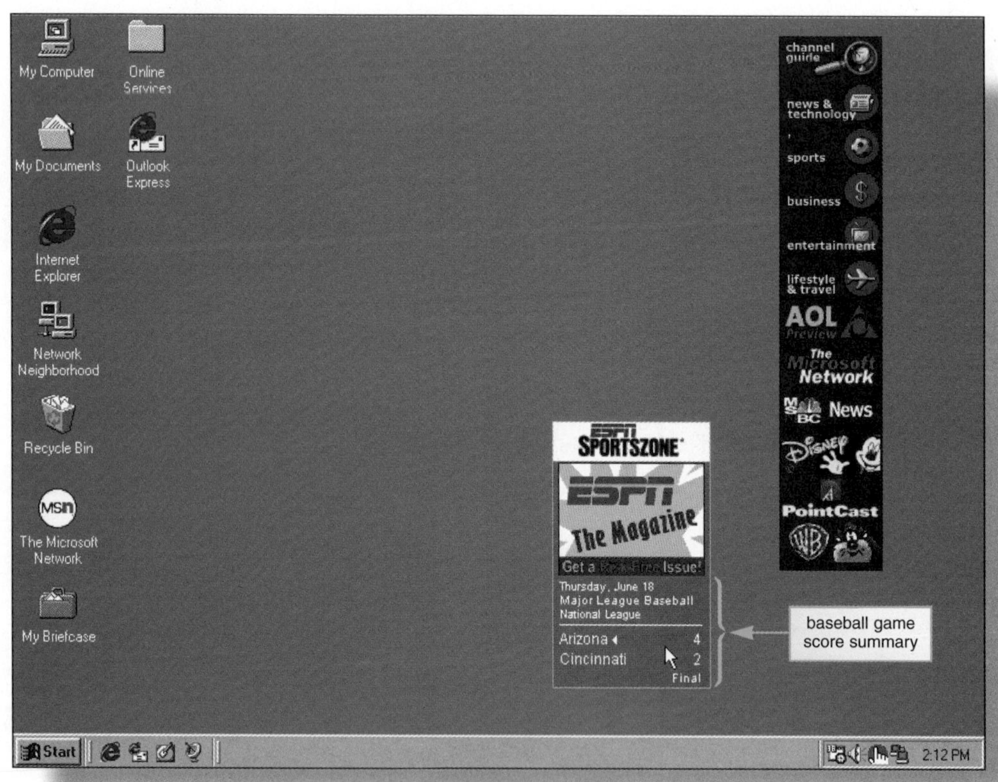

FIGURE 2-78

2 Click the score summary. Click the Maximize button in the Microsoft Internet Explorer window.

The Microsoft Internet Explorer window displays and maximizes (Figure 2-79). The window displays additional information about the sporting event.

3 Scroll the window to read the information about the sporting event. When finished, click the Close button in the Microsoft Internet Explorer window to close the window.

The Microsoft Internet Explorer window closes.

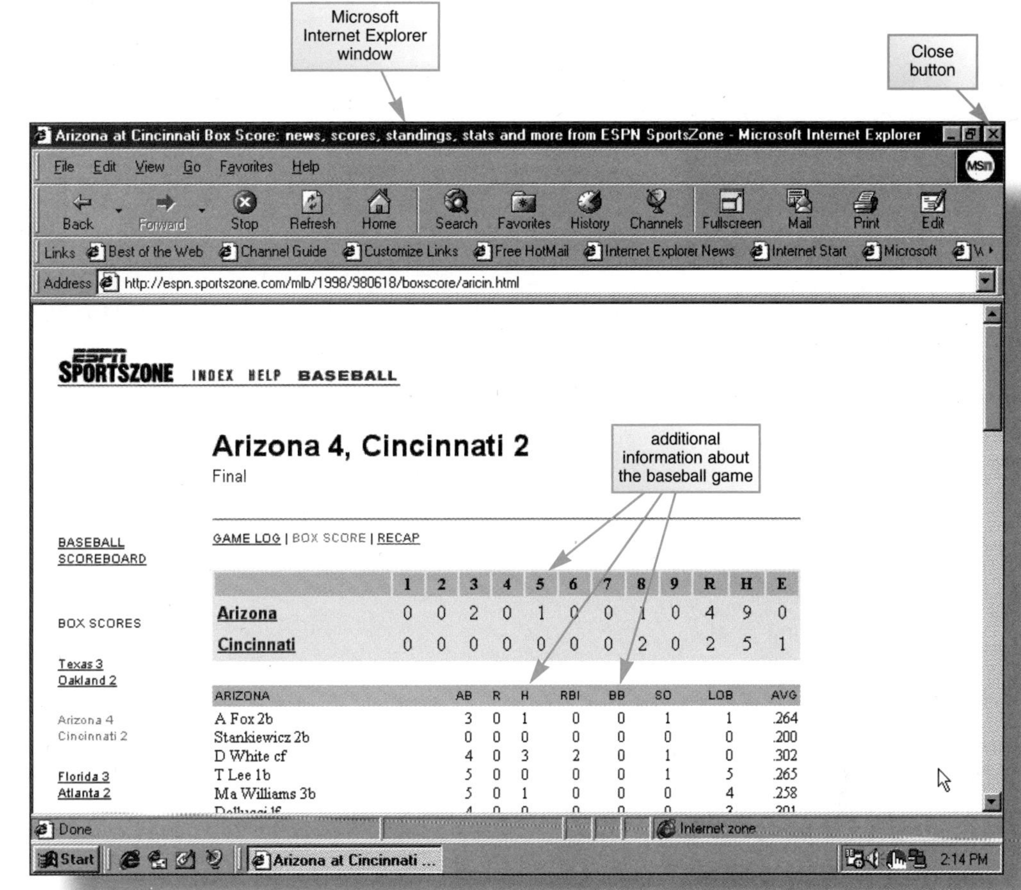

	1	2	3	4	5	6	7	8	9	R	H	E
Arizona	0	0	2	0	1	0	0	1	0	4	9	0
Cincinnati	0	0	0	0	0	0	0	2	0	2	5	1

ARIZONA	AB	R	H	RBI	BB	SO	LOB	AVG
A Fox 2b	3	0	1	0	0	1	1	.264
Stankiewicz 2b	0	0	0	0	0	0	0	.200
D White cf	4	0	3	2	0	1	0	.302
T Lee 1b	5	0	0	0	0	1	5	.265
Ma Williams 3b	5	0	1	0	0	0	4	.258

FIGURE 2-79

Removing a Desktop Item from the Active Desktop

When you no longer use a desktop item on the Active Desktop, remove the item from the desktop. In the process of removing the item from the desktop, the subscription to its associated channel also can be canceled. Perform the steps on the next two pages to remove the ESPN SportsZone™ item and cancel the subscription to the Scorepost: ESPN SportsZone™ channel.

More About

The Active Desktop™

After adding an Active Desktop item to the desktop, you can move the item. To move it, point to the desktop item name displayed at the top of the item and then drag the gray bar that displays to a new position on the desktop. Point anywhere off the gray bar to remove the gray bar.

To Remove a Desktop Item from the Active Desktop and Cancel a Subscription

1 Right-click an open area on the desktop. Click Properties on the shortcut menu. Click the Web tab in the Display Properties dialog box. Point to the Scorepost: ESPN SportsZone title.

The Display Properties dialog box displays (Figure 2-80). Check marks in the Internet Explorer Channel Bar and Scorepost: ESPN SportsZone check boxes and the two objects on the monitor indicate the Channel bar and ESPN SportsZone™ items display on the desktop.

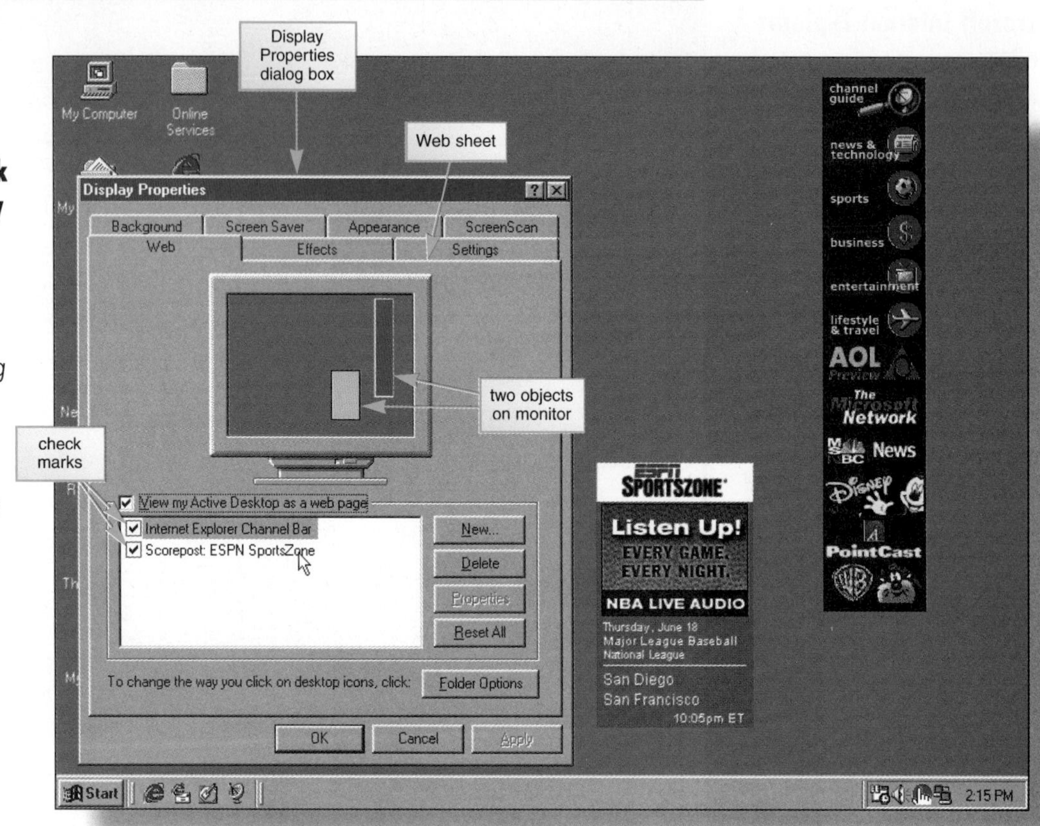

FIGURE 2-80

2 Click Scorepost: ESPN SportsZone to highlight the title. Point to the Delete button.

The Internet Explorer Channel Bar title no longer is highlighted. The Scorepost: ESPN SportsZone title is highlighted (Figure 2-81).

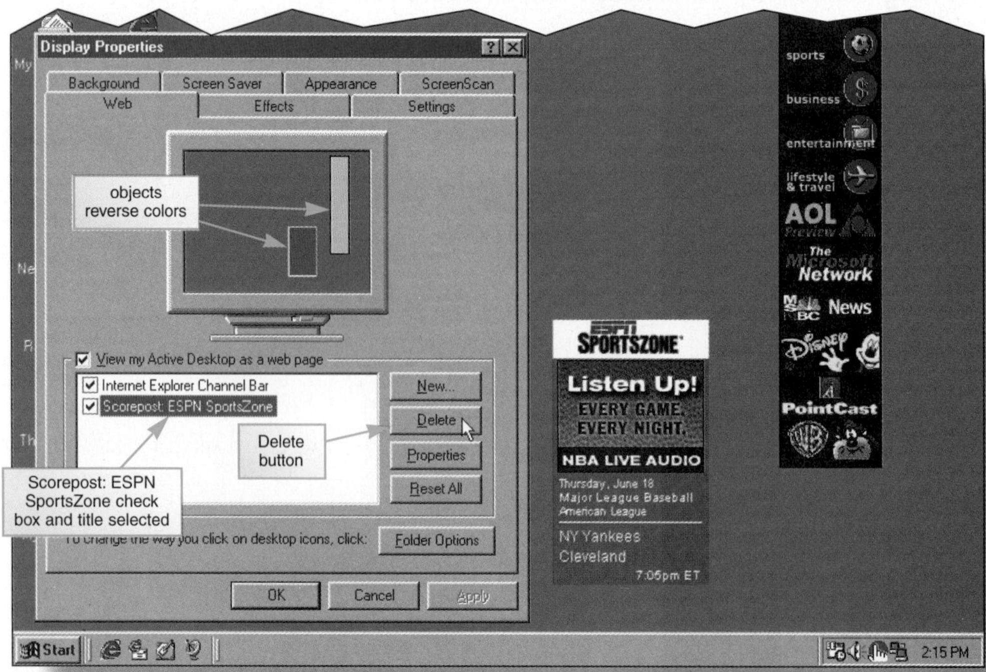

FIGURE 2-81

3 **Click the Delete button. Point to the Yes button in the Active Desktop Item dialog box.**

The Active Desktop Item dialog box displays (Figure 2-82). The question, Are you sure you want to delete this item from your Active Desktop?, displays in the dialog box. Clicking the Yes button will terminate the subscription to the Scorepost: ESPN SportsZone channel.

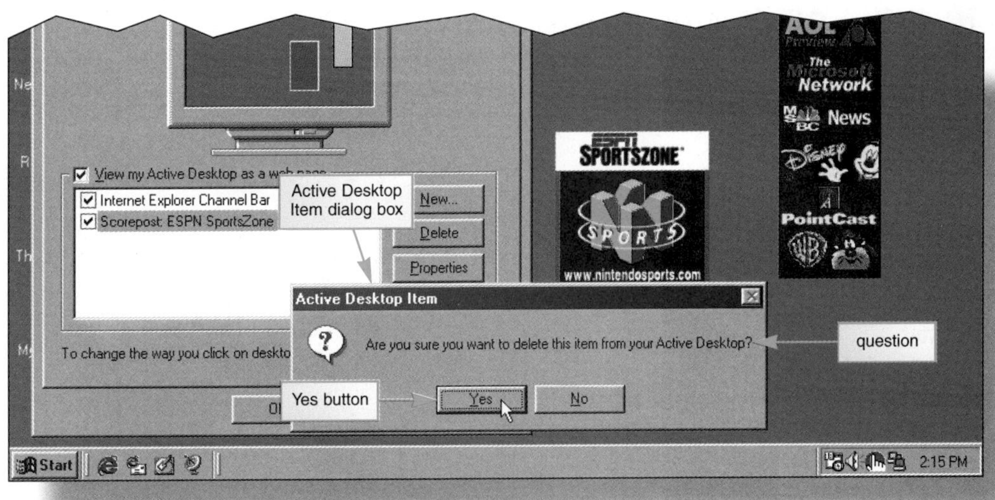

FIGURE 2-82

4 **Click the Yes button. Point to the OK button in the Display Properties dialog box.**

The Scorepost: ESPN SportsZone check box and title and the object that represents it are deleted from the Display Properties dialog box, and the subscription to the Scorepost: ESPN SportsZone channel is canceled (Figure 2-83).

**Click the OK button.**

The Scorepost: ESPN SportsZone item no longer displays on the desktop.

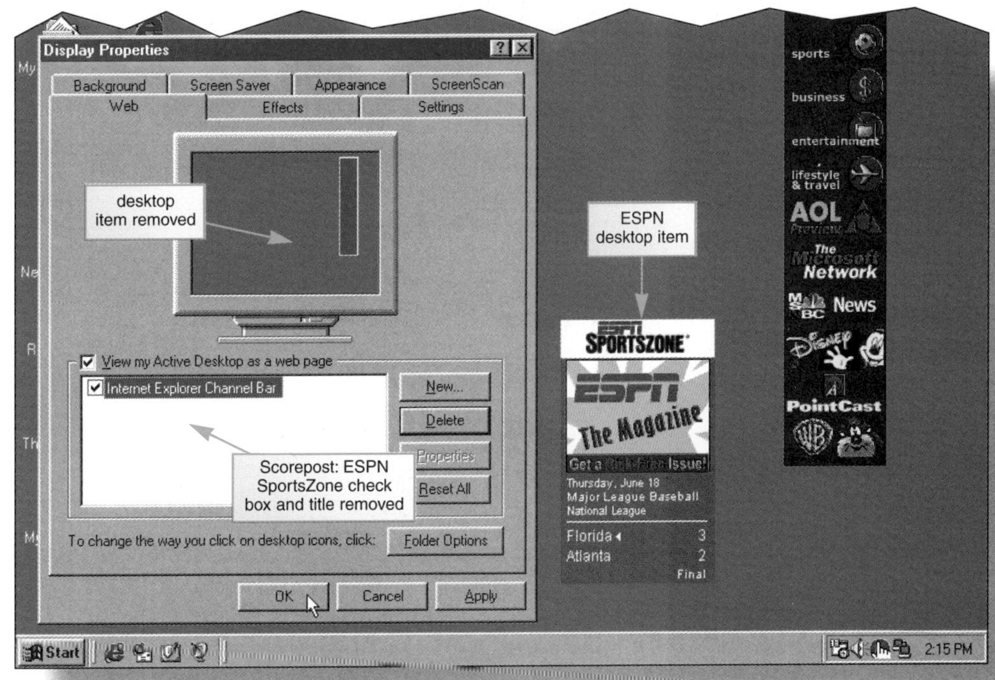

FIGURE 2-83

If after removing a desktop item from the Active Desktop, you wish to return the item to the desktop, follow the steps illustrated on pages WIN 2.49 through WIN 2.53 to add the item to the Active Desktop.

Other Ways

1. Point to desktop item name on Active Desktop item, click down arrow button on gray bar, click Customize My Desktop, click channel name, click Delete button, click Yes button, click OK button
2. Point to desktop item name on Active Desktop item, click Close button on gray bar

Turning Off the Active Desktop

When you no longer want the Channel bar or active content on the desktop, you can turn off the Active Desktop. When the Active Desktop is turned off, the Internet Explorer Channel bar is removed from the desktop and the desktop no longer is active. Perform the steps on the next page to turn off the Active Desktop.

To Turn Off the Active Desktop

1 Right-click an open area of the desktop, point to Active Desktop on the shortcut menu, and then point to View As Web Page on the Active Desktop submenu.

A shortcut menu and the Active Desktop submenu display (Figure 2-84). A check mark precedes the View As Web Page command on the Active Desktop submenu to indicate the Active Desktop is turned on.

Click View As Web Page.

The Active Desktop is turned off and the Internet Channel bar, shortcut menu, and Active Desktop submenu no longer display on the desktop.

Other Ways

1. Click Start button, point to Settings, point to Active Desktop, click View as Web Page
2. Click Start button, point to Settings, click Folder Options, click Settings button, click Use Windows classic desktop, click OK button, click Close button

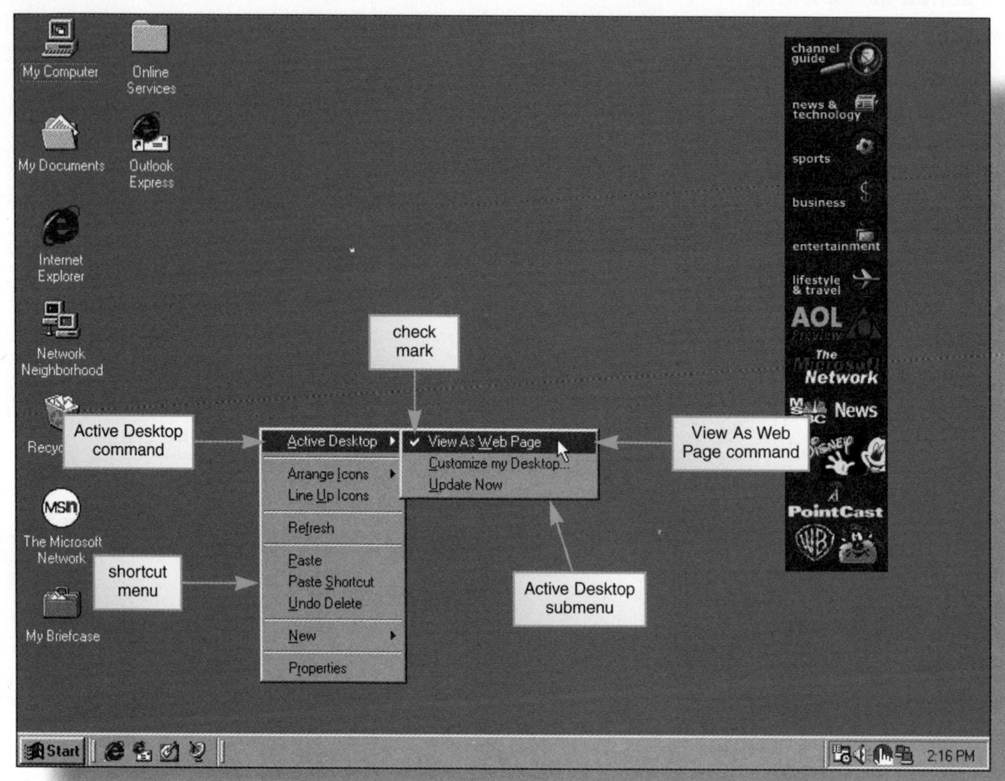

FIGURE 2-84

Using Microsoft Support Online

Windows Help provides a variety of ways in which to obtain information. In Project 1, you browsed through Help topics by category using the Contents sheet. Next, you found answers to questions about Windows 98 by searching entries in the Index sheet and viewing Help screens.

Another way to obtain information about Windows 98 is to use Microsoft Support Online. **Microsoft Support Online** allows you to use the Internet to search for Help about Windows 98 using the **Microsoft Windows Update Web site**. Because the information on the Internet can be easily updated, the information you obtain using Microsoft Support Online is more current than the information contained in the Windows Contents and Index sheets.

To obtain Help using **Microsoft Support Online**, you select the Microsoft product about which you want information and then construct a search inquiry. You can use a keyword, or Boolean, search or a natural language search to find the information. A **keyword**, or **Boolean, search** can consist of a single word (desktop), or a phrase (active desktop), while a **natural language search** uses keywords (How do I save changes to a document?). Words such as save, change, and document are keywords. Windows Support Online searches its collection of information, called the **Knowledge Database**, and displays a list of articles that relate to your search inquiry. The following table lists types of searches, examples of search inquiries, and the results of searching using the inquiries.

In this project, you will use Windows Support Online and the Internet to obtain Help about Windows Update. **Windows Update** is an application included with Windows 98 that allows you to keep the Windows 98 operating system on your computer up to date by obtaining current system information from the Microsoft Support Online site. The search inquiry to obtain help about Windows Update consists of the natural language question, What is Windows Update? Perform the following steps to obtain help about Windows Update.

Table 2-1

SEARCH TYPE	SEARCH INQUIRY	SEARCH RESULTS
Word	desktop	Articles containing the word, desktop
Phrase	active desktop	Articles containing the phrase, active desktop
Wild card (*)	hyper*	Articles containing words with the same first characters (hyperlink, hypertext, hypermedia)
Wild card (*.*)	close*.*	Articles containing all forms of the word (close, closing, closed, closes)
AND Boolean operator	open AND maximize	Articles containing both words (open, maximize)
NEAR Boolean operator	open NEAR maximize	Articles in which the two words are located closest to each other are listed first in the list of articles
AND NOT Boolean operator	close AND NOT a window	Articles containing the first word (close) but not the phrase (close a window)
Knowledge Database article number	Q155353	Articles identified by the Knowledge Database characters, Q155353
Natural language	How do I save changes to a document?	Articles containing the keywords in the search inquiry (save, change, document)

To Use Windows Support Online

1 Click the Start button on the taskbar. Click Help on the Start menu. Point to the Web Help button on the Help toolbar.

The Windows Help window opens (Figure 2-85).

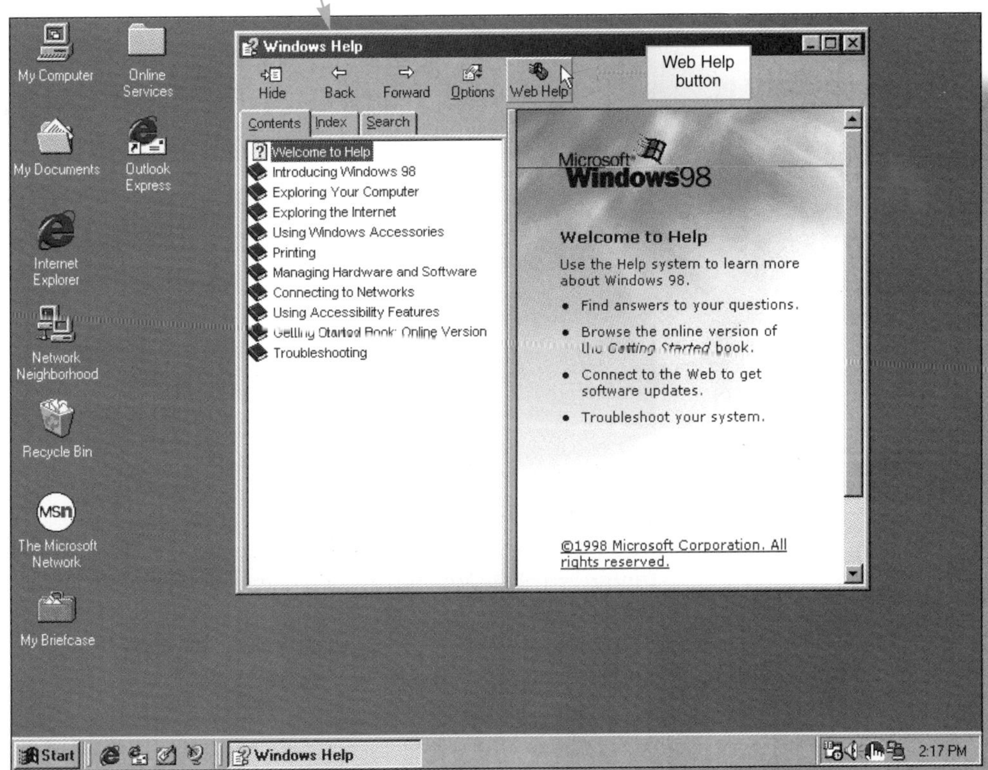

FIGURE 2-85

2 Click the Web Help button. Point to the Support Online hyperlink in the right frame.

Information about Support Online displays in the right frame of the Windows Help window (Figure 2-86).

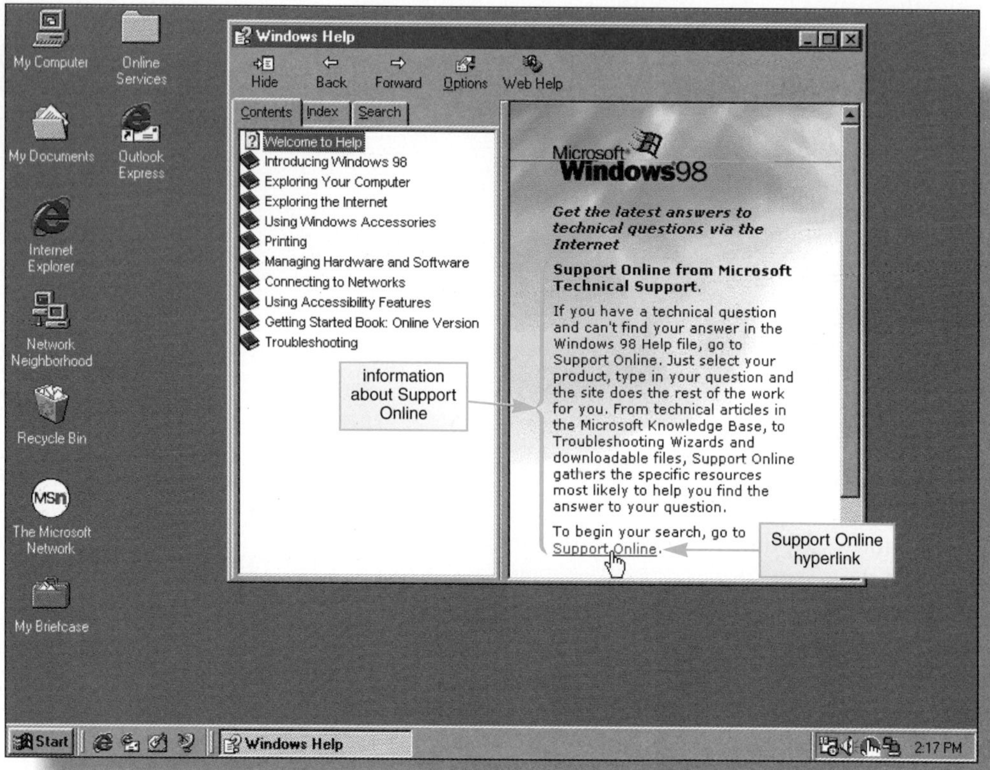

FIGURE 2-86

3 Click Support Online. Click the Asking a question using Natural Language Search option button. Type `What is Windows Update?` **in the My question is text box. Point to the find button.**

The Support Online window displays (Figure 2-87). A menu displays in the left frame and Advanced View options display in the right frame. Windows 98 displays in the My search is about box, the Asking a question using Natural Language Search option button is selected, and the My question is text box contains the search inquiry. The URL of the Web page displays in the Address bar.

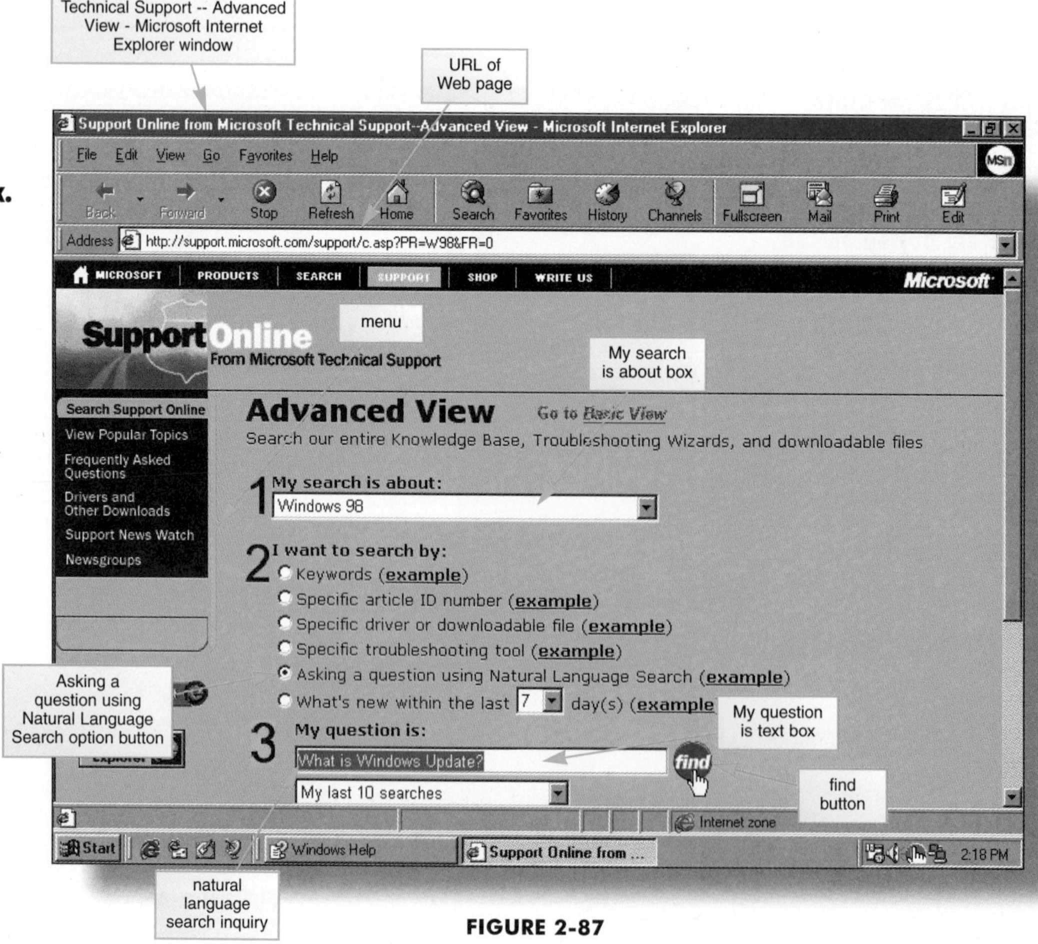

FIGURE 2-87

4 Click the find button. If necessary, scroll to display the Windows Update article. Point to the Windows Update article name. If this article name does not display, point to another article name.

Windows 98 searches the database of information about Windows 98 and displays a list of article names in the window (Figure 2-88). The URL changes to reflect the current Web page. Because information on the Internet can change frequently, the list of article names on your computer may be different.

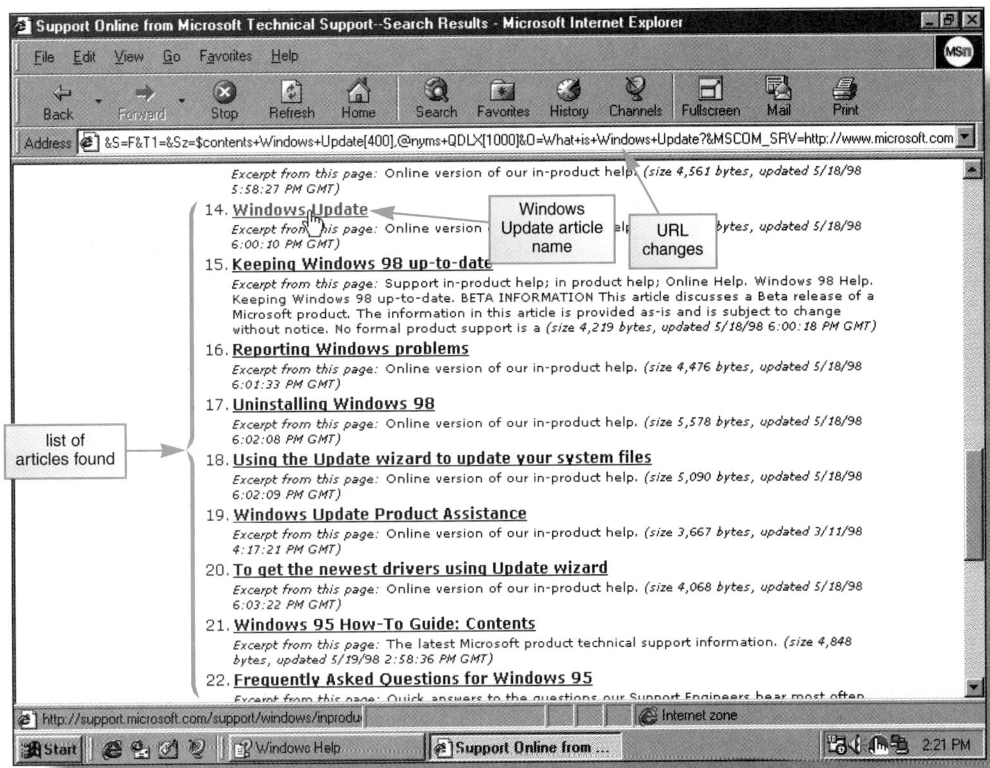

FIGURE 2-88

5 Click Windows Update. If necessary, scroll the window to read the information about Windows Update. Point to the Close button in the window.

The content of the Windows Update article displays in the window (Figure 2-89). The URL changes to reflect the current Web page.

6 Click the Close button. Click the Close button in the Windows Help window.

The Windows Update and Windows Help windows close.

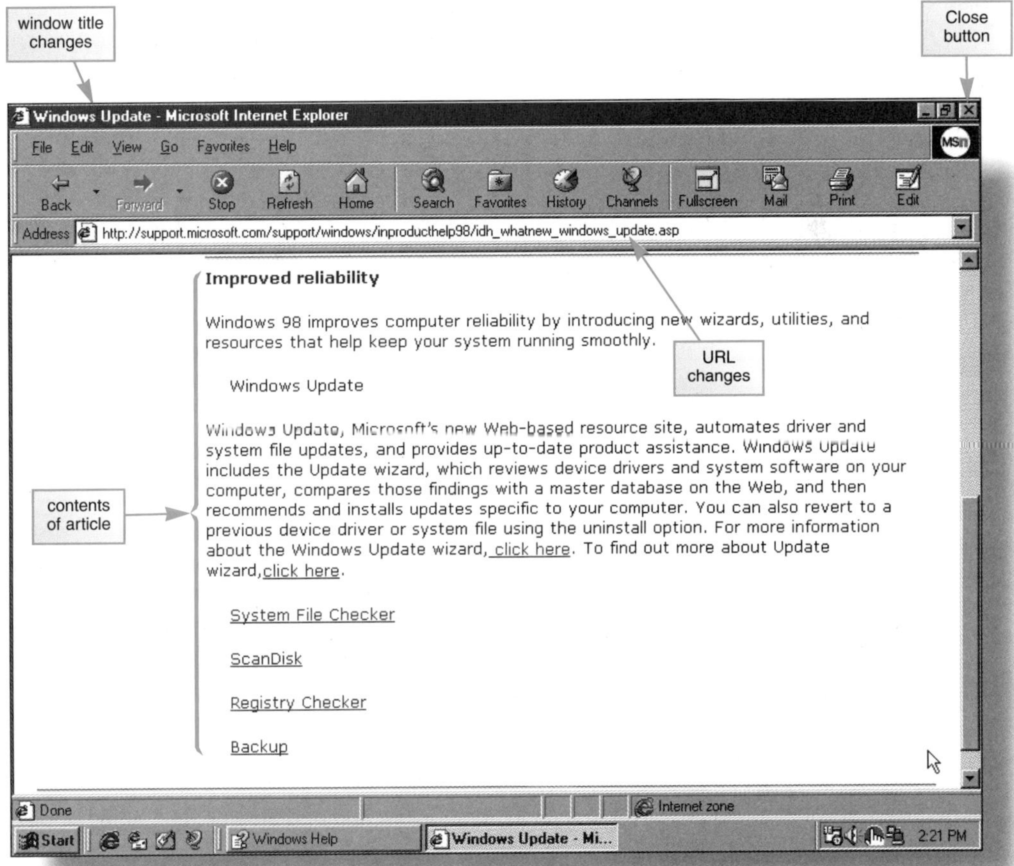

FIGURE 2-89

Windows 98 Web Help

Microsoft Support Online was not available in previous versions of Windows. Microsoft Support Online replaces the need for lengthy, hard-to-understand technical manuals. Because the Help information in Microsoft Support Online can be updated quickly by Microsoft, it provides the most up-to-date technical information, answers to frequently asked questions, and late-breaking tips about working with Windows 98.

Shutting Down Windows

After completing your work, you may wish to shut down Windows 98 using the Shut Down command on the Start menu. If you are sure you want to shut down Windows 98, perform the following steps. If you are not sure about shutting down Windows 98, read the following steps without actually performing them.

TO SHUT DOWN WINDOWS 98

1. Click the Start button on the taskbar and then point to Shut Down on the Start menu.
2. Click Shut Down and then click the OK button in the Shut Down Windows dialog box.

If you accidentally click Shut Down on the Start menu and you do not want to shut down Windows 98, click the Cancel button in the Shut Down Windows dialog box.

Project Summary

In this project you used the application-centric approach and document-centric approach to create two text documents on the desktop and then modified and printed these documents. Using a shortcut menu, you created a folder on the desktop and then placed the documents in the folder and copied the folder onto a floppy disk in drive A. You worked with multiple documents open at the same time. You placed a document shortcut on both the Start menu and desktop and removed the shortcuts. Using various methods, you deleted shortcuts, documents, and a folder from the desktop. You learned about the Active Desktop, turned on the Active Desktop, added an item to the Active Desktop, displayed additional information about a sporting event, removed the item, and turned off the Active Desktop. Finally, you used Windows Support Online to search for Help about Windows 98.

What You Should Know

Having completed this project, you now should be able to perform the following tasks:

- Close a Document *(WIN 2.12)*
- Close and Save a Modified Document on the Desktop *(WIN 2.16)*
- Close and Save Open Windows from the Taskbar *(WIN 2.27)*
- Copy a Folder on the Desktop onto a Floppy Disk *(WIN 2.30)*
- Create a Blank Document on the Desktop *(WIN 2.13)*
- Create a Shortcut on the Desktop *(WIN 2.39)*
- Create and Name a Folder on the Desktop *(WIN 2.18)*
- Delete a Folder from the Desktop *(WIN 2.47)*
- Delete a Shortcut from the Desktop *(WIN 2.43)*
- Delete Multiple Files *(WIN 2.45)*
- Display Additional Information About a Sporting Event *(WIN 2.54)*
- Display the Arrange Icons Submenu *(WIN 2.42)*
- Enter Data into a Blank Document *(WIN 2.16)*
- Launch a Program and Create a Document *(WIN 2.6)*
- Minimize All Open Windows *(WIN 2.26)*
- Move a Document into a Folder *(WIN 2.19)*
- Name a Document on the Desktop *(WIN 2.14)*
- Open a Document on the Desktop *(WIN 2.15)*
- Open a Document Using a Shortcut on the Desktop *(WIN 2.41)*
- Open a Document Using the Start Menu *(WIN 2.36)*
- Open a Folder *(WIN 2.21)*
- Open a Folder Stored on a Floppy Disk *(WIN 2.32)*
- Open an Inactive Window *(WIN 2.25)*
- Open and Modify a Document in a Folder *(WIN 2.22)*
- Open and Modify Multiple Documents *(WIN 2.23)*
- Place a Document Shortcut on the Start Menu *(WIN 2.34)*
- Print a Document *(WIN 2.11)*
- Print Multiple Documents from Within a Folder *(WIN 2.28)*
- Remove a Desktop Item from the Active Desktop and Cancel a Subscription (*WIN 2.56*)
- Remove a Shortcut from the Start Menu *(WIN 2.37)*
- Save a Document on the Desktop *(WIN 2.8)*
- Shut Down Windows 98 *(WIN 2.62)*
- Subscribe to a Channel and Add an Item to the Active Desktop (*WIN 2.49*)
- Turn on the Active Desktop (*WIN 2.48*)
- Turn off the Active Desktop (*WIN 2.58*)
- Use Windows Support Online *(WIN 2.59)*

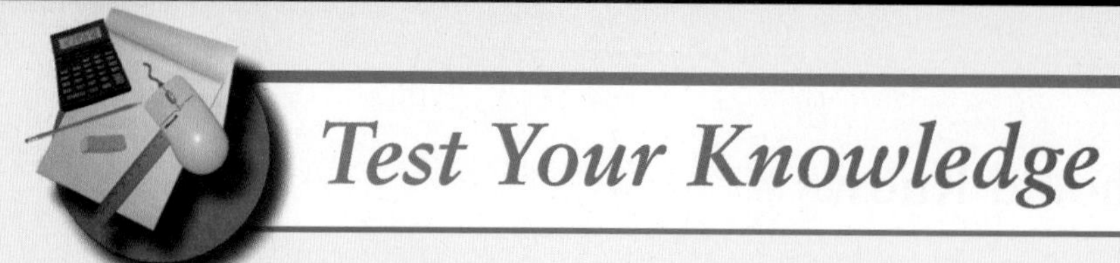

Test Your Knowledge

1 True/False

Instructions: Circle T if the statement is true or F if the statement is false.

T F 1. Application-centric means a user thinks in terms of the application program used to create a document rather than the document itself.

T F 2. To create a text document directly on the desktop, right-click the desktop, point to New on the shortcut menu, and click Text Document on the New submenu.

T F 3. To open a document stored on the desktop, click the Start button, point to Programs, and then click the document name on the Programs submenu.

T F 4. To create a folder on the desktop, right-click the desktop and then click Folder on the shortcut menu.

T F 5. When you drag a document into a folder on the desktop, you must click Move Here on the shortcut menu to place the document in the folder.

T F 6. To open a folder stored on the desktop, double-click the folder icon.

T F 7. The concept of multiple programs running at the same time is called multitasking.

T F 8. You can create a shortcut on both the desktop and Start menu.

T F 9. One way to view Active Web content on your desktop is to add an Active Desktop item to your desktop.

T F 10. The Help information you obtain while using Windows Support Online is located on the Internet.

2 Multiple Choice

Instructions: Circle the correct response.

1. A(n) __________ is a program that allows you to accomplish a specific task for which the program is designed.
   a. document
   b. operating system
   c. user interface
   d. application
2. To create a text document on the desktop, __________.
   a. click the desktop, click Text Document
   b. right-click the desktop, point to New, click Text Document
   c. click the desktop, point to Document, and click Text Document
   d. right-click the desktop, point to New, click Document
3. To open an inactive window, __________.
   a. click the inactive window's button in the taskbar button area
   b. press ALT+TAB until the name of the window displays, and then release the keys
   c. click the inactive window's button on the Start menu
   d. both a and b

Test Your Knowledge

4. To select two documents within a folder, __________.
   a. right-drag any single document
   b. click File on the menu bar and then click Select All
   c. click one document icon, hold down the SHIFT key, and click the other document icon
   d. click the folder title bar
5. A shortcut is __________.
   a. a program that makes your work easier and faster
   b. an icon that represents a document or an application program
   c. any icon found in an open window
   d. another name for a button in the taskbar button area
6. To open a document using the Start menu, __________.
   a. double-click the document name on the Start menu
   b. click the document name on the Start menu
   c. right-click the document name on the Start menu
   d. point to the document name on the Start menu
7. When you delete a shortcut from the desktop, __________.
   a. the shortcut is deleted permanently
   b. Windows 98 will display an error message in a dialog box because you cannot delete a shortcut from the desktop
   c. the shortcut and the related file are placed in the Recycle Bin
   d. the shortcut is placed in the Recycle Bin
8. Which of the following is not a way to delete an object from the desktop? __________.
   a. Right-drag the object to the Recycle Bin.
   b. Drag the object to the Recycle Bin.
   c. Click the object and then click Delete on the shortcut menu.
   d. Right-click the object and then click Delete on the shortcut menu.
9. Using the words, Start menu, as a search inquiry would result in the articles containing __________ to display.
   a. the phrase, Start menu
   b. both the word, Start, and the word, menu
   c. the word, Start, but not the word, menu
   d. Q155353
10. When you add an Active Desktop item to the Active Desktop, you also __________ to a __________.
    a. add a button, toolbar
    b. add active content, window
    c. subscribe, channel
    d. move a window, new location

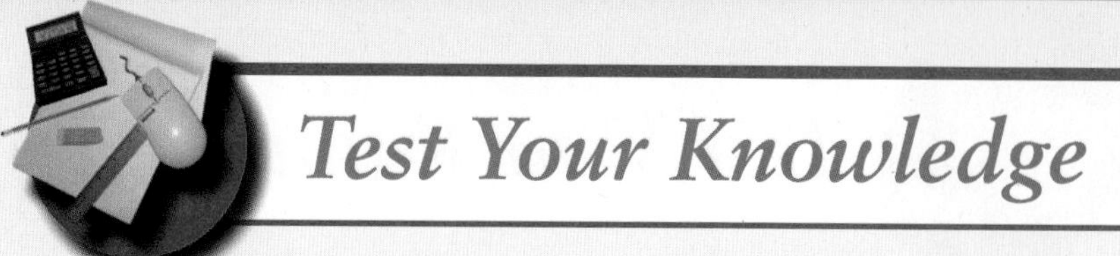

Test Your Knowledge

3 Working with Folders and Documents

Instructions: The open Business Documents folder displays on the desktop shown in Figure 2-90. The Address Book and Daily Appointments documents are stored in the Business Documents folder. In the spaces below, write the steps to accomplish the tasks indicated.

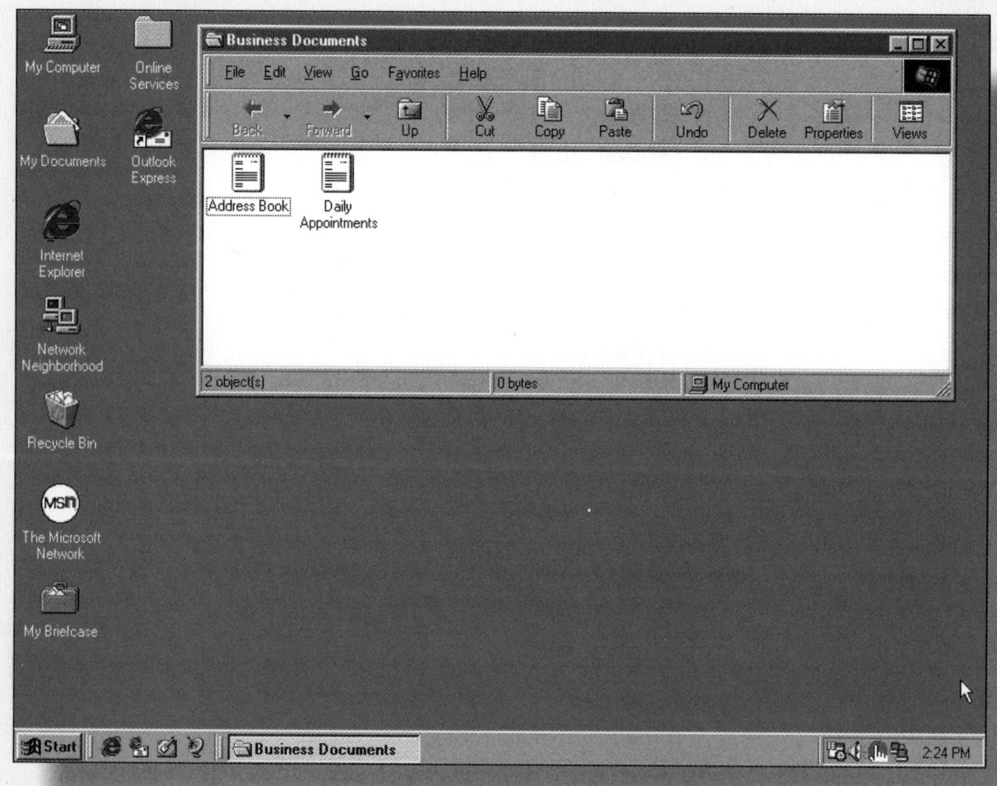

FIGURE 2-90

To Print the Address Book document

Step 1: Right-click on the Addressbook icon

Step 2: Click Print on the shortcut menu

To Copy the Daily Appointments document to the desktop

Step 1: Right click the Daily appointments icon & click copy

Step 2: Right click the Desktop & click paste + click Desktop as shortcut

To Delete the Address Book document from the Business Documents folder

Method 1:

Step 1: Right-click on the Adress Book icon

Step 2: Click Delete on the shortcut menu

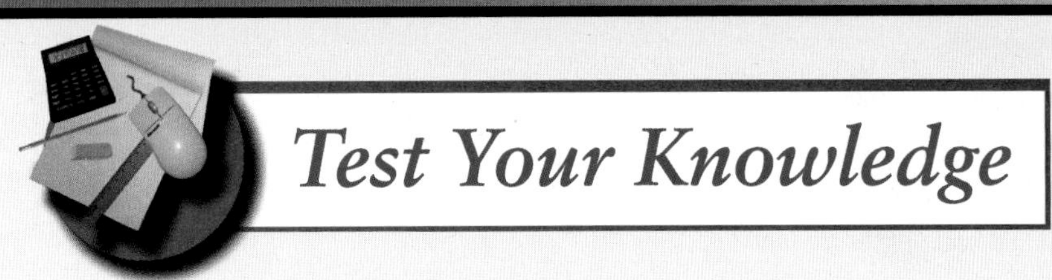

Test Your Knowledge

Method 2:

Step 1: Click on the Address book icon to select it

Step 2: click edit on the menu bar X No, click file

Step 3: click delete

Method 3:

Step 1: Drag the Address book icon to the recycle bin

To Delete the Business Documents folder from the desktop

Method 1: close folder 1st

Step 1: Right drag the Business Documents folder to the recycle Bin

Step 2: click move here, X

Method 2: close folder 1st

Step 1: Right click the Business Documents folder

Step 2: click Delete on the shortcut menu

Step 3: click yes to confirm

Method 3: close folder 1st

Step 1: Drag the Business Documents folder to the Recycle bin

4 Working with Document Shortcuts

Instructions: The closed Sales Document folder on the desktop contains the Monthly Sales document. In the spaces provided below, write the steps to accomplish the tasks indicated.

To place a document shortcut for the Monthly Sales document on the Start menu

Step 1: ________

Step 2: ________

To open the Monthly Sales document from the Start menu

Step 1: ________

Step 2: ________

To remove the Monthly Sales shortcut from the Start menu

Step 1: ________

Step 2: ________

Step 3: ________

Step 4: ________

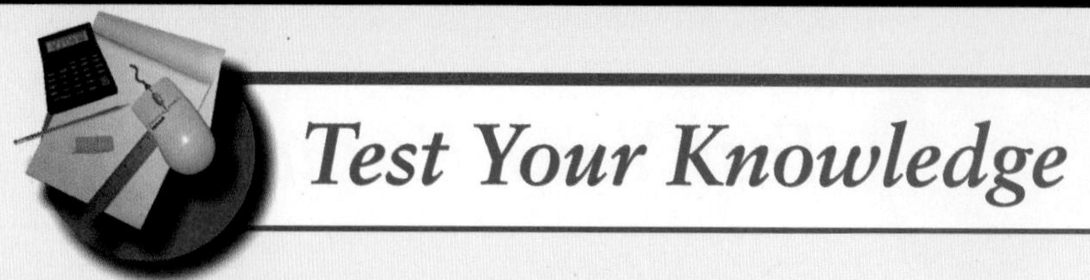

5 Adding a Desktop Item to the Active Desktop

Instructions: List the steps in the spaces provided to add the ESPN SportsZone™ desktop item to the Active Desktop.

Step 1: ____________________

Step 2: ____________________

Step 3: ____________________

Step 4: ____________________

Step 5: ____________________

Step 6: ____________________

Step 7: ____________________

Step 8: ____________________

Step 9: ____________________

Step 10: ____________________

Step 11: ____________________

1 Finding Terms and Definitions in the Windows Glossary

Instructions: Use a computer and Windows Help to perform the following tasks.

Part 1: ***Creating a Document on the Desktop***

1. Start Windows 98 and connect to the Internet if necessary.
2. Create a text document on the desktop. Name the document Windows Definitions.
3. Double-click the Windows Definitions document icon to open the document. Maximize the Windows Definitions - Notepad window.

Part 2: ***Launching Windows Help and Using the Glossary***

1. Click the Start button on the taskbar.
2. Click Help on the Start menu.
3. Click the Web Help button on the Help toolbar.
4. Click the Support Online hyperlink in the right frame of the Windows Help window.
5. Click the View Popular Topics command in the menu in the left frame.
6. Click the Choose a Popular Topic box arrow and then click Glossary in the list.
7. Click the go button.
8. If the Security Alert dialog box displays, click the Yes button.
9. If the Internet Redirection dialog box displays, click the Yes button. The title, Glossary, and the letters of the alphabet display in the window (Figure 2-91).

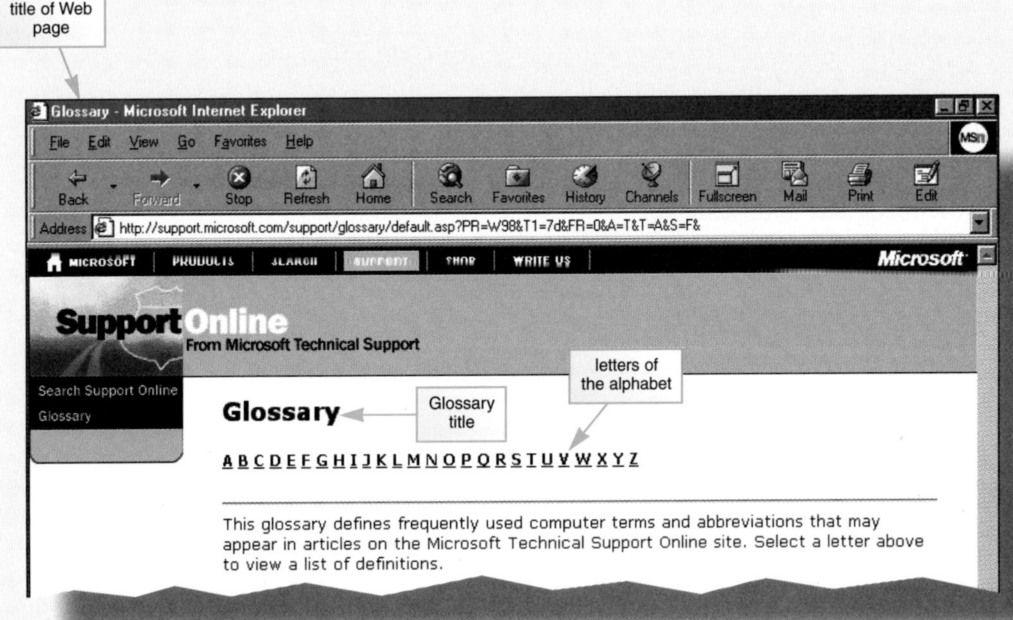

FIGURE 2-91

(continued)

Finding Terms and Definitions in the Windows Glossary *(continued)*

Part 3: *Copying a Term and Its Definition from the Glossary to the Notepad Window*

1. Click the first letter (A) in the list. A list of the terms beginning with the letter A and their definitions display.
2. Scroll the window to make the term, application-centric, and its definition visible.
3. Highlight the term and its definition by dragging.
4. Right-click the highlighted definition to display a shortcut menu.
5. Click Copy on the shortcut menu.
6. Click the Windows Definitions button in the taskbar button area to display the Windows Definitions - Notepad window.
7. Right-click the text area of the Notepad window to display a shortcut menu.
8. Click Paste on the shortcut menu. The term and definition display in the window. Click the Home button on the keyboard.
9. Position the insertion point between two words at the right side of the window and then press the ENTER key to move the text to the right of the insertion point to the next line in the document. Repeat this procedure until the entire definition is visible in the window.
10. Insert a blank line in the document following the definition.
11. Click File on the menu bar and then click Save to save the document.
12. Click the Glossary - Microsoft Internet Explorer button in the taskbar button area to display the Glossary - Microsoft Internet Explorer window.
13. Click the Back button on the Standard Buttons toolbar to display the alphabet list.

Part 4: *Copying Other Terms and Their Definitions to the Notepad Window*

1. Using the procedure shown in Part 3 above, copy the following terms and their definitions from the Glossary to the Notepad window: bit map, document-centric, and operating system. The definition for each term should be visible in the Notepad window.
2. Click File on the menu bar and then click Save to save the document.
3. Click File on the menu bar and then click Print to print the document.
4. Close the Windows Definition - Notepad window.
5. Close all open Windows Help windows.
6. Insert a floppy disk in drive A and copy the Windows Definition document onto the disk.
7. Delete the Windows Definition document on the desktop.

2 Performing Searches Using Windows Support Online

Instructions: Use Windows Support Online and a computer to perform the following tasks.

1. Design a search inquiry to search for articles about launching Notepad. List the names of the first three articles found in the spaces provided. Select an article that answers your inquiry and print the article.

   ____

   ____

   ____

2. Design a search inquiry to search for articles about creating a shortcut on the desktop. List the names of the first three articles found in the spaces provided. Select an article that you feel answers your inquiry and print the article.

   ____

   ____

   ____

3. Design a search inquiry to search for articles about Support Online. List the names of the first three articles found in the spaces provided. Select an article that you feel answers your inquiry and print the article.

   ____

   ____

   ____

4. Design a search inquiry to search for articles about retrieving a deleted shortcut. List the names of the first three articles found in the spaces provided. Select an article that you feel answers your inquiry and print the article.

   ____

   ____

   ____

1 Launching an Application, Creating a Document, and Modifying a Document

Instructions: Your boss asks you to create an office supplies shopping list for your department. You decide to use the application-centric approach to create the shopping list. Complete the following steps to accomplish this task.

Part 1: *Launching the Notepad Application*

1. Start Microsoft Windows 98 if necessary.
2. Click the Start button.
3. Point to Programs on the Start menu.
4. Point to Accessories on the Programs submenu.
5. Click Notepad on the Accessories submenu.
6. Enter the text shown in Figure 2-92.

Part 2: *Saving the Document onto a Floppy Disk and Printing the Document*

1. Insert a formatted floppy disk in drive A of your computer.
2. Click File on the menu bar and then click Save As to display the Save As dialog box.
3. Type `Office Supplies Shopping List` in the File name text box.

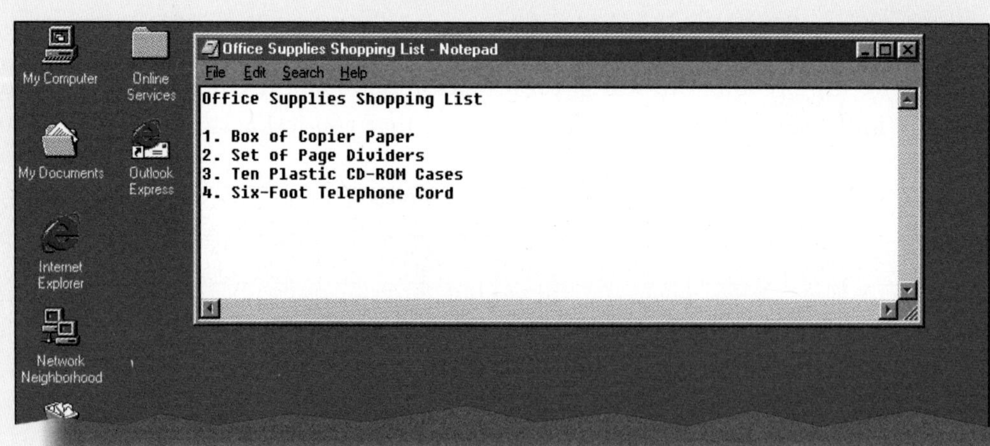

FIGURE 2-92

4. Click the Save in box arrow.
5. Click the 3½ Floppy (A:) icon.
6. Click the Save button in the Save As dialog box.
7. Click File on the menu bar and click Print.
8. Click the Close button on the Notepad title bar.
9. If you are not completing Part 3 of this assignment, remove your floppy disk from drive A.

Part 3: *Modifying a Document*

1. Click the Start button, point to Programs, point to Accessories, and then click Notepad.
2. Click File on the menu bar and then click Open.
3. Click the Look in box arrow and then click the 3½ Floppy (A:) icon.
4. Click Office Supplies Shopping List in the list.
5. Click the Open button in the Open dialog box.
6. Press the DOWN ARROW key six times.
7. Type `5. Crystal Clear Glaze (4 Ounce Bottle)` and then press the ENTER key.

8. Click File on the menu bar and then click Save.
9. Click File on the menu bar and then click Print.
10. Click the Close button on the Notepad title bar.
11. Remove the floppy disk from drive A.

2 Creating, Saving, and Printing Windows 98 Seminar Announcement and Schedule Documents

Instructions: A two-day Windows 98 seminar will be offered to all teachers at your school. You have been put in charge of developing two text documents for the seminar. One document announces the seminar and will be sent to all teachers. The other document contains the schedule for the seminar. Complete the following steps to prepare the documents using Notepad.

Part 1: ***Creating the Windows 98 Seminar Announcement Document***

1. Start Microsoft Windows 98 if necessary.
2. Create a blank text document on the desktop. Name the document Windows 98 Seminar Announcement.
3. Enter the text shown in Figure 2-93.

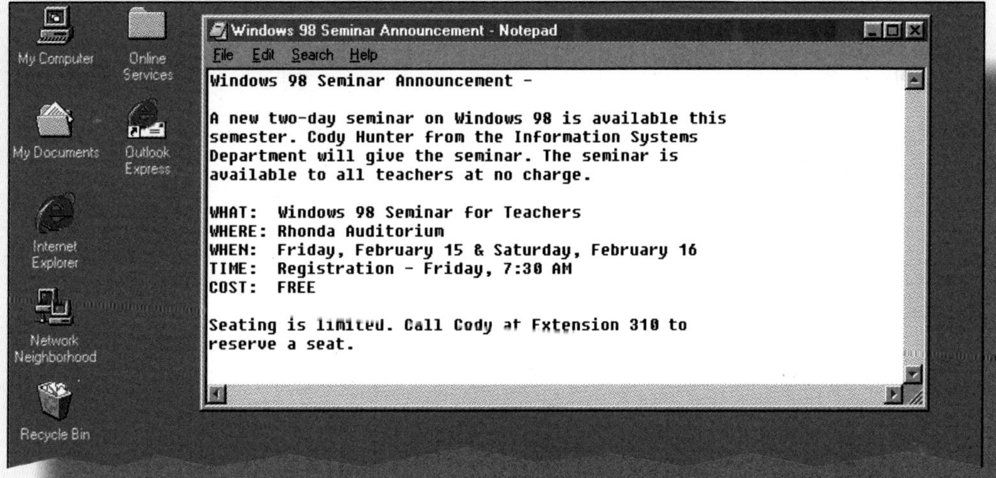

FIGURE 2-93

4. Save the document on the desktop.
5. Print the document.
6. Create a folder on the desktop called Windows 98 Seminar Documents.
7. Place the Windows 98 Seminar Announcement document in the Windows 98 Seminar Documents folder.

(continued)

Creating, Saving, and Printing Windows 98 Seminar Announcement and Schedule Documents *(continued)*

***Part 2:** Creating the Windows 98 Seminar Schedule Document*

1. Create a blank text document on the desktop. Name the document Windows 98 Seminar Schedule.
2. Enter the text shown in Figure 2-94.

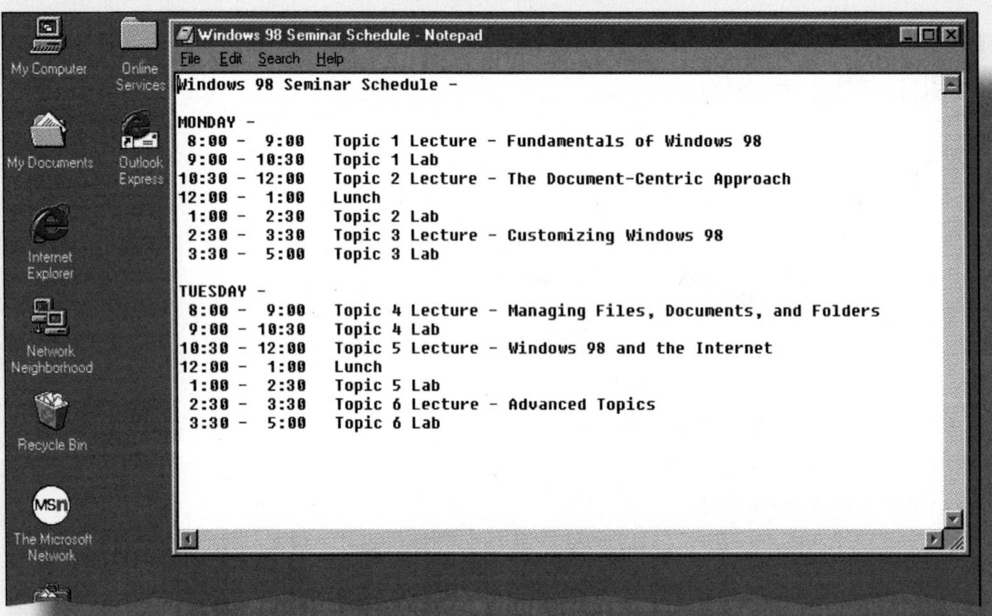

FIGURE 2-94

3. Save the document on the desktop.
4. Print the document.
5. Place the Windows 98 Seminar Schedule document in the Windows 98 Seminar Documents folder.
6. Move the Windows 98 Seminar Documents folder to a floppy disk.

3 Creating, Saving, and Printing Automobile Information Documents

Instructions: For almost a year, you have accumulated data about your 1999 Pontiac automobile. You have written some of the information on pieces of paper, while other information is in the form of receipts. Now you have decided to organize all this information on your computer. Create all documents using the document-centric approach. Complete the following steps to accomplish this task.

***Part 1:** Creating the Automobile Information Document*

1. Start Microsoft Windows 98 if necessary.
2. Create a text document on the desktop. Name the document Automobile Information.
3. Enter the text shown in Figure 2-95.

In the Lab

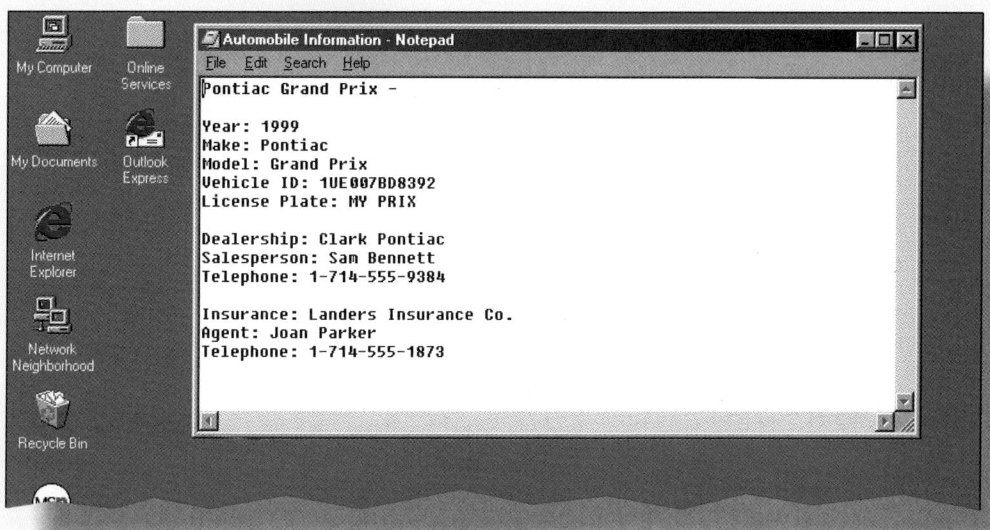

FIGURE 2-95

4. Save the document on the desktop.
5. Print the document.
6. Create a folder on the desktop called Automobile Documents.
7. Place the Automobile Information document in the Automobile Documents folder.

Part 2: ***Other Automobile Documents***

1. Create the Phone Numbers document (Figure 2-96), the Automobile Gas Mileage document (Figure 2-97 on the next page), and the Automobile Maintenance document (Figure 2-98 on the next page).
2. Save each document on the desktop.
3. Print each document.
4. Place each document in the Automobile Documents folder.
5. Move the Automobile Documents folder to a floppy disk.

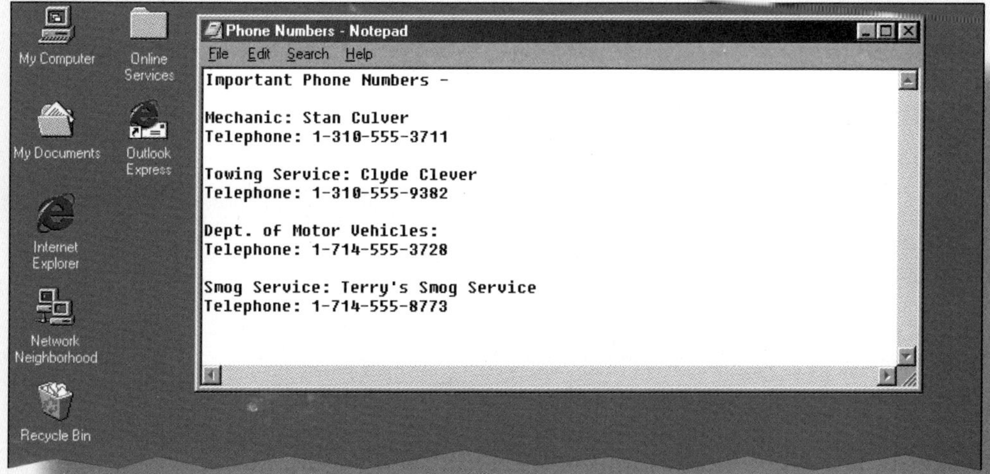

FIGURE 2-96

(continued)

Creating, Saving, and Printing Automobile Information Documents *(continued)*

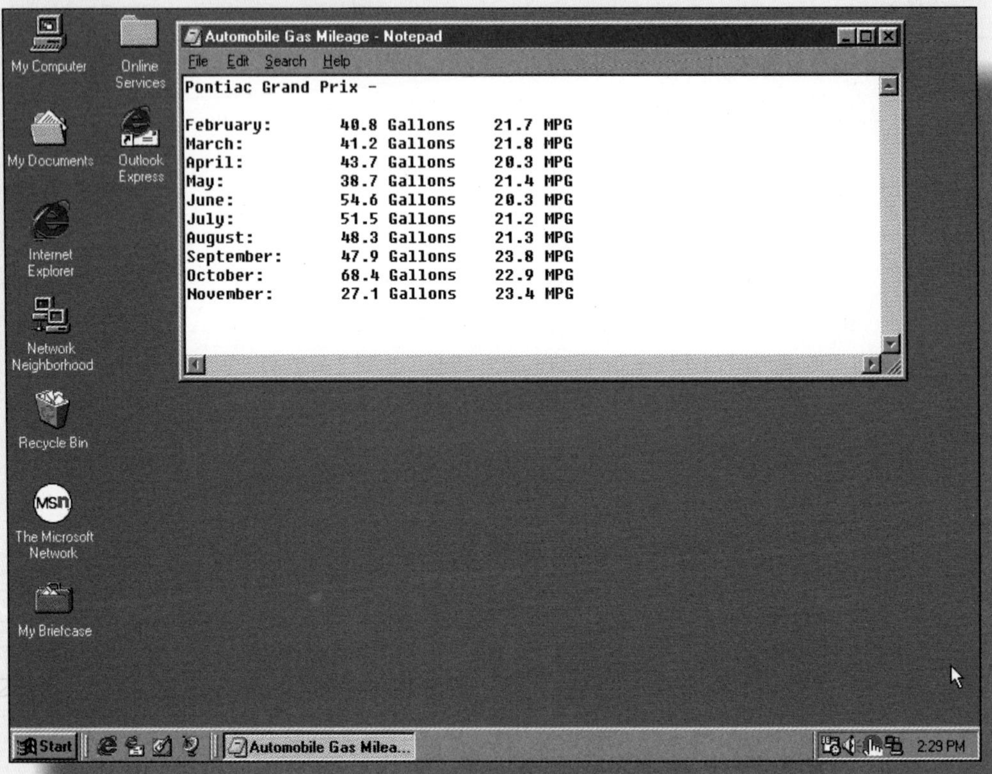

FIGURE 2-97

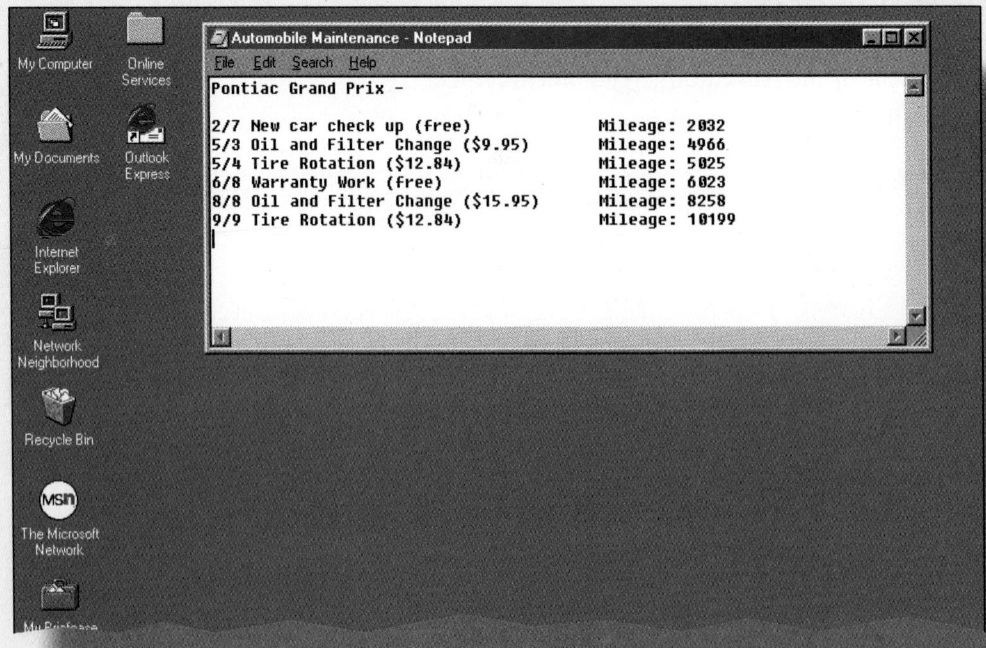

FIGURE 2-98

4 Adding a Desktop Item to the Active Desktop

Instructions: Perform the following steps to add a desktop item to the desktop, move the item on the desktop, display additional information about a news story, and remove the item from the desktop.

***Part 1:** Adding a Desktop Item to the Desktop*

1. Start Microsoft Windows 98 and connect to the Internet if necessary.
2. Right-click an open area on the desktop.
3. Click Properties on the shortcut menu.
4. Click the Web tab in the Display Properties dialog box and then click the New button.
5. Click the Yes button in the New Active Desktop Item dialog box.
6. Click the Maximize button in the Desktop Gallery window.
7. Click the travel icon in the Desktop Gallery window. Two channel names display in the window (Figure 2-99).

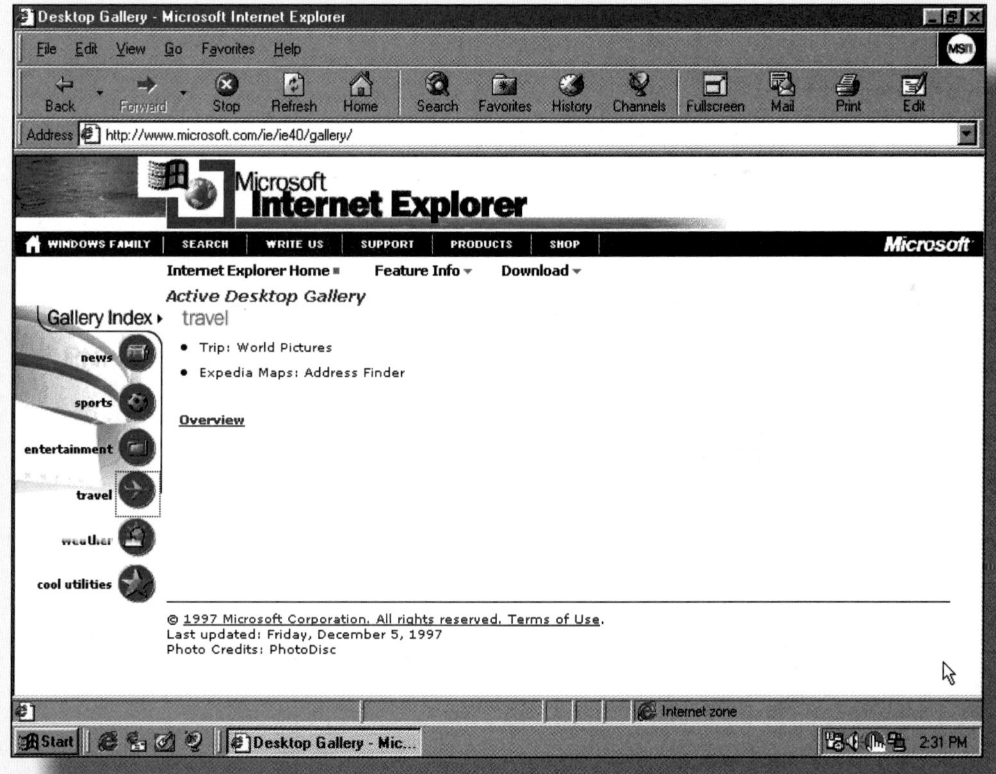

FIGURE 2-99

8. Click the Expedia Maps: Address Finder channel name.
9. Click the Add to Active Desktop button.

(continued)

Adding a Desktop Item to the Active Desktop *(continued)*

10. Click the Yes button in the Security Alert dialog box.
11. Click the OK button in the Add item to Active Desktop dialog box.
12. Click the Close button in the Desktop Gallery window.

Part 2:* *Sizing the Desktop Item

1. Point to the bottom window border to change the mouse pointer to a double-headed arrow.
2. Drag the border down until the Address, City, State, and ZIP boxes are visible.

Part 3:* *Displaying and Printing a Map

1. Click the Address text box and then type your street address in the text box.
2. Click the City text box and then type your city name in the text box.
3. Click the State box arrow. Click your state name in the list.
4. Click the ZIP text box and type your Zip code in the text box.
5. Click the Find button.
6. If the Security Alert dialog box displays, click the Yes button.
7. If the Internet Redirection dialog box displays, click the Yes button.
8. Maximize the Microsoft Expedia Maps window.
9. Click the Print hyperlink in the window.
10. Click the Print button on the Standard Buttons toolbar to print the map.
11. Close the browser window.

Part 4:* *Removing a Desktop Item on the Desktop

1. Right-click an open area on the desktop.
2. Click Properties on the shortcut menu.
3. Click the Web tab in the Display Properties dialog box.
4. Click the Expedia Address Finder check box title to highlight it and then click the Delete button.
5. Click the Yes button in the Active Desktop Item dialog box.
6. Click the OK button.

Cases and Places

The difficulty of these case studies varies:
◗ are the least difficult; ◗◗ are more difficult; and ◗◗◗ are the most difficult.

1 ◗ Your employer is concerned that some people in the company are not thoroughly researching software purchases. She has prepared a list of steps she would like everyone to follow when acquiring software (Figure 2-100).

You have been asked to use WordPad to prepare a copy of this list that can be posted in every department. Use the concepts and techniques presented in this project to create a WordPad document on the desktop. Save and print the document. After you have printed one copy of the document, try experimenting with different WordPad features to make the list more eye-catching. If you like your changes, save and print a revised copy of the document. If WordPad is not available on your computer, use Notepad.

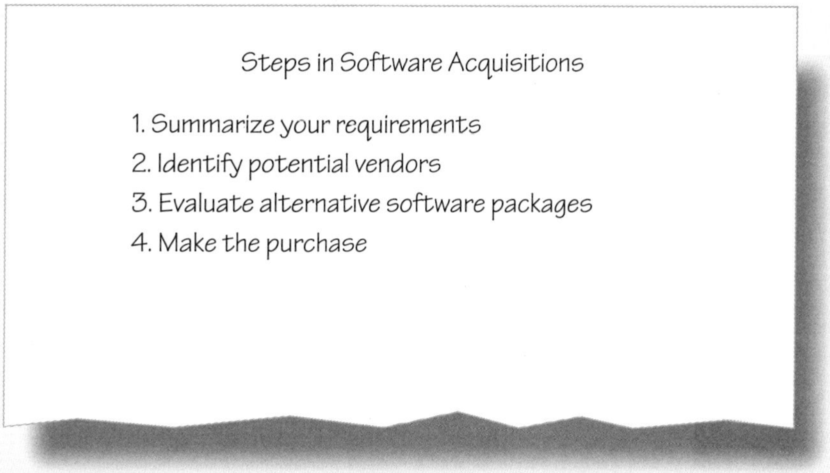

Steps in Software Acquisitions

1. Summarize your requirements
2. Identify potential vendors
3. Evaluate alternative software packages
4. Make the purchase

FIGURE 2-100

2 ◗ You volunteer to show your friend how to add desktop items to the Active Desktop. After explaining the concept of channels and showing several desktop items to your friend, he decides he would like for you to show him how to add the ESPN SportsZone™, CNET, and Microsoft Ticker Tape items. Add these three desktop items to your desktop. Move and size the desktop items on the desktop to make each item visible. Click a sporting event in the ESPN SportsZone™ item and print the event. Click a news story in the CNET item and print the story. Click a stock quote in the Microsoft Ticker Tape item and print the quote.

3 ◗◗ Document-centric versus application-centric: prepare a brief report about the two approaches. Explain what each approach means to the computer user, summarize the advantages and disadvantages of each approach, and indicate which is the better approach for you and why. Do you think one approach will be more popular in the future? Will future operating systems emphasize one approach over the other? Support your opinions with information from computer magazines, articles on the Internet, and other resources.

Cases and Places

4 ▶▶ Microsoft touts Windows 98 as an intuitive operating system. Webster's dictionary defines *intuitive* as knowing or perceiving by immediate apprehension or cognition. Using current computer magazines or other resources, prepare a brief report on the intuitive nature of Windows 98. Describe the features of Windows 98 that Microsoft feels help people instantly understand the operating system. Discuss the opinions that reviewers had about learning and using Windows 98. Finally, from your research and your own experience, explain whether you believe Windows 98 is an intuitive operating system.

5 ▶▶▶ Microsoft Corporation offers many ways to obtain information about its software products. In addition to Windows 98 Help, the Microsoft Web site (www.microsoft.com) contains helpful information about Microsoft products. Products include operating systems (Windows 3.1, Windows 95, Windows 98, and Windows NT), application software (Office, Word, Excel, Access, PowerPoint, NetMeeting, Bookshelf, and Outlook Express), and an online service (MSN). Using any two operating systems and any four application programs just mentioned and the online service, write a brief report summarizing each product's function. Write a single paragraph about each product.

6 ▶▶▶ Registering for classes can be a daunting task for incoming college freshmen. As someone who has gone through the process, prepare a guide for students who are about to register for the first time next semester. Your guide should be two or more documents and include a calendar and/or schedule of key dates and times, a description of the registration procedure, and suggestions for how students can make registration easier. Give the documents suitable names and save them in a folder on the Windows 98 desktop. Print each document.

7 ▶▶▶ In the course of a year, a typical business might save hundreds of document files. These files must be organized so they can be located and retrieved efficiently. Windows 98 provides an easy way to work with document files on personal computers. How are document files organized with other operating systems used by businesses? Visit a business that uses personal computers with an operating system different from Windows 98. Find out how document files are saved, organized, and accessed. Write a brief report describing the way document files are stored. Explain how the same files might be kept using Windows 98. Based on what you have learned, decide which operating system can be used to organize document files more effectively and explain why.

Microsoft Windows 98

File, Document, and Folder Management and Windows 98 Explorer

OBJECTIVES

You will have mastered the material in this project when you can:

- Display icons in various views in a window
- Open a folder, document, and application program from a window
- Cascade and tile open windows on the desktop
- Copy, move, and delete files from open windows
- Launch Windows 98 Explorer
- Display files and folders in Explorer
- Expand drives and folders in Explorer
- Open a drive and folder in Explorer
- Launch an application program from Explorer
- Close folder expansions
- Copy, move, rename, and delete files in Explorer
- Close Explorer
- Display drive and folder properties
- Find files or folders using Find on the Start menu
- Use the Run command

MOORE AND More Storage

Cramming Data in Small Places

Is it any doubt that you are an expert when it comes to cramming? You cram for final exams, cram books into heavy backpacks, and cram clothes into tiny closets. Only a few decades ago, college students held contests to see how many people could cram into telephone booths and Volkswagen Beetles. About the same time, Gordon Moore, a semiconductor engineer, realized cramming was a good thing when it came to computer chips.

In 1965, Moore observed a trend when he was drawing an illustration for a speech: every 18 to 24 months a new memory chip was being released with double the number of transistors as its predecessor. He predicted that this growth would continue exponentially, and he was correct. Today's Pentium II processor has 7.5 million transistors, which is nearly 3,200 times more than the 2,300 transistors found on a chip released in 1971.

7.5 MILLION

His theory became known as Moore's Law. In 1968, Gordon Moore became a cofounder of Intel Corporation, one of the world's largest microprocessor manufacturers.

Hard disk capacity has grown to impressive densities in recent years. In 1956, IBM's first hard drive stored five megabytes (five million bytes) of data. Subsequent drive capacity doubled every 30 months until 1991. At that time, IBM introduced new technology that doubled capacity every 18 months. IBM needed a truck to deliver that refrigerator-sized first hard drive, which consisted of fifty 24-inch disks, called platters, and cost more than $1 million, at the value of today's dollars. The hard drive in your computer probably has two 3½-inch platters, stores at least four gigabytes (four billion bytes), and costs less than $300.

With such increased disk capacity, computers store more data, programs, and files than ever before. Consider how in this project, you will manage and organize files and documents using tools supplied with Windows 98. You will master the operations of copying, moving, renaming, and deleting files stored on your computer's floppy disk and then display your computer's hard disk properties. Do you wonder how all the data files and programs fit on those disks?

Engineers use the term, *areal density,* when referring to capacity, which is a combination of the disk's magnetic properties, read/write head movement, and electronic principles. As the hard disk's platters whirl at 3,600 to 7,200 revolutions per minute, read/write heads attached to access arms move to the correct position on a particular platter and retrieve or record bits of data.

Technology gurus predict that Moore's Law for silicon chips will hold true until 2020. At that time, they will be forced to use new methods and materials, such as the optical technique of holography. As for disk drives, capacity may max out in 2010, when densities will reach 70 to 100 gigabytes per square inch, as compared with today's one gigabyte per square inch. Engineers are investigating holographic storage, which will hold 1,000 gigabytes per square inch, but they have set their sights on technologies that could lead to capacities of one million gigabytes per square inch.

With that capacity in your computer, just think of how many programs and data files you will be able to cram into that space. Be forewarned: you probably will need every bit (or byte) of this space to hold the progressive applications planned for the next decade and beyond.

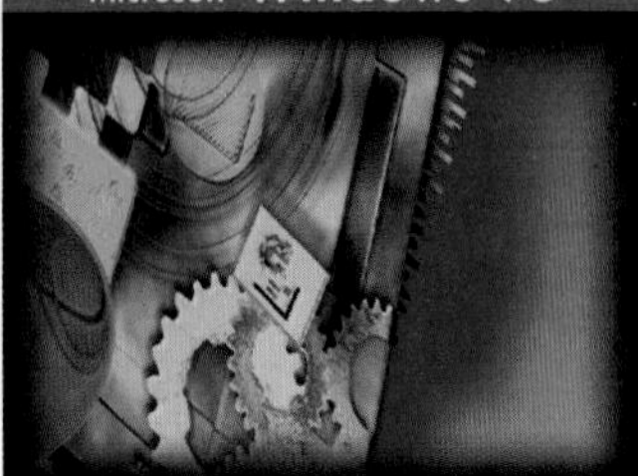

Microsoft Windows 98

File, Document, and Folder Management and Windows 98 Explorer

CASE PERSPECTIVE

Your organization has decided to switch to Windows 98 from Windows 95. Your supervisor has read in computer magazines that to use Windows 98 effectively, people must be able to control and manage windows on their Windows 98 desktop, and their proficient use of Windows 98 Explorer will be critical in the successful implementation of Windows 98. Although almost everyone is excited about the change, those who have little experience using Windows 95 are apprehensive about having to learn about file and window management. You have been asked to teach a class with an emphasis on file and desktop management to any employees who are not experienced Windows users. Your goal in Project 3 is to become competent using these features of Windows 98 so that you can teach the class.

Introduction

In Project 2, you used Windows 98 to create documents and store them on both a floppy disk and the desktop, and you created folders in which to place the documents. Windows 98 also allows you to examine the documents, files, and folders on your computer in a variety of ways, depending on the easiest and most accessible manner during your work on the computer. The two major ways for you to work with files and documents are using the My Computer window and Windows 98 Explorer, which is an application program provided with Windows 98. This project will illustrate how to manage and organize files and documents using the tools supplied by Windows 98.

My Computer Window

As noted in previous projects, the My Computer icon displays in the upper-left corner of the Windows 98 desktop. The **My Computer icon** represents a window that displays all the hardware components on your computer (disk drives, CD-ROM drives, and DVD drives) and system folders (Printers, Control Panel, Dial-Up Networking, and Scheduled Tasks). To open and maximize the My Computer window and view the components of your computer, complete the steps on the next two pages.

Steps To Open and Maximize the My Computer Window

1 Double-click the My Computer icon on the desktop. Point to the Maximize button in the My Computer window.

The My Computer window opens (Figure 3-1).

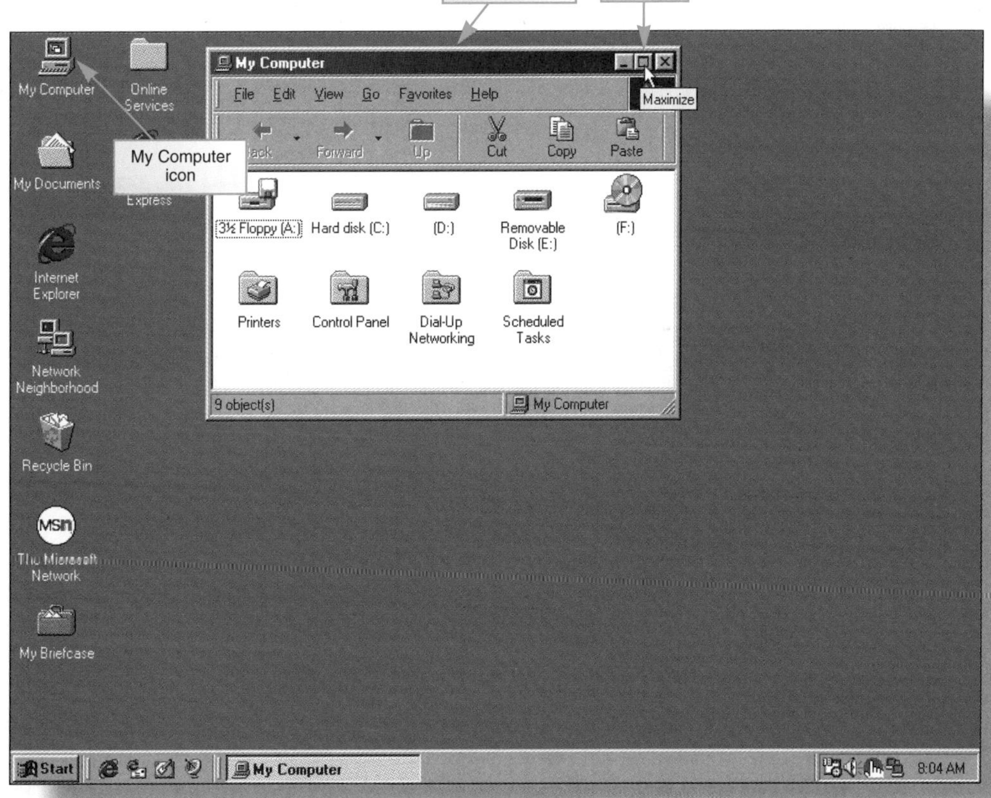

FIGURE 3-1

2 **Click the Maximize button.**

The My Computer window is maximized (Figure 3-2).

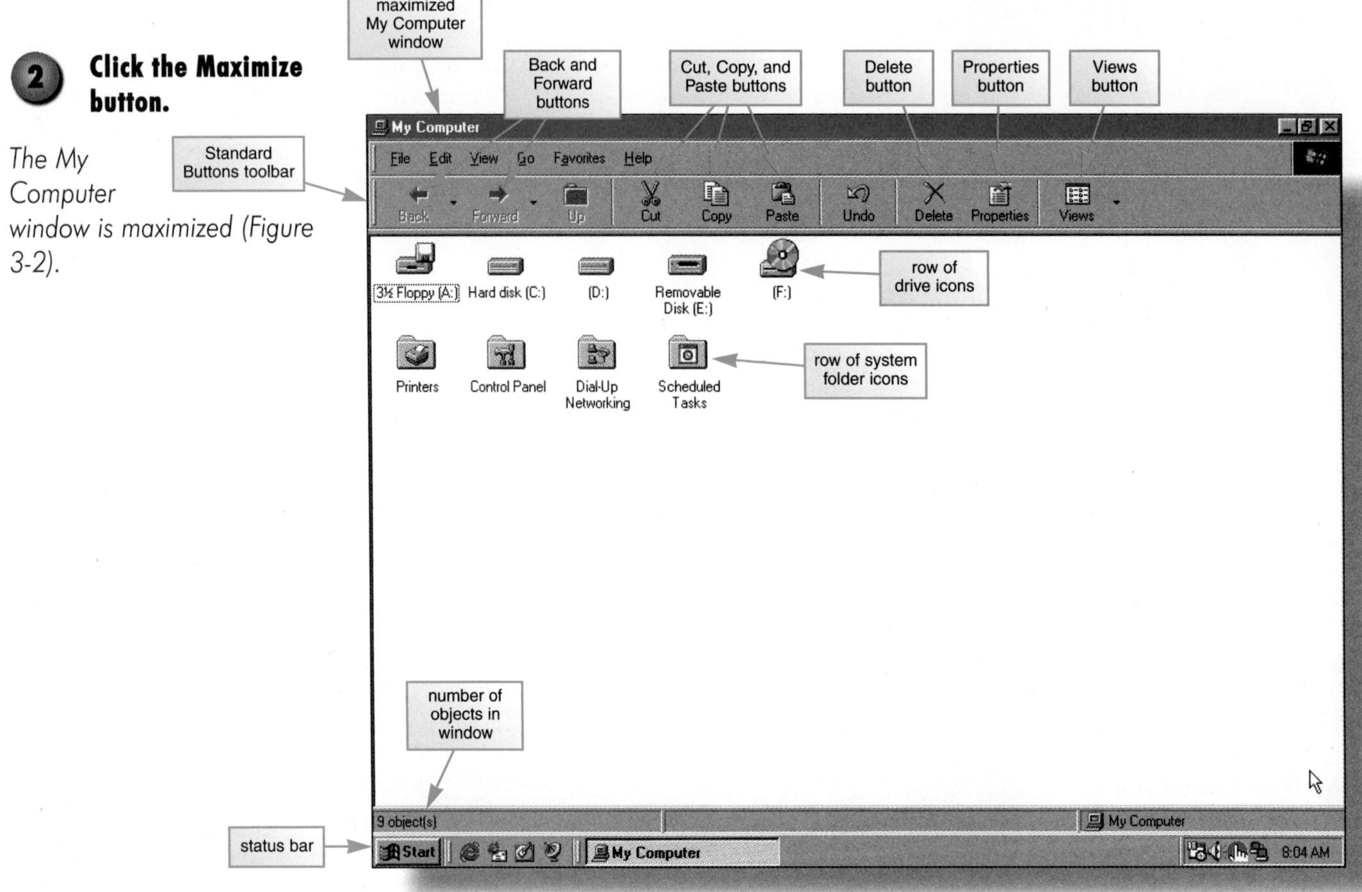

FIGURE 3-2

The Standard Buttons toolbar shown in Figure 3-2 contains buttons you will use in this project to navigate between windows (Back and Forward), copy and move files (Cut, Copy, and Paste buttons), delete files (Delete icon), display object properties (Properties), and change the appearance of the icons in a window (Views button).

The area below the Standard Buttons toolbar contains a row of drive icons (3½ Floppy (A:) icon, Hard disk (C:) icon, (D:) icon, Removable Disk (E:) icon, and (F:) icon) and a row of system folder icons (Printers icon, Control Panel icon, Dial-Up Networking icon, and Scheduled Tasks icon). The icons on your computer may be different and may display in a different format than the ones shown in Figure 3-2.

The **Hard disk (C:) icon** shown in Figure 3-2 represents the hard disk on your computer. The **hard disk** is where you can store files, documents, and folders if it is not necessary for you to transport them from one computer to another. Storing data on a hard disk often is more convenient than storing it on a floppy disk in drive A because using a hard disk is faster, and generally more storage room is available on a hard disk than on a floppy disk. Your computer always will have at least one hard disk drive, normally designated as drive C. On the computer represented by the My Computer window in Figure 3-2, the hard disk has been given a **disk label**, or title (*Hard disk*). The label is not required. Later in this project you will see how to give a drive a name.

Some computers may have additional hard drives or have a single hard drive that has been subdivided into two or more areas by the operating system. In Figure 3-2, the Hard disk (C:) icon and (D:) icon refer to different areas of the same hard drive. The Hard disk (C:) icon represents the area of the hard drive that contains the programs required by the operating system and the files, folders, and programs you want to save. The **(D:) icon** represents an area on the hard drive where additional files, folders, or programs can be stored. Some computers may have a separate second hard drive or a removable hard drive, such as the removable hard drive represented by the **Removable Disk (E:) icon** shown in Figure 3-2. Removable disk drives, such as a Jaz drive or a Zip drive, allow you to store large files or a large number of files on a cartridge that can be removed from the disk drive.

The **(F:) icon** is a CD-ROM drive. In Figure 3-2, the label for the drive is blank because the drive does not contain a CD-ROM. If you insert a CD-ROM in the drive, such as an **audio CD** containing music, then Windows 98 changes the label to reflect the type of CD in the drive and musical notes are added to the icon.

The status bar at the bottom of the My Computer window indicates the window contains nine objects.

Viewing Icons in the My Computer Window

The icons in the My Computer window shown in Figure 3-2 are displayed in a format called **Large Icons**, which means the icons are relatively large. The icons can, however, display in other formats. Complete the following steps to display icons in all the different formats available in the My Computer window.

To Change the Format of the Icons in a Window

1 Point to the Views button on the Standard Buttons toolbar (Figure 3-3).

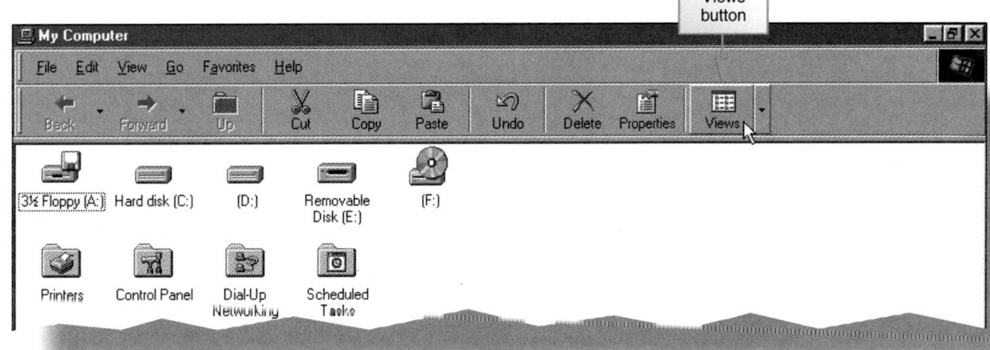

FIGURE 3-3

2 Click the Views button.

The icons display in Small Icons format with the icon title adjacent to the icon (Figure 3-4). The icons display in five columns.

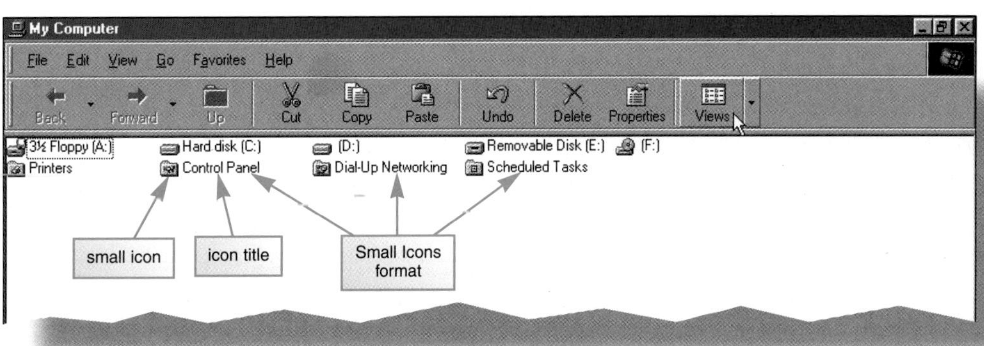

FIGURE 3-4

Click the Views button.

The icons display in the window in List view using the Small Icons format (Figure 3-5). The ***List view*** *places the drive and folder icons in a list.*

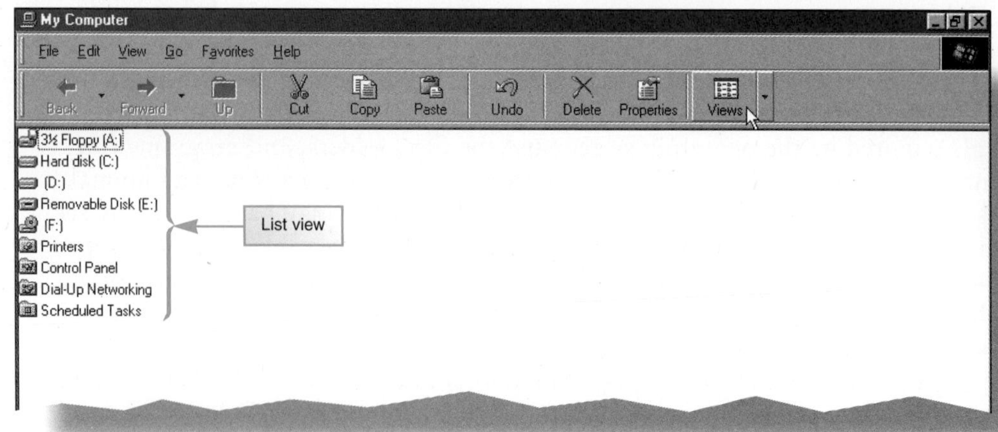

FIGURE 3-5

Click the Views button.

The icons display in a list in Details view using the Small Icons format (Figure 3-6).The ***Details view*** *provides detailed information about each drive or folder*

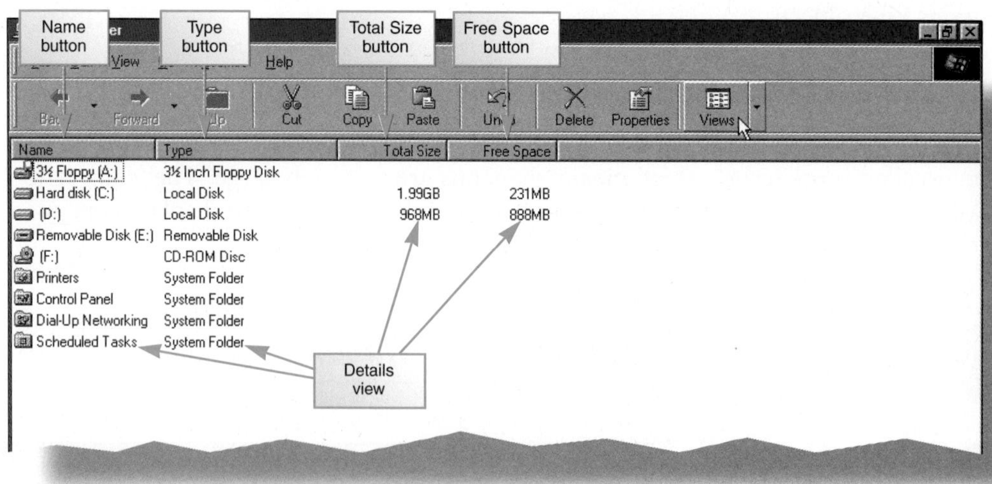

FIGURE 3-6

1. Right-click open area of My Computer window, point to View, click icon format
2. On Views button, click down arrow, click icon format
3. On View menu click icon format
4. Press ALT+V, select icon format

The manner in which you display folder contents in the My Computer window is a matter of personal preference. You also can sequence the icons in the My Computer window when detailed information is displayed using the buttons below the Standard Buttons toolbar. If you click the **Name button**, the items will display in alphabetical sequence by name either in ascending or descending sequence. If you click the Name button again, the alphabetical sequence is reversed. If you click the **Type button**, the items will display in alphabetical sequence by type. Although only two entries have the total size and free space values displayed, you also can sequence the icons by total size and free space. Clicking the **Total Size button** causes the items to display in size sequence, from the smallest to the largest or from largest to smallest, while clicking the **Free Space button** causes items to display from smallest to largest based on free space.

In Figure 3-6, the Type column tells you the type of object for each icon. The first five objects are 3½ Inch Floppy Disk, Local Disk, Local Disk, Removable Disk, and CD-ROM Disc, respectively. Each of the last four items is a system folder. The Total Size column states the size of the hard disks (1.99GB and 968MB) and the Free Space column states the amount of space that is not being used on the disks (231MB and 888MB). The values for the total size and free space may be different on your computer.

Viewing Icons

The icons in any window can be displayed as large icons, small icons, in a list, or with details. You also can increase the size of the icons on the desktop and decrease the size of the icons on the Start menu. For detailed instructions for making these changes, consult Windows 98 Help.

The view you use to display icons in a window is a matter of personal preference. The Windows 98 default setting for viewing the icons in a window is the Large Icons view. When you close a window, Windows 98 remembers the format of the icons in the window and uses that format to display the icons the next time you open the window. For example, if you close the My Computer wiindow shown in Figure 3-6 (Details view) and then open the window, the icons in the window will display in Details view.

More About

Icons

In many cases, you may not recognize a particular icon because hundreds of icons are developed by software vendors to represent their products. Each icon is supposed to be unique and eye-catching. You can purchase thousands of icons on floppy disk or CD-ROM that you can use in documents you create.

Viewing the Contents of Drives and Folders

In addition to the contents of My Computer, the contents of drives and folders also can be viewed. In previous projects, you have seen both windows for folders and windows for floppy drive A. In fact, the contents of any folder or drive on your computer can display in a window.

The default option for opening drive and folder windows, called the **single window option**, uses the same window to display the contents of a newly opened drive or folder. Because only one window displays on the desktop at a time, the single window option eliminates the clutter of multiple windows on the desktop. To illustrate the single window option and view the contents of hard drive C, complete the following step.

Steps To View the Contents of a Drive

1 Point to the Hard disk (C:) icon in the My Computer window.

2 Double-click the Hard disk (C:) icon.

The maximized Hard disk (C:) window opens in the same window as My Computer was displayed (Figure 3-7). The objects in the window display in the Large Icons format. The button on the taskbar is now for the Hard disk (C:) window, not for the My Computer window.

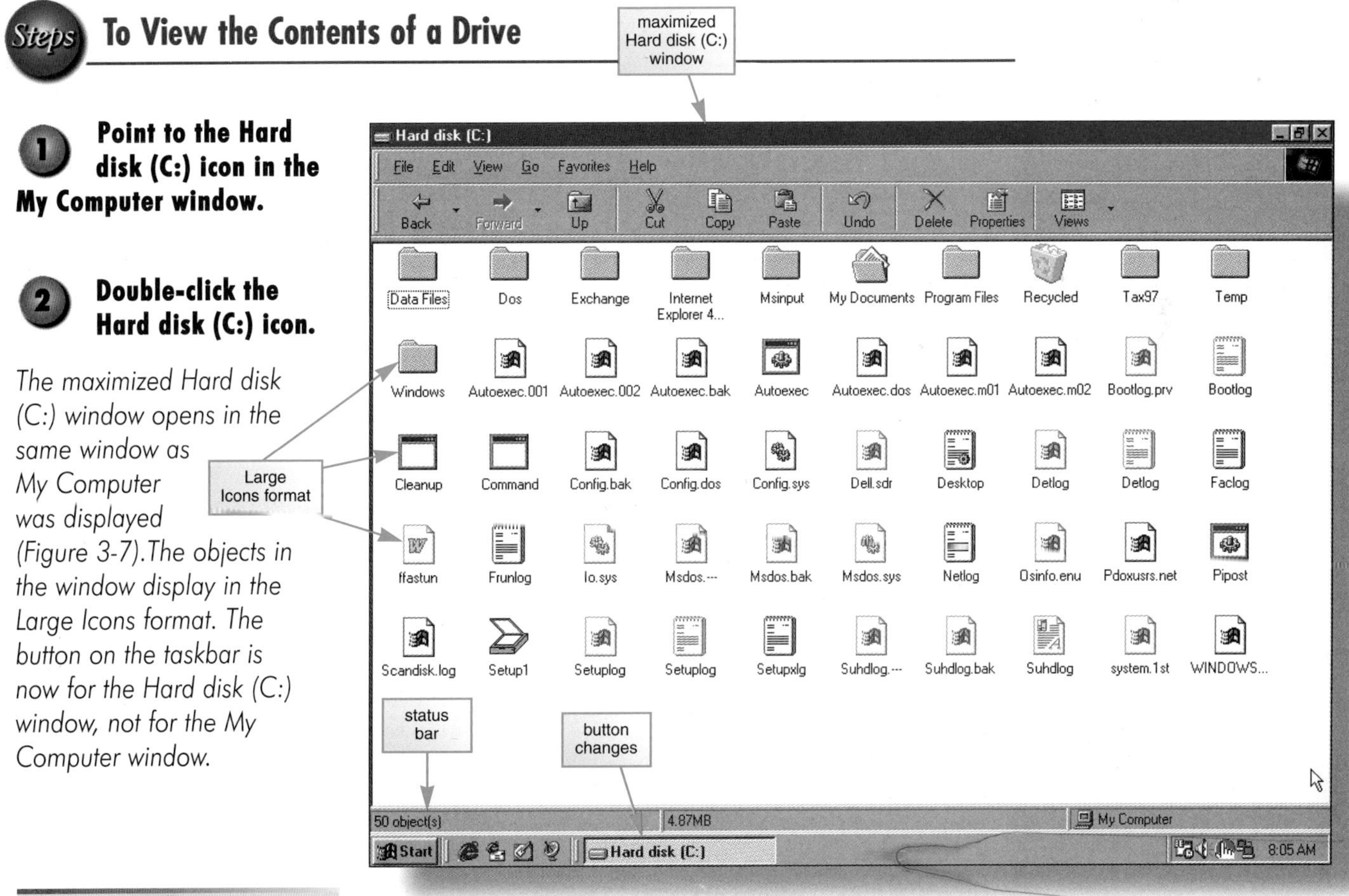

FIGURE 3-7

Other Ways

1. Right-click Hard disk (C:) icon, click Open
2. Click Hard disk (C:) icon, press ENTER

A yellow folder icon represents each folder in the Hard disk (C:) window. Application programs and documents are represented by icons unique to the application program or to the application program that can open the document.

The contents of the hard disk window you display on your computer can differ considerably from the contents shown in Figure 3-7 on the previous page because each computer has its own application programs and documents. The manner in which you interact with and control the programs and documents in Windows 98 is the same, however, regardless of the actual programs or documents.

The status bar in Figure 3-7 contains information about the folders, programs, and documents displaying in the window. Fifty objects (folders, programs, and documents) display in the window.

Hidden Files

Sometimes the status bar will indicate that a folder contains hidden files. Hidden files usually are placed on your hard disk by software vendors such as Microsoft and often are critical to the operation of the software. Rarely will you designate a file as hidden. You should almost never delete a hidden file.

The designation, 4.87MB, on the status bar in Figure 3-7 indicates the objects in the window consume 4.87 megabytes on the hard disk. This number does not include the contents of any of the folders displayed in Figure 3-7. Recall from Figure 3-6 on page WIN 3.8 that the entire drive C, which is 1.99 gigabytes in size, has only 231 megabytes free. Therefore, considerably more storage space is used on drive C than 4.87 megabytes.

If the My Computer window in Figure 3-6 was not maximized before double-clicking the Hard disk (C:) icon, the Hard disk (C:) window would display in the same physical window as My Computer, be the same size, and be located at the same place on the desktop.

Opening a Folder Window

In Figure 3-7 on the previous page, ten folder icons display. Each of the folders can be opened to display the contents of the folder. One folder in the Hard disk (C:) window, the **Windows folder**, contains programs and files necessary for the operation of the Windows 98 operating system. As such, caution should be exercised when working with the contents of the Windows folder because changing the contents of the folder may cause your programs to stop working correctly. To open the Windows folder, complete the following steps.

To Open a Folder Window

1 If necessary, scroll the window to view the Windows folder in the Hard disk (C:) window. Point to the Windows folder icon (Figure 3-8).

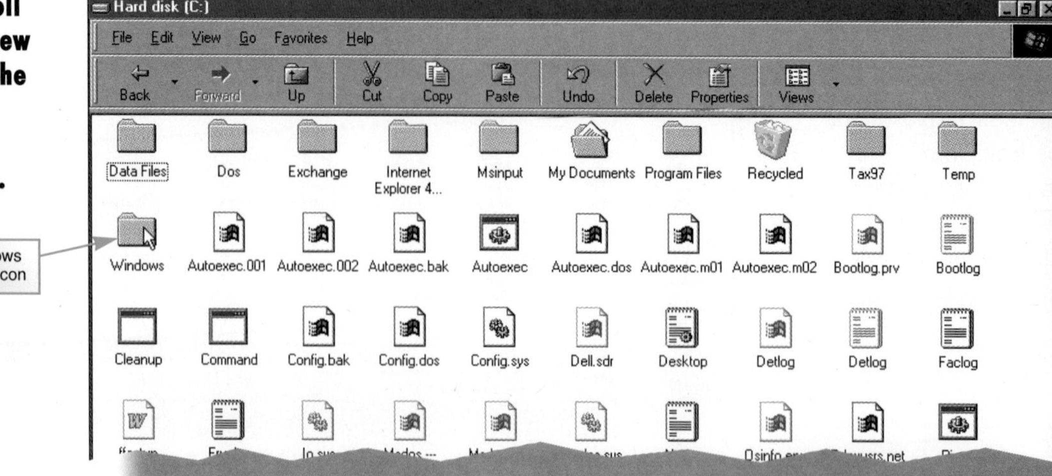

FIGURE 3-8

Double-click the Windows folder.

The maximized Windows window opens in the same window that contained the Hard disk (C:) window, and the Hard disk (C:) button in the taskbar button area is replaced with the Windows button (Figure 3-9). The window displays folder and file icons but the scroll box in the window is small, indicating many more objects are contained within the window. The status bar indicates the objects in the window consume 51.7 megabytes.

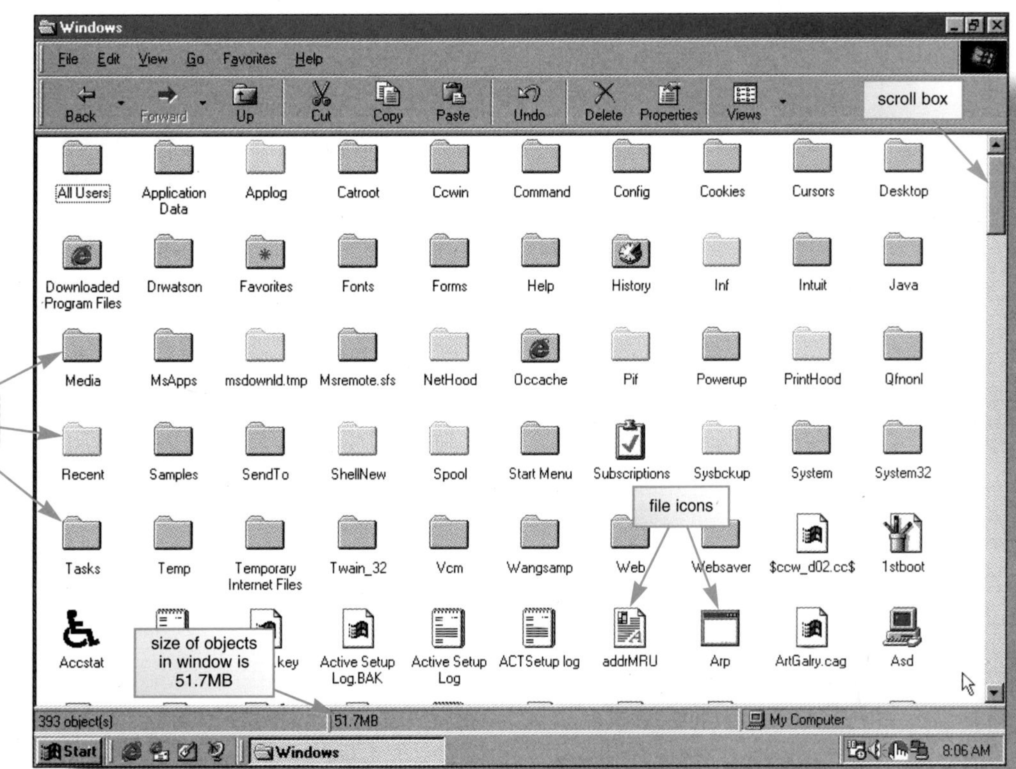

FIGURE 3-9

The majority of objects shown in Figure 3-9 are folder icons. As you can see, folder icons always display first in the window. File icons display after the folders. As with every window you will see in the steps within this book, the contents of the windows on your computer may be different. Every effort has been made, however, to ensure that the files used in the steps within this book also will be found on any computer you are using.

Other Ways

1. Right-click Windows icon, click Open
2. Click Windows icon, press ENTER

Opening a Document from a Window

In Project 2, you created a text document on the desktop and then opened the document by double-clicking the document icon on the desktop. In addition to opening a text document on the desktop, you can open a Paint document in a folder in a similar fashion. Paint documents contain graphics images, called **bitmap images**, and are created using the **Paint program**, which is a program that is supplied with Windows 98. Several Paint documents are included with Windows 98 and stored in the Windows folder on the hard drive. A Paint icon identifies each Paint document. To open a Paint document from the Windows window, complete the following steps.

To Open a Document from a Window

1 Scroll down the Windows window until the Forest icon displays. Point to the Forest icon. If your computer does not contain the Forest icon, find and point to one of these Paint icons: Gold Weave, Leaves, Tartan, and Winlogo, or any other Paint icon.

*The mouse pointer points to the Forest icon (Figure 3-10). This icon, called a **Paint icon**, is associated with all document files that can be opened by the Paint application program. Thus, you can identify all Paint documents because they all are represented by this icon.*

FIGURE 3-10

2 **Double-click the Forest icon. If the Forest - Paint window is maximized, click the Restore button and then size the window to approximately the size shown in Figure 3-11.**

Windows 98 launches the Paint application program, the Paint window containing the Forest document opens on top of the Windows window, and the recessed Forest - Paint button displays in the taskbar button area (Figure 3-11).

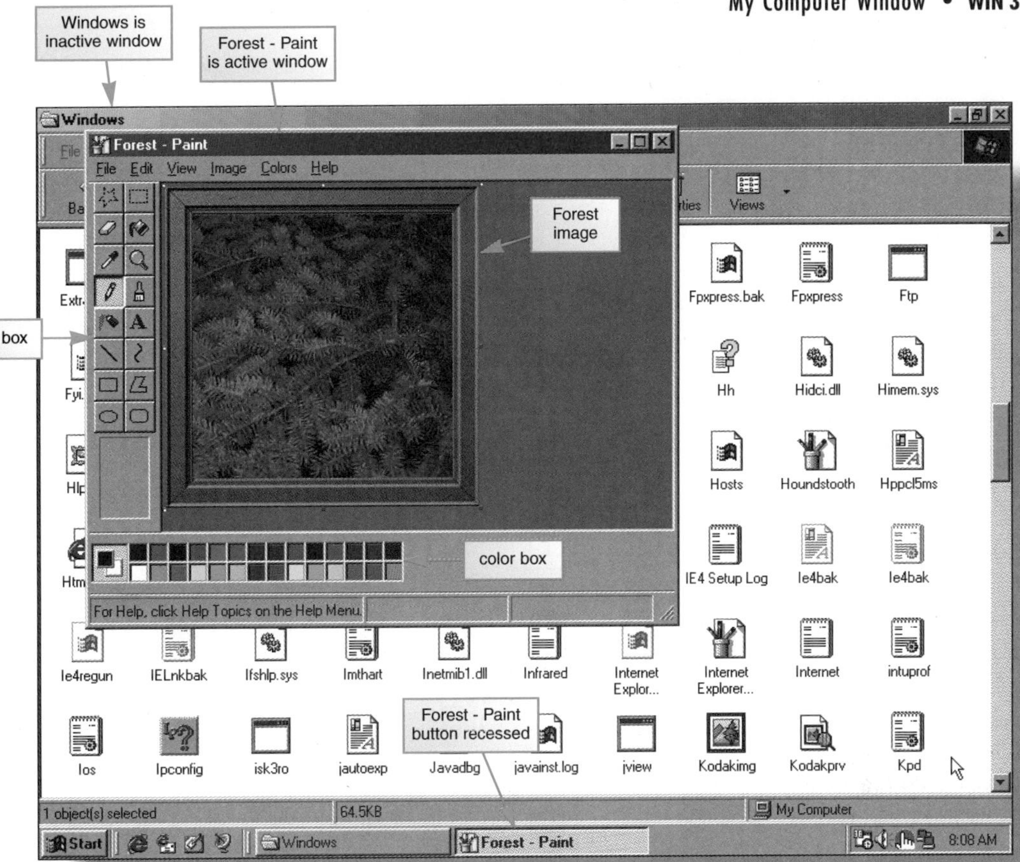

FIGURE 3-11

The Forest - Paint window displays on top of the Windows window on the desktop. The Forest - Paint window consists of a title bar and menu bar. On the left of the window is the **tool box**, which contains tools used to create images. At the bottom of the window is the **color box**, where colors can be selected for an image. The Forest - Paint window is the active window and the Windows window is the inactive window. Currently, a folder window and a document window are open on the desktop.

Other Ways

1. Right-click document icon, click Open
2. Click document icon, press ENTER

Launching an Application Program from a Window

In addition to opening a document from a window, you also can launch an application program from a window. To launch the Notepad application program, complete the steps on the next page.

More About

The Paint Program

An image with color usually has more impact than one without color. The Paint program allows you to create color images. To learn about the Paint program, click Help on the menu bar in the Paint window, click Help Topics, and use the Contents or Index sheet to read about the features of Paint.

To Launch an Application Program from a Window

1 Click the Windows button in the taskbar button area. When the maximized Windows window displays, scroll until the Notepad icon displays in the window. Point to the Notepad icon.

The maximized Windows window displays as the active window and its button is recessed in the taskbar button area (Figure 3-12). You can switch between one open window and another open window by clicking the button in the taskbar button area.

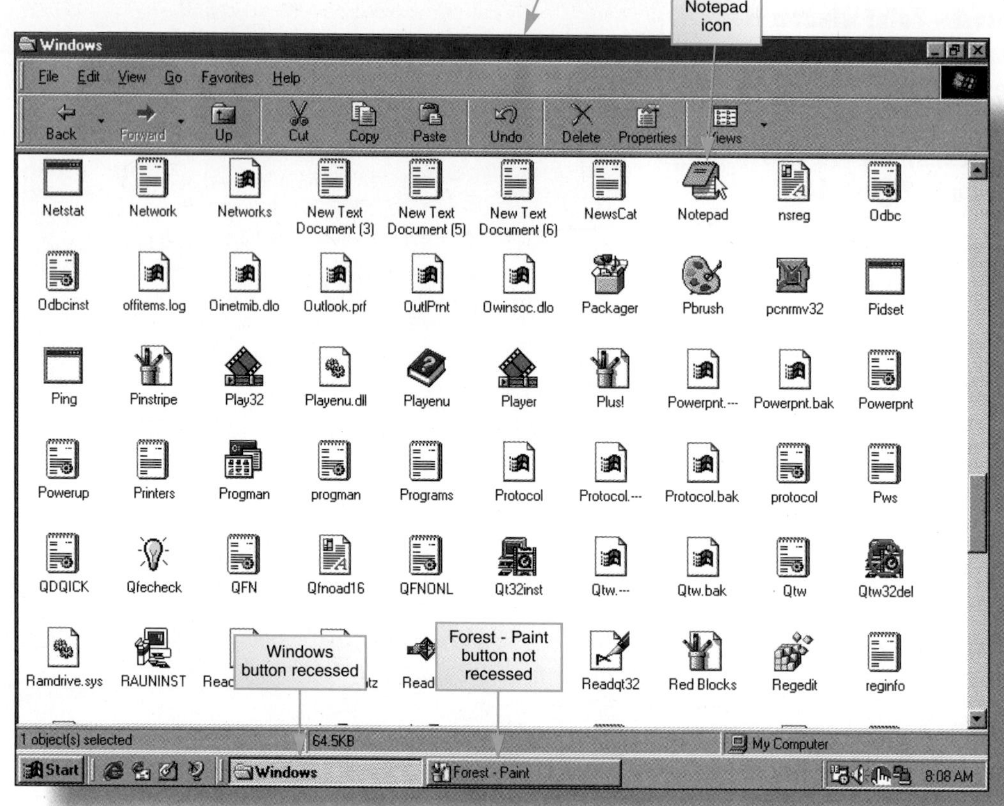

FIGURE 3-12

2 Double-click the Notepad icon.

Windows 98 launches the Notepad application program (Figure 3-13). The Untitled - Notepad button in the taskbar button area is recessed, indicating it is recessed, indicating it is active. Three windows now are open on the desktop. Although, the Forest - Paint window is not visible on the desktop, its button displays in the taskbar button area.

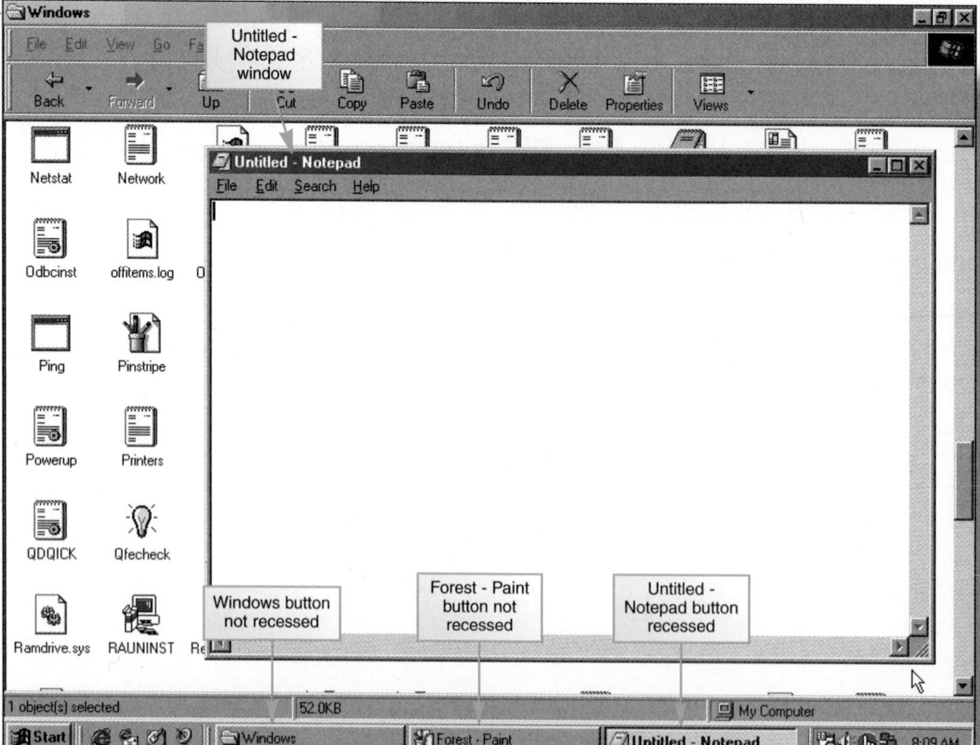

FIGURE 3-13

As seen in Figure 3-12, whenever you click a button for an open window in the taskbar button area, the window displays and becomes the active window. Windows 98 provides another method to switch between windows, as mentioned in the Other Ways box. If you press and hold the ALT key and then press the TAB key, a box showing an icon for each open window displays on the screen, together with the name of the active window. If you continue to hold the ALT key, each time you press the TAB key the name of the next open window will display and the associated icon in the box will be highlighted by a colored square. When you release the ALT key, the window associated with the highlighted icon will become the active window.

In this section, you have opened the My Computer window, the Hard disk (C:) window, a folder window (Windows), a document window (Forest - Paint), and an application program window (Notepad).

Other Ways

1. Click Windows button or press ALT+TAB until Windows displays in box on screen, right-click Notepad icon, click Open
2. Click Windows button or press ALT+TAB until Windows displays in box on screen, click Notepad icon, press ENTER

Managing Open Windows

In Figure 3-13, three windows are open. Windows 98 allows you to open many more windows, depending on the amount of RAM you have on your computer. As you can see in Figure 3-13, however, many open windows on the desktop can be cluttered and difficult to use. Therefore, Windows 98 provides some tools with which to manage open windows. You already have used one tool — the capability of maximizing a window. When a window is maximized, it occupies the entire screen and cannot be confused with other open windows.

In some cases, however, it is important that multiple windows display on the desktop. Windows 98 allows you to arrange the windows in specific ways. The following sections describe the ways in which you can manage open windows.

Cascading Windows

One way to organize windows on the desktop is to **cascade** them, which means they are displayed on top of each other in an organized manner. To cascade the open windows on the desktop shown in Figure 3-13, complete the steps on the next page.

More About

ALT+TAB

In Windows 3.1, a previous version of Windows, the most convenient way to switch between open windows was pressing the ALT+TAB keys. Microsoft discovered that most users either did not know about this method or were wary about using it. Therefore, few people were using the multitasking capabilities of Windows 3.1. Microsoft tried to solve the problem by placing the buttons of open windows on the taskbar.

More About

Managing Windows

Probably the most intimidating aspect of the Windows operating system is multiple windows open on the desktop. In addition to the techniques shown in this section, always remember that if you maximize a window, it is the only window you will see on the desktop. Then, if you want to switch to another open window, merely click its button in the taskbar button area and maximize it. Many people find working with one maximized window at a time the easiest way to contend with window clutter.

To Cascade Open Windows

1 Right-click an open area on the taskbar. Point to Cascade Windows on the shortcut menu.

A shortcut menu displays (Figure 3-14). The commands on the menu apply to the open windows on the desktop. The Notepad window no longer is the active window (light blue title bar and button not recessed).

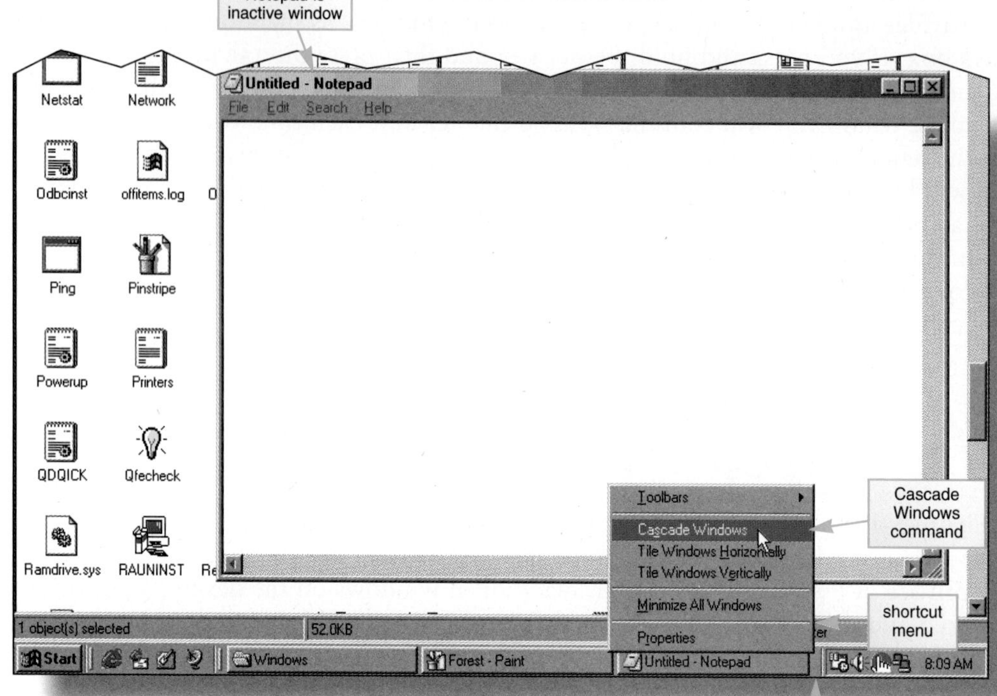

FIGURE 3-14

2 Click Cascade Windows.

The open windows display cascaded on the desktop (Figure 3-15). You can see the title bar of each window and the top two windows are moved slightly to the right. None of the windows is the active window (all light blue title bars and no recessed buttons).

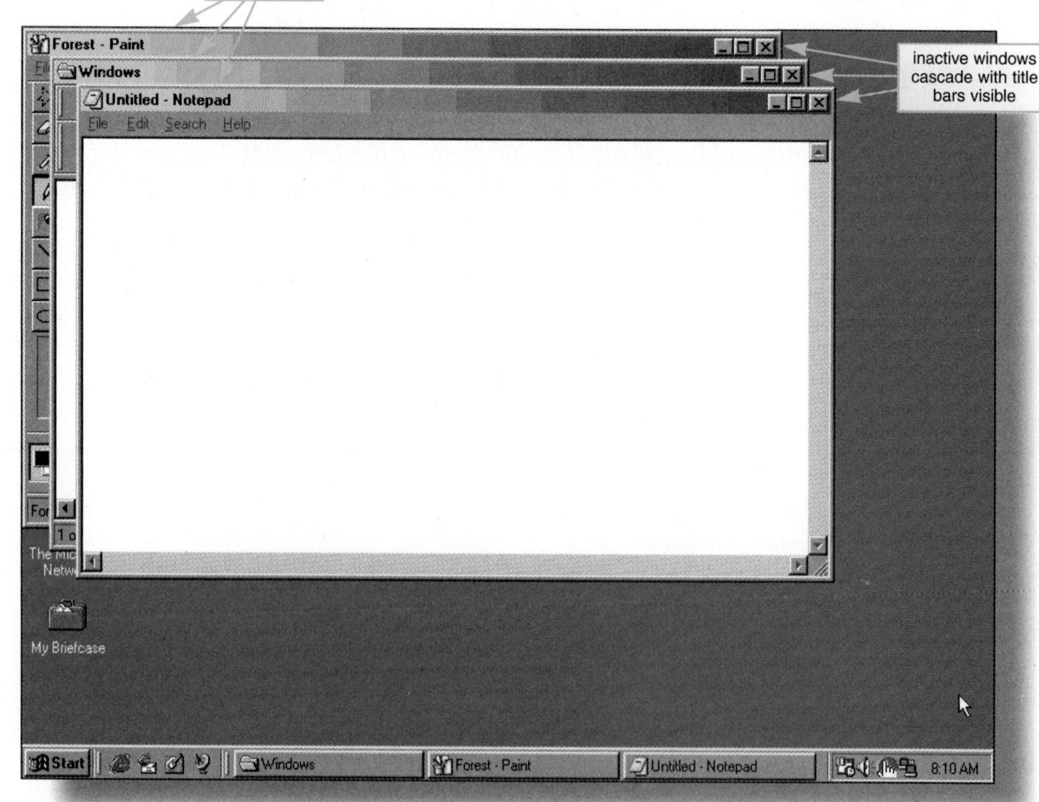

FIGURE 3-15

Other Ways

1. Right-click open area on taskbar, press S

Windows 98 cascades only windows that are open. Windows that are minimized or closed will not be cascaded on the desktop. When you cascade the open windows, the windows are resized for cascading. In Figure 3-15, all windows have been resized to be the same size.

More About

The Taskbar

When you cascade windows, you must right-click an open area of the taskbar to display a shortcut menu. Sometimes it is difficult to find an open area on the taskbar. If so, try right-clicking the area to the left or right of the taskbar buttons in the taskbar button area, the area to the left of the first icon on the Quick Launch toolbar, or a blank area in the status tray area.

Making a Window the Active Window

When windows are cascaded as shown in Figure 3-15, they are arranged so you see them easily, but you must make one of the windows the active window in order to work in the window. To make the Forest - Paint window the active window, complete the following step.

Steps To Make a Window the Active Window

1 Point to the Forest - Paint window title bar.

2 Click the Forest - Paint window title bar.

The Forest - Paint window moves to the top of the desktop indicating it is active (dark blue title bar) and the Forest - Paint button is recessed in the taskbar button area (Figure 3-16).

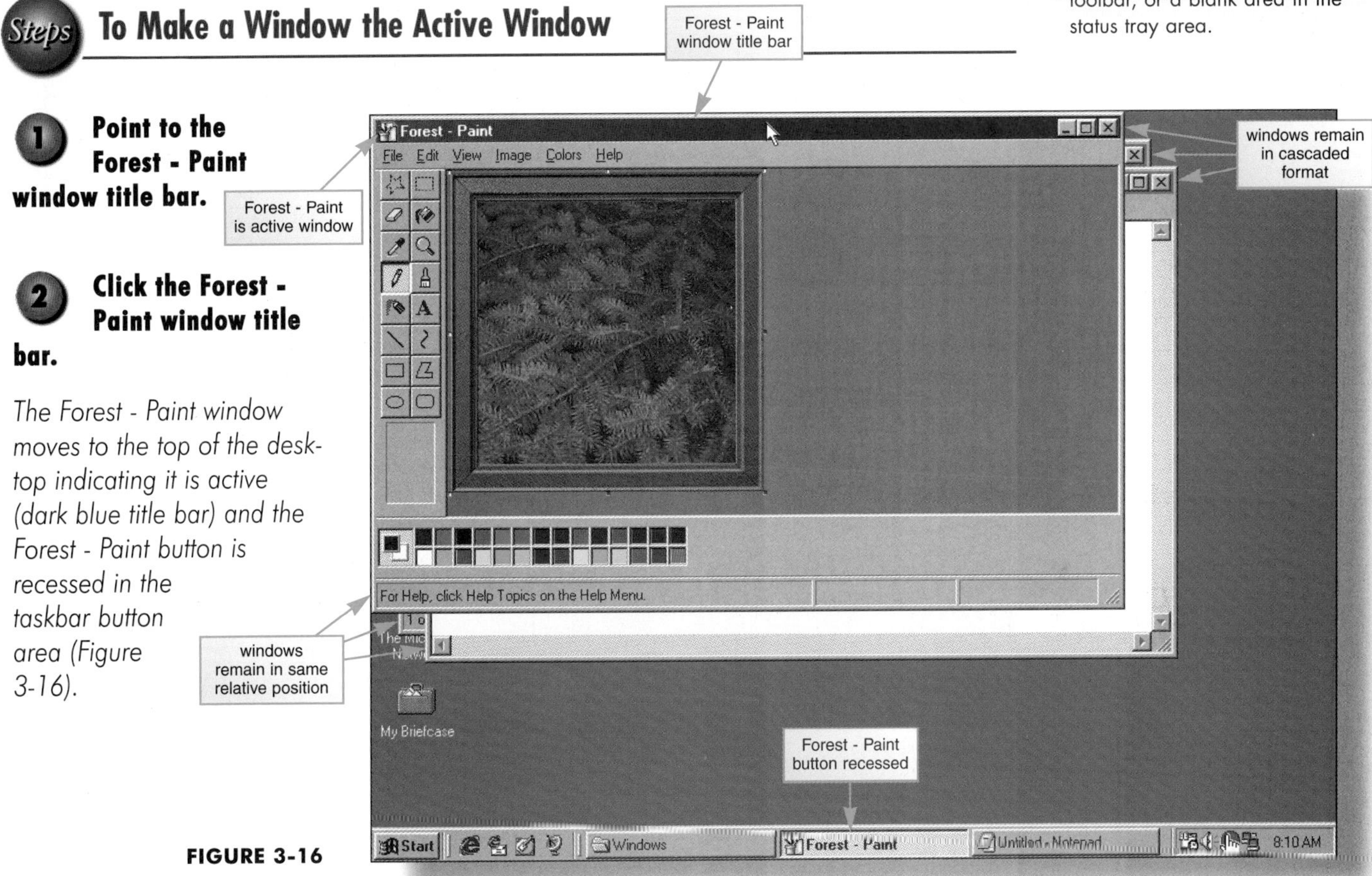

FIGURE 3-16

Other Ways

1. Click Forest - Paint button in taskbar button area
2. Press ALT+TAB until Forest - Paint displays in box, release ALT key
3. Click anywhere in window to make it active

The size of the Forest - Paint window in Figure 3-16 does not change and the other windows remain in a cascaded format. The Forest - Paint window title bar remains just above the Windows title bar, which is in the same relative position as it was when it was not the active window (see Figure 3-15).

To make a window the active window, you clicked the title bar of the window. You also can click the button in the taskbar button area of the window you want to make active, or you can click anywhere in the window that you want to be active. You do not necessarily have to click the title bar of the window.

Undo Cascade

Sometimes after you have cascaded the windows, you may want to undo the cascade operation and return the windows to their size and location before cascading. To undo the previous cascading, complete the following steps.

To Undo Cascading

1 Right-click an open area on the taskbar. Point to Undo Cascade on the shortcut menu (Figure 3-17).

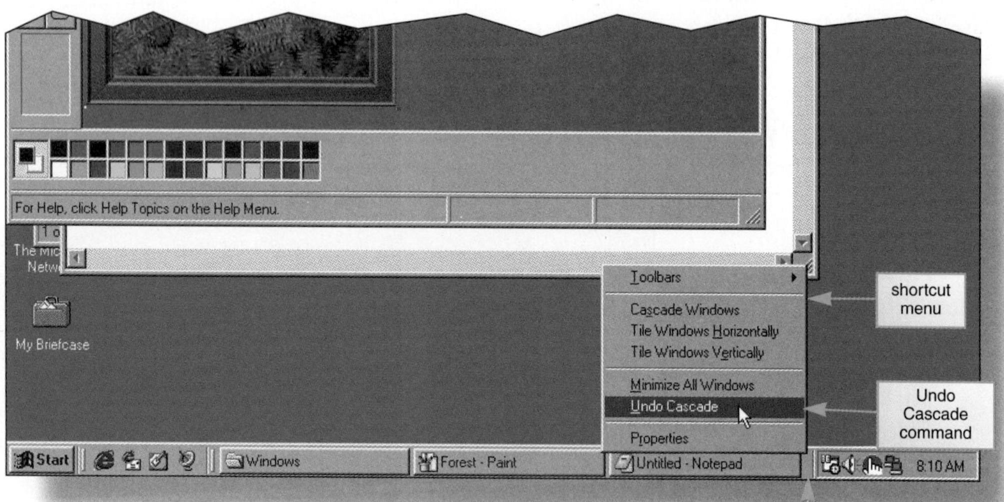

FIGURE 3-17

2 Click Undo Cascade.

The maximized Windows window displays on top of the other windows on the desktop (Figure 3-18). Although not visible in Figure 3-18, the windows on the desktop display as if they had never been cascaded. The only difference is the maximized Windows window remains on top instead of placing Notepad on top as before the windows were cascaded (see Figure 3-13 on page WIN 3.14 for the desktop prior to cascading).

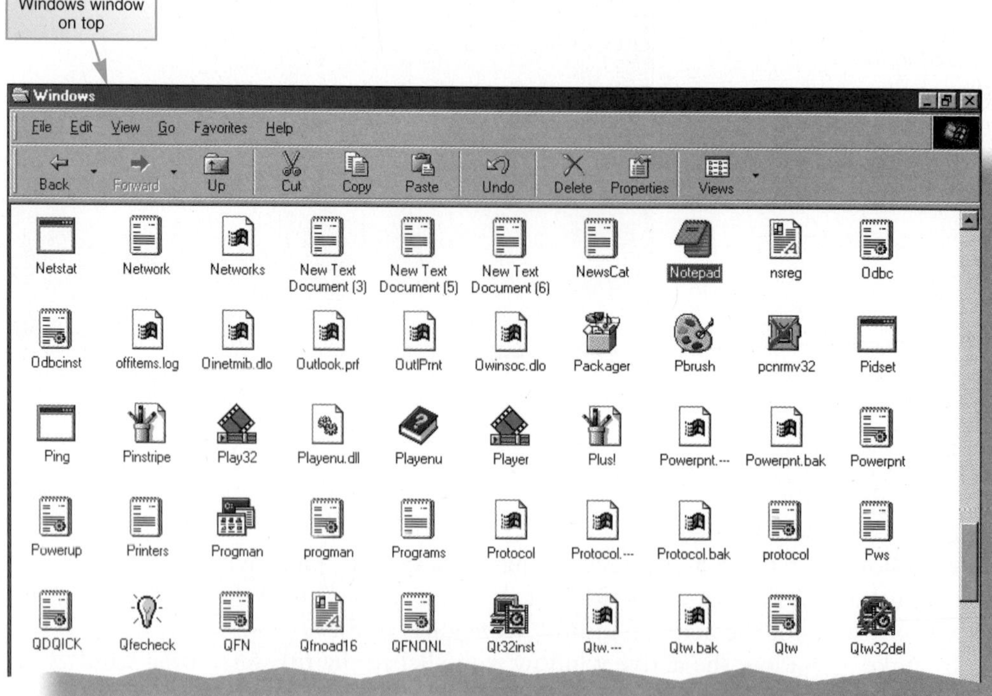

FIGURE 3-18

Other Ways

1. Right-click open area on taskbar, press U

Tiling Open Windows

While cascading arranges the windows on the desktop so each of the title bars in the windows is visible, it is impossible to see the contents of each window. Windows 98 also can **tile** the open windows, which allows you to see partial contents of each window. To tile the open windows in Figure 3-18, complete the following steps.

To Tile Open Windows

1 Right-click an open area on the taskbar. Point to Tile Windows Vertically on the shortcut menu (Figure 3-19).

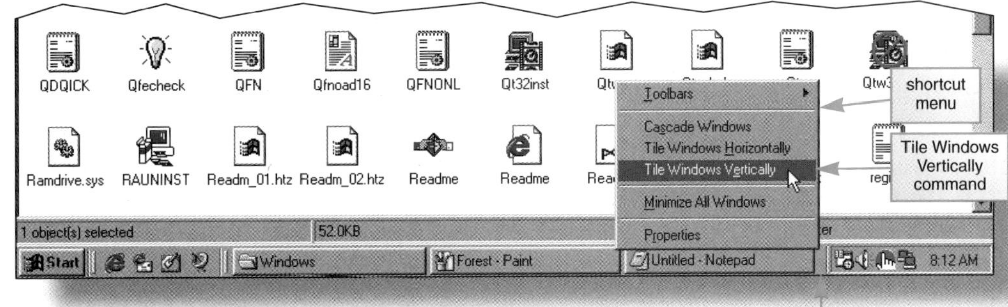

FIGURE 3-19

2 Click Tile Windows Vertically.

The three open windows are arranged in a tile format (Figure 3-20). The Paint window takes a slightly larger portion of the space in the middle because of the color box and covers the title bar of the Notepad window. None of the windows is active (no recessed buttons).

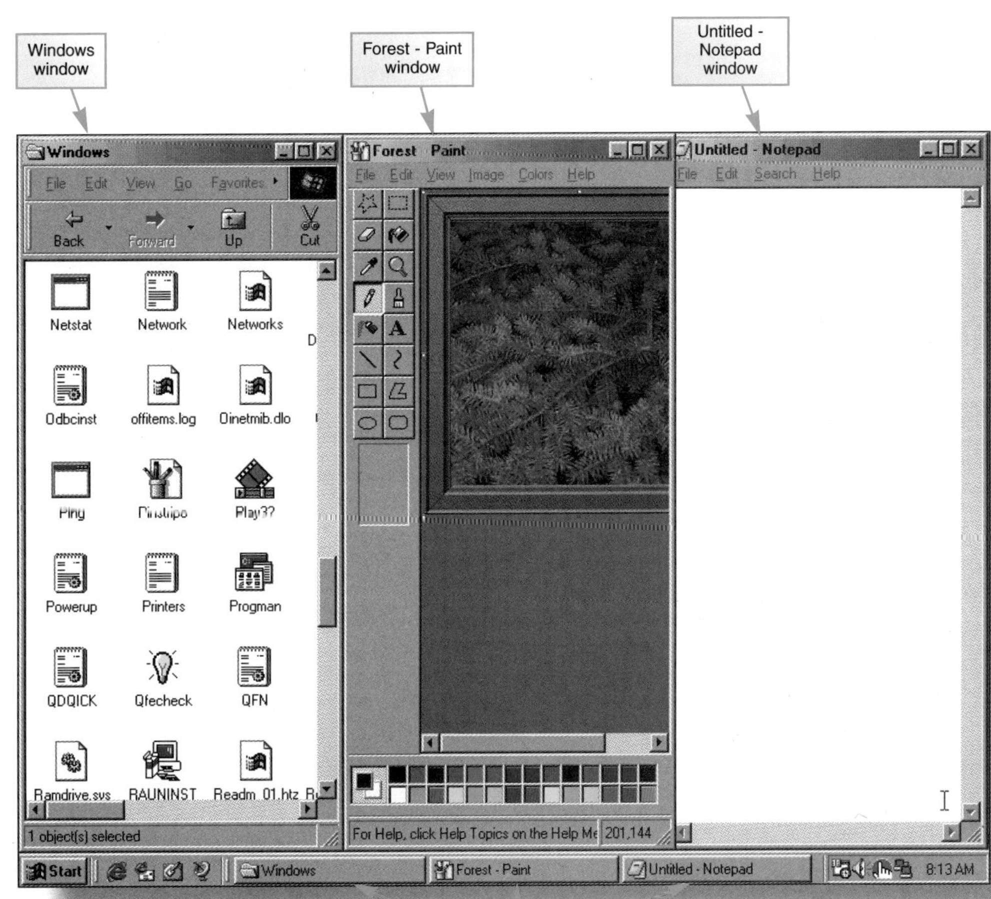

FIGURE 3-20

Other Ways

1. Right-click open area on taskbar, press E

While the windows shown in Figure 3-20 on the previous page are arranged so you can view all of them, it is likely that the size of each one is not useful for working. You can undo the tiling operation if you want to return the windows to the size and position they occupied prior to tiling. If you want to work in a particular window, you may want to click the Maximize button in that window to maximize the window.

To undo the tiling operation and return the windows to the format shown in Figure 3-18 on page WIN 3.18, complete the following steps.

Steps To Undo Tiling

1 Right-click an open area on the taskbar. Point to Undo Tile (Figure 3-21).

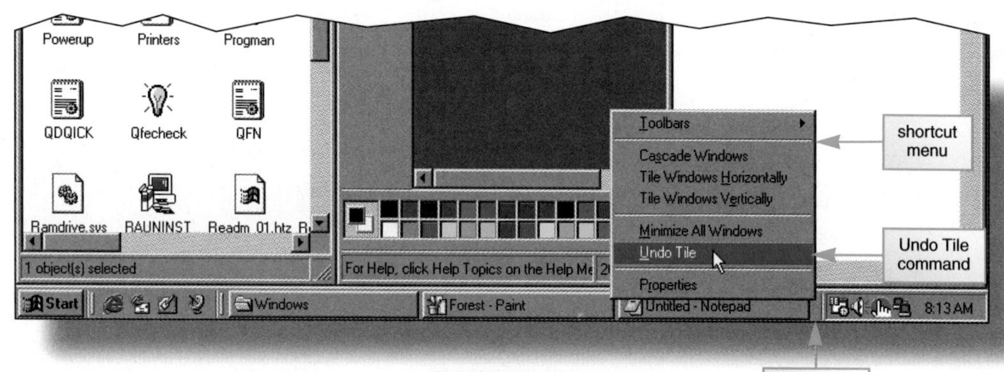

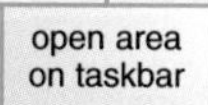

FIGURE 3-21

2 Click Undo Tile.

The windows no longer are tiled and display as if they had never been tiled (Figure 3-22). The maximized Windows window displays on top of the other windows on the desktop.

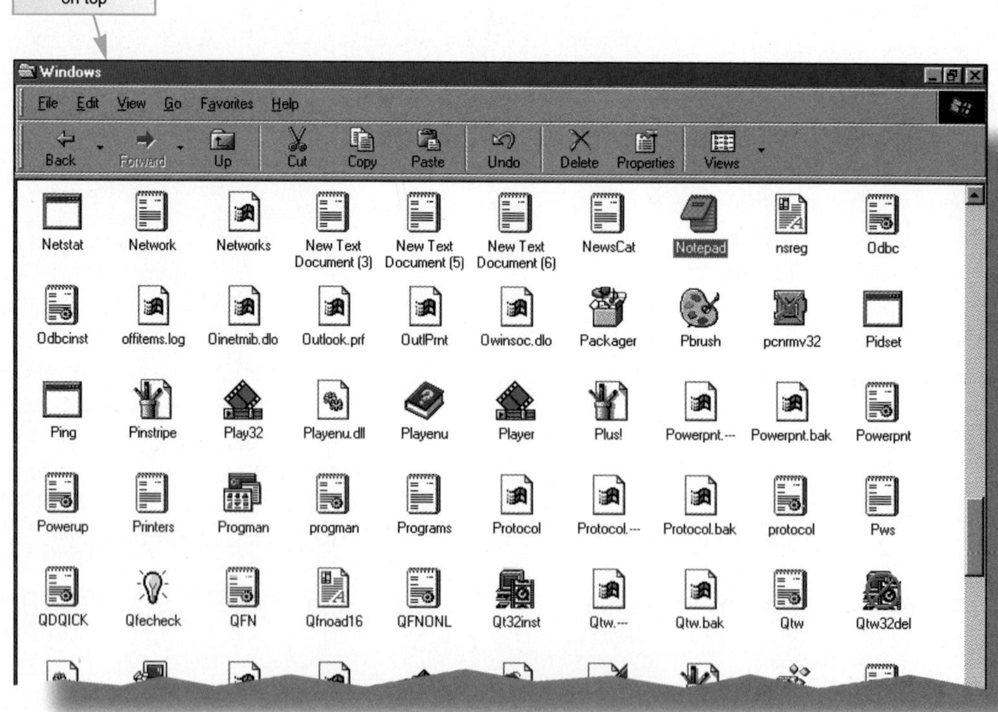

FIGURE 3-22

Other Ways

1. Right-click open area on taskbar, press U

Closing Windows

When you have finished working with windows, normally you should close the windows so your desktop remains as uncluttered as possible. To close the three open windows, complete the following steps.

TO CLOSE OPEN WINDOWS

1. Click the Close button in the Windows window.
2. Click the Close button in the Untitled - Notepad window.
3. Click the Close button in the Forest - Paint window.

All the windows are closed and the buttons no longer display in the taskbar button area (Figure 3-23).

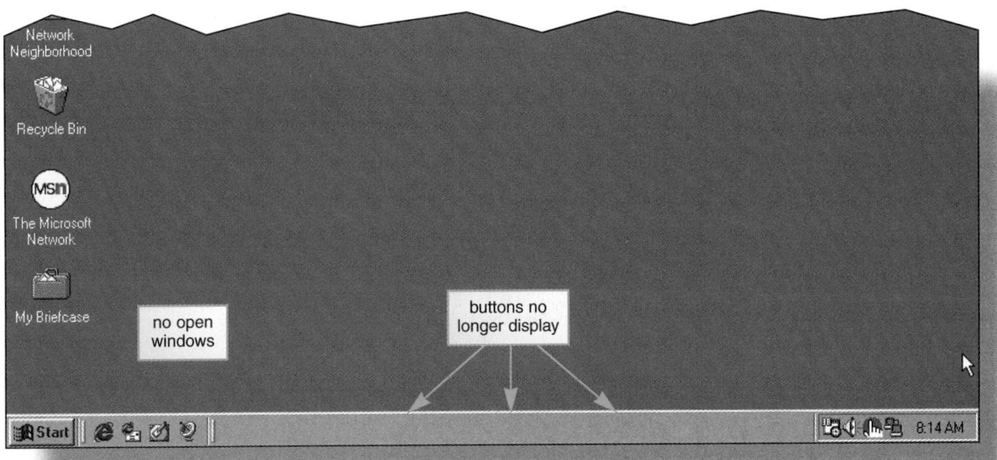

FIGURE 3-23

Copying, Moving, and Deleting Files in Windows

In Project 2, you learned how to move and copy document files on the desktop to a folder on the desktop, how to copy a folder from the desktop onto a floppy disk, and how to delete files from the floppy disk. Another method you can use to copy a file or folder is called the **copy and paste method**. To copy a document file from a folder to another folder or drive, open the window containing the file, point to the file to copy, and then click the Copy button on the Standard Buttons toolbar to place a copy of the file in a storage area of the computer called the **Clipboard**. Then, open the folder or drive window to contain the file, and click the Paste button on the Standard Buttons toolbar to copy the file from the Clipboard to the window. The following section explains how to perform these tasks.

> **More About**
>
> **Copying and Moving**
>
> "Copying, moving, it's all the same to me," you might be tempted to say. They are not the same at all! When you copy a file, it will be located in two different places: the place to which it was copied and the place from which it was copied. When a file is moved, it will be located in only one place, the location to which it was moved. Many users have been sorry they did not distinguish the difference when a file they thought they had copied was moved instead.

Copying Files from a Folder to a Drive

Assume you want to copy three files, Black Thatch, Bubbles, and Carved Stone, from the Windows folder onto the floppy disk in drive A. To copy from a folder, the folder window must be open on the desktop. To open the Windows window on drive C and display in the window the icons for the files to be copied, complete the steps on the next page.

TO OPEN A FOLDER WINDOW

1. Double-click the My Computer icon on the desktop.
2. Double-click the Hard disk (C:) icon in the My Computer window.
3. Double-click the Windows icon in the Hard disk (C:) window.
4. Scroll down in the Windows window until the icons for the Black Thatch, Bubbles, and Carved Stone files are visible in the window. If one or more of these icons is not in the Windows window on your computer, display any other icons.

The Black Thatch, Bubbles, and Carved Stone icons are visible in the Windows window (Figure 3-24). The Back button does not appear dimmed and this indicates more than one window has been opened. The Forward button appears dimmed indicating it is not available.

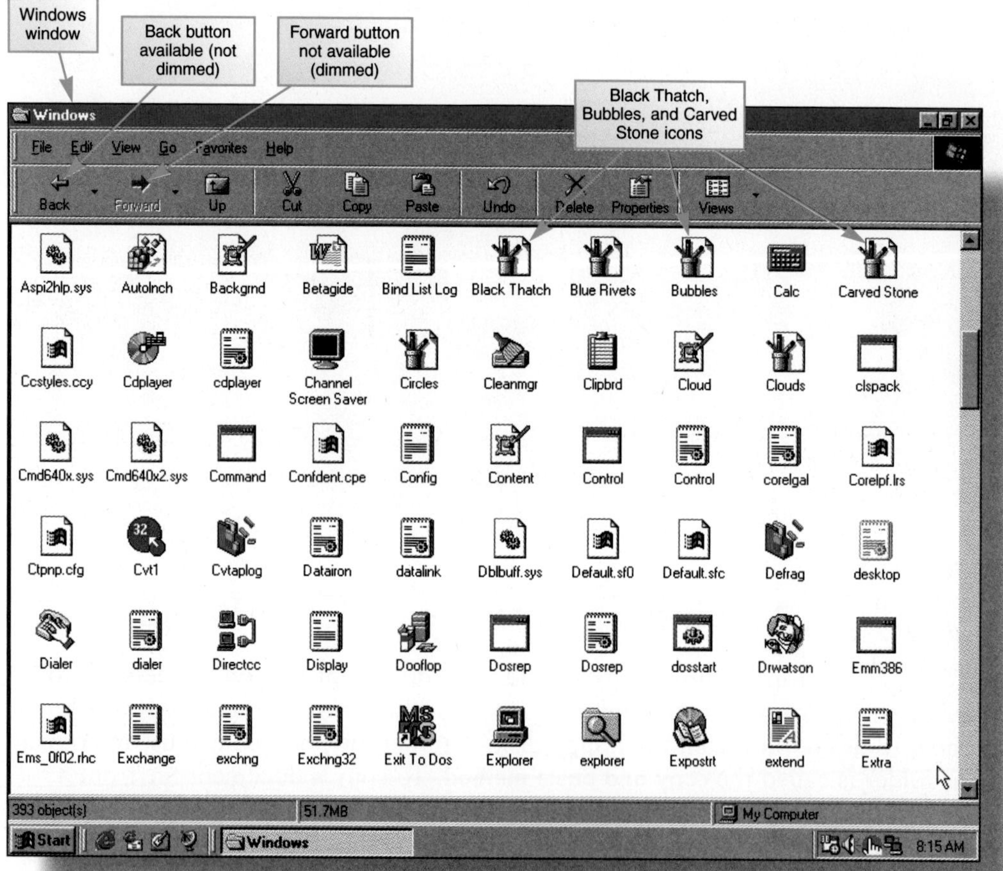

FIGURE 3-24

Once you have opened the folder window and the icons for the files to be copied display, you can select the files and then copy them. To copy the Black Thatch, Bubbles, and Carved Stone files onto the floppy disk in drive A, complete the following steps.

Steps To Copy Files from a Folder onto a Floppy Disk

1 Insert a formatted floppy disk in drive A of your computer.

2 Press and hold the CTRL key and click the Black Thatch icon, Bubbles icon, and Carved Stone icon. Release the CTRL key. Point to the Copy button on the Standard Buttons toolbar.

The Black Thatch, Bubbles, and Carved Stone icons are selected (Figure 3-25).

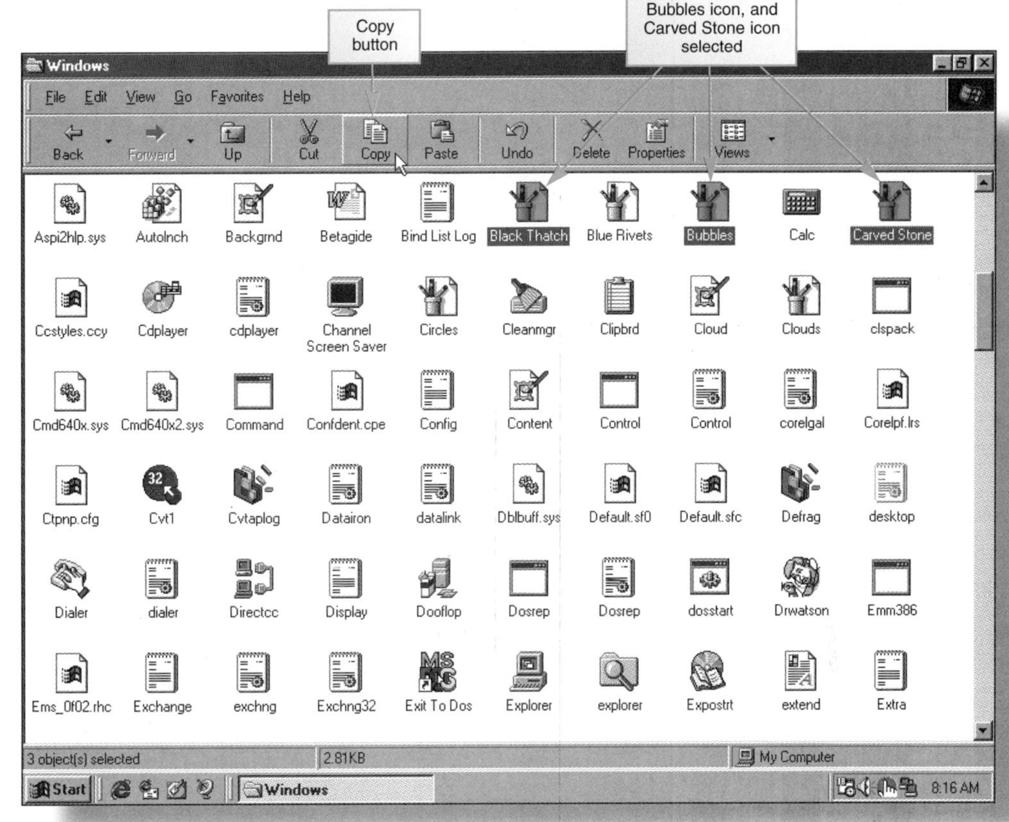

FIGURE 3-25

3 Click the Copy button. Point to the Back button arrow on the Standard Buttons toolbar (Figure 3-26).

Windows 98 copies the three files to the Clipboard. The Back button and arrow become three-dimensional.

FIGURE 3-26

4 **Click the Back button and then point to My Computer.**

The Back button menu displays containing the names of the previously opened windows (Hard disk (C:) and My Computer) (Figure 3-27).

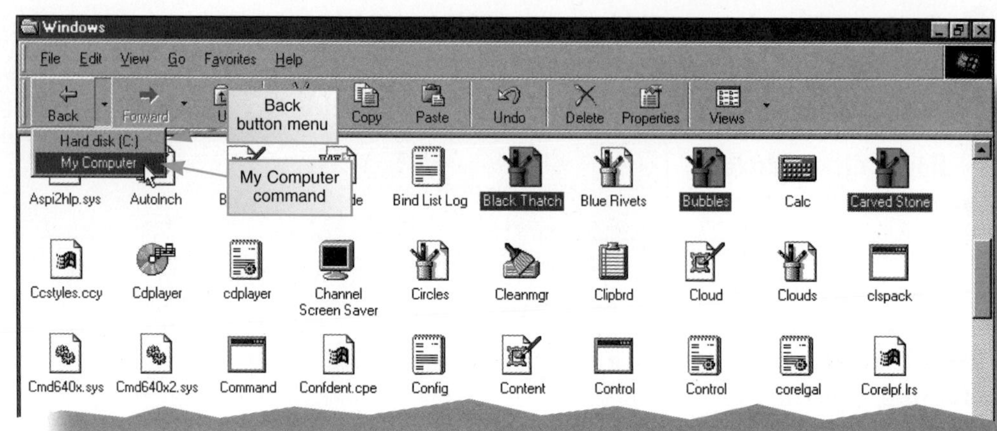

FIGURE 3-27

5 **Click My Computer. Point to the 3½ Floppy (A:) icon in the My Computer window.**

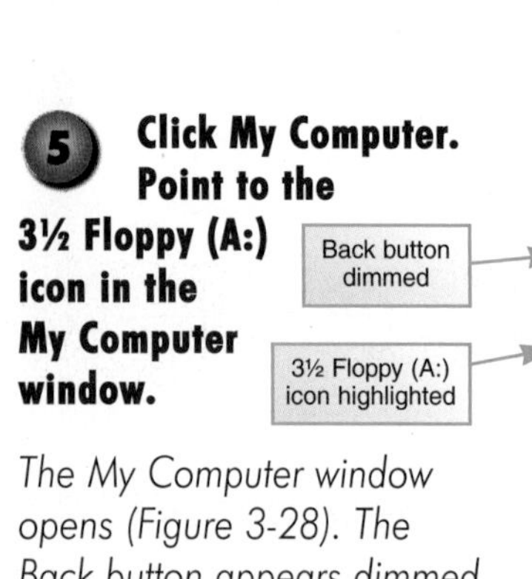

The My Computer window opens (Figure 3-28). The Back button appears dimmed indicating the My Computer window was the first window opened. The Forward button no longer appears dimmed.

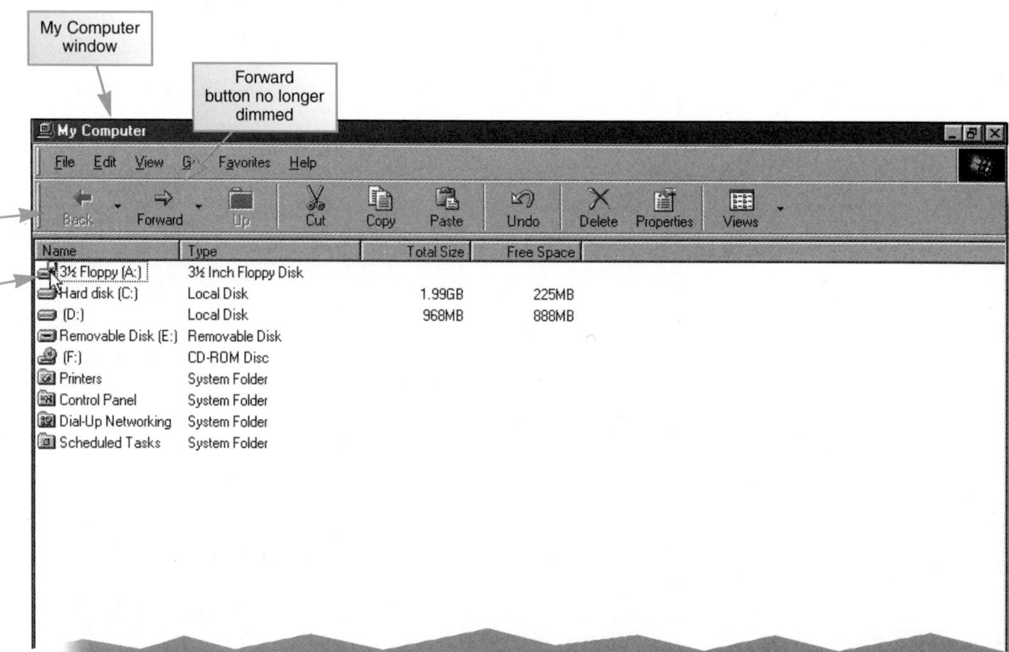

FIGURE 3-28

6 **Double-click the 3½ Floppy (A:) icon. Point to the Paste button on the Standard Buttons toolbar.**

The 3½ Floppy (A:) window opens (Figure 3-29).

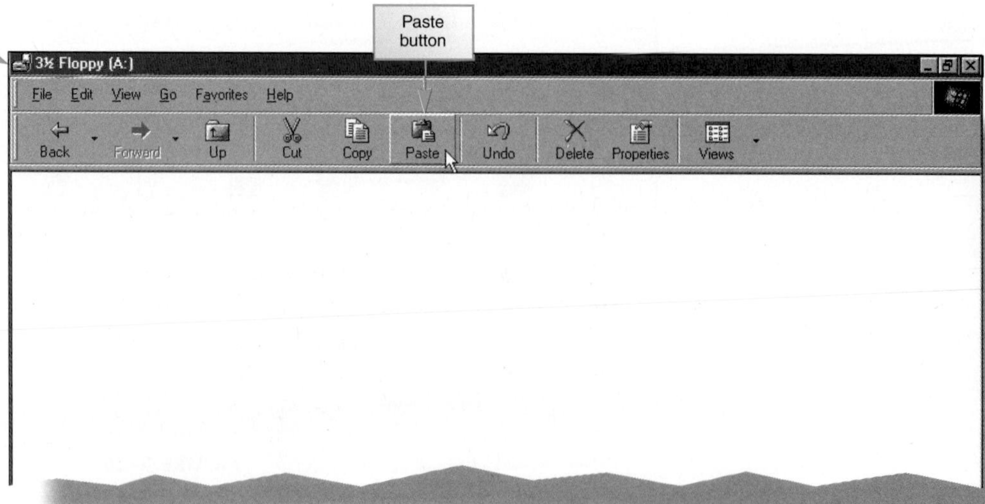

FIGURE 3-29

Click the Paste button.

While the files are being copied, the Copying dialog box displays indicating the files are being copied from the Windows folder to the disk in drive A (Figure 3-30). The dialog box contains the name of the file being copied, where the file is from, and to where the file is being copied. If you wish to terminate the copying process before it is complete, you can click the Cancel button.

8 Click the Close button to close the 3½ Floppy (A:) window.

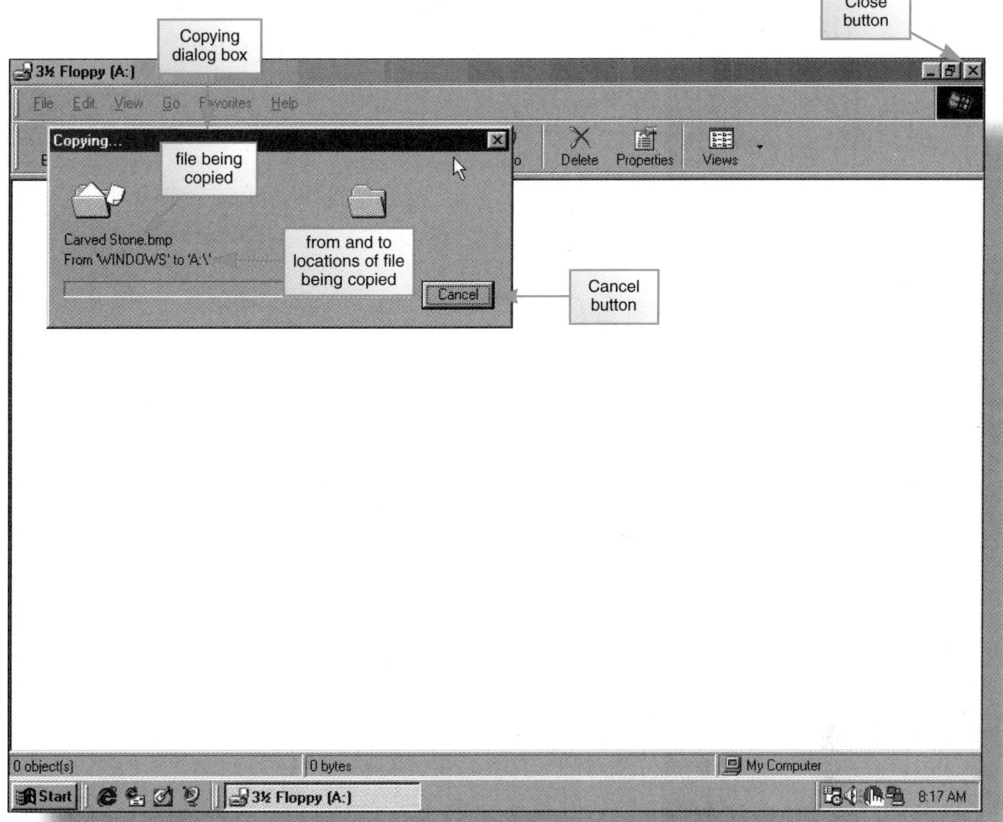

FIGURE 3-30

After copying the three files onto the floppy disk, the files are stored on both the floppy disk and in the Windows folder on drive C. If you want to move a file instead of copy a file, use the **Cut button** on the Standard Buttons toolbar to move the file to the clipboard and the Paste button to copy the file from the Clipboard to the new location. When the move is complete, the files are moved onto the floppy disk and are no longer stored in the Windows folder.

Moving and copying files is a common occurrence when working in Windows 98 and should be understood. Later in this project, you will see how to accomplish these same tasks using a Windows 98 program called Explorer.

Deleting Files in Windows

In Project 2, you saw how to delete shortcuts, folders, and files from the desktop. You can use the same techniques when deleting shortcuts, folders, and files from an open window. To review, the methods are: (1) right-drag the object (shortcut icon, folder icon, or file icon) to the Recycle Bin and then click Move Here on the shortcut menu; (2) right-click the object, click Delete on the shortcut menu, and then click the Yes button in the Confirm File Delete dialog box; and (3) drag the object to the Recycle Bin and then click the Yes button in the Confirm File Delete dialog box. A fourth method is available when deleting shortcuts, folders, or files from an open window: (4) click the object to be deleted, click File on the menu bar, click Delete, and then click the Yes button in the Confirm File Delete dialog box.

Other Ways

1. Select icons of file(s) to be copied, right-click an icon, click Copy, display window to contain file(s), right-click window, click Paste
2. Select icons of file(s) to be copied, on Edit menu click Copy, display window to contain file(s), on Edit menu click Paste
3. Select icons of file(s) to be copied, press CTRL+C, display window to contain file(s), press CTRL+V

More About

Deleting Files

Someone proposed the Delete command be removed from operating systems after an employee, who thought he knew what he was doing, deleted an entire database, which cost the company millions of dollars. The Delete command should be considered a dangerous weapon.

Copying, moving, and deleting shortcuts, folders, and files is an important part of using Windows 98. You should be completely comfortable with all these operations. In addition, your ability to manage windows on the Windows 98 desktop can make the difference between an organized approach to dealing with multiple windows and a disorganized, confusing mess of windows on your desktop.

More About

Windows 98 Explorer

For those familiar with Windows 3.1, Windows 98 Explorer bears some resemblance to File Manager. With the introduction of Windows 95, Microsoft made significant improvements and changed the basic way the program works. Those who passionately disliked File Manager found Explorer a better way to perform file maintenance.

Windows 98 Explorer

Windows 98 Explorer is another program that is part of Windows 98. It allows you to view the contents of your computer, including drives, folders, and files, in a hierarchical format. In Explorer, you also can move, copy, and delete files in much the same manner as you can when working with open windows. The following section explains how to work with Windows 98 Explorer.

Launching Windows 98 Explorer

As with many operations, Windows 98 offers a variety of ways in which to launch Explorer. To launch Explorer using the My Computer icon, complete the following steps.

Steps To Launch Explorer

1 Right-click the My Computer icon and then point to Explore on the shortcut menu.

A shortcut menu displays (Figure 3-31). The **Explore command** *will launch Windows 98 Explorer.*

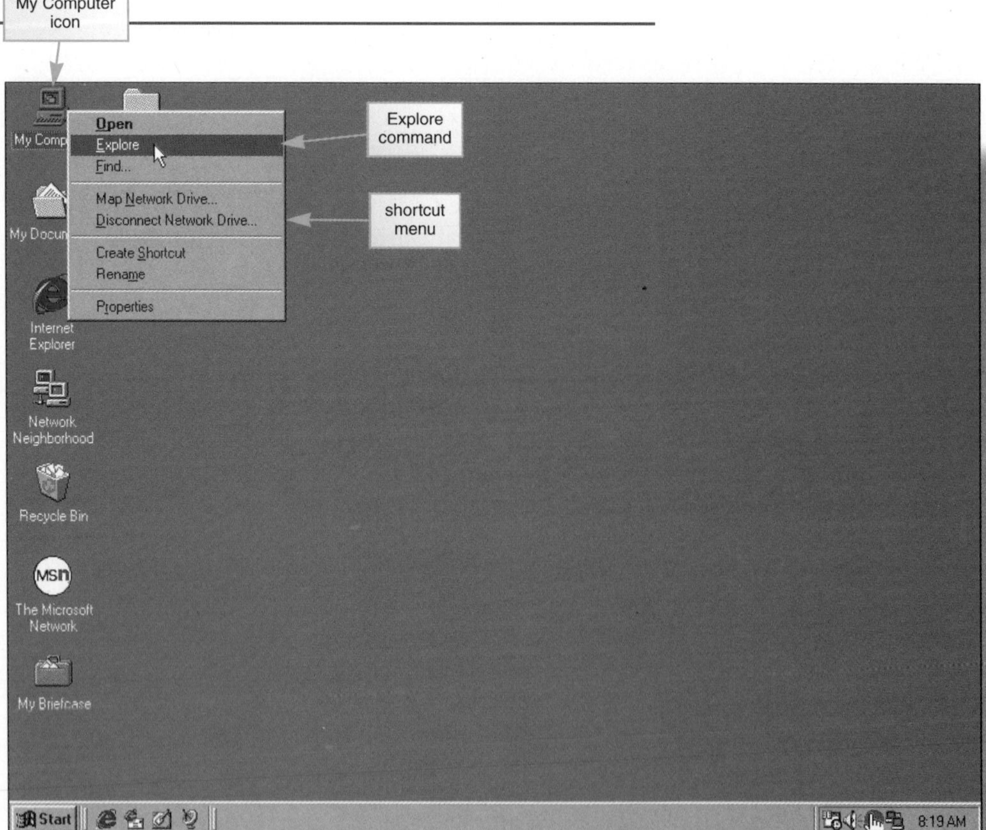

FIGURE 3-31

2 Click Explore. If necessary, maximize the Exploring - My Computer window.

The maximized Exploring - My Computer window displays (Figure 3-32).

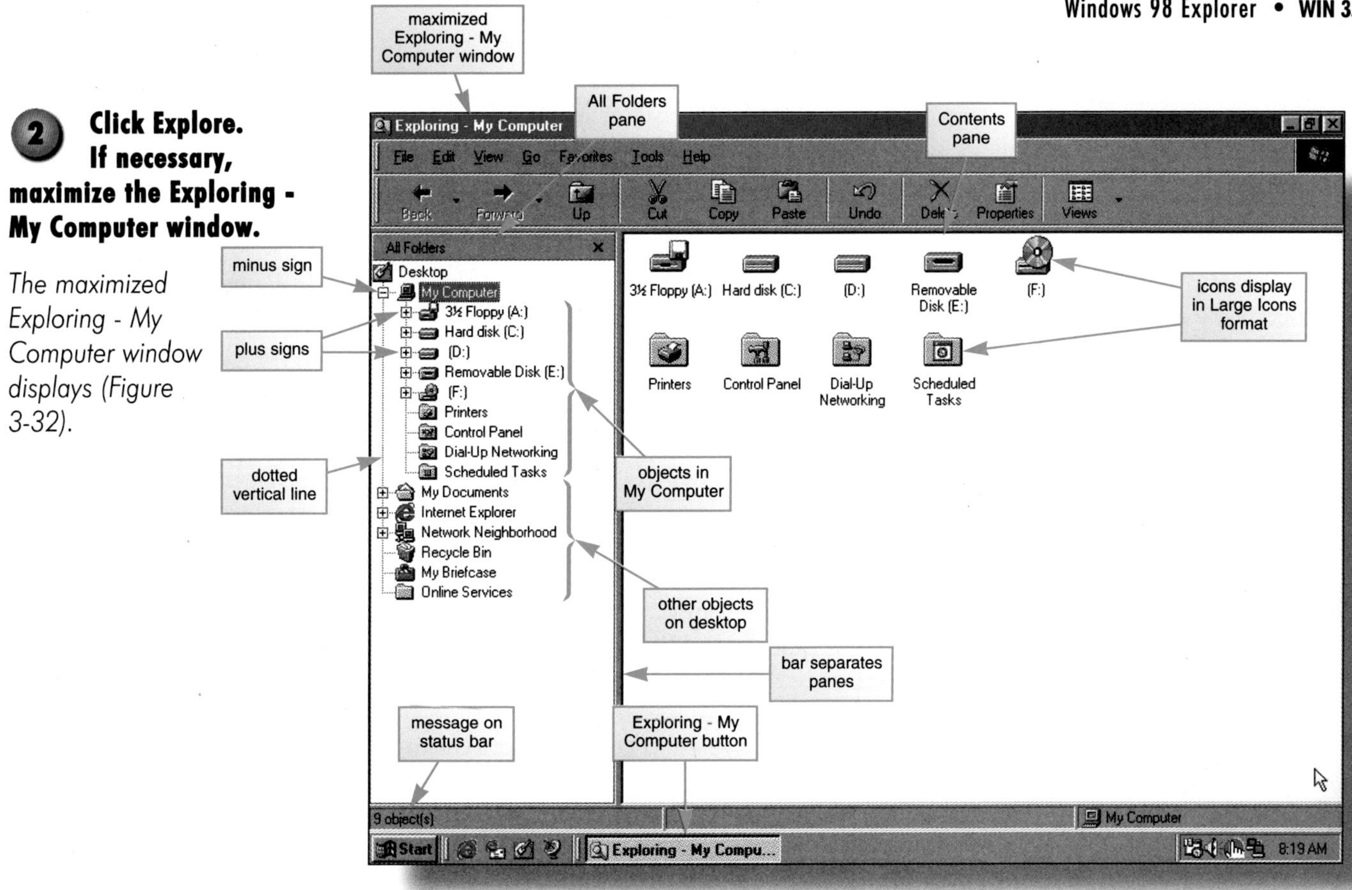

FIGURE 3-32

Explorer Window

The Exploring window in Figure 3-32 contains a number of elements, some of which should be familiar and some of which are new. The title bar in the window is the same as seen in other windows, and the menu bar contains the File, Edit, View, Go, Favorites, Tools, and Help menu names. The use of some of these menus will be explained later in this project. The Standard Buttons toolbar displays below the menu bar.

The main window is divided into two panes – the All Folders pane on the left and the Contents pane on the right. A bar separates the panes. You can drag the bar left or right to change the size of the two panes.

In the **All Folders pane**, Explorer displays, in a **hierarchical structure**, the icons and titles on the computer. The highest level in the hierarchy is the Desktop. Connected by a dotted vertical line below the Desktop are the My Computer, My Documents, Internet Explorer, Network Neighborhood, Recycle Bin, My Briefcase, and Online Services icons. These icons are found on the desktop. Your computer may have other icons.

Other Ways

1. Right-click Start button, click Explore on shortcut menu
2. Click Start button, point to Programs, click Windows Explorer
3. Right-click any icon on desktop (except The Microsoft Network icon and Outlook Express icon) or any button on Channel bar, click Explore on shortcut menu
4. Right-click Start button or any icon on desktop (except The Microsoft Network icon and Outlook Express icon) or any button on Channel bar, press E

More About

Large Icons

Research by Microsoft Corporation indicates that the Large Icons format is easier to work with and less confusing than the other icon formats. For this reason, the files and folders in the Exploring - My Computer window in Figure 3-32 display in the Large Icons format.

A Hierarchy

One definition of hierarchy in *Merriam Webster's Collegiate Dictionary Tenth Edition* is a division of angels. While no one would argue angels have anything to do with Windows 98, some preach that working with a hierarchical structure as presented by Explorer is less secular (of or relating to the world) and more spiritual (of or relating to supernatural phenomena) than the straightforward showing of files in windows. What do you think?

To the left of the My Computer icon and title is a minus sign in a small box. The **minus sign** indicates that the drive or folder represented by the icon next to it, in this case My Computer, contains additional folders or drives and these folders or drives are displayed below the icon. Thus, below the My Computer icon, again connected by a dotted vertical line, are the 3½ Floppy (A:) icon, Hard disk (C:) icon, (D:) icon, Removable Disk (E:) icon, (F:) icon, and the Printers, Control Panel, Dial-Up Networking, and Scheduled Tasks folder icons. These drives and folders are contained within the My Computer window, as seen in previous examples.

The 3½ Floppy (A:) icon, Hard disk (C:) icon, (D:) icon, Removable Disk (E:) icon, and (F:) icon each have a small box with a plus sign next to it. The **plus sign** indicates that the drive or folder represented by the icon has more folders within it but the folders are not displayed in the All Folders pane of the Exploring window. As you will see shortly, clicking the box with the plus sign will display the folders within the drive or folder represented by the icon. If an item contains no folders, such as Recycle Bin and My Briefcase, no hierarchy exists to display and, therefore, no small box displays next to the icons.

The **Contents pane** in the Exploring window is identical to the My Computer window (see Figure 3-1 on page WIN 3.5). The Contents pane contains the 3½ Floppy (A:) icon, Hard disk (C:) icon, (D:) icon, Removable Disk (E:) icon, (F:) icon, and the Printers, Control Panel, Dial-Up Networking, and Scheduled Tasks folder icons. These icons may be different and may display in a different format on your computer. A message on the left of the status bar located at the bottom of the window indicates the Contents pane contains nine objects.

Windows 98 Explorer displays the drives and folders on the computer in hierarchical structure. This arrangement allows you to move and copy files and folders using only the Exploring - My Computer window. In the following sections, you will learn how to accomplish these tasks.

Displaying Files and Folders in Windows 98 Explorer

You can display files and folders in the Contents pane of the window as large icons, small icons, a list, or with details. Currently, the files and folder in the Contents pane display in Large Icons format. The manner in which you display folder contents in the Contents pane largely is a matter of personal preference.

Displaying Drive and Folder Contents

Explorer is used to display both the hierarchy of items in the All Folders pane of the window and the contents of drives and folders in the Contents pane of the window. To display the contents of a drive or folder, you need only click the drive or folder icon in the All Folders pane of the window. To display the contents of the Hard disk (C:) drive, complete the following step.

To Display the Contents of a Drive

1 Click the Hard disk (C:) icon in the All Folders pane.

The Contents pane of the Exploring window contains the contents of drive C (Figure 3-33). Notice that all the folder icons display first and then the file icons display.

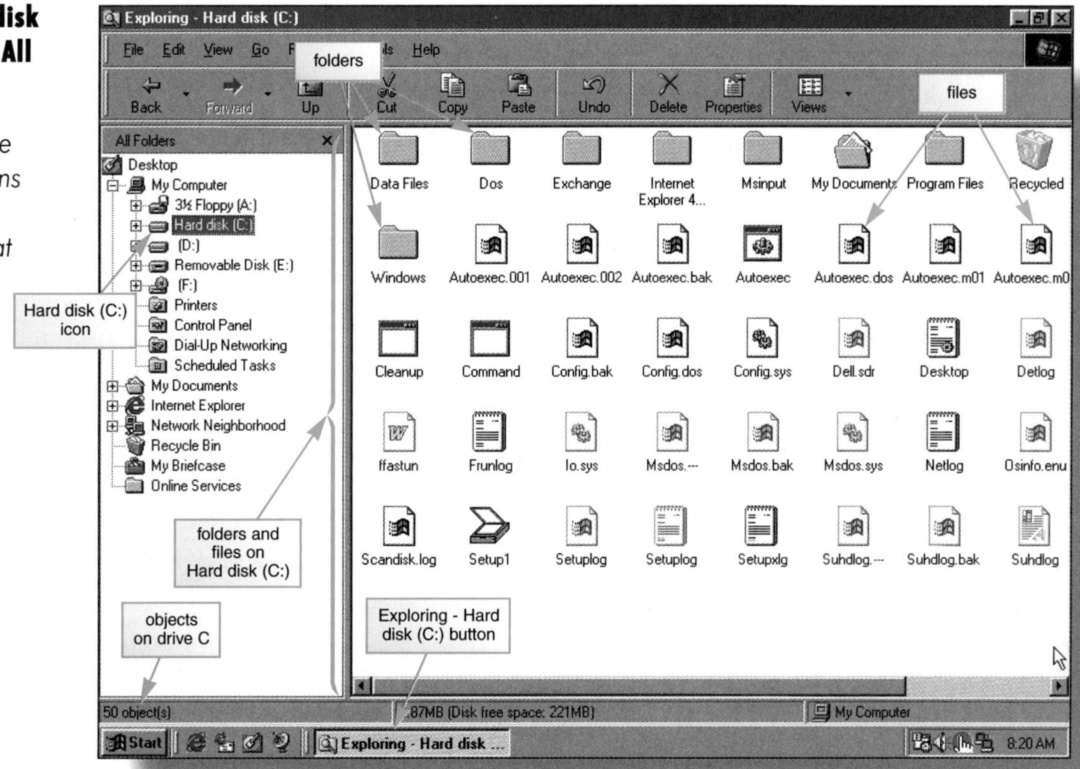

FIGURE 3-33

Other Ways

1. Double-click Hard disk (C:) icon in Contents pane
2. Press TAB to select any drive icon in All Folders pane, press DOWN ARROW or UP ARROW to select drive C icon in Contents pane
3. Press TAB to select any drive icon in Contents pane, press DOWN ARROW or UP ARROW to select drive C icon in Contents pane, press ENTER

The status bar shown in Figure 3-33 contains information about the folders and files displaying in the window. Fifty folders and files display in the window.

Expanding a Selected Drive or Folder

When a plus sign in a small box displays to the left of a drive or folder icon in the All Folders pane of the window, the drive or folder can be expanded to show all the folders it contains. To expand drive C and view the folders on drive C, complete the steps on the next page.

To Expand a Drive

1 Point to the plus sign in the small box to the left of the Hard disk (C:) icon (Figure 3-34).

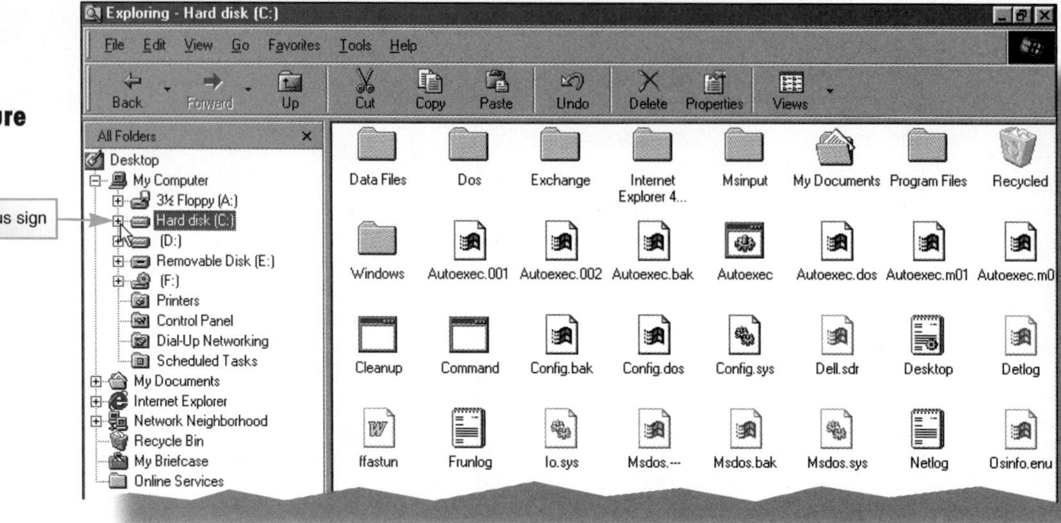

FIGURE 3-34

2 Click the plus sign.

The hierarchy below the Hard disk (C:) icon expands to display folders contained on drive C (Figure 3-35). A dotted vertical line connects these folders. A folder without a plus sign to the left of it contains no more folders. A folder with a plus sign to the left of it contains more folders. The minus sign to the left of the Hard disk (C:) icon indicates the drive has been expanded.

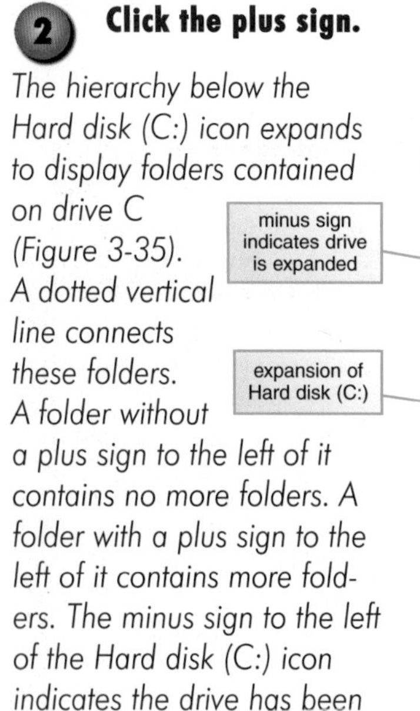

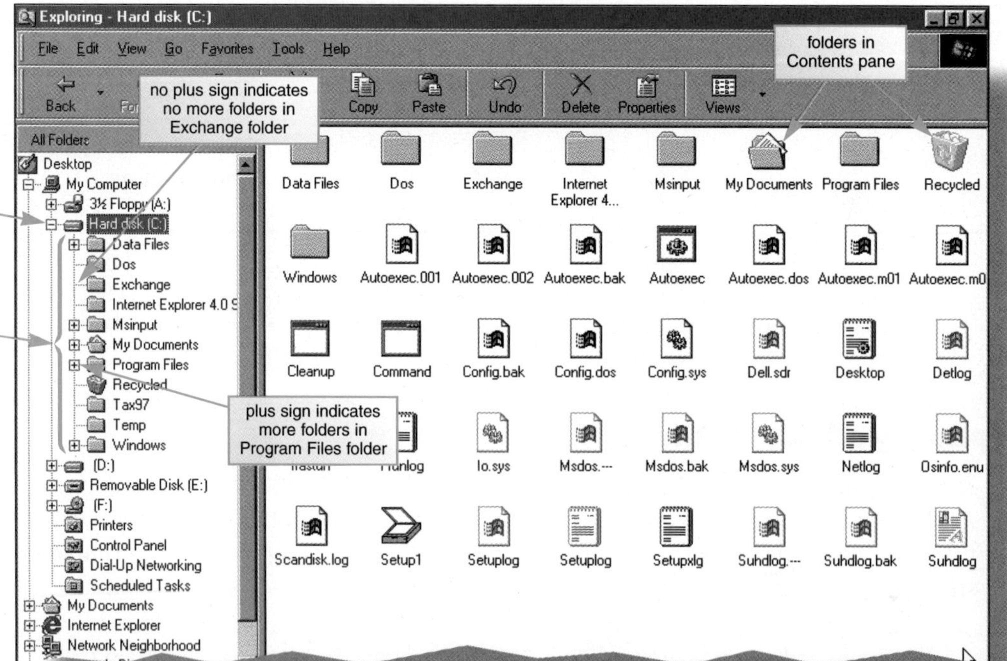

FIGURE 3-35

Other Ways

1. Double-click highlighted drive icon in All Folders pane
2. Select drive to expand, press PLUS on numeric keyboard
3. Select drive to expand, press RIGHT ARROW

With a drive or folder expanded, folders contained within the expanded drive or folder display in the All Folders pane of the window. You can continue this expansion to view further levels of the hierarchy. To expand the Windows folder, complete the following steps.

Steps To Expand a Folder

1 Point to the plus sign in the small box to the left of the Windows icon (Figure 3-36).

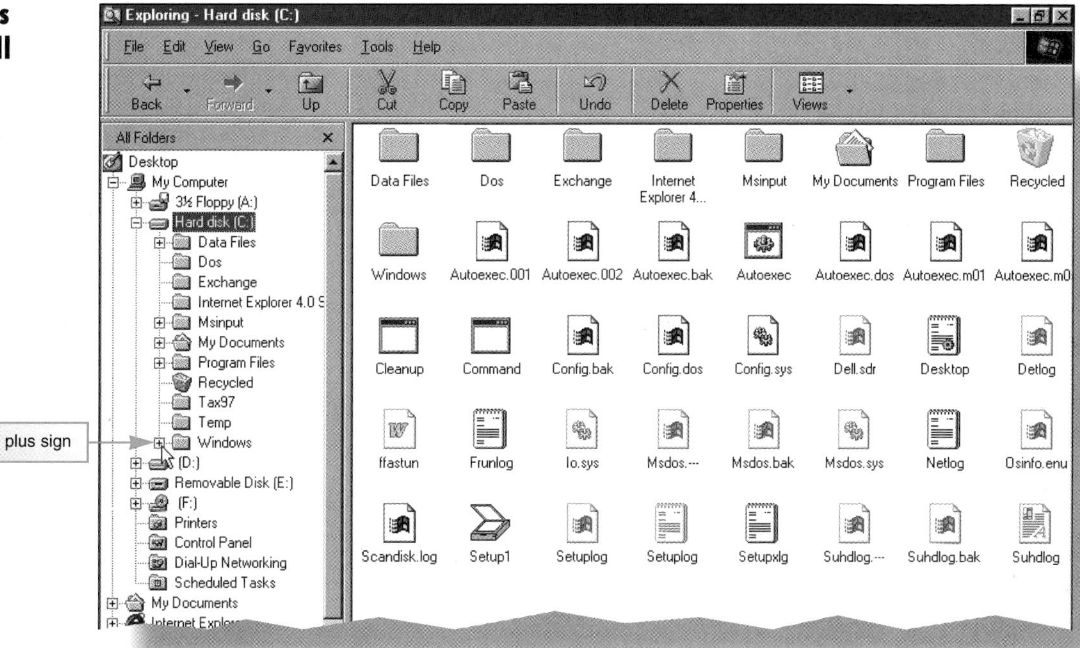

FIGURE 3-36

2 Click the plus sign.

The Windows icon displays at the top of the All Folders pane and the Windows folder expands (Figure 3-37). Some of the folders in the Windows folder contain more folders and others do not. The minus sign to the left of the Windows folder indicates it is expanded.

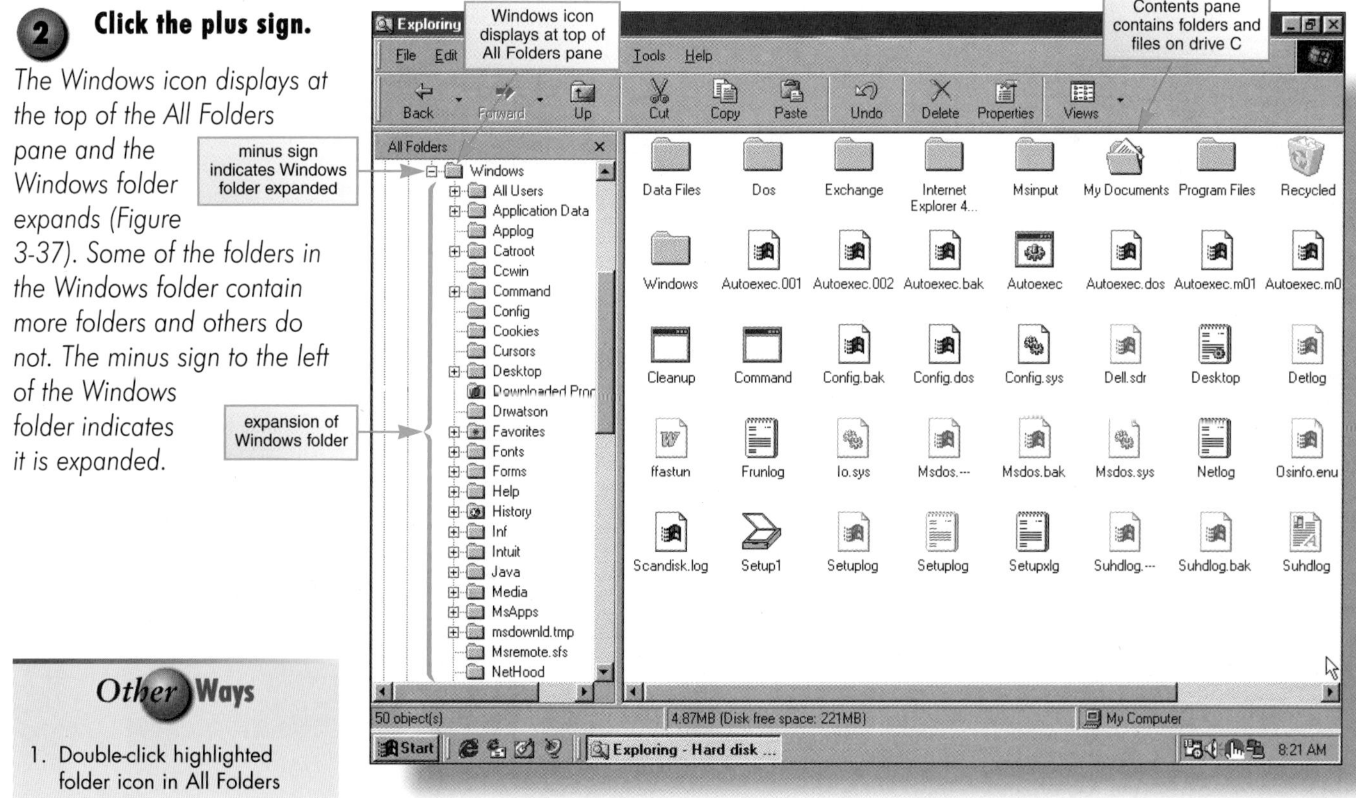

FIGURE 3-37

Other Ways

1. Double-click highlighted folder icon in All Folders pane
2. Select folder to expand, press PLUS
3. Select folder to expand, press RIGHT ARROW

In Figure 3-37 on the previous page, the Windows folder is expanded but the Contents pane of the window still contains the contents of Hard disk (C:) because the Windows folder was not opened. It was expanded but not opened by clicking the plus sign next to the Windows icon.

Opening Folders in Explorer

Whenever you display folders and files in the Contents pane of the Exploring window, you can open these folders and files in a separate window on the desktop. For example, to open the Programs window, complete the following steps.

Steps To Open a Folder Window in Explorer

1 If the Start Menu icon is not visible in the All Folders pane, scroll to make the icon visible. Click the Start Menu icon. Right-click the Programs icon in the Contents pane of the window. Point to Open on the shortcut menu.

The open Start Menu icon displays in the All Folders pane and a shortcut menu displays in the Contents pane (Figure 3-38).

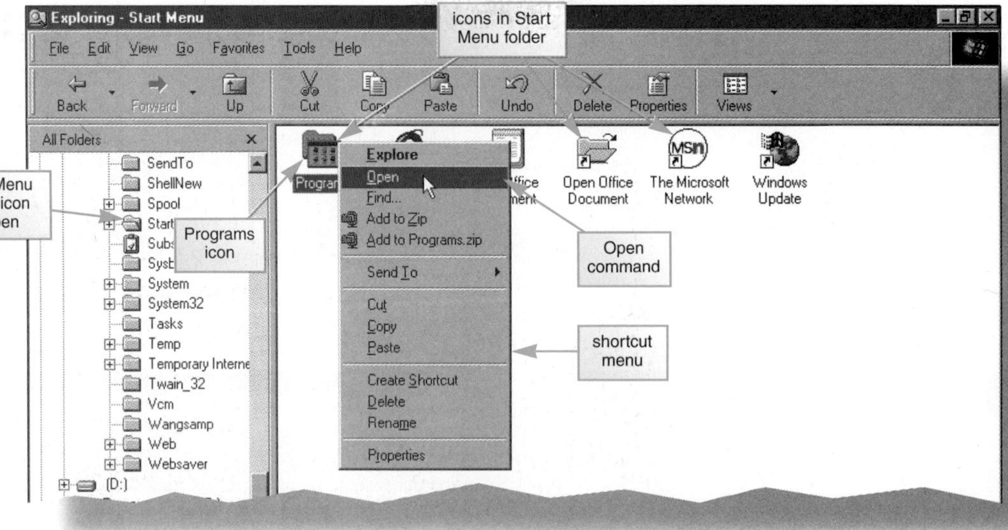

FIGURE 3-38

Click Open.

The Programs window opens on top of the Exploring window (Figure 3-39). The Programs window contains folders and shortcuts.

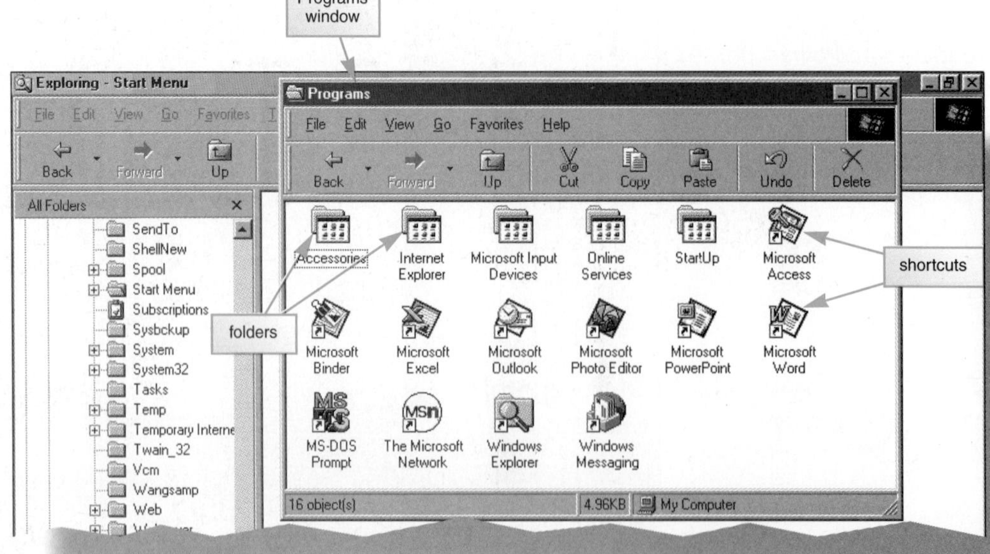

FIGURE 3-39

Other Ways

1. Right-click Programs icon in Contents pane, press O

In Figure 3-38, the Explore command on the shortcut menu is in bold (dark) font. This means Explore is the default command on the shortcut menu. If you double-click the Programs icon in the Contents pane of the Exploring window, the Explore command will be executed. When it is, the contents of the Programs folder will display in the Contents pane of the Exploring window.

Programs Folder

The **Programs folder** contains all the folders and shortcuts found on the Programs submenu when you click the Start button and point to Programs. Figure 3-40 illustrates the Programs submenu and the corresponding objects in the Programs folder. Notice that Accessories on the Programs submenu corresponds to the Accessories folder in the Programs window. Similarly, the Internet Explorer, StartUp, and Microsoft Outlook folders and shortcut correspond to the entries on the Programs submenu. Thus, you can see that the entries on the Programs submenu actually are folders and shortcuts in the Programs folder.

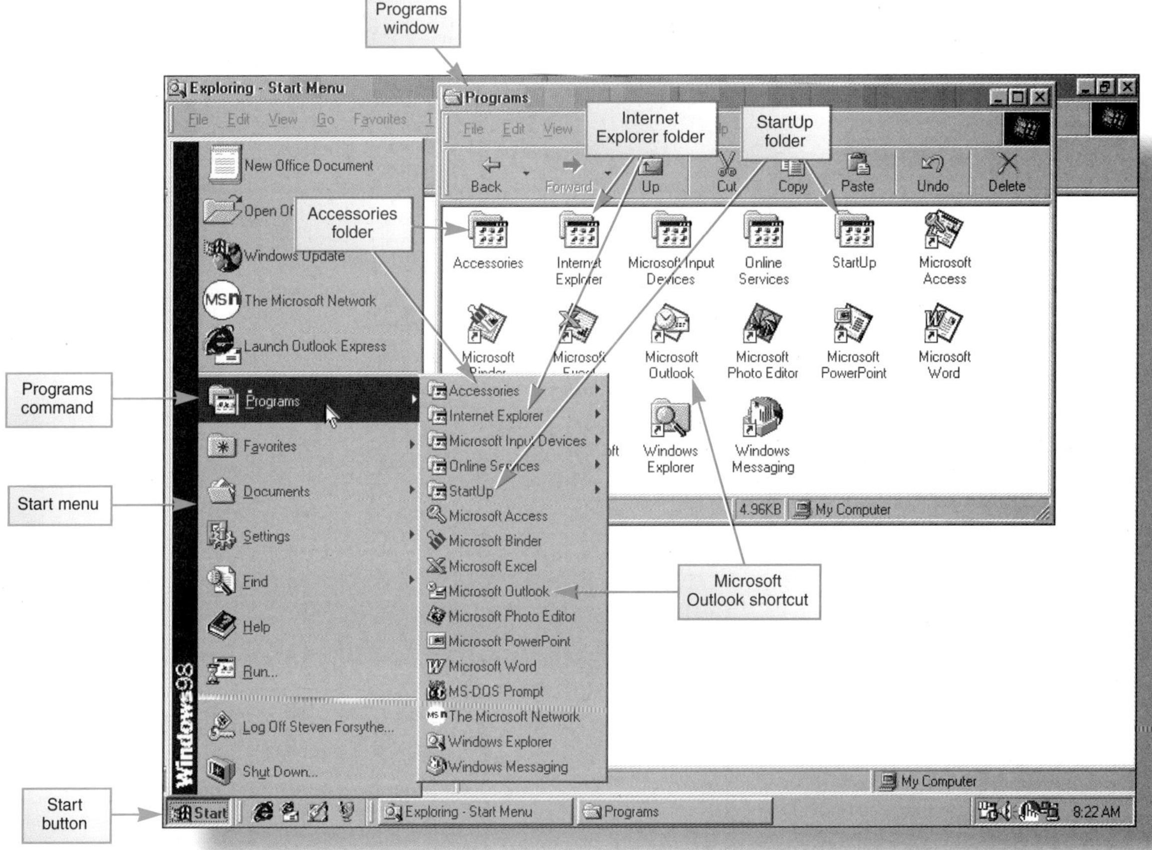

FIGURE 3-40

The Programs window shown in Figure 3-39 must be closed. To close the Programs window, complete the following step.

TO CLOSE A WINDOW

 Click the Close button on the Programs window title bar.

The Programs window closes and the Start menu no longer displays.

Launching an Application Program from Windows 98 Explorer

You can launch an application program from the Contents pane of the Exploring window using the same techniques you used for launching an application program from an open window earlier in this project (see Figure 3-12 and Figure 3-13 on page WIN 3.14). To launch the Internet Explorer program stored in the Internet Explorer folder from the Contents pane of the Exploring window, complete the following steps.

To Launch an Application Program from Explorer

1 Click the plus sign to the left of the Start Menu icon in the All Folders pane. Click the plus sign to the left of the Programs icon. If necessary, scroll the All Folders pane to the right to see the icon titles. Click the Internet Explorer folder icon in the All Folders pane. Point to the Internet Explorer shortcut icon in the Contents pane.

The Start Menu and Programs folders are expanded and the contents of the Internet Explorer folder display in the Contents pane (Figure 3-41).

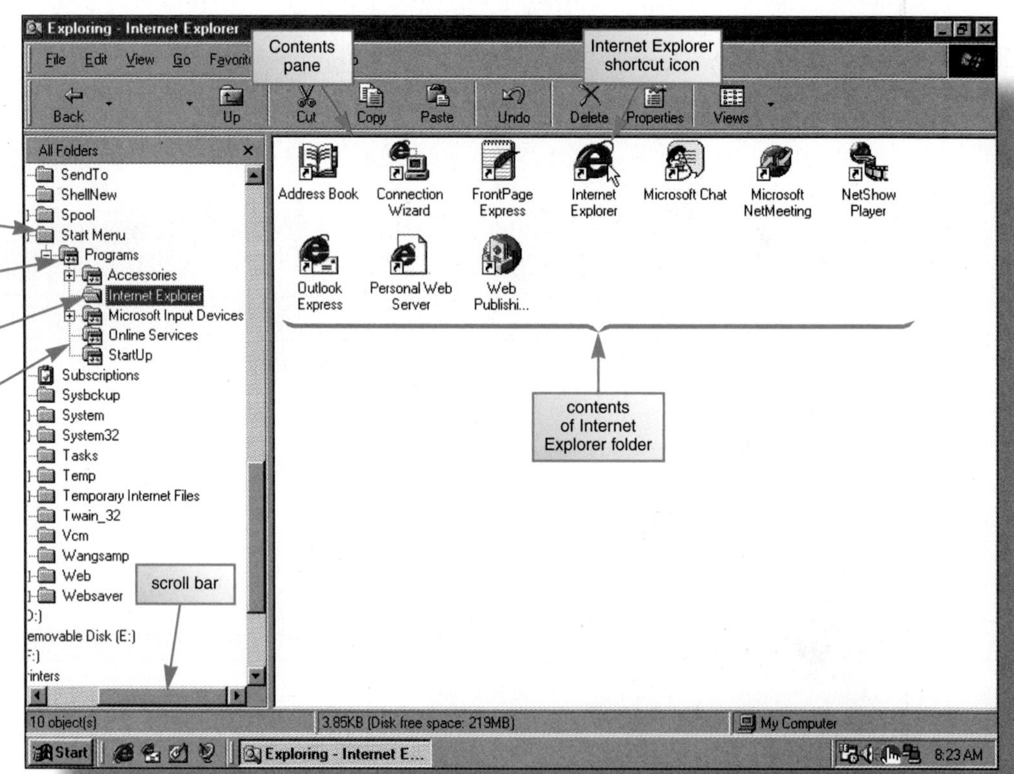

FIGURE 3-41

Double-click the Internet Explorer shortcut icon.

Windows 98 launches the Internet Explorer program. The MSN.COM, Welcome Page - Microsoft Internet Explorer window opens and the Welcome to MSN.COM page displays (Figure 3-42). Because Web pages are modified frequently, the Web page that displays on your desktop may be different from the Web page in Figure 3-42. The URL for the Web page displays in the Address bar.

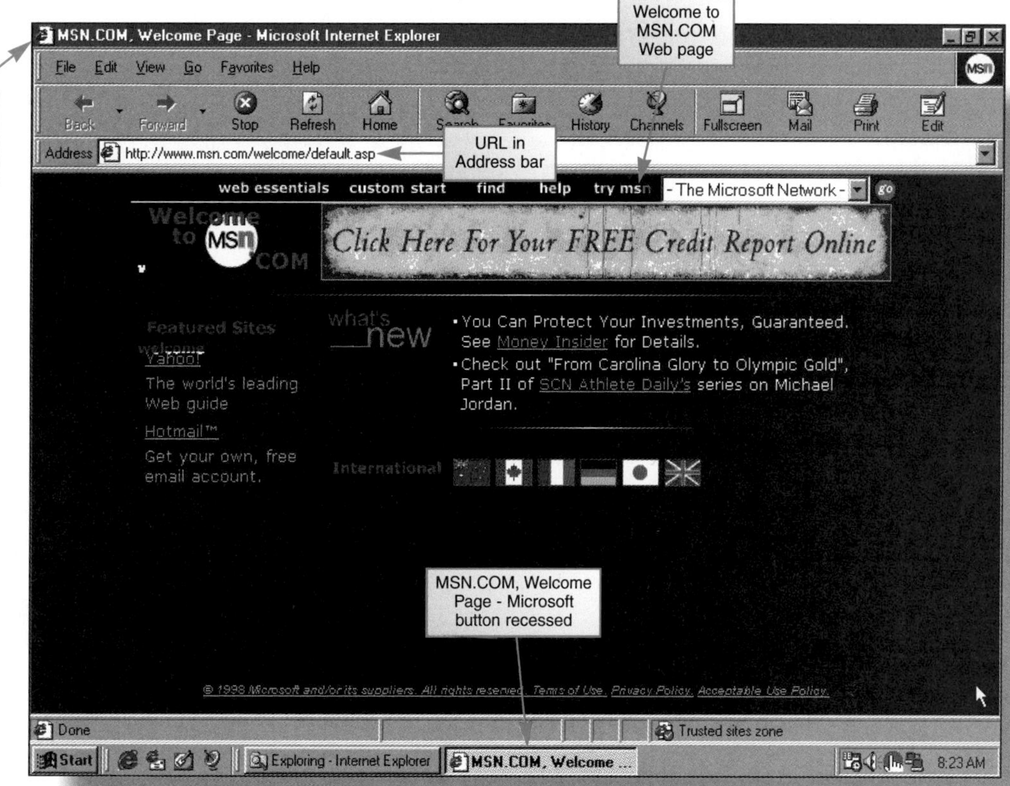

FIGURE 3-42

Other Ways

1. Right-click Internet Explorer shortcut icon, click Open
2. Click Internet Explorer shortcut icon, press ENTER

You can use the Internet Explorer program for any purpose you want, just as if you had launched it from the desktop or Quick Launch toolbar. When you are finished with the Internet Explorer program, you should close the program. To close the Internet Explorer program, complete the following step.

TO CLOSE AN APPLICATION PROGRAM

Click the Close button on MSN.COM, Welcome Page - Microsoft Internet Explorer title bar.

Closing Folder Expansions

Sometimes, after you have completed work with expanded folders in Explorer, you will want to close the expansions while still leaving Explorer open. To close the open folders shown in Figure 3-41, complete the steps on the next two pages.

Launching Programs in Explorer

Usually, people find starting application programs from the Start menu or from a window easier and more intuitive than starting programs from Explorer. In most cases, you will not be launching programs from Explorer.

To Close Expanded Folders

1 If necessary, scroll to the left in the All Folders pane so the Programs and Start Menu icons are visible. Click the minus sign to the left of the Programs icon. Click the minus sign to the left of the Start Menu icon.

The expansion of both folders close (Figure 3-43). The minus sign to the left of the Start Menu icon changes to a plus sign. When you close the expansion of a folder by clicking the minus sign, the contents of the folder display in the Contents pane of the Exploring window, so the contents of the Start Menu folder display in the Contents pane.

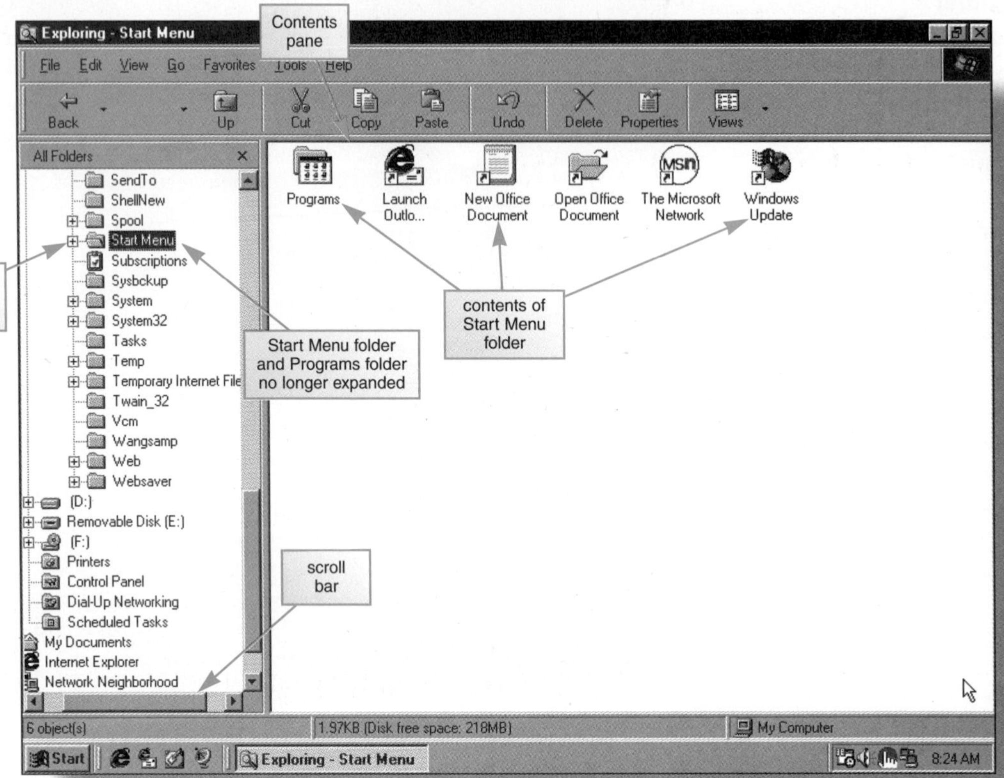

FIGURE 3-43

2 Scroll up in the All Folders pane so the Windows folder is visible. Point to the minus sign in the small box to the left of the Windows icon.

The Windows icon displays in the All Folders pane (Figure 3-44). The minus sign indicates the Windows folder is expanded.

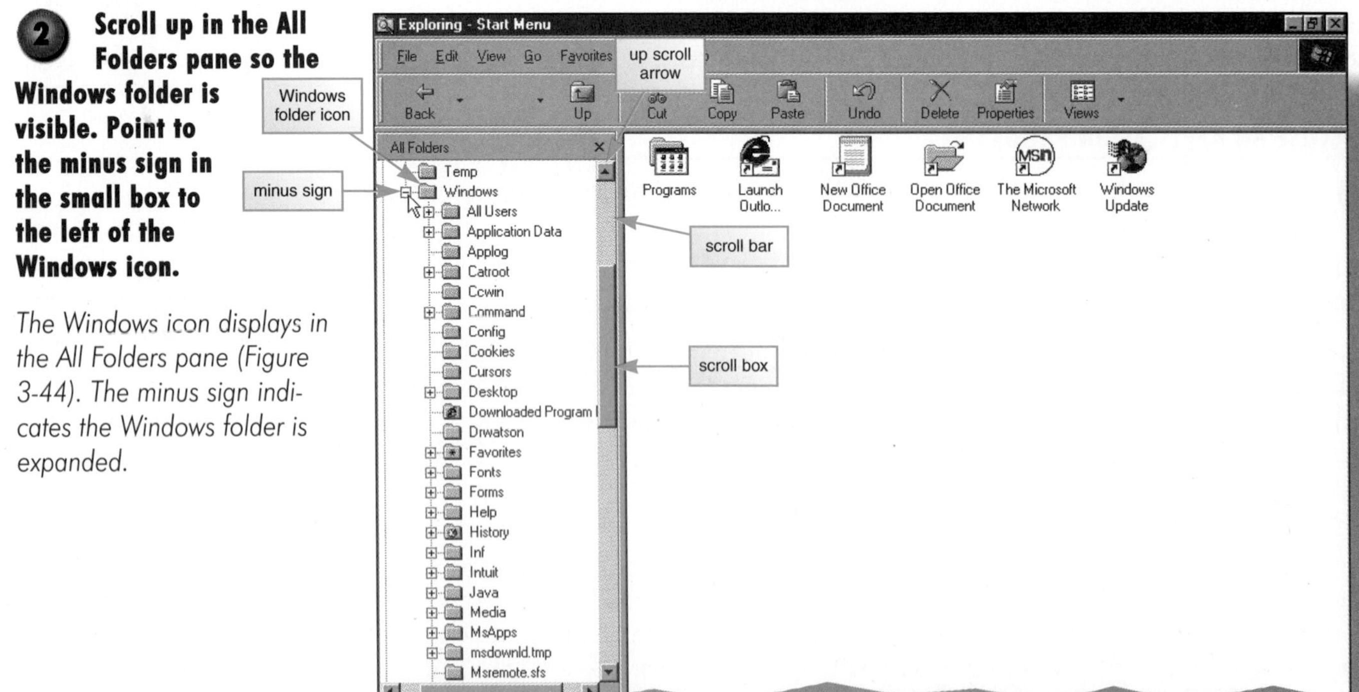

FIGURE 3-44

3 Click the minus sign

The expansion of the Windows folder closes (Figure 3-45). The minus sign changes to a plus sign to indicate the Windows folder is not expanded. The Windows entry in the All Folders pane is highlighted and the contents of the Windows folder display in the Contents pane of the window. The button in the taskbar button area and the open Windows icon reflect this.

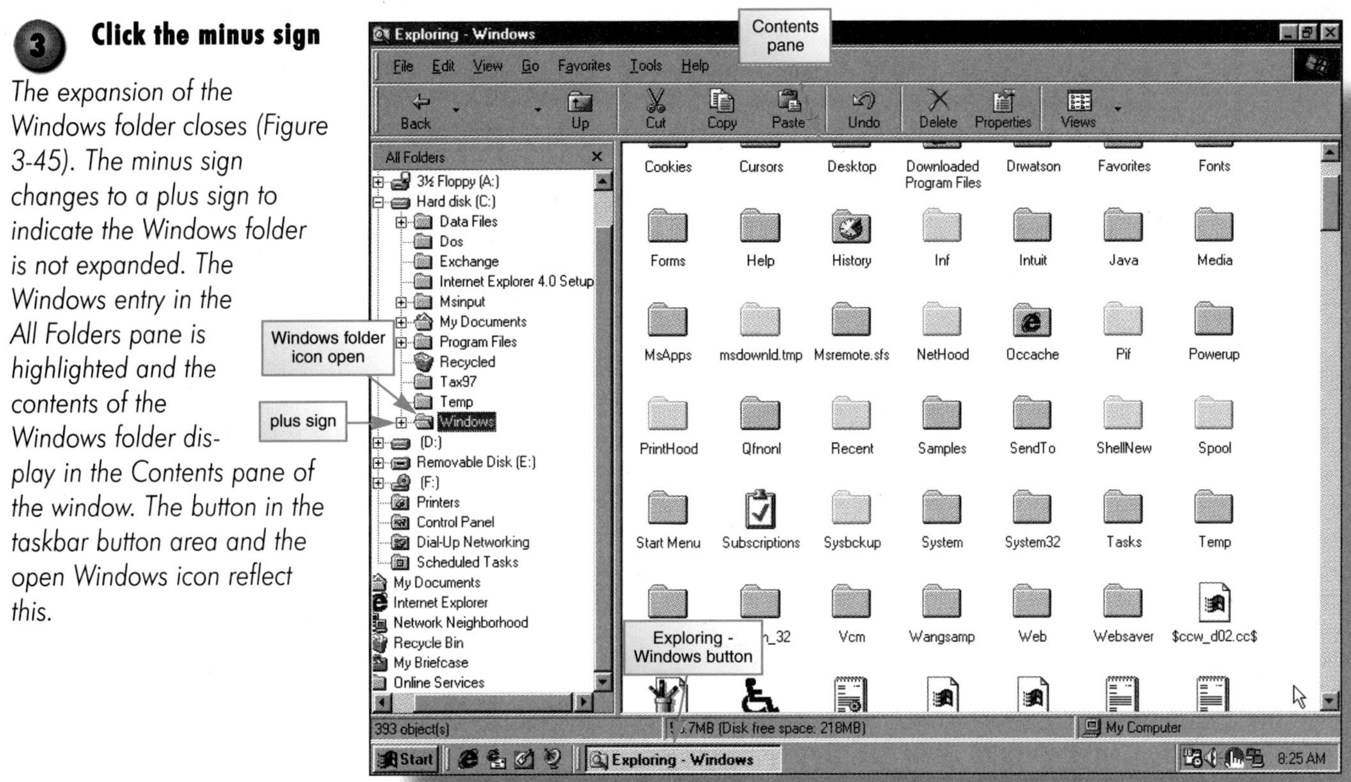

FIGURE 3-45

Moving through the All Folders and Contents panes of the Exploring window is an important skill because you will find that you use Explorer to perform a significant amount of file maintenance on your computer.

Other Ways

1. Click expanded folder icon, press MINUS SIGN
2. Click expanded folder icon, press LEFT ARROW
3. Click expanded folder icon, double-click folder icon

Copying, Moving, Renaming, and Deleting Files and Folders in Windows 98 Explorer

You can copy, move, rename, and delete files and folders in Windows 98 Explorer using essentially the same techniques as when working in folder windows. To a large extent, whether you perform these activities in folder windows, in Explorer, or in a combination of the two is a personal preference. Nonetheless, it is important for you to understand the techniques used in both cases so you can make an informed decision about how you want to perform file maintenance when using Windows 98.

Copying Files in Windows 98 Explorer

In previous examples of copying files, you used the copy and paste method to copy a document file from a folder to a drive. Although you could use the copy and paste method to copy files in Windows 98 Explorer, another method of copying a file is to right-drag a file (or folder) icon from the Contents pane to a folder or drive icon in the All Folders pane. To copy the Circles bitmap image file from the Windows folder onto a floppy disk in drive A of your computer, complete the steps on the next two pages.

To Copy a File in Explorer by Right-Dragging

1 **Insert a formatted floppy disk in drive A of your computer.**

2 **Scroll down the Contents pane until the Circles icon displays. If the Circles bitmap image file is not on your computer, scroll the Contents pane to display any other bitmap image file icon. If necessary, scroll the All Folders pane until the 3½ Floppy (A:) icon displays.**

The Circles icon displays in the Contents pane and the 3½ Floppy (A:) icon displays in the All Folders pane (Figure 3-46).

FIGURE 3-46

3 **Right-drag the Circles icon on top of the 3½ Floppy (A:) icon. Point to Copy Here on the shortcut menu.**

The dimmed image of the Circles icon displays on top of the 3½ Floppy (A:) icon and a shortcut menu displays (Figure 3-47).

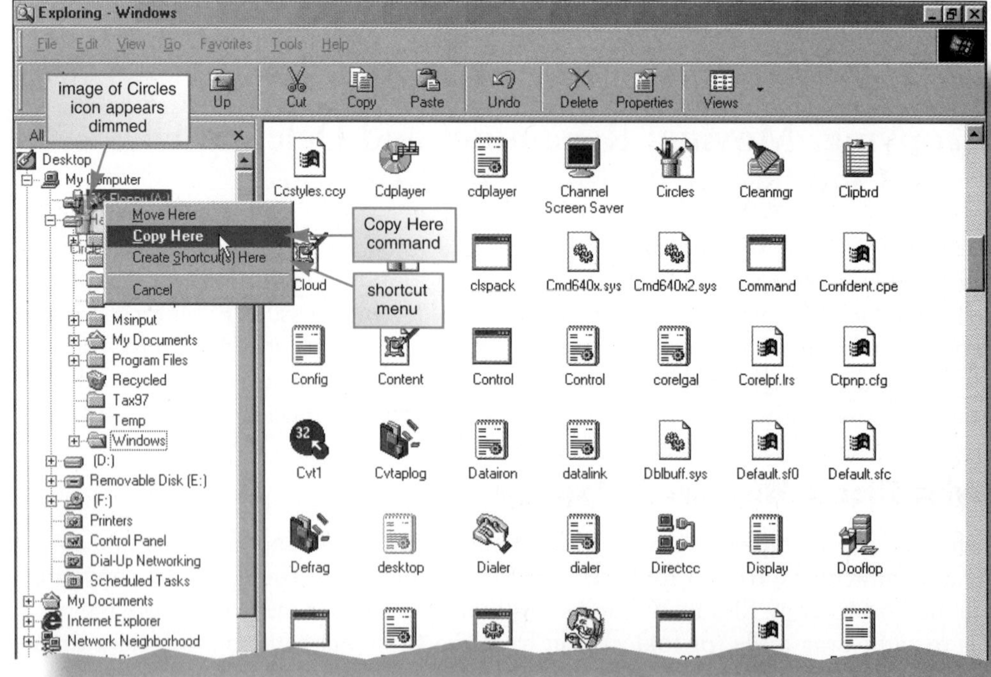

FIGURE 3-47

Click Copy Here.

The Copying dialog box displays while the file is being copied (Figure 3-48). The file being copied (Circles.bmp) and the from (WINDOWS) and to (A:\) locations are identified in the dialog box. After the file is copied, it is stored on the floppy disk in drive A.

FIGURE 3-48

Files can be moved using the same techniques just discussed except that you click **Move Here** instead of Copy Here on the shortcut menu (see Figure 3-47). The difference between a move and a copy, as mentioned previously, is that when you move a file, it is placed on the destination drive or in the destination folder and is removed from its current location. When a file is copied, it is placed on the destination drive or in the destination folder as well as remaining stored in its current location. Use caution when moving a file so that you will not remove it from a location where you want to keep it.

In general, you should right-drag or use the copy and paste method to copy or move a file instead of merely dragging a file. If you drag a file from one folder to another on the same drive, Windows 98 moves the file. If you drag a file from one folder to another on a different drive, Windows 98 copies the file. Because of the different ways this is handled, it is strongly suggested you right-drag or use copy and paste when moving or copying files.

Other Ways

1. Right-click file to copy, click Copy, right-click 3½ Floppy (A:) icon, click Paste
2. Drag file to copy on top of 3½ Floppy (A:) icon
3. Click file to copy in Contents pane, on Edit menu click Copy, click 3½ Floppy (A:) icon, on Edit menu click Paste
4. Select file to copy in Contents pane, press CTRL+C, select 3½ Floppy (A:) icon, press CTRL+V

Displaying the Contents of a Floppy Disk

After copying a file, you might want to examine the folder or drive where the file was copied to ensure it was copied properly. To see the contents of the floppy disk in drive A, complete the step on the next page.

To Display the Contents of a Floppy Disk

1 Click the 3½ Floppy (A:) icon in the All Folders pane.

The contents of the floppy disk in drive A display in the Contents pane (Figure 3-49). The Circles file is stored on the floppy disk. If you have additional files and/or folders on the floppy disk you are using, their icons and titles also will display.

FIGURE 3-49

Other Ways

1. Right-click 3½ Floppy (A:) icon, click Explore

Renaming Files and Folders

In some circumstances you may want to **rename** a file or a folder. This could occur when you want to distinguish a file in one folder or drive from a copy, or if you decide you need a better name to identify a file. To change the name of the Circles file on the floppy disk to Blue Circles, complete the following steps.

To Rename a File

1 **Right-click the Circles icon in the Contents pane. Point to Rename on the shortcut menu.**

The Circles icon is selected and a shortcut menu displays (Figure 3-50).

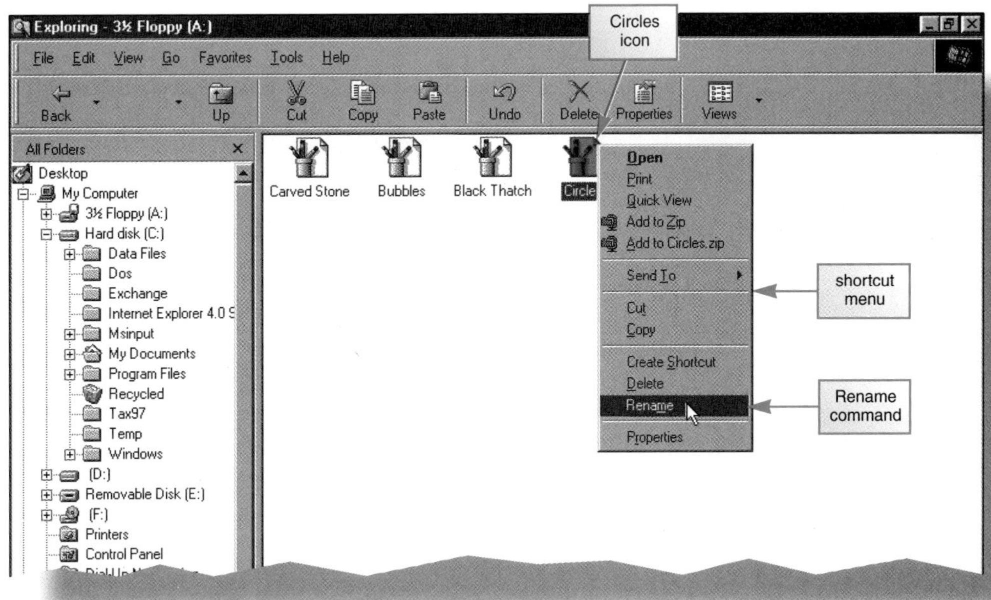

FIGURE 3-50

2 **Click Rename. Type** `Blue Circles` **and then press the ENTER key.**

The file is renamed Blue Circles (Figure 3-51). Note that the file on the floppy disk in drive A is renamed, but the original file in the Windows folder on drive C is not renamed.

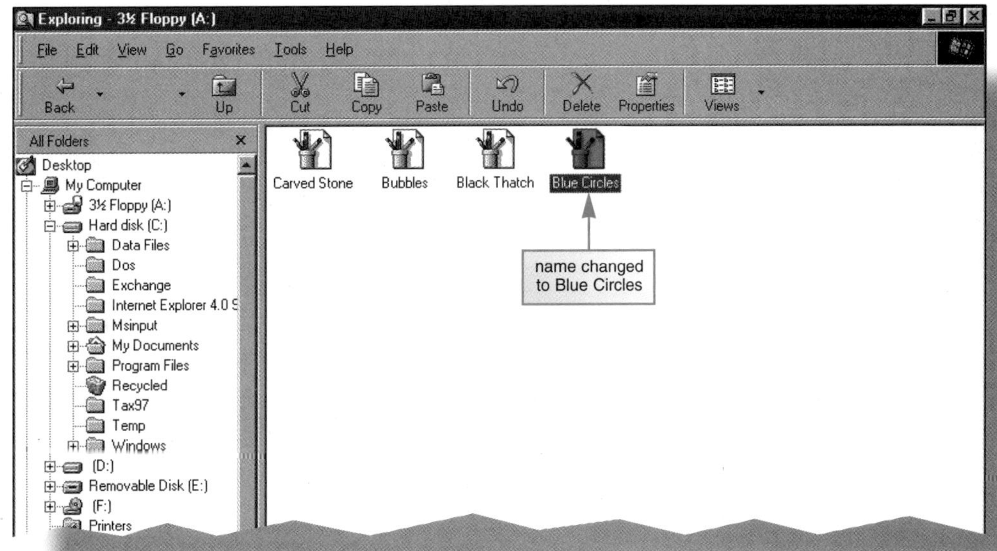

FIGURE 3-51

Other Ways

1. Right-click icon in Contents pane, press M, type name, press ENTER
2. Click icon in Contents pane, press F2, type name, press ENTER
3. Click icon, on File menu click Rename, type name, press ENTER
4. Select icon, press ALT+F, press M, type name, press ENTER

Renaming files in the manner shown above also can be achieved in other windows. For example, if you open the My Computer window and then open the 3½ Floppy (A:) window, you can rename any file stored on the floppy disk using the technique just shown.

You also can rename files on a hard disk using the techniques shown, but you should use caution when doing so. If you inadvertently rename a file that is associated with certain programs, the programs may not be able to find the file and, therefore, may not execute properly.

If you change a file name for which a shortcut exists on a menu, in a folder, or on the desktop, Windows 98 will update the shortcut link so the shortcut points to the renamed file. The name of the shortcut, however, is not changed to reflect the name change of the linked file.

More About

Deleting Files

Warning! This is your last warning! Be EXTREMELY careful when deleting files. Hours and weeks of hard work can be lost with one click of a button. If you are going to delete files or folders from your hard disk, consider making a backup of those files to ensure that if you inadvertently delete something you need, you will be able to recover.

Deleting Files in Windows 98 Explorer

A final function that you may want to use in Windows 98 Explorer is to delete a file. As has been mentioned, you should exercise extreme caution when deleting a file or files. When you delete a file from a floppy disk, the file is gone once you delete it. If you delete a file from a hard disk, the deleted file is stored in the Recycle Bin where you can recover it until you empty the Recycle Bin. Nevertheless, be very careful when deleting files, whether from a floppy disk or from a hard disk.

Assume you have decided to delete all four files from the floppy disk in drive A. To delete the files, complete the following steps.

Steps To Delete Files from a Floppy Disk

1 Click the Carved Stone icon in the Contents pane. Press and hold the SHIFT key and then click the Blue Circles icon. Point to the Delete button on the Standard Buttons toolbar.

The four icons are selected (Figure 3-52). Holding the SHIFT key and then pointing to a second icon selects all the icons between the two you have clicked.

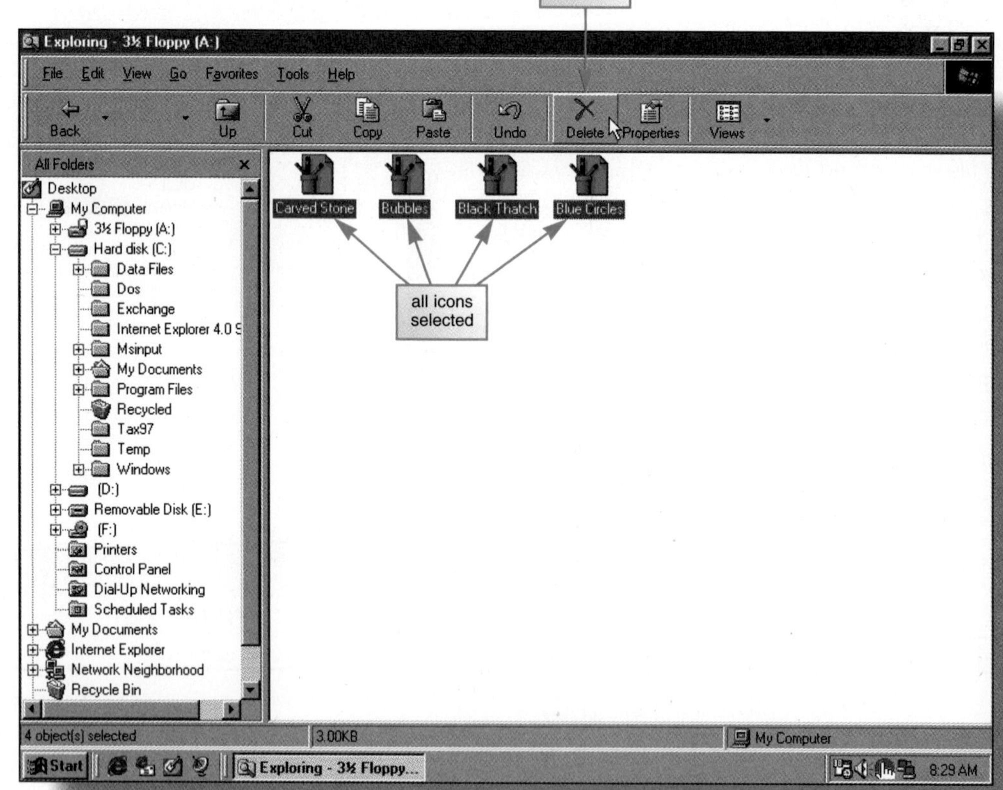

FIGURE 3-52

2 Click the Delete button. Point to the Yes button.

The Confirm Multiple File Delete dialog box displays (Figure 3-53). The dialog box asks if you are sure you want to delete the four items.

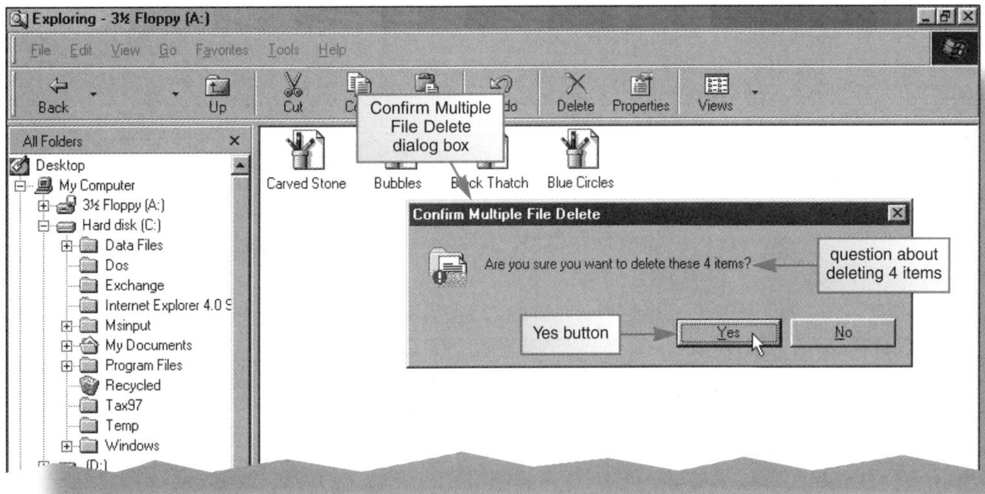

FIGURE 3-53

3 Click the Yes button.

A Deleting dialog box displays while the four files are being deleted (Figure 3-54). The Deleting dialog box indicates the file being deleted (Black Thatch.bmp) and where the file is being deleted from (A:\). If you wish to terminate the deleting process before it is complete, you can click the Cancel button.

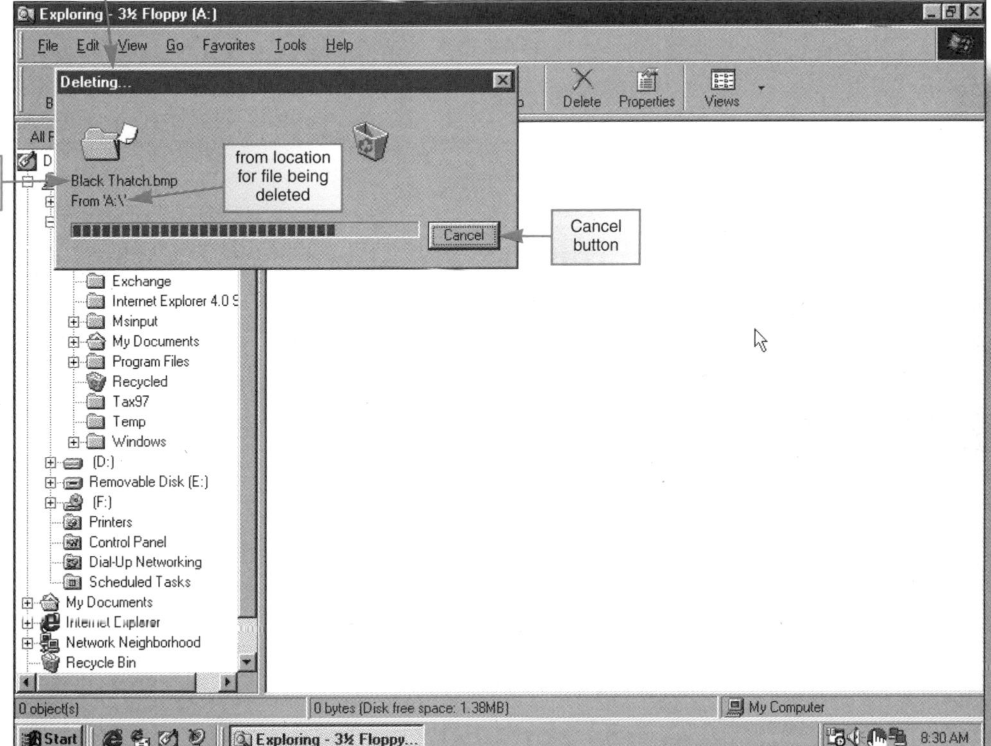

FIGURE 3-54

Other Ways

1. Right-drag icon to Recycle Bin, click Move Here, click Yes button
2. Drag icon to Recycle Bin, click Yes button
3. Right-click icon, click Delete, click Yes button.
4. Click icon, on File menu click Delete, click Yes button
5. Select icon, press ALT+F, press D, press Y

You can use the same methods just specified to delete folders from a floppy disk or a hard disk. Again, however, you should use extreme caution when deleting folders and files to ensure you do not delete something you may not be able to recover.

Closing Windows 98 Explorer

When you are finished with file maintenance, normally you will close the Exploring window. To close the Exploring window, complete the step below.

TO CLOSE THE EXPLORING WINDOW

 Click the Close button on the Exploring window title bar.

Windows 98 closes the Exploring window.

Summary of Windows 98 Explorer

Windows 98 Explorer gives you the capability of performing file maintenance in a single window without displaying additional windows or worrying about windows management on the desktop. In addition, it provides a hierarchical view of all drives, folders, and files on your computer. Whether you choose to use Explorer or My Computer to perform file maintenance is a personal choice. You may find that some tasks are easier using Explorer and others are easier using My Computer.

More About

Properties

Properties are something new with Windows 95 and Windows 98. The Properties dialog boxes allow you to customize not only your desktop and working environment, but also control how devices respond and operate. They provide useful information as well. Right-click/Properties is a sequence you should become familiar with in Window 98.

Properties of Objects

Every object in Windows 98 has **properties**, which describe the object. In some cases, you can change the properties of an object. Each drive, folder, file, and program in Windows 98 is considered an object and, therefore, has properties. In the following section, the properties of objects will be shown.

Drive Properties

Each drive on your computer has properties. To display the properties for drive C, complete the following steps.

Steps To Display Hard Disk Properties

1 Double-click the My Computer icon on the desktop. Click the Hard disk (C:) icon in the My Computer window. Point to the Properties button on the Standard Buttons toolbar.

The My Computer window opens on the desktop (Figure 3-55).

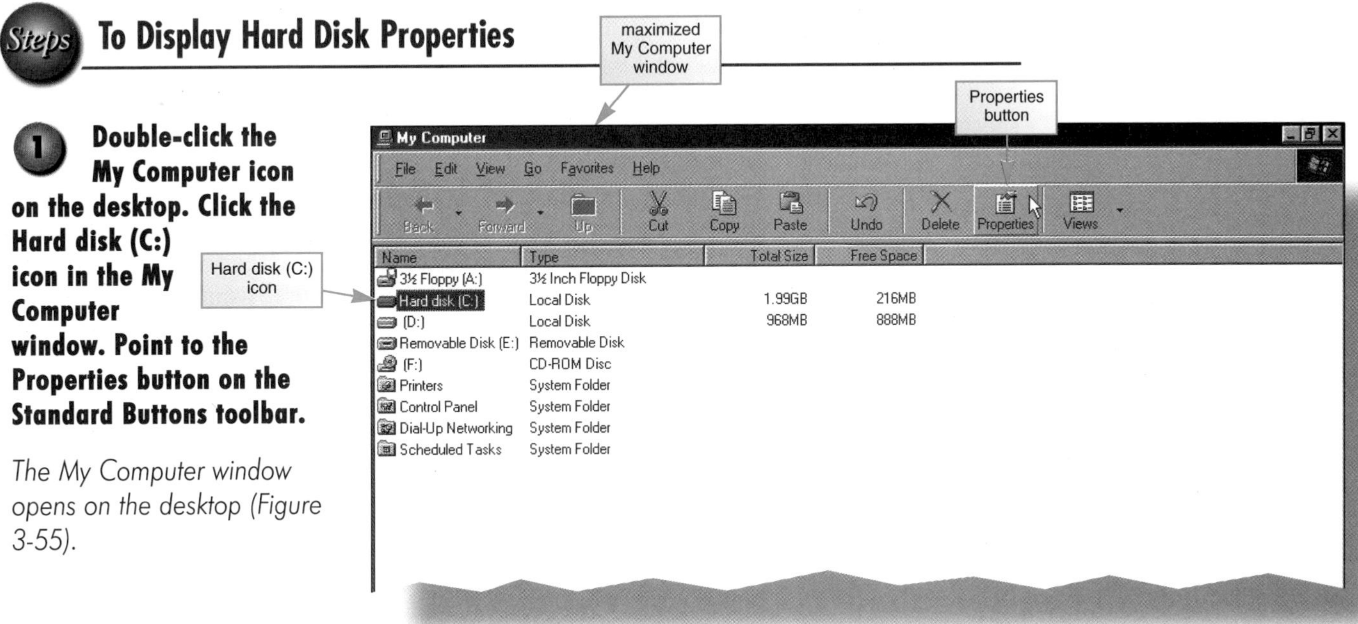

FIGURE 3-55

2 Click the Properties button. Point to the Cancel button.

The Hard disk (C:) Properties dialog box displays with the General sheet on top (Figure 3-56). On the **General sheet,** *the Label text box allows you to change the label name given to the drive (HARD DISK). The name on your computer may be different. The type of drive (Local Disk) and File system (FAT) display below the Label text box. The used space on the drive (dark blue box) is the space on the disk holding files and folders. The free space (magenta box) is the space available for more folders and files. The total capacity of the disk is specified and a pie chart graphically represents the used and free space on the disk.*

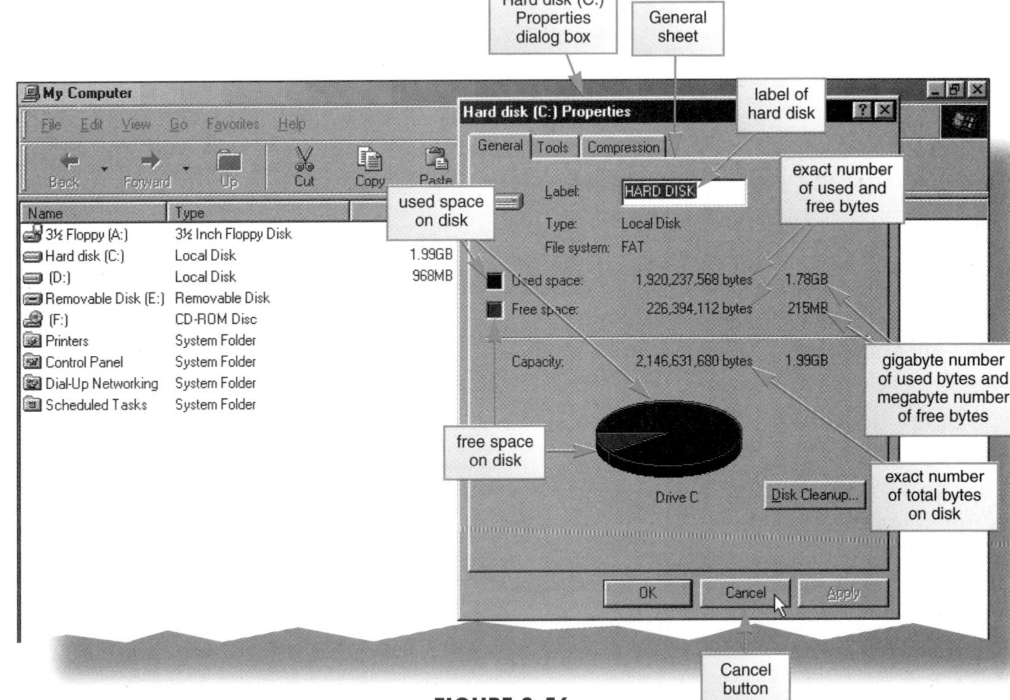

FIGURE 3-56

3 Click the Cancel button.

The Hard disk (C:) dialog box no longer displays.

Other Ways

1. Right-click drive icon, click Properties, click Cancel button
2. Click drive icon, on File menu click Properties, click Cancel button
3. Select drive icon, press ALT+ENTER, press ESC

The **Tools sheet** in the Hard disk (C:) Properties dialog box in Figure 3-56 on the previous page, accessible by clicking the Tools tab, allows you to check errors on the hard disk, back up the hard disk, or defragment the hard disk. The **Compression sheet**, accessible by clicking the Compression tab, allows you to increase free space on the hard disk by compressing the hard disk or creating a new compressed drive.

In Figure 3-56, you might think the number of bytes specified for used space and for free space do not correspond with the megabyte or gigabyte specification shown, but in fact they do. A **gigabyte of RAM** or disk space is not exactly one billion characters, or bytes. Because addresses are calculated on a computer using the binary number system, a gigabyte of RAM or disk space actually is 1,073,741,824 bytes, which is equal to 2^{30}. In Figure 3-56, if you multiply 1.78 times 1,073,741,824, the answer is just less than 1,920,237,568, which is shown as the total number of bytes of used space on drive C. Therefore, 1.78 GB is the closest estimate, expressed as gigabytes, for the total amount of unused space on drive C.

The same is true of the megabyte specification for free space. A **megabyte of RAM** or disk space is 1,048,576 bytes and not exactly one million bytes, which is equal to 2^{20}. In Figure 3-56, if you multiply 215 times 1,048,576, the answer is just less than 226,394,112, which is shown as the total number of bytes of free space on drive C. Therefore, 215 MB is the closest estimate, expressed as megabytes, for the total amount of free space on drive C.

Properties of a Folder

Folders also have properties. To display the properties of the Windows folder, complete the following steps.

Steps To Display Folder Properties

1 Double-click the Hard disk (C:) icon in the My Computer window. Click the Windows icon in the Hard disk (C:) window. Point to the Properties button on the Standard Buttons toolbar.

The Hard disk (C:) window opens and the Windows icon is selected (Figure 3-57).

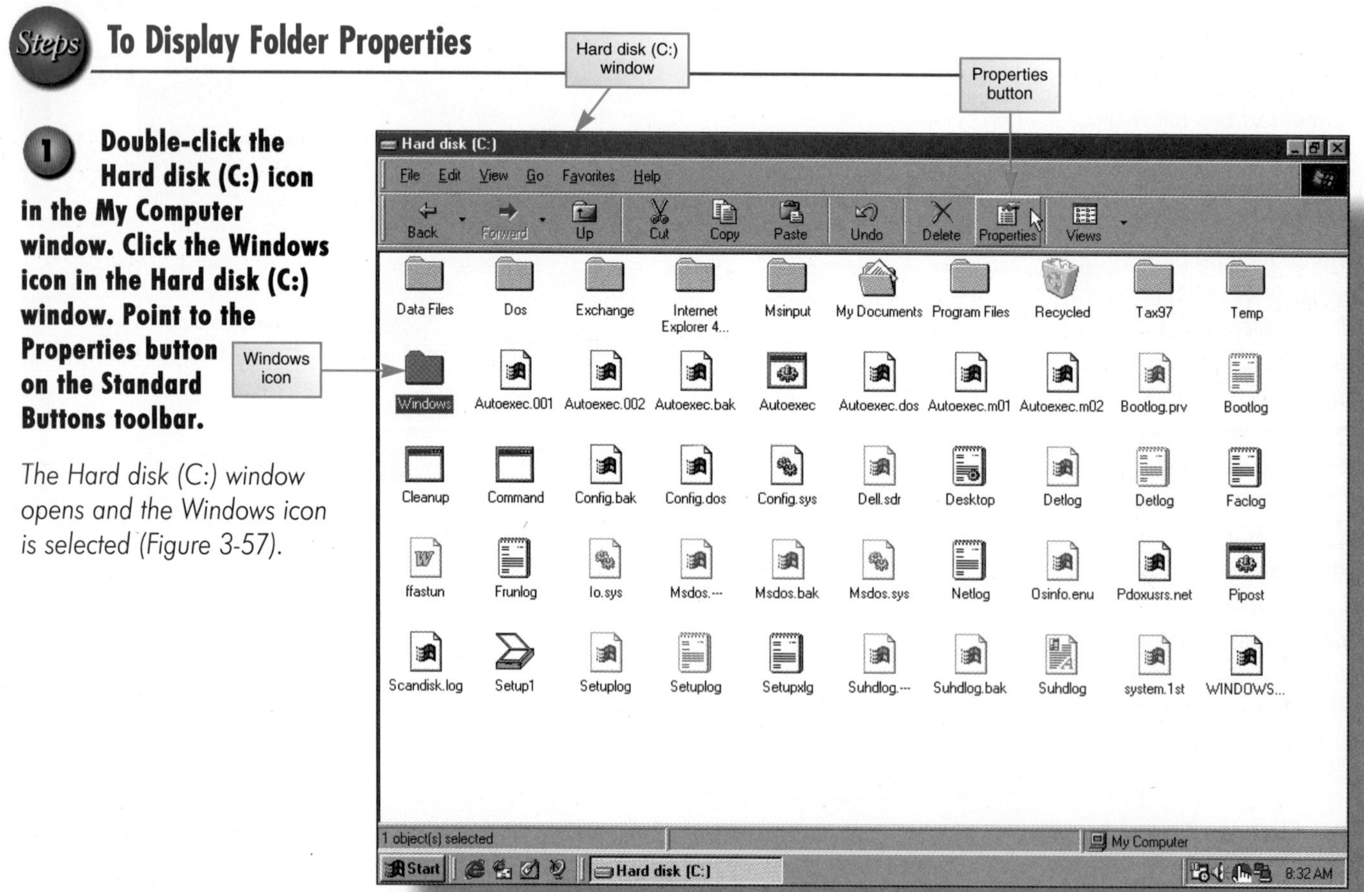

FIGURE 3-57

2 Click the Properties button. Point to the Cancel button.

The Windows Properties dialog box displays (Figure 3-58). The Windows folder name displays near the top of the dialog box. The type, File Folder, is specified. The location of the folder is shown. The size in megabytes and actual bytes displays. The Windows folder contains 8,686 files and 186 folders. These values may be different on your computer. The MS-DOS name (WINDOWS) is the name used for the folder in Microsoft DOS, an operating system available before Windows.

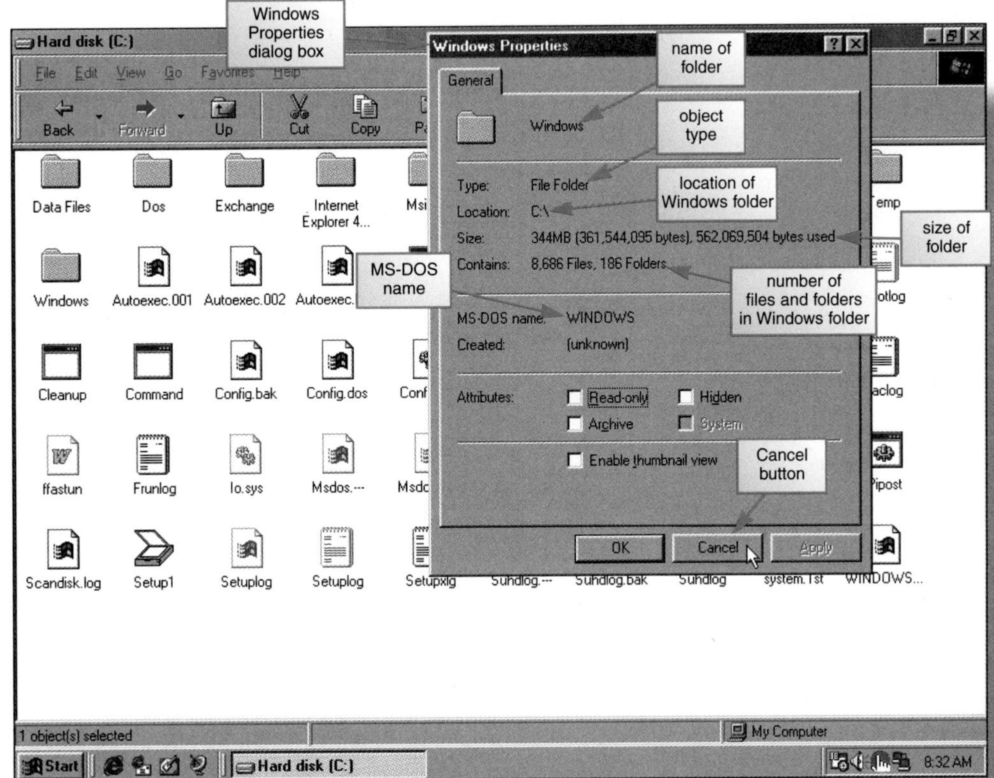

FIGURE 3-58

3 Click the Cancel button and then close all open windows.

In the examples of drive and folder properties, you opened windows, pointed to the object, and then clicked the Properties button on the Standard Buttons toolbar. These same steps can be performed in Windows 98 Explorer. Thus, if you have Explorer open and want to display the properties of drive C, point to the drive C icon and then click the Properties button on the Standard Buttons toolbar.

Files and programs also have properties, although these properties are different from the properties for a hard disk and the properties for a folder. As you can see, each object on the desktop and in folder windows has properties.

Other Ways

1. Right-click folder icon, click Properties, click Cancel button
2. Click folder icon, on File menu click Properties, click Cancel button
3. Select folder icon, press ALT+ENTER, press ESC

Find

Some would argue that Find is the handiest Windows 98 tool. If an application program is not represented by an icon on the desktop or on the Start menu, many people use Find to display the icon in the Find dialog box and then double-click the icon to launch the program.

Finding Files or Folders

The Windows folder shown in Figure 3-58 on the previous page contains 8,686 files in 186 folders. Your entire computer, however, will contain many more files and folders. In many instances, you will know the location of files you use often and can open the folder that contains them. In some cases, however, you might know you have a certain file on your computer but you have no idea in what folder it is located. To manually search every folder on your computer to find the file would be time-consuming and, perhaps, impossible. Fortunately, Windows 98 provides a **Find command** that allows you to find the location of a file if you know its name or even if you know some text that is included in the file.

Finding a File by Name

If you know the name or partial name of a file, you can use Find to locate the file. Assume, for example, you know a wallpaper bitmap image file named blue rivets exists somewhere on your computer. You want to open the file to see what the image looks like. To find the file, complete the following steps.

To Find a File by Name

1 Click the Start button on the taskbar. Point to Find on the Start menu. Point to Files or Folders on the Find submenu.

The Start menu and Find submenu display (Figure 3-59).

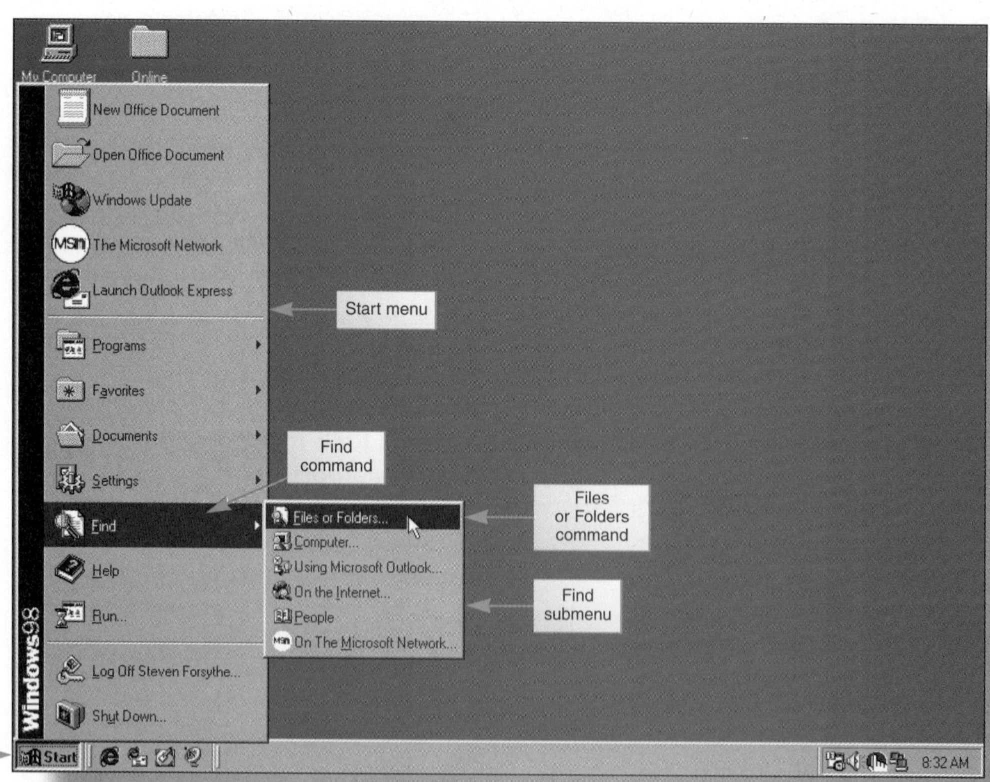

FIGURE 3-59

2 Click Files or Folders. Type `blue rivets` **in the Named text box and then point to the Find Now button.**

The Find: All Files window opens (Figure 3-60). On the Name & Locations sheet, the words you typed and a blinking insertion point display in the Named text box. The Look in box specifies where the search will take place (all of drive C will be examined).

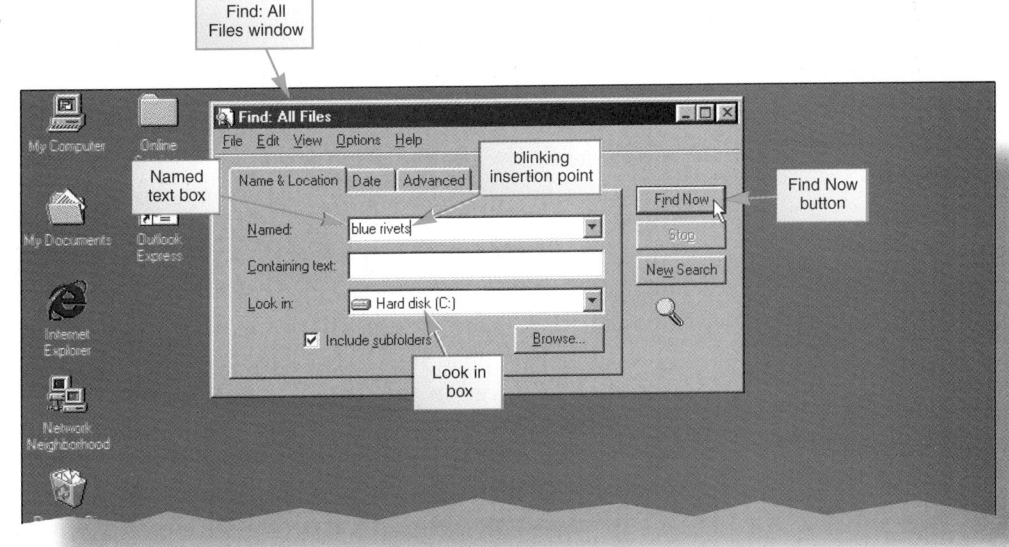

FIGURE 3-60

Click the Find Now button.

Windows 98 searches all of drive C looking for files with the term, blue, or the term, rivets, in their names. Any files that are found are listed in the window. Several files were found in this search (Figure 3-61). The first file in the list is named Blue Rivets. The Find window displays the names of the files, the folder where the file is located, the size of the file, the type of files, and the date and time the files were last modified. The file sizes, files types, and modified dates and times are not visible in the dialog box shown in Figure 3-61.

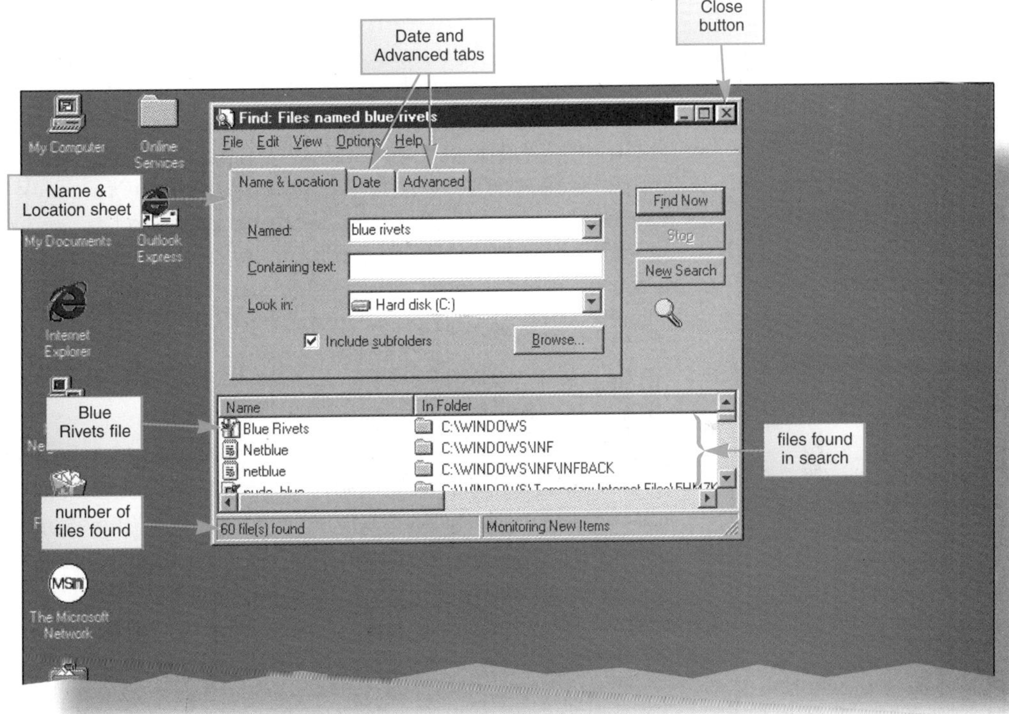

FIGURE 3-61

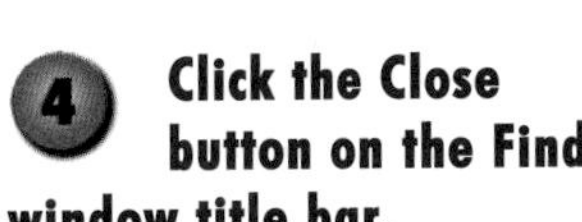

4 Click the Close button on the Find window title bar.

Other Ways

1. Right-click Start button, click Find, type file name, click Find Now button, click Close button
2. Right-click drive icon in All Folders pane, click Find, type file name, click Find Now button, click Close button
3. Press F3 (or CTRL+ESC, press F, press F), type file name, press ENTER

In the Find window in Figure 3-61 on the previous page, after the search is complete you can work with the files found in any manner desired. For example, you can open the file by double-clicking the file icon or by right-clicking the file icon and then clicking Open on the shortcut menu. You can print the file by right-clicking the file icon and then clicking Print on the shortcut menu. You can create a shortcut on the desktop by right-dragging the file icon to the desktop and then clicking Create Shortcut(s) Here on the shortcut menu. You can copy or move the file in the same manner shown for files in My Computer or in Explorer. In summary, any operation you can accomplish from My Computer or from Explorer can be accomplished on the files displayed in the Find window.

If the file you are searching for is an executable program file, such as Notepad, you can launch the program by double-clicking the file icon in the Find window in the same manner as when you double-click the file icon in a window on the desktop.

If you know only a portion of a file's name, you can use an asterisk in the name to represent the remaining characters. For example, if you know a file starts with the letters MSP, you can type `msp*` in the Named text box. All files that begin with the letters msp, regardless of what letters follow, will display.

The Date and Advanced tabs identify sheets that provide different criteria for a search. On the **Date sheet**, you can specify you want to display all files that were created or modified before or after a certain date. On the **Advanced sheet**, you can specify that you want to find all files that contain the text you enter. If no files are found in the search, the window is empty and the message, 0 file(s) found, displays on the status bar. In this case, you might want to check the file name you entered or examine a different drive to continue your search.

The Find capability of Windows 98 can save much time when you need to locate a file on your computer.

Run Command

You have seen how to launch programs by double-clicking the program icons in a window or on the desktop, and by clicking the shortcut icons on the Programs submenu or other submenus. Windows 98 also offers the **Run command**, located on the Start menu, to launch programs. The Run command is particularly useful when you are installing new software on your computer.

For example, assume you just purchased a new piece of software from Microsoft. Often, on the CD-ROM or floppy disk containing the software, the instructions will state something such as, Click Start button, click Run, type `a:\setup`, and click OK. These instructions are common when you buy an application program.

To use the Run command to launch the Paint program (the actual name of the program is MSPAINT), complete the following steps.

More About

Run

You often will use the Run command with programs stored on a floppy disk that you run one time but do no save on your hard disk. Run has its origins from text-based operating systems such as MS-DOS where the only way to cause a program to execute was to type the name of the program and press the ENTER key.

To Launch a Program Using the Run Command

1 Click the Start button on the taskbar and then point to Run.

Windows 98 displays the Start menu (Figure 3-62).

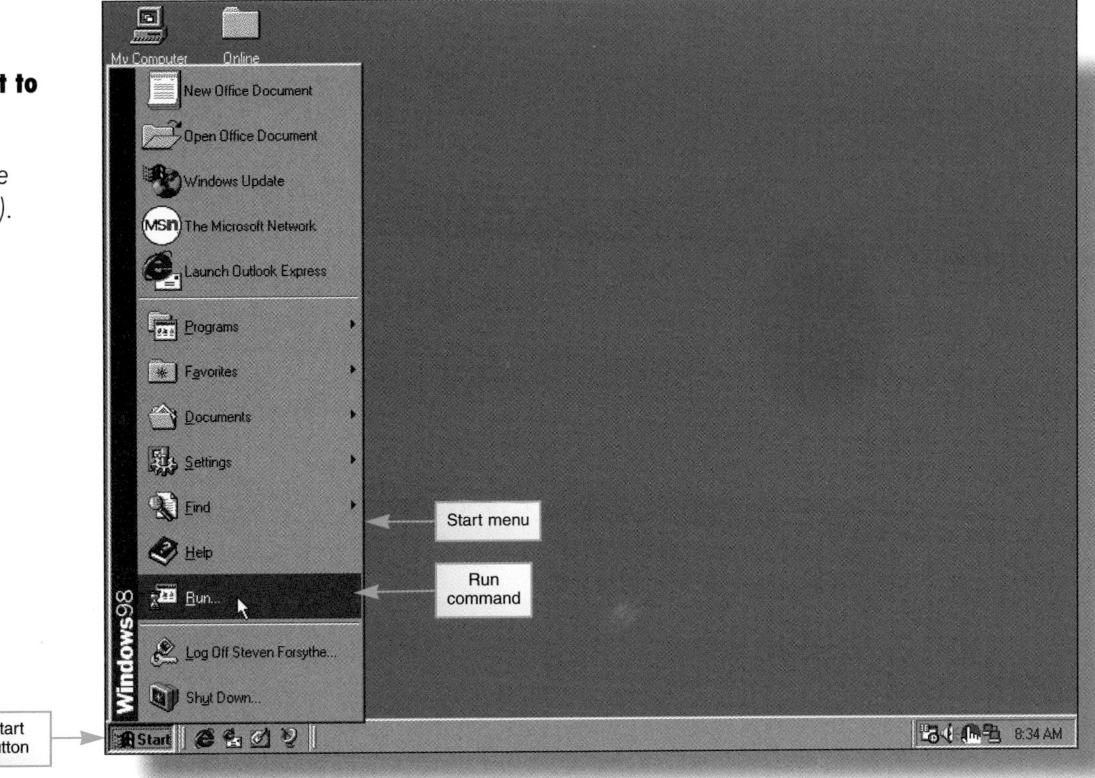

FIGURE 3-62

2 Click Run. Type `mspaint` **in the Open text box and then point to the OK button.**

The Run dialog box displays (Figure 3-63). The entry, mspaint, displays in the Open text box.

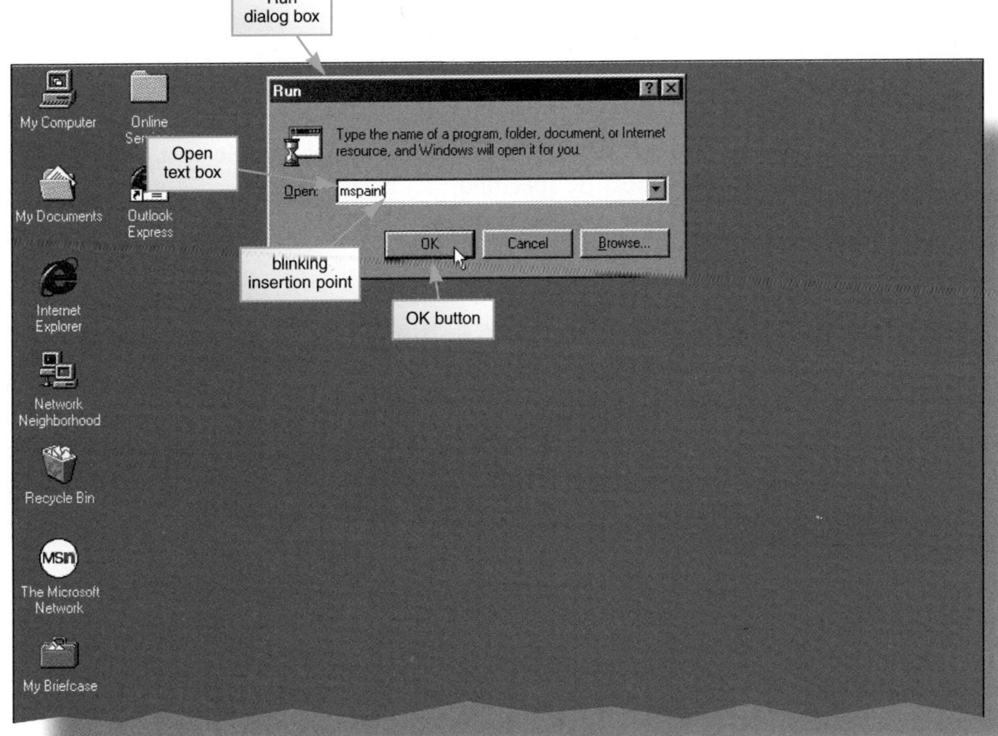

FIGURE 3-63

Click the OK button.

Windows 98 launches the mspaint program (Figure 3-64). You can perform any activities you want with the Paint program.

Click the Close button on the Paint window title bar.

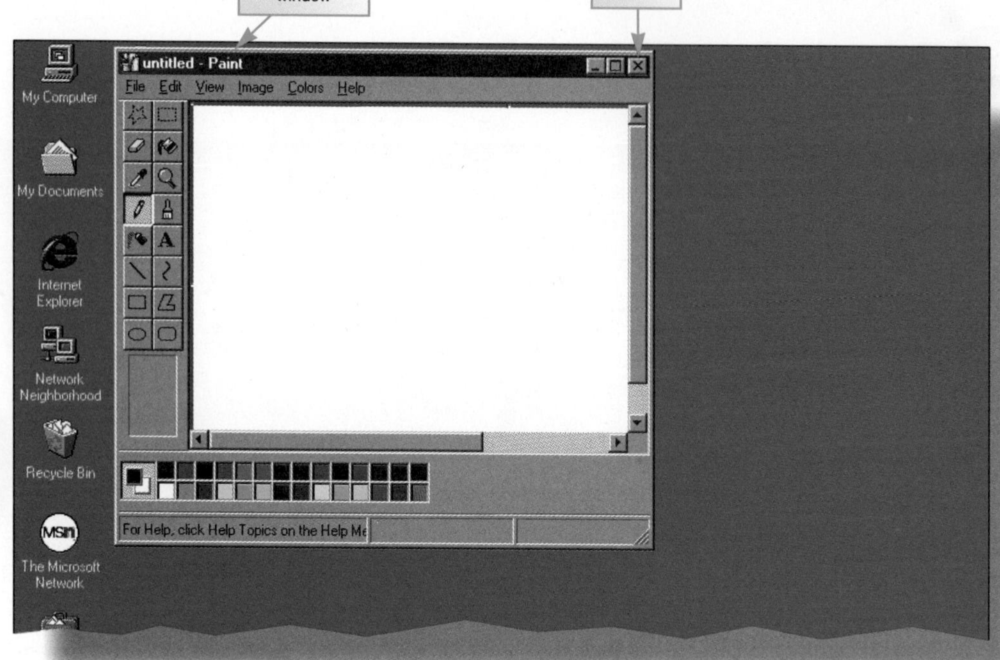

FIGURE 3-64

Other Ways

1. Press CTRL+ESC, press R, type program name, press ENTER

You can use the Run command to open folders and files as well as executable programs. If the program, file, or folder is located in the Windows folder, you simply type the name of the program, file, or folder. If the file is located elsewhere, you must type the path for the file. A **path** is the means of navigating to a specific location on a computer or network. To specify a path, you must type the drive letter, followed by a colon (:) and a backslash (\). Then type the name of the folders and subfolders that contain the file. A backslash should precede each folder name. After all the folder names have been typed, type the file name. The file name should be preceded by a backslash. For example, the path name for the Bubbles bitmap image file stored in the Windows folder on drive C is: C:\WINDOWS\BUBBLES.BMP. The file extension (.bmp) identifies the file as a bitmap image file. File extensions always must be specified in a path name.

The Run command is useful to open programs. It also can be used to open files and folders.

More About

Paths

Paths are left over from MS-DOS and the manner in which you had to identify where a file was stored for access. In Windows 98, you merely need to open a window or, in Explorer, open the folder to access the file. You normally will not be concerned about paths, although you will see them specified often.

Shutting Down Windows 98

After completing your work with Windows 98, you may wish to shut down Windows 98 using the Shut Down command on the Start menu. If you are sure you want to shut down Windows 98, perform the following steps. If you are not sure about shutting down Windows 98, read the steps without actually performing them.

TO SHUT DOWN WINDOWS 98

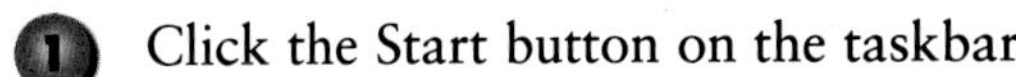

1. Click the Start button on the taskbar.
2. Click Shut Down on the Start menu.
3. Click the OK button in the Shut Down Windows dialog box.

If you accidentally click Shut Down on the Start menu and you do not want to shut down Windows 98, click the Cancel button in the Shut Down Windows dialog box.

Project Summary

In this project, you viewed icons in windows in different formats. After opening a document and launching an application program, you learned to manage windows on the desktop. Next, you saw how to copy, move, and delete files from an open window. You gained knowledge of Windows 98 Explorer, both in how to display drives, folders, and files, and how to copy, move, rename, and delete files. Finally, you learned about the Find and Run commands.

What You Should Know

Having completed this project, you now should be able to perform the following tasks:

- Cascade Open Windows *(WIN 3.16)*
- Change the Format of the Icons in a Window *(WIN 3.7)*
- Close a Window *(WIN 3.33)*
- Close an Application Program *(WIN 3.35)*
- Close Expanded Folders *(WIN 3.36)*
- Close Open Windows *(WIN 3.21)*
- Close the Exploring Window *(WIN 3.44)*
- Copy a File in Explorer by Right-Dragging *(WIN 3.38)*
- Copy Files from a Folder onto a Floppy Disk *(WIN 3.23)*
- Delete Files from a Floppy Disk *(WIN 3.42)*
- Display Folder Properties *(WIN 3.46)*
- Display Hard Disk Properties *(WIN 3.45)*
- Display the Contents of a Drive *(WIN 3.29)*
- Display the Contents of a Floppy Disk *(WIN 3.40)*
- Expand a Drive *(WIN 3.30)*
- Expand a Folder *(WIN 3.31)*
- Find a File by Name *(WIN 3.48)*
- Launch a Program Using the Run Command *(WIN 3.51)*
- Launch an Application Program from a Window *(WIN 3.14)*
- Launch an Application Program from Explorer *(WIN 3.34)*
- Launch Explorer *(WIN 3.26)*
- Make a Window the Active Window *(WIN 3.17)*
- Open a Document from a Window *(WIN 3.12)*
- Open a Folder Window *(WIN 3.10, WIN 3.22)*
- Open a Folder Window in Explorer *(WIN 3.32)*
- Open and Maximize the My Computer Window *(WIN 3.5)*
- Rename a File *(WIN 3.41)*
- Shut Down Windows 98 *(WIN 3.53)*
- Tile Open Windows *(WIN 3.19)*
- Undo Cascading *(WIN 3.18)*
- Undo Tiling *(WIN 3.20)*
- View the Contents of a Drive *(WIN 3.9)*

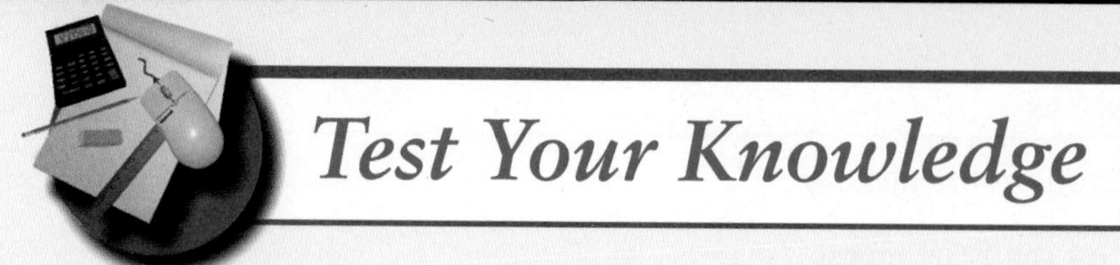

Test Your Knowledge

1 True/False

Instructions: Circle T if the statement is true or F if the statement is false.

T F 1. A floppy disk generally is faster and has more storage capacity than the hard disk on your computer.

T F 2. To open a folder, double-click the folder icon.

T F 3. You can open documents from a window, but to launch an application program you must click the Start button and use the Programs submenu.

T F 4. After you cascade or tile windows, you must restart Windows 98 in order for the windows to display as they did before you cascaded or tiled them.

T F 5. A major feature of Windows 98 is that more than one window can be open at the same time.

T F 6. You can copy files from a folder on the desktop onto a floppy disk, but you cannot copy files from the floppy disk into a folder on the desktop.

T F 7. The best way to open Windows 98 Explorer is to right-click the My Computer icon and then click Explore.

T F 8. To display the contents of drive C on your computer in the Contents pane of the Exploring window, click the plus sign in the small box next to the drive C icon.

T F 9. After you expand a drive or folder, the information displayed in the Contents pane of the Exploring window is the same as the information displayed below the drive or folder icon in the All Folders pane.

T F 10. To find a file by its name, you can use the Find command on the Start menu.

2 Multiple Choice

Instructions: Circle the correct response.

1. To display within a folder window the details of the files found in the folder, __________.
   a. click View on the menu bar and then click List
   b. click Edit on the menu bar and then click Details
   c. right-click the folder, point to View, and click Details
   d. click View on the menu bar
2. To cascade all the open windows on the desktop, __________.
   a. click File on the menu bar and then click Cascade Windows
   b. right-click the taskbar, click Cascade Windows on the shortcut menu
   c. right-click the Start button, click Properties, click Cascade Windows, and click the OK button
   d. right-click the desktop, click Cascade Windows on the shortcut menu
3. When using the single window option to browse windows, __________.
   a. clicking the BACK button will display one window back from the window you are currently viewing
   b. you increase the probability of window clutter on your desktop
   c. you cannot use the copy and paste method
   d. the window size changes depending on the number of files and folders you want to display

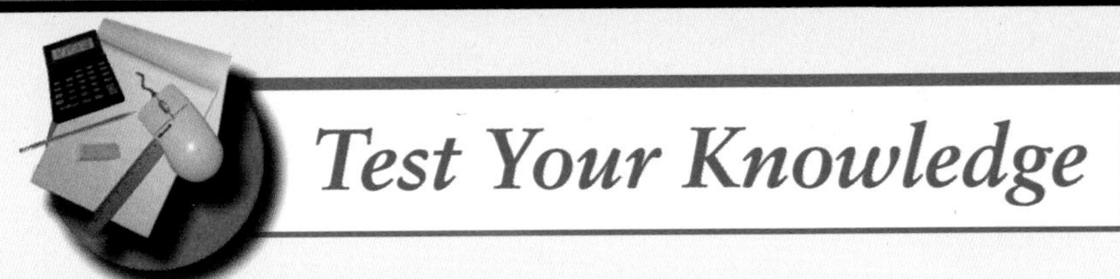

Test Your Knowledge

4. To select multiple icons in a folder at one time, __________.
   a. right-click each icon
   b. press and hold the SHIFT key and point to each icon you want to select
   c. press and hold the CTRL key and double-click each icon you want to select
   d. press and hold the CTRL key and click each icon you want to select
5. When you right-click an icon and a shortcut menu displays, the command in bold means __________.
   a. this command cannot be used at the current time
   b. this command will be executed if you double-click the icon
   c. this is the only command you can use at this time
   d. this is the preferred command to use and if you click another command, Windows 98 may not be able to carry out the command successfully
6. To display the contents of a folder in the Exploring window, __________.
   a. click the plus sign next to the folder icon
   b. right-click the folder icon in the All Folders pane of the window
   c. point to the folder icon in the Contents pane of the window
   d. click the folder icon in the All Folders pane of the window
7. The Programs folder contained within the Start menu folder contains __________.
   a. all the programs available on the computer
   b. all shortcuts and folders found on the Programs submenu
   c. programs you can execute only if you have a special password
   d. only programs placed on your computer when Windows 98 was loaded onto your computer
8. When you close an expanded folder in the All Folders pane of the Exploring window, __________.
   a. the expansion closes in the All Folders pane and the contents of the folder display in the Contents pane
   b. the Exploring window closes
   c. the computer beeps at you because you cannot perform this activity
   d. the My Computer window displays
9. Before you can copy a file from one folder to another folder in Windows Explorer by right-dragging, you must __________.
   a. display the icon for the file you want to copy in the Contents pane of the Exploring window
   b. display the icon for the file you want to copy in the All Folders pane of the Exploring window
   c. open the My Computer window to display the folder where you want to copy the file
   d. display the folder where you want to copy the file in the Contents pane.
10. The Run command on the Start menu __________.
    a. can be used only when no other way to launch a program is available
    b. is most useful when you are not sure of the actual name of the program
    c. is useful when installing new software on your computer
    d. must be used if the program is stored with a specific path on your hard disk

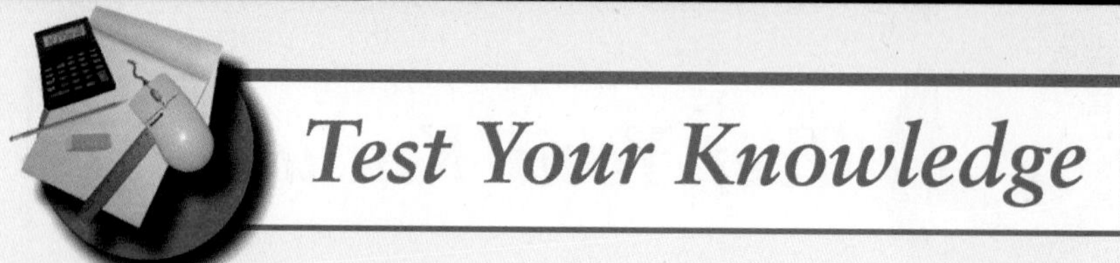

3 Understanding the Exploring Window

Instructions: In Figure 3-65, arrows point to several items in the Exploring window. Identify the items or objects in the spaces provided.

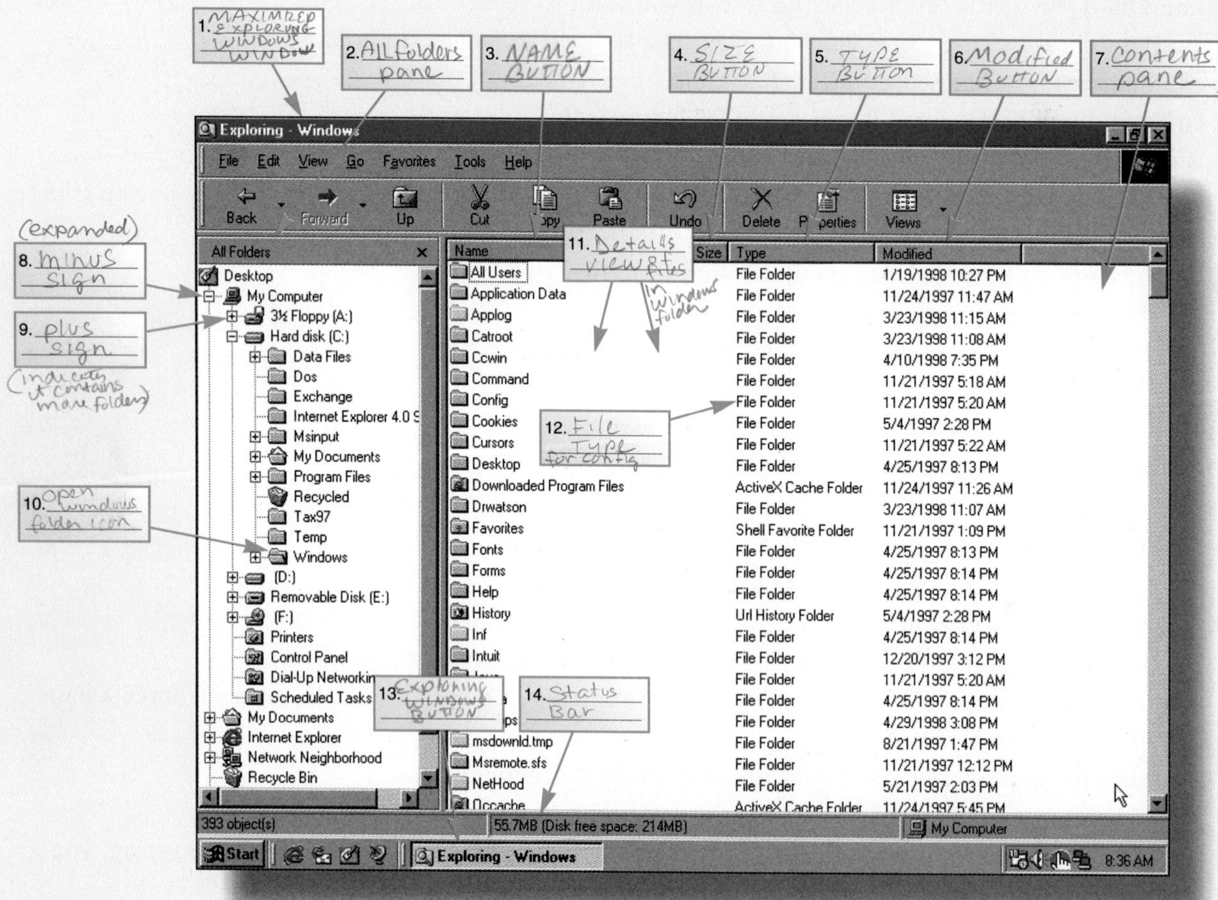

FIGURE 3-65

4 Copying Files

Instructions: Copy the Blue Rivets file shown in Figure 3-66 onto a floppy disk in drive A. In the space below, list all the methods you can use to copy the file and write the specific steps for each method.

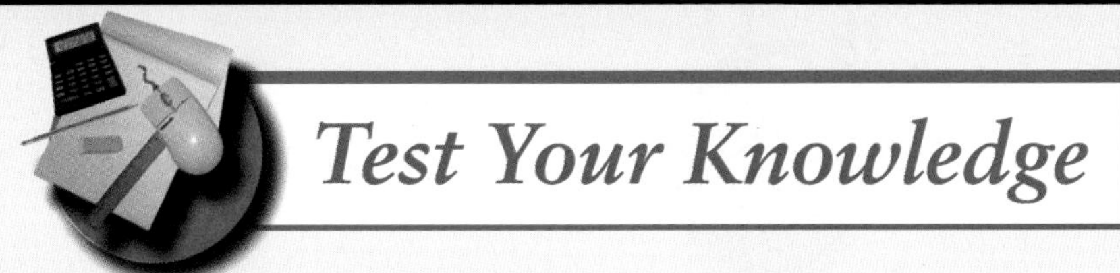

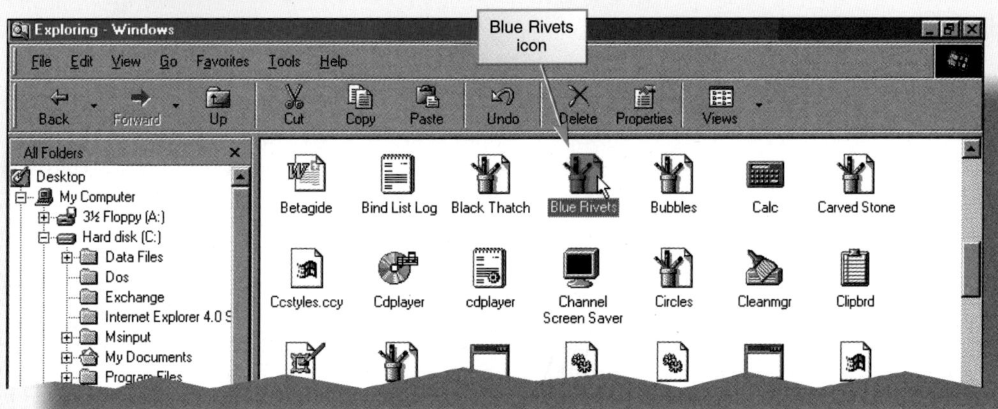

FIGURE 3-66

1 Using Windows Help

Instructions: Use Windows Help and a computer to perform the following tasks.

1. Start Microsoft Windows 98 if necessary.
2. Answer the following questions about paths.
   a. What is a path? ______________________________
   b. What can a path include? ______________________________
   c. How do you specify a path? ______________________________
   d. Specify the path for a file named Harriet's Research Paper that is stored in the My Files folder within the Office folder within the Program Files folder on drive C of your computer. ______________________________
3. Open Windows Help. In the Help Topics: Windows Help dialog box, click the Index tab if necessary, and then type `windows explorer` in the text box. Answer the following questions about Windows Explorer.
   a. How do you create a folder in Windows Explorer? ______________________________
   b. How do you copy a disk in Windows Explorer? ______________________________
   c. How do you display the full path of a file in the title bar? ______________________________
   d. How do you print an unopened file from Windows Explorer? ______________________________

(continued)

Using Windows Help *(continued)*

4. You have recently written a business letter to a manager named Laura Chaney. You explained DVD drives to her. You want to see what else you said in the letter, but you cannot remember the name of the file or where you stored the file on your computer. You read something in your Windows 98 manual that said the Find command could be used to find lost files. Using Help, determine what you must do to find your letter. Write those steps in the spaces provided.
   Step 1: ____________________
   Step 2: ____________________
   Step 3: ____________________
   Step 4: ____________________
5. You and a friend both recently bought computers. She was lucky and received a color printer as her birthday gift. You would like to print some of your more colorful documents on her color printer. You have heard that for a reasonable cost you can buy a network card and some cable and hook up your computers on a network. Then, you can print documents stored on your computer on her color printer. Using Windows Help, determine if you can share her printer. If so, what must you do in Windows 98 to make this become a reality? Print the Help pages that document your answer.
6. You can hardly believe that last week you won a laptop computer at a charity dance. The application programs on the laptop are the same as those on your desktop computer. The only trouble is that when you use your laptop computer to modify a file, you would like the same file on your desktop also to be modified. In that way, you can work on the file either on your desktop computer or on your laptop computer. A friend mentioned that the My Briefcase feature of Windows 98 allows you to do what you want to do. Using Windows Help, find out all you can about My Briefcase. Print the Help pages that specify how to keep files on both your desktop and laptop computers synchronized with each other.

1 File and Program Properties

Instructions: Use a computer to perform the following tasks and answer the questions.

1. Start Microsoft Windows 98 if necessary.
2. Double-click the My Computer icon. Double-click the drive C icon.
3. Double-click the Windows icon.

4. Scroll until the Blue Rivets icon is visible (Figure 3-67). If the Blue Rivets icon does not display on your computer, find another Paint icon.

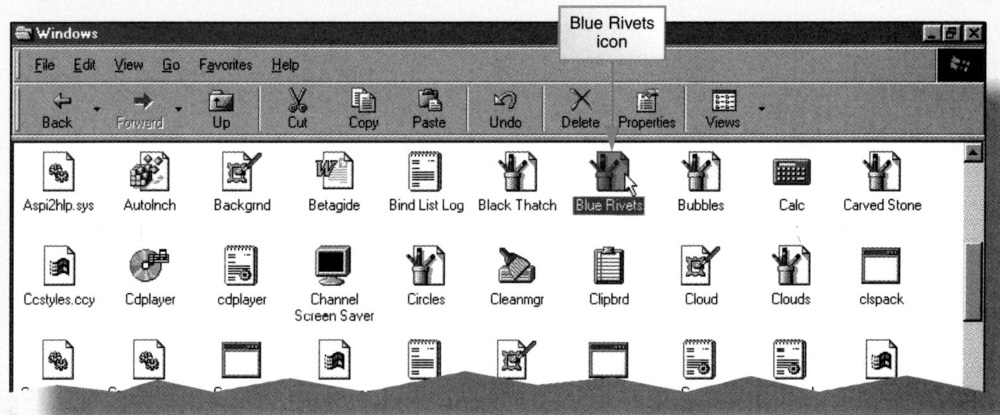

FIGURE 3-67

5. Right-click the Blue Rivets icon. Click Properties on the shortcut menu.
6. Answer the following questions about the Blue Rivets file:
   a. What type of file is Blue Rivets? ______________________
   b. What is the path for the location of the Blue Rivets file? ______________________
   c. What is the size (in bytes) of the Blue Rivets file? ______________________
   d. What is the MS-DOS name of the Blue Rivets file? ______________________ The tilde (~) character is placed in the MS-DOS file name when the Windows 98 file name is greater than eight characters. Windows 98 uses the first six characters of the long file name, the tilde character, and a number to distinguish the file from other files that might have the same first six characters.
   e. When was the file created? ______________________
   f. When was the file last modified? ______________________
   g. When was the file last accessed? ______________________
7. Click the Cancel button in the Blue Rivets Properties dialog box.
8. Scroll in the Windows window until the Notepad icon displays.
9. Right-click the Notepad icon. Click Properties on the shortcut menu.
10. Answer the following questions:
    a. What type of file is Notepad? ______________________
    b. What is the path of the Notepad file? ______________________
    c. How big is the Notepad file? ______________________
    d. What is the file extension of the Notepad file? What does it stand for? ______________________
    e. What is the file version of the Notepad file? ______________________
    f. What is the file's description? ______________________
    g. Who is the copyright owner of Notepad? ______________________
    h. What language is Notepad written for? ______________________
11. Click the Cancel button in the Notepad Properties dialog box.
12. Close all open windows.

2 My Computer

Instructions: Use a computer to perform the following tasks.

1. Start Microsoft Windows 98.
2. Double-click the My Computer icon. Double-click the drive C icon. Double-click the Windows icon.
3. Double-click the Notepad icon in the Windows window to start the Notepad application program. Create the text document illustrated in Figure 3-68.
4. Perform the following steps to save the Notepad document in the My Documents folder using the name, Big Ten Tournament Results. Click File on the menu bar and then click Save As. When the Save As dialog box displays, type `Big Ten Tournament Results` in the File name text box, verify that My Documents displays in the Save in box, and click the Save button in the Save As dialog box.

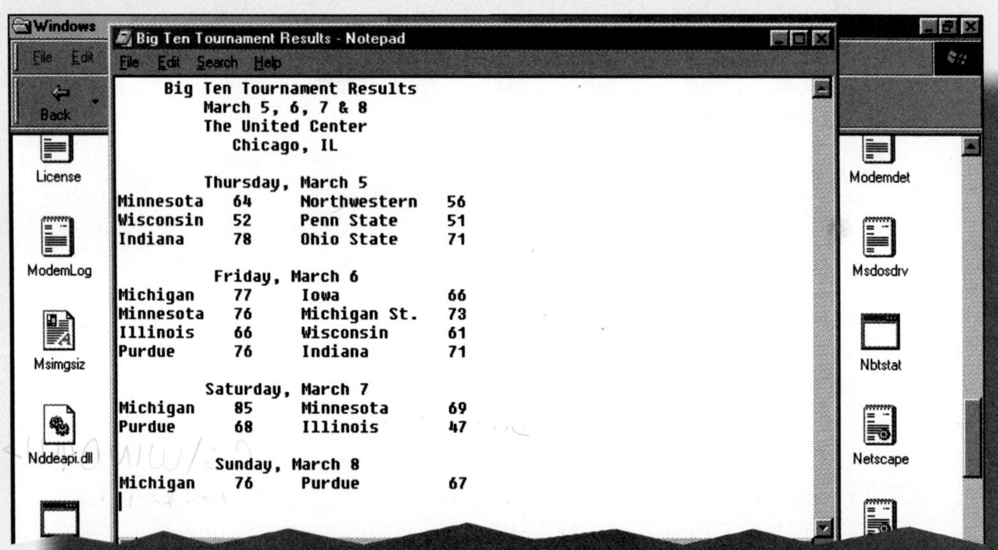

FIGURE 3-68

5. Click the Close button in the Notepad window. Click the Close button in the Windows window.
6. Double-click the My Documents icon on the desktop. Is the Big Ten Tournament Results icon in the My Documents folder? ______________________
7. Double-click the Big Ten Tournament Results icon to open its window.
8. Right-click the taskbar and click Tile Windows Horizontally on the shortcut menu. What does the desktop look like? ______________________
9. Click the Big Ten Tournament Results - Notepad button on the taskbar. Using the DOWN ARROW key, move the insertion point to the end of the document. Press the ENTER key. Type `Tournament MVP: Robert Traylor` and then press the ENTER key.
10. Save the modified document. Print the modified document.
11. Close the Big Ten Tournament Results - Notepad window.
12. Click the My Documents icon on the taskbar.
13. Insert a formatted floppy disk in drive A of your computer.
14. Double-click the My Computer icon on the desktop. Double-click the 3½ Floppy (A:) icon. Are the two windows tiled on the desktop? ______________________

15. Right-click the taskbar and then click Tile Windows Horizontally on the shortcut menu.
16. Right-drag the Big Ten Tournament Results icon in the My Documents window to an open area of the 3½ Floppy (A:) window. Click Move Here on the shortcut menu. What window(s) contains the Big Ten Tournament Results icon?
17. Close all open windows on the desktop.

3 Windows Explorer

Instructions: Use a computer to perform the following tasks:

1. Start Microsoft Windows 98.
2. Right-click the Start button on the taskbar, click Explore on the shortcut menu, and maximize the Exploring - Start Menu window (Figure 3-69).

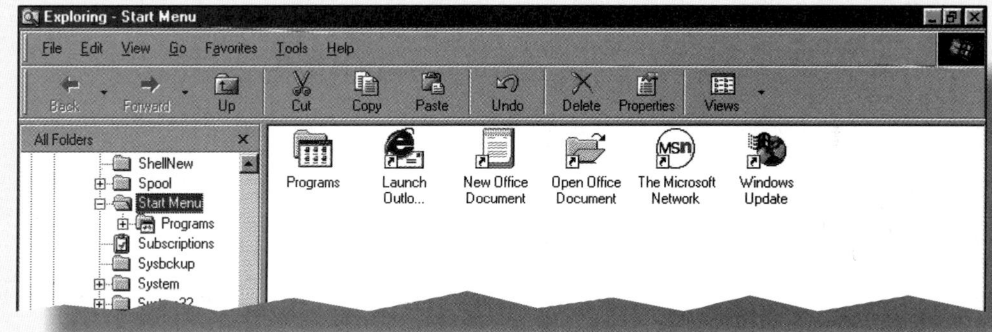

FIGURE 3-69

3. If necessary, scroll to the left in the All Folders pane so the Start Menu and Programs icons are visible. Click the plus sign in the small box to the left of the Programs icon.
4. Click the Internet Explorer icon in the All Folders pane.
5. Double-click the Internet Explorer icon in the Contents pane to launch the Internet Explorer application. What is the URL of the Web page that displays in the Internet Explorer window? On my computer it is www.google.com
6. Click the URL in the Address bar in the Internet Explorer window to select it. Type `www.scsite.com/win98` and then press the ENTER key.
7. Right-click the Space Needle clip art image on the Web page, click Save Picture As on the shortcut menu, and click the Save button in the Save Picture dialog box to save the image in the My Documents folder.
8. Click the Close button in the Microsoft Internet Explorer window.
9. Click the minus sign to the left of the Programs folder.
10. Scroll the All Folders pane to make the Windows folder visible and click the minus sign to the left of the Windows folder.
11. Scroll to the top of the All Folders pane to make the 3½ Floppy (A:) icon and My Documents icon visible.
12. Click the My Documents folder.
13. Right-click the Space Needle icon and click Properties.
    What type of file is the Space Needle file? JPEG Image
    When was the file last modified? Today, December 21, 2002, 1:47.58pm
    What is the size of the file? 17.6 KB
14. Click the Cancel button in the Space Needle Properties dialog box.

(continued)

Windows Explorer *(continued)*

15. Insert a formatted floppy disk in drive A of your computer.
16. Right-drag the Space Needle icon over the 3½ Floppy (A:) icon. Click Move Here on the shortcut menu. Click the 3½ Floppy (A:) icon in the All Folders pane. Is the Space Needle file stored on drive A? ______________________
17. Click Tools on the menu bar, point to Find, and click People on the Find submenu.
18. Click the Look in box arrow and then click MSN in the Look in list box.
19. Click the Name text box and then type `Steven Forsythe` in the text box. Click the Find Now button. How many entries are listed for Steven Forsythe? ______________________
What is the first e-mail address listed for Steven Forsythe? ______________________
20. Click the Close button in the Find People dialog box.
21. Click the Close button in the Exploring - 3½ Floppy (A:) window.

4 Windows Toolbars

Instructions: Use a computer to perform the following tasks.

1. Open and maximize the My Computer window.
2. Display the icons in the My Computer window using the Large Icons format
3. Click View on the menu bar and then point to Toolbars (Figure 3-70).

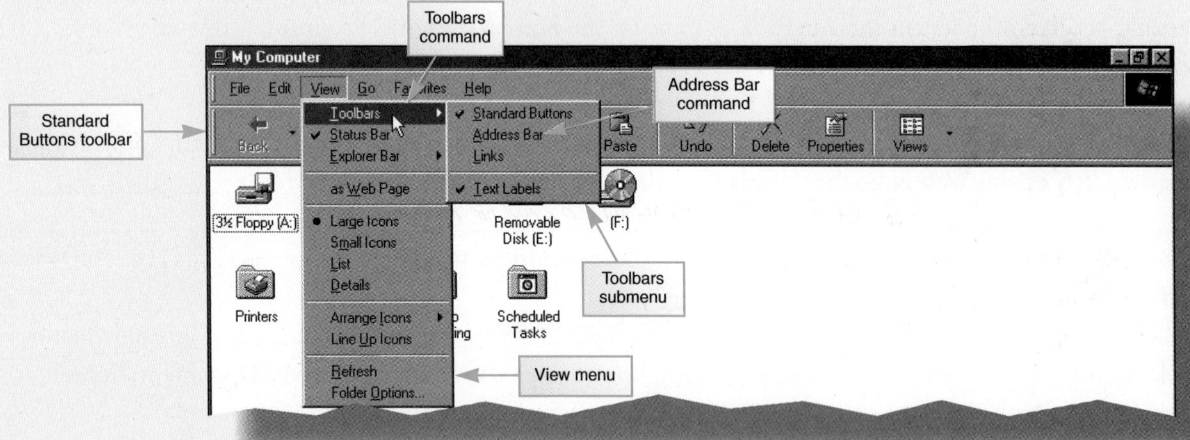

FIGURE 3-70

4. If a check mark does not display to the left of the Address Bar command on the Toolbars submenu, click Address Bar. The Address bar displays in the My Computer window.
5. Click the Address bar arrow.
6. Click the drive C icon in the Address list box. How did the window change? ______________________
____
7. Double-click the Windows icon. What happened? ______________________
____

8. In the Windows window, if the Standard Buttons toolbar does not display, click View on the menu bar, point to Toolbars, and then click Standard Buttons on the Toolbars submenu.
9. Scroll down if necessary until the Black Thatch icon displays in the window. If the Black Thatch icon does not display on your computer, find another Paint icon. Click the Black Thatch icon and then click the Copy button on the Standard Buttons toolbar.
10. Insert a formatted floppy disk in drive A of your computer.
11. Click the Address bar arrow.
12. Click the 3½ Floppy (A:) icon in the Address bar list box. What happened? ______________________

____
13. In the 3½ Floppy (A:) window, click the Paste button on the Standard Buttons toolbar. The Black Thatch icon displays in the 3½ Floppy (A:) window (Figure 3-71).

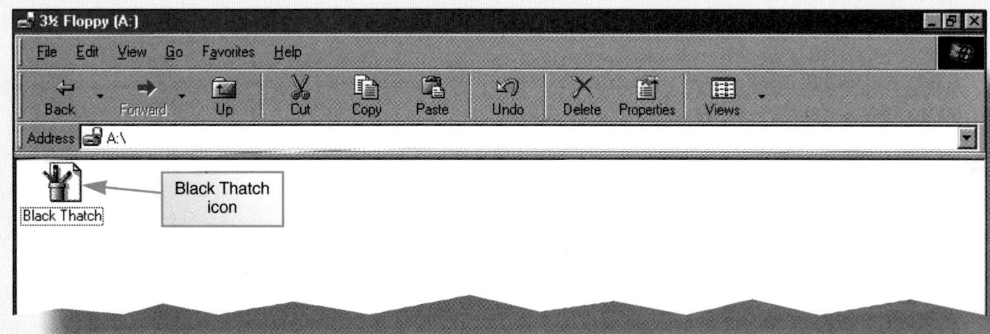

FIGURE 3-71

14. Click the Black Thatch icon in the 3½ Floppy (A:) window to select the icon, click the Delete button on the Standard Buttons toolbar, and then click the Yes button in the Confirm File Delete dialog box.
15. In the 3½ Floppy (A:) window, return the toolbar status to what it was prior to step 4.
16. Close the 3½ Floppy (A:) window.

The difficulty of these case studies varies:
◗ are the least difficult; ◗◗ are more difficult; and ◗◗◗ are the most difficult.

1 ◗ Your seven-year old brother is a graphics nut. He cannot get enough of the graphics that display on computers. Lately, he has been hounding you to show him all the graphics images that are available on your computer. You have done your best to put him off but finally have agreed to show him. Using techniques you learned in Project 3, display the icons for all the graphics image files that are stored on your computer (*Hint*: Many graphics files on Windows 98 computers contain a file extension of .bmp. Others may have a file extension of .pcx, .tif, or .gif). Once you have found the graphics files, display all of them and then print the three you like best.

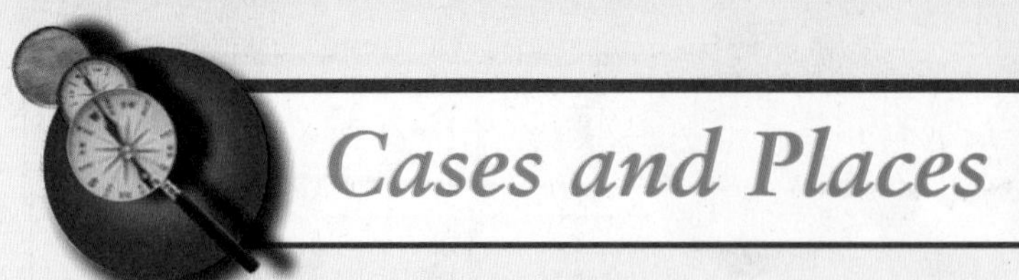

Cases and Places

2 ▶ Your employer suspects that the computer you use normally has been used by someone else during off-hours for non-company business. She has asked you to search your computer for all files that have been created or modified during the last ten days. When you find the files, determine if any of them are Notepad files or Paint files that you did not create or modify. If so, summarize the number of them and the date on which they were created or modified in a brief report to your employer.

3 ▶▶ Backing up files is an important way to protect data and ensure it is not lost or destroyed accidentally. File backup on a personal computer can use a variety of devices and techniques. Using the Internet, a library, personal computer magazines, or other resources, determine the types of devices used to store backed up data, the schedules, methods, and techniques for backing up data, and the consequences of not backing up data. Write a brief report of your findings.

4 ▶▶ A hard disk must be maintained to be used most efficiently. This maintenance includes deleting old files, defragmenting a disk so it is not wasteful of space, and from time to time, finding and attempting to correct disk failures. Using the Internet, a library, Windows 98 Help, or other research facilities, determine the maintenance that should be performed on hard disks, including the type of maintenance, when it should be performed, how long it takes to perform the maintenance, and the risks, if any, of not performing the maintenance. Write a brief report on the information you obtain.

5 ▶▶ The quest for more and faster disk storage continues as application programs grow larger and create sound and graphics files. One technique for increasing the amount of data that can be stored on a disk is disk compression. Disk compression programs, using a variety of mathematical algorithms, store data in less space on a hard disk. Many companies sell software you can load on your computer to perform the task. Windows 98 has disk compression capabilities as part of the operating system. Visit a computer store and find two disk compression programs you can buy. Write a brief report comparing the two packages to the disk compression capabilities of Windows 98. Discuss the similarities and differences between the programs and identify the program that claims to be the most efficient in compressing data.

6 ▶▶▶ Some in the computer industry think the Windows 98 operating system is deficient when it comes to ease of file management. Therefore, they have developed and marketed software that augments the operating systems to provide different and, they claim, improved services for file management. Visit a computer store and inquire about such products for Windows 98. Try a few of the activities in Project 3 using some of these products. What do you think? Write a brief report comparing the products you tested with Windows 98. Explain which you prefer and why.

7 ▶▶▶ Data stored on disk is one of a company's more valuable assets. If that data were to be stolen, lost, or compromised so it could not be accessed, the company literally could go out of business. Therefore, companies go to great lengths to protect their data. Visit a company or business in your area. Find out how it protects its data against viruses, unauthorized access, and even against such natural disasters as fire and tornadoes. Prepare a brief report that describes the company's procedures. In your report, point out any areas where you see the company has not protected its data adequately.